D0805671

Prime Time and Misdemeanors

Prime Time and Misdemeanors

INVESTIGATING THE 1950S
TV QUIZ SCANDAL
—A D.A.'s ACCOUNT

Joseph Stone and Tim Yohn

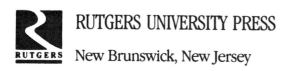

RUTGERS UNIVERSITY PRESS

New Brunswick, New Jersey

Library of Congress Cataloging-in-Publication Data

Stone, Joseph, 1912–
   Prime time and misdemeanors : investigating the 1950s TV quiz
scandal: a D.A.'s account / Joseph Stone and Tim Yohn.
     p. cm.
   Includes bibliographical references and index.
   ISBN 0-8135-1753-2
   1. Quiz shows—United States—History. 2. Fraud—United States—
History. I. Yohn, Tim, 1940–   . II. Title.
PN1992.8.Q5S7   1992
791.45'3—dc20   91-19782
                                                     CIP

British Cataloging-in-Publication information available

Dedicated to the memory of
Erica Stone Kaper

CONTENTS

ACKNOWLEDGMENTS

The ideal editor is a good cop and a bad cop rolled into one, as we found out in the months after Rutgers University Press first looked at our manuscript. It was nearly three times as long as the final version and included elaborate digressions on the history and functions of grand juries, the law of perjury, the workings of the Manhattan district attorney's office in the political context of the 1950s, the government regulation of broadcasting, as well as the colorful history of radio and television quiz programs. We are grateful to Marlie Wasserman of Rutgers Press and William Boddy of New York University for guiding us in paring the book down to the essential—Joseph Stone's inside story of the 1950s television quiz-rigging affair from his point of view as a senior assistant district attorney in charge of his office's investigation of the quizzes.

We want to acknowledge the following people for the help and encouragement they gave us at various stages of the project: Nicholas Barrett, Lawrence Bernstein, Frank Brenner, Robert Burstein, Philip Cates, Ken Cobb, Robert Coren, Harold Craig, Thomas DeLong, Robert Donnelly, Vivian Erdreich, Lawrence Freundlich, Fred Friendly, David Fuller, David Gelman, Jay Goldberg, Richard Goodwin, Marion Hepp, Milton Hirschorn, Michael Juviler, Dorothy Karchin, Doris Kearns, Evelyn Konrad, Julian Krainin, Herman Land, Michael Lanza, Kevin Lewis, Mark Miller, Joyce Power, Robin Rue, Jeffrey Rutledge, Jerry Slater, Jonathan Stone, Melvin Stein, Jacqueline Williams, and Marshall Witten.

We also thank Ilene Slater Stone and Mary Malott for their fortitude and patient support of this effort.

Prime Time and Misdemeanors

Introduction
Mere Entertainment?

In July 1987, during the congressional hearings into the Iran-Contra affair, Senator Daniel Inouye asked then-U.S. Attorney General Edwin Meese why he, Meese, had not put to the late director of Central Intelligence, William Casey, "the $64,000 question" concerning the diversion of funds to the U.S.-backed Nicaraguan rebels. Most likely it was inadvertent, but with his phrase Senator Inouye paid homage to another scandal, which thirty years ago had entranced the American public every bit as much as the Watergate and Iran-Contra affairs would in later decades.

From 1955 to 1958, in the midst of the television medium's most dynamic growth as an industry, big-money quiz programs dominated the airwaves. If today viewers turn on a popular TV quiz to see what the show's hostess is wearing, thirty years ago they tuned in to see contestants, whose names were household words, appear week after week on live broadcasts and roll up huge winnings—in some cases hundreds of thousands in 1950s preinflation dollars—by answering difficult questions requiring unusual knowledge.

For weeks on end, seemingly ordinary people who had become celebrities overnight on programs like "The $64,000 Question," "The $64,000 Challenge," and "Twenty-One" enthralled national audiences conservatively estimated at fifty million at the peak of the shows' popularity. From children to octogenarians, people from all walks of life, some with apparent "genius" levels of knowledge in fields often unrelated to how they made their living— scores of quiz show contestants became national heroes, living embodiments of the American dream. Tens of millions of viewers awaited the reappearances of the contestants and agonized as they sweated in "isolation booths" for the right answers, then rejoiced in victory or sympathized when their heroes were defeated or took their winnings and retired. All this translated into bonanzas for the shows' creators, broadcasters, commercial sponsors, and advertising agencies.

When a young part-time actor named Edward Hilgemeier came into the office of the District Attorney of New York County to complain that a minor quiz called "Dotto" was fixed, I was chief of the district attorney's Complaint Bureau, reporting to District Attorney Frank S. Hogan. I had been associated with the office for over twenty years and was a specialist in various kinds of commercial and consumer fraud, but I had never heard anything like the complaint Hilgemeier was making and was inclined to dismiss him as a crank. When bits of his story appeared several days later in a newspaper—and "Dotto" was taken off the air—I still had no idea that I soon would be engulfed in a uniquely American scandal, which, because it involved television, ranks only after the Watergate and the Iran-Contra affairs in terms of the furor and national soul-searching it would bring about.

The publicizing of Hilgemeier's complaint had the immediate effect of encouraging another whistle-blower to come forward, Herbert Stempel, an ex-G.I. college student and the first big champion of "Twenty-One" until his dethronement by the Columbia College English instructor, Charles Van Doren. Stempel told us and the press that not only had he been given questions and answers in advance, but he claimed that he was also ordered by "Twenty-One"'s head producer, Daniel Enright, to throw the match to Van Doren by deliberately giving the wrong answer to a key question. Stempel's allegations as well as denials by broadcasters, producers, and other contestants created a fire storm of publicity. When Enright came into the office in person to counter Stempel's allegations with a charge of blackmail, we had no choice but to begin a formal investigation to determine what crimes if any had been committed in connection with the operation of the quiz programs.

Despite the uproar, if the first dozen people we questioned about their connection with "Twenty-One" had told the truth, the entire matter would have been resolved in a few weeks. Instead, our investigation and its aftermath lasted for years. The first phase involved a nine-month grand jury inquiry, a legal battle over the grand jury's report, and circuslike public hearings of a subcommittee of the U.S. House of Representatives. These culminated in the voluntary public confession by Van Doren of his participation in quiz fixing, which marked the high point of public interest in the affair. If initial lying by Van Doren and other key figures drew out the affair in the first phase, it was doubly ironic that Van Doren's turnabout prompted confessions of perjury by others and opened an extended second phase, overlooked by the public and covered in part V of this book: another grand jury inquiry lasting five months, the prosecution of twenty people that dragged on until 1962, and a long proceeding before the Federal Communications Commission.

My last official act in connection with the quiz affair was in October 1962, more than four years after my first involvement. Some, professionals in the television business, were blacklisted by the industry for years afterward. The damage to the lives of still others ended only with their deaths. For a handful, the ordeal has continued down to the present day, some three decades after the events this book describes. This then is a story of extortion, of larceny, of obstruction of justice, of perjury, of lying so pervasive that it was woven into the fabric of American life.

PRIME TIME AND MISDEMEANORS recounts in detail the quiz-rigging affair from my point of view as an investigator and prosecutor. The great mystery became for my associates and me not how or why the shows were fixed—this emerged early in the investigation—but why so many people were willing to break the law by lying about an activity, quiz rigging, which, when they were engaged in it, was *not* illegal, even after we advised them of this fact. When Frank Hogan informed newspapers late in 1959 that, of the 150 people who testified before the first quiz grand jury, perhaps 50 told the truth, *Christian Century* magazine commented editorially by asking, "Are we a nation of liars and cheats?"

From my perspective, I would have to say the answer is yes. Part of the reason is that lying is endemic in our society. For instance, income tax laws, with their subtle distinction between avoidance (legal) and evasion (illegal) have helped create a nation of liars. Add to this the red tape that encourages millions of small businesses and independent entrepreneurs to lie about tax withholding, social security deductions, and other items relating to incomes and tax liability. Advertising is riddled with misleading and outright false claims, while salespeople routinely pitch lies and half truths. Radio and TV lay down a barrage of commercials that exaggerate at best, lie at worst. Political campaign commercials are filled with half-truths and false promises; "sound bites" are hit-and-run distortions of the truth. Puffery and lying on employment resumés, applications for health and life insurance policies, fraudulent claims for workers' compensation, the giving of false addresses by parents in order to register children in preferred schools, cheating by students on examinations, and faking of research by scholars and scientists . . . the list is endless. Even journalists claim the need to fabricate quotations from interview subjects, to provide "flow" to their writing. Caught in lies, writers and politicians torture meaning by calling their lies "misspeaking" (a term frequently employed by the White House) or "untruth," supposedly a good-faith device used to get at the actual truth.

These subtleties aside, there is a difference between lying and perjury. A lie is a false statement deliberately presented as true. Perjury is defined as knowingly making a false statement under oath in any proceeding where the oath is required by law. "Oath" includes an affirmation that a person, who for religious or other reasons cannot "swear" to do so, will tell the truth. Documents submitted to courts or other officially designated bodies in which an affiant has to swear to the truthfulness of statements made in such documents are also the subject of perjury laws. In New York State it is not perjury to lie to the police or to the district attorney, because neither has the authority to administer the oath to people questioned. The law does require witnesses who appear before a grand jury or testify in a court of law to swear or affirm under oath to tell the truth, under the penalty of the crime of perjury.

It is noteworthy in this regard that though the Ten Commandments don't bar lying per se, perjury is predicated on two of the Commandments:

> Thou shalt not take the name of the Lord thy God in vain; for the Lord will not hold him guiltless that taketh His name in vain.

> Neither shalt thou bear false witness against thy neighbor.

In more recent times, in 1942, Judge Matthew J. Troy of New York City's Court of Special Sessions called perjury "a well-recognized form of indoor sport." An Irish wit with a knack for publicity, Judge Troy was being serious, pointing up the fact that the crime of perjury undermines our entire system of law and prevents the true administration of justice. It is committed with what amounts to impunity in all our courts, criminal and civil, and by all groups of people, not the least of which are the police.

Except in rare cases involving investigations of racketeering and political crimes, perjury is seldom the subject of vigorous prosecution. It is not even considered important enough to be included in the FBI's annual Uniform Crime Statistics report, which, in addition to listing major crimes, issues figures for vagrancy, loitering, and drunkenness. Likewise the annual crime reports of New York State's Division of Criminal Justice Services do not carry figures relating to perjury. In more than two decades as a Manhattan assistant district attorney helping prosecute thousands of crimes, I handled exactly twenty-eight cases of perjury; twenty-one of these were connected with the quiz investigation and would not have taken place except for the tremendous publicity generated by the affair.

NOTHING in my experience prepared me for the mass perjury that took place before the first grand jury investigating TV quiz rigging, on the part of scores of well-educated people who had no trouble understanding what was at stake. Several of them in fact had law degrees. None of these people had ever been in trouble with the law as far as I could determine. With only one exception, the twenty who ultimately became defendants against charges of perjury had been interviewed in the office prior to testifying before the grand jury, and the exception was a lawyer. Each was assured of immunity from prosecution, except for the crime of perjury; each was emphatically warned of the consequences of lying under oath. As was our policy in every case, we strongly recommended that the witnesses seek legal advice on their own before testifying. The law relating to grand jury secrecy was explained to them; they were all assured that the D.A. would not leak anything they had told us. And we kept our word; all the details the press learned about our investigation came from the witnesses themselves. Eventually, however, after the grand jury investigation was closed, the testimony passed into the hands of congressional investigators, and we lost the ability to keep it secret. This was a development we could never have foreseen.

My exhortations and assurances fell on deaf ears. When the quizlings, as newspaper columnist Art Buchwald dubbed them, testified before the grand jury, they politely, firmly, and confidently repeated the lies they had told me in my office. Not until six months after the investigation began, when one of the quiz producers who had lied at his first appearance before the grand jury decided to recant, did I realize that my skills and techniques were not at fault. I had failed to grasp that the bond of loyalty between the former contestants and the producers was strong enough for the contestants to break the law by committing perjury at the producers' behest.

This was possible in part because of the personal characteristics for which the contestants had been chosen by the producers of the shows. In order for the public to believe the shows were genuine in the first place, the winners had to project integrity. For this reason, the choice of champions ran to college professors, graduate students, military officers (who wore their uniforms on the shows), housewives, and children. On a program like "Twenty-One," which required the contestants' conscious participation in the rigging, the producers had to resort to considerable pressure to secure the cooperation of contestants. But once this was achieved, the contestants were locked in; it was in their interest to avoid exposure because their professional reputations and status in their communities were at stake.

To the extent that they were able to corrupt people who seemed highly respectable, the quiz producers were consummate psychologists. They forged deep friendships with the contestants that resulted in varying degrees of emotional dependence on them. When a crisis developed, the contestants turned not to competent professionals for advice or even to their own spouses, but to the producers. Thus the producers and contestants of certain quiz shows had become a form of extended family, linked by the power of a secret guilt. Against this, our admonitions and assurances about the importance of telling the truth were abstractions at best, hostile threats at worst.

Complicating matters was the fact that some lawyers consulted by the contestants we questioned were former colleagues of mine in the district attorney's office—retained by the producers in the hope that such a connection to the office could be employed to soft-pedal the investigation. Ultimately I learned that these lawyers played a role in orchestrating perjury before the grand jury, drawing out an affair that would have been over in a matter of weeks with little or no damage to anyone's reputation if all the producers had come clean at the outset. A few lawyers involved went so far as to assure their clients that they had me in their pockets, that the quiz investigation was a political ploy on the part of the district attorney, and advised their clients that since they were not required to tell us anything at all in the D.A.'s office, they could say what they pleased without breaking the law. Meanwhile, the producers promised former contestants that they themselves would be telling both the district attorney and the grand jury the "truth"—that they had not given questions and answers in advance to contestants. With the help of their lawyers, the producers convinced the contestants that their interests were the same; once they all had their act together, it was show business as usual and a short step for all concerned to repeat the lies they had told us in the office to the grand jury under oath.

THE FATE of the quiz affair as a piece of history has been instructive and ironic. In a sense, those who at the time dismissed quiz fixing as "mere entertainment" ultimately won the battle, since the story was largely consigned to the status of trivia, in the form of error-riddled chapters in nostalgia picture books about television. In three decades only two writers attempted to treat the subject at length and in depth: Meyer Weinberg in *TV in America: The Morality of Hard Cash* (1962) examined quiz fixing along with other practices in the context of the failure of federal agencies to regulate rampant commercial broadcasting interests; and Kent Anderson, in *Television Fraud: The History and Implications of the Quiz Show Scandals* (1978), presented the affair as a case study in American self-perception. The sources for these studies were the official public record of deliberative bodies (principally the 1959 congressional hearings), magazine articles and press coverage, and books on television in general and on the sociology and politics of the era of the 1950s. Both able writers and intelligent scholars, Weinberg and Anderson lacked an insider's perspective, left large gaps in the story, especially as regards the behind-the-scenes roles played by lawyers at various stages, and inadvertently repeated many errors in their sources.

As a result of neglect, the quiz affair, even for people who vaguely remember seeing the rigged quizzes on television, has taken on the aura of a silly episode in the wacky, self-absorbed, and, above all, innocent era connoted by the term "the 1950s." In great part, this misapprehension reflects the fact that, by contrast to what followed in the wake of Watergate, for example, practically no one personally involved in the quiz affair has written about his or her experience for publication. There seem to be only two exceptions, both brief chapters in recent autobiographies. One exception is Patty Duke's 1987 memoir, *Call Me Anna*. Duke was a successful child actress in early 1958 when she was given questions and answers in advance as a contestant on "The $64,000 Challenge"; with justification, she blamed her Svengali-like manager for involving her in the fixing. The second is the introduction to Richard Goodwin's 1988 account of his exploits as an insider in the Kennedy and Johnson presidencies, *Remembering America: A Voice from the Sixties*. Here Goodwin breezily sketched his experience as an ambitious young counsel to the congressional subcommittee that investigated the quiz shows.

Otherwise, even after thirty years, the reluctance of people connected with the quiz shows to discuss their involvement remains formidable. A circle of wagons has been drawn up to protect the memory of one of the top quiz show producers, the late Louis Cowan, who twenty years before the scandal pioneered "control" techniques in his successful radio program, "Quiz Kids." Frank Stanton, the head of CBS at the time of the scandal, declined to be interviewed by us on the ground that Cowan was no longer around to tell his side of the story. On the other hand, another central figure, Daniel Enright, was able quietly and very successfully to reestablish himself in the television business. Until only relatively recently, when he was interviewed on television on the occasion of the thirtieth anniversary of the Washington quiz hearings, Enright maintained silence on the details of the quiz rigging he had masterminded. The enduring secretiveness on the part of so many of the people connected with the shows has been a key factor in the trivializing of the affair, perpetuating the myth that the quiz show rigging really hurt no one, a myth that this book is intended to correct.

PART ONE

Scandal

CHAPTER ONE

Connecting the Dots

(AUGUST 16–27, 1958)

Saturday, August 16, 1958, was a typical New York summer dog day when I went in to my office on the seventh floor of the huge Criminal Courts Building at 100 Centre Street in lower Manhattan. The art deco-style colossus was best known to the public for the notorious Tombs, the principal men's jail of Manhattan, at its north end. Separated from the jail by seventeen floors of courtrooms and judges' chambers were the offices of the district attorney of New York County, the Manhattan prosecutor.

As the senior assistant district attorney in charge of the Complaint Bureau and one of seven bureau chiefs reporting to District Attorney Frank Hogan, I rated a large, bright corner office with an air conditioner. A Saturday morning in summer, with only the Arraignments Part of the courts in operation and a skeleton crew in the office, was a good time to catch up on the paperwork that piled up during the routinely tumultuous work weeks I spent supervising ten junior assistant D.A.s plus staff who comprised the Complaint Bureau and provided the main point of contact between the D.A.'s office and the general public.

I was making headway on the pile of papers on my desk, when Melvin Stein, one of my junior associates on duty that morning, asked me to sit in as he took a statement from a man who had just walked in off the street with an unusual complaint—a TV quiz show was fixed. Stein was a recent Columbia Law School graduate, with the D.A.'s office only a few months; I had fifteen years' experience as a city prosecutor dealing with more kinds of fraud than most people could imagine existed, but I had never heard this one before. But after spending an hour with the complainant, a tall, thin aspiring actor in his mid-twenties named Edward Hilgemeier, I was not inclined to give much credence to his story: discovering that a contestant on a daytime quiz called "Dotto" was given answers in advance to questions used on the air, he complained to the producers who then paid him $1,500 in return for his signature on documents that waived any further claim against them.

Neither Stein nor I was aware of anything about TV quiz shows except that they were very popular. Beyond that, as far as I knew, there was nothing illegal about giving answers to contestants or paying someone to keep quiet about the practice. At the heart of Hilgemeier's complaint seemed to be the fear that he was being blacklisted as an actor in television because of his knowledge concerning "Dotto." "I have been hearing things about myself," he said, "and I want them to stop so I can continue to get work." When complainants got around to saying they were "hearing things," I usually had heard enough. I thanked Hilgemeier for his visit and promised to let him know what action, if any, we could take.

Judging from Hilgemeier's appearance and manner, the easiest thing was to dismiss him as one of those people who crawl out of the woodwork into the Complaint Bureau when the weather is hot and the moon becomes full. I gave him no more thought until late Monday morning, August 18, when I was summoned to Hogan's office and his secretary, Ida Delaney, handed me a newspaper clipping to read before going in to see him. It was an inside item from the early edition of the *New York Post,* headlined "Next Question: Why Did 'Dotto' Die?" According to the piece, the two "Dotto" television quiz programs, a daytime version on the CBS network and a Tuesday night version on NBC, had been canceled by the networks and the programs' commercial sponsor, the Colgate-Palmolive Company. At the same time, according to *Post* reporter Jack O'Grady, an unnamed contestant had filed an affidavit with the Federal Communications Commission charging that one of the show's "champions" had been furnished with answers in advance.

At age fifty-five, Frank S. Hogan had been district attorney of New York County since succeeding Thomas E. Dewey in the job in 1942. A paragon of staunchly upright and vigilant public service as well as a superb administrator, Hogan, whom we called "the Chief," had made the office the model for public prosecutors nationwide. Reelected against only token opposition to four terms as D.A., Hogan was now in the midst of a faltering campaign as the Democratic nominee for the U.S. Senate, but that did not interfere with the smooth running of his office, which he carried out with an obsession for detail. Every day he scanned the newspapers for items worthy of the office's attention, and the cancelation of a TV show amid hints of fraud was the sort of thing to catch his eye. He had called me in because of my background in handling business and consumer frauds involving deceptive advertising, mislabeling, and commercial bribery.

I told the Chief we had already heard about "Dotto" and quickly sketched Hilgemeier's visit to the office on Saturday, not concealing my skeptical first impression. But then, Hilgemeier had not mentioned filing an affidavit with the FCC; now his complaint looked as if it might have been concocted in cahoots with O'Grady to help make a newspaper story printable. Nevertheless, something real was afoot with the sudden cancelation of "Dotto." Hilgemeier's tale warranted another look.

On Friday, August 22, Hilgemeier was back in the office, in the company of a lawyer named Irving Tannenbaum, having been assured that he was not a "target" or potential defendant in a prosecution. Right off, Hilgemeier admitted to telling his story to O'Grady over a month before, and that the reporter had helped him write the affidavit sent to the FCC. Hilgemeier handed us a copy of the affidavit, which ran to some twenty-eight numbered items. Melvin Stein and I scanned this, then had Hilgemeier tell us his story again, which he did, adding considerable detail.

Hilgemeier, a native of Indianapolis, had been an aspiring actor in New York for several years and earned money by doing odd jobs and appearing as a contestant on quiz shows. Since October 1957 he had won small sums of money and merchandise on five shows, the largest amount being $3,000 on "The Price Is Right." Thus he was looking for work when he joined the audience of daytime "Dotto" at a midtown CBS broadcast studio on May 16 or 17, 1958. He and several others who had filled out audience-member application cards were asked to remain after the broadcast for an interview, then were directed to the offices of "Dotto"'s producers, Marjeff, Inc., in a midtown hotel, to take a test of general knowledge and a "famous persons" picture identification test. A day or two later, he was notified he had been selected to be a standby contestant on May 20.

Based on the children's game of connecting dots to make a picture, the "Dotto" quiz pitted two contestants—each working from separate dot pictures of a celebrity—in a race to connect enough dots to recognize the face first. The contestants took turns answering questions in various categories of knowledge, which changed after every round. A correct answer by a contestant connected a certain number of dots in that contestant's picture. Upon being told the upcoming category, the contestant had the option to ask for a question from three levels of difficulty, such that a correct answer was rewarded with five, eight, or ten dots connected in the picture. Each face was composed of fifty dots, and the sooner a contestant made the identification, the more he or she won—$20 for each dot on the picture that was left unconnected.

Being a standby contestant meant Hilgemeier was not scheduled to go on the air but, depending on the tempo of the turnover of others ahead of him, he would eventually go on. Having contestants stand by was a means of familiarizing them with the program so that by the time they did go on they would not freeze up. On May 20 Hilgemeier was in the dressing room of the "Dotto" studio before air time, along with other standbys and two women scheduled as contestants for that day's broadcast. One of the two was Marie Winn, a student at Columbia University, who was the reigning champion of "Dotto," having won matches for two days in a row; the other was Yeffe Kimball Slatin, a self-styled American Indian princess, Winn's first challenger for the day.

As Hilgemeier related it, two "Dotto" staff members, associate producers named Art Henley and Gil Cates, came in to take the two women separately to another room for "warm-up" sessions, during which they went over scripted dialogue to be used in the so-called interview segment or chat before the actual quizzing; material used in the interviews was based on personal background information provided to the producers by the contestants. After returning to the dressing room from her warm-up, Hilgemeier observed, Winn spent some time writing in a notebook, holding it tightly on her knee to keep what she was writing to herself.

Shortly before the broadcast, a dress rehearsal took place before the cameras, and Hilgemeier noted what he called "an undue amount of familiarity" between Winn and the studio personnel. When the broadcast began, he watched from the wings and thought that Winn "had everything on the tip of her tongue." Suspicious, he returned to the dressing room and found Winn's notebook on a table, where she had left it, and thumbed through it. On one page he saw what he thought could be answers to the questions Winn was being asked on the broadcast, and he tore the page out. He now handed us a photostat of a piece of paper, which had on it the following in scrawled handwriting:

Bing Crosby
Barry Fitzgerald—Abbie Players
Donald Duck—3 nephews
Dagwood—Mr. Dithers

Short stories—[illegible]
Zhukhov

Alexanders Ragtime Band
Band Played On

MacNamaras Band
Johnson's Polar Garden
Sewards Folly— [1]

Returning to the stage area, Hilgemeier encountered Slatin coming off the set, having just been defeated by Winn. He took Slatin aside and showed her the notebook page he had torn out. At her insistence, they returned to the dressing room to see Winn's notebook, then left the studio as the broadcast continued and Winn competed against another challenger. Hilgemeier and Slatin had the page photostatted, then went to see Slatin's lawyer, Arthur Seiff, in his office. Seiff told them he didn't have time to handle the situation but suggested another lawyer, Sidney Hoffman, whom they called, making an appointment for two days later.

Instead of waiting, Slatin and Hilgemeier that evening proceeded to the "Dotto" office, found Gil Cates, and told him their story. Cates called his boss, Edward Jurist, "Dotto"'s producer, who arrived shortly and took over, interviewing Slatin and Hilgemeier separately. Jurist professed to be amazed at the situation, according to Hilgemeier, but said he could not put Slatin back on the show because her reappearance could not be explained to the audience. He promised to make it up to her, though. He did not want to put Hilgemeier on the show at this time, but if Hilgemeier cared to wait, he could be a contestant on a new nighttime version of "Dotto" set to start in July. The prize money would be bigger and Jurist all but promised a substantial reward if Hilgemeier would keep quiet about Winn's notebook. At this point, Hilgemeier claimed, he indicated to Jurist he was not interested in anything they could offer him.

When Hilgemeier and Slatin met with Sidney Hoffman, the lawyer agreed to see what kind of settlement he could obtain from "Dotto," and had them sign a retainer agreement giving him one-third of whatever money might be recovered for them. He then took from them the original page from Winn's notebook. On May 31 Hoffman reported that Marjeff's parent firm, Frank Cooper Associates, a "packager" or independent producer of programs for television, was offering $2,000 to Slatin and $500 to Hilgemeier if they would sign an agreement not to sue. Hilgemeier declined the offer, telling Hoffman he was more interested in continuing to work in television. On June 18 Hoffman informed Hilgemeier that even though he and Slatin had no real case against "Dotto," Cooper had upped its offer to Slatin to $4,000, which she had accepted; Hilgemeier would receive $1,000 if he settled now. Hilgemeier again refused and now demanded back the original notebook page, but Hoffman said he had already turned this over to Frank Cooper Associates.

Beginning to wonder whose side Hoffman was on, Hilgemeier turned to lawyer Irving Tannenbaum, a neighbor, who advised him he did have a case and he should withdraw from the retainer agreement he had with Hoffman. Hoffman refused to accede, insisting any settlement must be through him. By July 10, not hearing anything more from Tannenbaum, Hilgemeier on his own made contact with reporter O'Grady. Then without consulting Tannenbaum, Hilgemeier went to see Jurist to "resolve the matter" and mentioned that he was talking to a newspaper reporter. Jurist asked Hilgemeier to hold off and talk to Sy Fischer, Jurist's own boss, and O'Grady advised Hilgemeier to play along.

On July 11 Hilgemeier met with Fischer, a partner in Frank Cooper Associates and manager of the packager's New York operations, in his office on East 54th Street. With Jurist and Walter Schier, Cooper's attorney, present, Fischer offered Hilgemeier $1,500 to settle. When Hilgemeier balked, Fischer accused Hilgemeier of blackmail, picked up the phone, and said he was calling the police. When Hilgemeier revealed he was in touch with the *Post,* Fischer put down the phone and asked Hilgemeier to go home, think it over, and call him back.

O'Grady advised Hilgemeier to take the $1,500 and sign a release, which would be proof of the whole affair—and the story would be worth $500 to the *Post.* O'Grady accompanied Hilgemeier back to see Fischer, who sent them to see Schier. At Schier's office, while O'Grady waited outside, Hilgemeier signed several documents and was given fifteen $100 bills, but Schier refused to give Hilgemeier copies of the documents. During the next two weeks, O'Grady helped Hilgemeier draft an affidavit covering events up to the payment. O'Grady then submitted it to the *Post*'s legal department, which gave the opinion that without copies of the releases Hilgemeier had signed, the story was not printable. Without informing Tannenbaum or O'Grady, Hilgemeier went to the Park Avenue offices of Colgate-Palmolive, "Dotto"'s sponsor, on August 7, where he showed a copy of the affidavit to two executives whose names he could not recall, telling them he did not want money but only to have "the bad talk about him in the industry stopped." He followed up with another visit to Colgate on August 11 and told another executive that O'Grady was "pressuring" him to print a story. Then, on August 13, he was called back to Colgate, where seven executives spent two and a half hours going over his story. Finally, on August 16, after his first visit to us, he brought Tannenbaum and O'Grady up to date. On Monday, August 18, as the story was breaking in the *Post*, O'Grady called Hilgemeier to reveal he had sent the affidavit to the FCC as far back as July 31. This, Hilgemeier claimed, was the first he had heard of this action.

After we were through with Hilgemeier, he and his lawyer departed, leaving us with the copies of the affidavit and Winn's notebook page. Little had happened to change my initial assessment of Hilgemeier as an undependable witness, but the affidavit, the involvement of O'Grady, and above all the fact of the cancelation of "Dotto" pointed to scandal. What did it mean for the district attorney's office? First, there was the possibility of extortion by Hilgemeier and Slatin. Second, though I had no idea of the contractual relations among CBS, Colgate, and the "Dotto" producers, an element of larceny might have been involved if the producers had misrepresented the show as a genuine contest, but were rigging the outcome in favor of one contestant over another. Third, there was the possibility that if contestants like Winn were given answers by "Dotto" staff people, it was in return for bribes or kickbacks of part of the prize money. If this were done without the knowledge of the staff people's superiors, then the crime of commercial bribery would have been committed. These possibilities were enough for us to dig deeper. The next step would be to summon Slatin and Winn for questioning. We also needed to find out precisely how "Dotto" worked and what kind of records existed for a defunct TV show, specifically a list of the questions asked and, if possible, the answers given on the May 20 broadcast. That was the only way we could assess the significance of the page from Winn's notebook.

ON MONDAY MORNING, August 25, I talked to Thomas Fisher, a CBS vice-president and the network's general attorney, and Walter Schier, the Frank Cooper Associates attorney, who assured me of the eagerness of their organizations to cooperate with the district attorney. Fisher arranged for CBS to send over a kinescope, a 16-millimeter film made by a movie camera placed before a monitor during transmission, of the May 20 "Dotto" broadcast. Yeffe Slatin, reached by telephone at her home in Greenwich Village, agreed to come for an interview the following day. When we couldn't reach Marie Winn by phone at her apartment on the Upper West Side, we sent out a detective to find her. At noon, the early edition of the *Post* was on the streets with a new story by O'Grady, revealing that we had questioned the still unnamed "Dotto" whistle-blower. Later in the afternoon, the "Dotto" kinescope was in our hands and Detective Nicholas Barrett of the Office Squad was threading it into a movie projector set up in my office for an audience consisting of Stein, some very curious junior assistant D.A.s, secretaries, and me.

The "Dotto" stage set consisted of two walls jutting out from the back and meeting at a right angle center stage, so that each of two competing contestants, standing behind lecterns on either side, could see one wall but not the other. On each wall was an electric scoreboard, a large windowlike square for the "Dotto" drawing and, below that, a smaller rectangular space, called the "Dotto-graph," where the contestant could write in a guess as to the drawing's identity; it was big enough for the audience to see without tipping off the opponent. Next to the drawing square were slots where the clues to the drawing's identity would appear when the contestant earned enough points to be given clues.

Jack Narz, a suntanned and slender master of ceremonies, bounded onto the set and took his place behind another lectern, downstage center, with the word "Dotto" in script affixed to it and a tube of Colgate toothpaste prominently displayed. Narz welcomed the first two contestants, who walked on from opposite sides and took their places behind the desklike lecterns. Marie Winn was young, dark haired, and vivacious and spoke with a very slight European accent; Yeffe Kimball—her married name, Slatin, was not given— was older, taller, and more serious, and she wore a beaded American Indian dress.

Narz reminded the audience that Winn was returning to the show after having won $440 the previous day. We then learned that Slatin was from Oklahoma and was part Osage Indian; her husband was an atomic scientist, and the name Yeffe meant "wandering star." She gave a demonstration, in Indian sign language, of riding a horse to New York City to be on the program, which gave Narz the opportunity to crack a joke about New York traffic. After a toothpaste commercial, the contestants tried out the buzzers they would sound when they believed they could identify the "Dotto" drawing, and the quiz began. They would then take turns answering questions in various categories, having the appropriate number of dots automatically connected in their respective drawings after giving correct answers. A wrong answer by a contestant would result in the connecting of a number of dots in her opponent's picture. After a correct identification, the winner would receive $20 for each of the fifty dots left unconnected on her drawing.

In the first round, both women answered questions correctly in the category of history; then Slatin failed to answer a question about short stories, while Winn answered correctly, giving her an advantage and enough dots connected on her board to be given a clue. So far none of the questions had related to material on Winn's notebook page, but the clue now shown to Winn and the audience ("Abbey Player") as well as the name Winn wrote on the "Dotto-graph" (Barry Fitzgerald) were both on Winn's notebook page. Narz congratulated Winn for the right answer to the "Dotto" picture. Slatin still had the opportunity, without having been provided the clue, to guess the identity and tie Winn; to help her, ten more dots were connected in her picture. She squinted, then guessed Winston Churchill. She was wrong and was presented with a check for $25 in consolation. Having identified the picture with twenty-five dots still unconnected, Winn won $500, giving her a total of $940.

After a soap commercial, the "Home Dotto" feature, in which a viewer reached by telephone failed to identify correctly the Home Dotto drawing, and another commercial in which a model named Bess Myerson demonstrated a room deodorant, Winn faced her second challenger of the day. Michael Hayden, an airline pilot from Greenwich, Connecticut, walked on stage. After some patter about Hayden's job, the game began, with Winn and Hayden answering questions in the category of "songs about bands." Their answers, "McNamara's Band" and "Alexander's Ragtime Band," were on Winn's notebook page. After answering a question in the category of "Russia, Now and Yesterday," Hayden had eighteen dots connected and he pressed his buzzer and wrote down Huey and Dewey, two of the three nephews of the cartoon character Donald Duck. There was confusion on Narz's part, for this was a partial answer and he asked for a "ruling" from the producer offstage. Meanwhile, he gave Winn the opportunity to guess.

> WINN: It looks to me by that thing down there, something like a duck. So is it Donald Duck? Or little ducks?
> NARZ: Well, I can accept one answer from you, Marie. Could you give me just one?
> WINN: Donald Duck's little nephews?
> NARZ: Well, you are right. Now that is right—it is Donald Duck's little nephews. And I think we have—well, I know we have a tie game now, so that solves our problem.[2]

Winn and Hayden were invited to return the following day to play "Double Dotto" at stakes of $40 a point, and the broadcast ended with a new clue to the Home Dotto picture and a commercial for a sink cleaner. "Donald Duck—3 nephews" was one of the entries on Winn's notebook page.

It struck me as ironic that there was a conspiracy to cover up any fixing of "Dotto," because the *real* problem of the show—its sheer absurdity, underscored by the frequency of commercials and their exaggerated claims for the products advertised—was already there for all to see. But now, in addition, it seemed apparent that "Dotto" was fixed. The clues to both pictures that Winn identified were on her notebook page, as were answers to questions in the categories of "Songs about Bands" and "Russia, Now and Yesterday"; presumably Winn would have given "Zhukov" or "Seward's Folly" as answers to a question in the Russia category if Hayden had not guessed at the picture of Donald Duck's nephews. My guess was that Winn's notation "Dagwood—Mr. Dithers" was the identity of another drawing that might have been used in the event of a third game.

TWO DAYS LATER, we had talked to both Slatin and Winn, and the "Dotto" affair became front-page news—with Hilgemeier's identity as whistle-blower revealed and our own investigation made known—as the CBS network embarked upon a public relations campaign to protect its image. The first step was on August 26, when David Worgan, a senior assistant district attorney and Hogan's executive assistant, who was fielding press questions for the Chief about "Dotto," received a call from a top outside attorney for CBS, Samuel I. Rosenman, a one-time aide to Franklin Roosevelt. Rosenman assured Worgan of CBS's determination to deny its facilities to programs "which operate as a fraud or mislead the public"; the network had been pressing its own investigation of "Dotto" for a week and had uncovered "no improper procedures" so far.[3] Later in the day, CBS executive vice-president Hubbell Robinson, Jr., followed up with a telegram to Worgan expressing more eagerness to cooperate with us and requesting that we make available to them "any information which you may develop with respect to any irregularity in any quiz show on our network."[4] The Rosenman and Robinson statements were released to the press by CBS, with the result that reporters and photographers set up camp on Leonard Street across from our lobby entrance to keep an eye out for people coming to talk to us about "Dotto."

Slatin, who appeared in the office on August 26 without a lawyer, was in her early forties and had a lithe, athletic build and angular features; she was an artist, had spent time in Paris during the war studying with Fernand Léger, and now painted American Indian themes and served as a consultant to museums on Indian culture. She took the attitude that she was being put upon by us in an essentially private matter, but she was not uncooperative.

Winn, on the other hand, had secured the services of Murray Edelbaum, a highly competent criminal lawyer. Although I assured him that Winn was wanted as a witness only, Edelbaum insisted on my promise that, if she was brought before a grand jury, she would formally be granted immunity from prosecution. Before making such a promise, I had to weigh the possibility that Winn might have committed bribery by kicking back part of her "Dotto" winnings to someone on the production staff, but in that event the person taking the bribe—and likely soliciting it—would be a better target. I knew Edelbaum and trusted him to extract the whole story from Winn and to play straight with me; therefore, when he said she had not committed any crime, I acceded to his demand since her role was that of a witness and we wanted the whole truth from her. On August 27 Edelbaum brought his client to the D.A.'s floors without being spotted by the reporters on Leonard Street. Nervous as she was, it was not hard to see what would attract TV producers to Winn. A twenty-one-year-old native of Czechoslovakia, she was bright and animated; her faint accent added to her charm. She was in her last year at Columbia University, majoring in Slavic languages. When we showed her our copy of her notebook page, she confirmed the handwriting was hers and that she had written it after a private meeting with an associate producer of "Dotto" before the May 20 broadcast.

One thing Winn and Slatin had in common was how they were recruited to "Dotto"; both had been tapped by the same talent scout. In the case of Winn, she was at a ballet performance at the Metropolitan Opera House, when, during intermission, a woman approached her, identified herself as Diane Lawson, a "people getter" for quiz shows, and invited Winn to her office for an interview. That led to Winn's taking tests for "Dotto" and being interviewed by the show's staff. She was a standby on four broadcasts before her first appearance as a contestant, on May 19, 1958.

Before the broadcast, Winn recounted, she was taken from the dressing room by an associate producer, Stan Green, to a private room to go over her personal background for her introduction on the show. But there was more to it than that. As Winn now put it, Green wanted "to give me a sort of idea as to what kind of questions they were going to ask so that I wouldn't go in there cold." How much did she know about automobiles, he asked her; for example, did she know where the antifreeze was put? He also asked if she had ever seen Arthur Godfrey's "Talent Scouts" television show. Winn appeared in the second half of the broadcast, with time to play one game, which she won. Several of the questions were among those Green had asked her in the warm-up, and the "Dotto" drawing was of Arthur Godfrey.

Yeffe Slatin's name had been given by a friend to Diane Lawson, who called her and arranged for interviews and testing by "Dotto" personnel in a room rented for the purpose at Steinway Hall on West 57th Street. Slatin was a standby on May 6, then selected to be a contestant on May 20. As instructed, she arrived at the studio sometime after 9 A.M. and was taken to the dressing room, where she was introduced to Winn, Hilgemeier, and the airline pilot, Michael Hayden. At one point, Stan Green took her outside to discuss cues, how the "Dotto" buzzer worked, and so on, but he did not warm her up with practice questions.

Winn's experience was therefore clearly different. When Green had called her out, he took her to another room and asked her the name of the Irish actor who played with Bing Crosby in *Going My Way?* She asked him if he meant Barry Fitzgerald. He said yes, and asked her how she liked the movie. Then he asked her other questions, including whether she knew of the three nephews of Donald Duck. She told us that, by now, "I had sort of an idea that the conversation had some bearing on the show. I would say it was likely that the questions might come up in some form or other."

Slatin remembered Winn jotting something in her notebook when she returned to the dressing room. Trying to strike up a conversation, she asked Winn what she was doing. "Studying for my exams at Columbia" was the curt reply. Another "Dotto" staff member whose name she couldn't recall now took Slatin outside to rehearse her demonstration of Indian sign language. She told him she was nervous, that she felt weak in certain categories, but he told her not to worry.

After her defeat by Winn, Slatin left the stage and saw Hilgemeier waiting for her. Her account of what happened subsequently differed on some points from Hilgemeier's. According to Slatin, Hilgemeier did not have Winn's notebook page with him. "Get upstairs and get that book," he whispered, "the answers are in that book." They hurried to the dressing room; she found Winn's notebook, looked through it, and she was the one who tore out the page. She put it in her purse and left the studio, followed by Hilgemeier. Later, when they went to see Edward Jurist and she was alone with the producer, Slatin showed him the notebook page and complained that since Winn had all the answers she herself didn't have a chance. She wanted compensation and "some justification," and he wanted to know how it had happened, whether it was a leak. She told him she had no idea and he promised her satisfaction.

Winn meanwhile did not learn anything was wrong until she returned that evening to her apartment, discovered a page was missing from her notebook, and received a phone call from Diane Lawson telling her that another contestant had found the page and was trying to make trouble. She told Winn not to return to "Dotto" and that an announcement would be made that she was ill. In due course, she received a check for her winnings of $940. She was firm in her denial that neither Lawson nor anyone else connected with "Dotto" had asked for or even hinted that she kick back any of the money.

Slatin's involvement in all this ended a mere four days after her and Hilgemeier's visit to the lawyer, Sidney Hoffman. She agreed to "Dotto"'s offer, which was $4,000 to start with, not $2,000 as Hilgemeier was first told by Hoffman. After signing a release, she was given a check by Hoffman on May 26 for $2,666, the promised amount minus Hoffman's fee. She claimed to have had no further contact with Hilgemeier and no idea how much had been offered to him. She was never called upon by Colgate to tell her side of the story.

Winn, on the other hand, was not out of the woods. On August 8 Lawson called her in to her office to announce that Hilgemeier had taken his complaint to Colgate, and the jobs of everyone at "Dotto" were at stake. Winn agreed to accompany Lawson to Colgate and deny receiving answers in advance by claiming she made the notes *after* the broadcast. The meeting took place at the Cooper offices, with lawyers present for Cooper, for Ted Bates & Co., the advertising agency that handled "Dotto" for Colgate, and for CBS. The allegations in Hilgemeier's affidavit were read to Winn, and she was shown her notebook page. She confirmed it was hers but said she did not realize until that moment that the page was missing from her notebook. She had such a poor memory, she told the lawyers, that after the broadcast she wrote things down in order to write a letter about the show to her sister in Philadelphia, who did not have a TV set. Finishing her story for us, Winn showed no emotion when I said we would let her know through Edelbaum if we wanted to see her again or call her before a grand jury.

At this point, we had accounts of the May 20 "Dotto" rigging from three people: Hilgemeier, Slatin, and Winn. The contradictions among the accounts were minor ones of timing and sequence. The important thing was that we had corroboration of wrong-doing and cover-up if not an actual crime, and a long list of people to call in for interviews. I sent my associate Melvin Stein off to set these up, starting at the top if possible with the producers, Jurist and Fischer. Before I could call David Worgan, Frank Hogan's executive assistant, with a report, he called me, to say he was sending down Marty Steadman, a reporter for the *Journal-American*, with someone who wanted to make a new complaint against another quiz show. I met them at the elevator. The reporter introduced himself and then a short, stocky man of around thirty, named Herbert Stempel, as if I should have known the name, which I did not. Steadman excused himself and departed, leaving Stempel with me. I spent the evening and the better part of the next two days with Stempel as the simmering scandal initiated by the cancelation of "Dotto" exploded into a fire storm of charges concerning the biggest of the big-money quizzes, "Twenty-One."

CHAPTER TWO

"I'm Perfectly Willing to Need Help"

(AUGUST 27–SEPTEMBER 5, 1958)

I took Herbert Stempel to my office, dragooned Robert Donnelly, another junior assistant district attorney under my supervision, and listened as Stempel recounted his experience as a contestant on the big-money quiz, "Twenty-One," broadcast on Monday nights on NBC. Stempel, a resident of Forest Hills in the borough of Queens, a graduate of the City College of New York, and most recently employed as a trainee with the New York City Welfare Department, had been the show's champion from October 17 to December 5, 1956, when he was defeated by a challenger named Charles Van Doren, though Stempel took home $49,500 in winnings. Like everyone else, I knew the name of Charles Van Doren, an English instructor in his late twenties at Columbia College, scion of a distinguished American literary family, whose appearances on "Twenty-One" had made him a national celebrity.

In June 1955 the debut and overnight success of "The $64,000 Question" on CBS had created the big-money TV quiz craze. In this program, unlikely experts—a shoemaker–opera buff, a marine captain whose field was food and cooking, a housewife who knew boxing inside and out—took turns entering a windowed "isolation booth" that cut them off from help by the audience. Here they answered difficult questions for a top prize of $64,000 and became celebrities in the process. The instant popularity of "The $64,000 Question" had prompted imitations from other producers, the most successful of which was "Twenty-One." Modeled on the card game of blackjack, "Twenty-One" differed from the "Question" in important ways: two contestants competed, they weren't merely experts in a single field but answered difficult questions in scores of different subjects, and the format was open-ended: as long as one contestant defeated challengers, he or she could stay on the program indefinitely, in theory, and there was no limit to winnings.

After being introduced on the air, the two competing contestants entered separate isolation booths and donned earphones to receive instructions from the master of ceremonies, Jack Barry, who along with his partner, Daniel Enright, had created "Twenty-One." The contestants did not choose the subjects; instead, Barry announced them, reading from cards that popped up from a dispensing machine, apparently at random. Like blackjack, the game went in rounds. When Barry announced the subject, the contestants in turn gambled on their knowledge by selecting a number of points from one to eleven, then were asked a question—an easy one for a low number of points, a hard one for a high number. The idea was to amass twenty-one points in two or more rounds. The isolation booths functioned to keep contestants from knowing each other's score and from hearing each other's question and answer, since the same question was used for both if they asked for the same number of points in a round. The category of knowledge changed with each round. If a player missed a question in an early round, he or she had the chance to recover in a subsequent round. On the other hand, after the first round, a wrong answer meant deducting the number of points the question was worth from points previously won.

As in blackjack, contestants could stop the game by "knocking" after the second round if they felt their score was higher than their opponents'. At the end of a game, the winners were credited with $500 for each point they had more than the losers. A winner could retire with the winnings or remain as champion to face a new challenger. A losing challenger departed with a small consolation prize. If the champion lost, previous winnings were trimmed accordingly. If there was a tie, then the worth of the prize was raised an extra $500 per point in the spread in the next game. Thus a series of ties, during which a champion could not retire, would quickly raise the overall stakes into tens of thousands of dollars.

After four months on "Twenty-One," Van Doren left with $129,000, twice the top prize of the "Question," and in July 1958, a Columbia University student named Elfrida Von Nardroff had left after six months as champion with $226,500. But now, in my office, Stempel was claiming he was given the questions and answers in advance for all the games he had played on the air, by Enright, the chief producer; every moment of his appearances, including those during which he gave wrong answers that occasioned his defeat by Van Doren, had been scripted and rehearsed with him by Enright.

The story began for Stempel on September 27, 1956, the morning after he watched the third broadcast of "Twenty-One," when he sat down to write a letter to Barry and Enright Productions asking to be considered as a contestant.

I am married and have a 14-month-old son. I am a veteran of 8 years of Army service, part of which was spent with Army Criminal Investigation, and have been stationed in many parts of the world. I am aged 29 and am at present a senior at the City College of New York. Doctors have told me and many of my friends say that I have a very retentive, if not photographic memory, and I have thousands of odd and obscure facts and many facets of general information at my fingertips. I have sat home continuously watching many television shows and I answer the so great bulk of the questions that my wife has continually urged me to try out for your fine show.[1]

In fact, Stempel had a supergenius IQ of 170, but, I learned, he was very far from "finding himself" in terms of what to do with his gift. He was an only child and three years old when his father, a seasonal factory worker, died. Stempel's mother had to work and left him alone during the day in their Bronx tenement apartment. After graduating from the prestigious Bronx High School of Science, he worked briefly for the Post Office before going into the army in 1944, where he remained until 1952, when he left to go to college on the G.I. Bill. Enrolled at City College, he met and married his wife Toby, whose father had founded a successful hosiery business. After her father died, Toby became beneficiary of a trust fund administered by her brother. With his brilliant mind, Stempel did not have to spend much time on his studies. He had vague ambitions of becoming an actor or playwright, but, he freely admitted, his overriding short-term goal was to find a way out from under the financial thumb of his wife's family.

A few days after writing his letter, he received a phone call from the Barry and Enright office, went in, and took a written test of general knowledge devised to screen prospective contestants. The next day, he was called back by Howard Merrill, a staff producer, who congratulated him on answering correctly 251 items out of the 363 on the test, the best performance by an applicant up to that point. Merrill then introduced him to Enright, in the latter's office. There Enright and Merrill, along with Jack Barry and other members of Enright's staff, spent two hours probing Stempel's background as well as barraging him with questions like "What is the capital of Nepal?", "Name the classifications of fingerprints," "What is the width of a football field goalpost?"—all of which Stempel had little trouble answering. He was told they would be in touch.

On October 16, 1956, Stempel received a personal call from Enright asking him to come down to the office immediately. Toby Stempel had gone to a movie with a friend, leaving her husband to baby-sit, so he could not leave the apartment. Enright asked directions, then arrived half an hour later at Stempel's door carrying an attaché case. As Stempel recounted it, Enright sat down, opened the attaché case, and took out a stack of square cards. "The category is Science," said Enright, "for one point, answer the following question . . . ," then he read a simple question from a card, which Stempel answered. Enright next read a slightly harder Science question worth two points, then one for three points, all the way up to eleven points. Enright repeated the sequence in six or seven other categories of knowledge and told Stempel the answers to the few questions he did not know. Then, according to Stempel, Enright smiled and asked him how he would like to make a lot of money. When Stempel said why not, Enright told him, "Play ball with me, kid, and you'll win $24,000 just like that." He would be a contestant on "Twenty-One" the following night; on the broadcast he would request a nine-point question in the first round of the game, and a nine-point question in the second round, and he would win.

Without waiting for an answer, Enright asked to see Stempel's wardrobe. Stempel took Enright into the bedroom, where Enright went through the closet and pulled out an old blue double-breasted suit, shiny and shabby, which had belonged to Stempel's father-in-law. "You'll wear this," Enright said and asked to see his shirts. Stempel opened a bureau drawer and Enright pulled out a blue and white striped shirt with a frayed collar. "It's blue. That's what you wear on television." Enright told him to have his hair cut in a white-wall, marine-style, and asked about his watch. Stempel was wearing an old $6 watch that ticked as loudly as an alarm clock. Enright listened, then said it would do fine.

Overwhelmed as Enright kept talking, Stempel told us, he immediately took it for granted that being given the number of points to ask for, being rehearsed with the questions and answers, being told what to wear, was how a quiz show was run. After a few minutes, Toby Stempel walked in and met Enright. They chatted a bit, then Enright said, "Everything is going to be all right. We are all going to make a lot of money."

The following day, alone with Enright in his office, Stempel was handed paper and pencil and ordered to write down exactly what he was told. "You'll be given the category, then take five seconds, pause, stutter, then say nine points." Enright demonstrated how to stutter, then told him what the questions would be and the answers he was to give. "When you are nervous and tense, you are supposed to act nervous and tense. When you get the question, I want you to bite your lip and close your eyes"—again Enright demonstrated—"and pretend that you are concentrating and really trying to dredge up the answer." Enright took out a handkerchief and showed Stempel how he should mop his brow—not smear it, but pat it—to create a more tense atmosphere. Stempel was told how to sigh and breathe heavily into the isolation booth microphone. On the air, Barry would call him "Herb," but he was to be deferential and always address the emcee as "Mr. Barry."

That evening Stempel went to NBC Studio 6B in the RCA Building in Rockefeller Center at quarter to eight. After being made up, he was shown to a private dressing room to wait. Enright came in to check on him and run through the stage directions once more. After the broadcast began, Stempel waited twenty minutes while two contestants played to a scoreless tie and a new rule was invoked on the air, whereby scoreless contestants were eased off with $100 consolation prizes. Then Stempel was on against an accountant named Maurice Peloubet. He played as instructed, won by eighteen points to nothing, racking up winnings of $9,000 in three or four minutes.

During the next five weeks, Stempel demolished challengers and swelled his winnings to over $50,000. In two sessions every week before the upcoming broadcast, he met alone with Enright to go over the number of points he would select for each round, the questions, and the answers he would give, including an occasional deliberate miss to vary the pace. What Enright called the "mechanics"—stage directions, gestures, timing, and wording of responses—were rehearsed and performed exactly for the desired effect and to keep games from running over into the time allotted for commercials. Every motion, sigh, and word uttered on the air was part of the script and had to be down pat. An eleven-point question could consist of seven or eight parts. Stempel might be instructed to answer the first, second, and third parts, skip the fourth and fifth, answer the rest, then return to the fourth and fifth, close his eyes, count off the answers on his fingers. Then he would strain for the hardest part to heighten the drama. He was told always to count off a certain number of "beats," extra pauses before each answer, to increase tension to the maximum. Then he was suddenly to open his eyes, give the answer with a dazzling smile, and explode with pleasure when Barry said, "That's right!"

And to make sure Stempel knew his lessons, there was a run-through in the dressing room before each broadcast, one last check to see that the script was being followed. After this session, Stempel tore up his notes and flushed them down the toilet of the backstage men's room. During the actual broadcast, to make things more convincing, the air conditioning in the isolation booth was turned off to make Stempel sweat.

So complete was Enright's control that Stempel remained the passive pupil even when he knew he was right and Enright was wrong. For the November 7, 1956, broadcast he was told he would be asked the name of the Pacific island the bomber "Enola Gay" left from to drop the first atom bomb on Hiroshima in August 1945. Stempel said he knew the island was Tinian, in the Marianas group. No, it was Okinawa, Enright said; his research people couldn't be wrong. On the broadcast, playing against a Cuban physician named Carlos Carballo, Stempel followed orders and answered "Okinawa" when the question came, and Barry declared his answer correct. The reaction from the public rolled in, including a phone call from the widow of the Enola Gay's copilot to correct the answer. Barry and Enright scrambled to find Dr. Carballo and bring him back the following week, when Barry announced his mistake, claiming he had read the answer from the wrong card, because Okinawa was the correct answer to another, unused question about islands. The flawed game was declared a tie, and Stempel won the rematch.

When Stempel had pushed his winnings up to the $50,000 level, he received from Enright an explanation of the economic facts of life about "Twenty-One": Pharmaceuticals, Inc., manufacturer of Geritol and other products, the show's sponsor, budgeted $10,000 a broadcast for prize money, and the producers had to stay within the budget. Enright now showed Stempel a letter addressed to Enright in which Stempel would agree to accept only $40,000 if he left the show with posted winnings of between $60,000 and $80,000; $50,000 on sums between $80,000 and $100,000; and $60,000 on sums over $100,000. According to Stempel, Enright made it clear at this point that he was to sign this agreement, retroactively, or suddenly find himself a loser. Stempel did not hesitate to sign, but by now he was so reluctant to rock the boat that he did not even ask Enright for a copy.

On the broadcast of November 28, 1956, when his winnings totaled $69,500, Stempel played arranged ties against a challenger who Stempel sensed immediately was his nemesis, Charles Van Doren. Stempel could not tell us with certainty if Van Doren was being given the questions and answers in advance, for Enright never told him anything about what his opponents would do, and he knew better than to ask. Nevertheless, he was told there would be three ties and followed his instructions to the letter. Since the result indeed was three ties, he could only assume that Van Doren was also being fixed. They were scheduled to return to play again, with the stakes raised to $2,000 a point.

On December 4, one day before the return match, Stempel went to Enright's office for their usual session. Enright took a piece of chalk and went to a blackboard near his desk. "You brought this show up very, very well," Enright acknowledged to Stempel as he drew a diagonal line going up the blackboard, then leveled it off. "But now we find we're sort of at a plateau, and we feel it is time for a change. We need another winner to take over from you, a new champion. So tomorrow night's the night you have to go." It was nothing personal, Enright explained, but he could not argue with the ratings; they needed "a new face." He promised to make Stempel a research consultant for "Twenty-One," at a salary of $250 a week.

Next, Enright outlined the upcoming scenario. The first game would be a 21–21 tie. After winning sixteen points in the first two rounds, in the third round Stempel would be asked, for five points, which movie won the Oscar for Best Picture in 1955. Stempel would answer incorrectly *On the Waterfront*, which galled him, because he had seen *Marty*, the Best Picture of 1955, three times and identified with the love story of two ordinary, unglamourous New Yorkers, but Stempel understood the cute twist. He would miss an easy question, so the public could think the great genius, for all his erudition, had overlooked something just about anybody could answer. But then, he would recover in the next round and tie with Van Doren at twenty-one.

In the first round of the second game, the category would be Newspapers, and Stempel would ask for eleven points. Enright read the question: "Name the famous newspaper and its editor, who died in 1944, and give us the title of the editorial that made him and his paper nationally known." Stempel's American history course had covered it just a few days before, and he told Enright that William Allen White was the editor, the newspaper was the *Emporia Gazette*, and the name of the editorial was "What's the Matter with Kansas?" But Enright said, "Well, forget 'What's the Matter with Kansas.' You don't know the answer and you can't even hazard a guess on it."

Between the session with Enright and the broadcast, Stempel went over the angles. According to his agreement with Enright, even if he was allowed to go over $100,000, he would receive only $60,000. Following orders, he would come off the show with announced winnings of $49,500, of which the agreement would give him $40,000. Given his tax situation and the promise of a job paying $250 a week from Enright, he would do best to play along. Nevertheless, just before the broadcast, Stempel told Enright he wanted the opportunity to play straight against Van Doren, because it was a college fight—CCNY versus Columbia. Enright refused; Stempel had to go for the good of the show, and he repeated the offer to find Stempel a position with the firm.

On the air, in the first round of the second game, as instructed, Stempel did not attempt to guess the name of the editorial that made the *Emporia Gazette* famous. Later in the game, when he correctly answered the names of the wives of Henry VIII, then was asked to describe their fates, he wise-cracked, "Well, they all died," before going on to say precisely and correctly how. It was a little piece of sardonic humor he thought up himself and asked Enright if it was okay to use. Enright gave his approval.

It was an extraordinary story, besides which Hilgemeier's revelations about "Dotto" paled, but what kind of proof did Stempel have? At his meetings with Enright, Stempel confirmed, no one else was ever present. Once when he and Enright were working, Barry looked in; Enright immediately shoved the question cards into his desk drawer, and Barry hastily departed. When Stempel asked Enright if Barry knew what they were doing, Enright told him to mind his own business. As for the nominal producer of "Twenty-One," Howard Merrill, Stempel had no dealing with him beyond going over the script for the "interview" chatter; Merrill soon left "Twenty-One" for another job and was replaced by another staff member, Albert Freedman, with whom Stempel had little contact.

But, Stempel revealed, even before the advent of Van Doren, he told friends and acquaintances what was going on in great detail. These included several neighbors in Queens, one of his instructors at CCNY, his doctor, his druggist, and the barber he visited once a week to keep his whitewall haircut trimmed. He also made friends with Al Davis, one of Enright's public relations men, also a Queens resident and a CCNY graduate, and told him what was happening. When he left Enright's office on December 4, after learning he would lose, Stempel visited his doctor, his druggist, and barber and told them he would be taking the dive. On the day of the broadcast, he dropped into Davis's office, showed him the notes he had made during the session with Enright—a rundown of that night's show with the questions and answers to be used—and confided that the show was fixed and he was going to lose.

WHEN DONNELLY and I had heard this much of Stempel's story, it was late at night, so we scheduled him for another session the following afternoon, August 28. That morning I learned he had already told his story to the *Journal-American*, which reported on its front page that an unnamed "star" of "Twenty-One" was talking to the district attorney. My guess was that the newspaper had been unable to corroborate Stempel's account to them and, following the lead of the *Post* in connection with Hilgemeier and "Dotto," was using a visit to the D.A. as a pretext for breaking the story. In the morning, I briefed Hogan, who had reasons beyond professional instinct to be skeptical of Stempel. A graduate of both Columbia College and Law School, Hogan lived near the university campus, was active as a booster of his alma mater, and had social links with its administrators and faculty. He knew personally Charles Van Doren's father, Mark Van Doren, a distinguished poet and long-time professor of English at the college. He now said to me he could not conceive of the possibility that someone of the character and background of Charles Van Doren, whom he had met, could be involved in something like the fixing of a quiz program.

Nevertheless, I stood by that afternoon in the large office Hogan used only on formal occasions as he met the press and acknowledged that "Twenty-One" as well as "Dotto" was being investigated. From what we had determined so far, Hogan told the reporters, he didn't believe that "the people viewing the quiz shows have any basis to lodge a formal complaint under the penal law, although they have a right to be angry." If the shows were fixed, however, "It might be proper to recommend legislation or to send the matter to the FCC. . . . A lot more digging will be needed before I can say there is anything serious or not. It is unfair to say this is a burgeoning scandal."[2] The newspapers thought otherwise. The following morning, August 29, in addition to Hogan's remarks, they carried strong rebuttals issued by NBC and Barry and Enright of the unnamed contestant's charges. NBC claimed specifically that the charges concerning "Twenty-One"

> first came to our attention over a year ago. At that time we made an investigation and found them to be utterly baseless and untrue. We are completely convinced of the integrity of *Twenty-One* as a program and of the integrity of its producers. . . .
>
> At the time these charges were first brought to our attention, and shortly thereafter, two major newspapers made thorough investigations of them and apparently concluded, as we did, that they had no basis in fact. As a result, they printed nothing.[3]

As soon as I arrived at the office, I was summoned to David Worgan's office. In addition to Worgan, I found four people named by Stempel in his story: Jack Barry, in his early forties, jowly and intense; Arthur Franklin, a public relations man, also in his forties, lean and nervous; Franklin's partner, Alfred Davis, younger, a family-man type; and Daniel Enright, at forty, polished, earnest, and cultivated. Also present were two lawyers: representing NBC was Lawrence McKay, a partner of John Cahill, a former U.S. attorney for the Southern District of New York and one of Frank Hogan's closest friends; representing Barry and Enright was Irving Cohen.

McKay and Cohen wasted no time making clear what was at stake. There was no beating about the bush about an unnamed contestant; instead, they stated that the outrageous allegations of Stempel were damaging the reputation, credibility, and existence of "Twenty-One," which Barry and Enright produced for NBC, the owner of the program since it was purchased from its creators in May 1957, and it was essential that the charges be cleared up as quickly as possible. Then Enright took over and, frequently yessed by Franklin, did most of the talking. Enright and Barry had been partners since the late 1940s, creating and selling program concepts for radio and television, then producing them for broadcast under leasing arrangements with commercial sponsors or directly with broadcasting networks. The most successful of their early television packages was "Juvenile Jury," in which a panel of children discussed problems and answered questions submitted by home viewers, studio audience members, and celebrity guests, and was followed by a similar show with elderly panelists called "Life Begins at 80"; later the format yielded "Wisdom of the Ages," a combined panel of youngsters and oldsters. In July 1956 they introduced their first successful quiz program—"Tic Tac Dough," based on the game of tic-tac-toe, broadcast weekdays at midday on NBC and, later on, in a weekly evening prime-time higher-stakes version, also on NBC. This was followed by "Twenty-One," beginning in September 1956. Barry and Enright currently produced two other small-stakes daytime quizzes for NBC, "Concentration" and "Dough Re Mi."

Enright stressed that the continuing success of a program like "Twenty-One" depended upon the public's perception of the absolute integrity and honesty of the quiz. Unsubstantiated allegations like Stempel's, if not repudiated, could seriously damage the reputation of the show and destroy it. According to Enright, Stempel was a disturbed person and a blackmailer; aware from the start that something was wrong with Stempel, Enright had signed him on as a contestant because he was an unusual combination they believed would appeal to an audience. He was, in Franklin's words, "extraordinarily ordinary"; at the same time, he was an offbeat character so intent on collecting knowledge that there was practically nothing he did not know.

Stempel became a big winner and caught on with the public, but, as Enright and Franklin now told it, things began going wrong after Stempel lost to Van Doren on December 5, 1956, and entered a state of emotional upheaval as a result of being cut off from the celebrity. They were fond of Stempel and wanted to help him out, even though Enright had made no promises to him. They tried using him to warm up the "Twenty-One" studio audience with patter before air time, but Stempel was so wooden that the audience froze up and he had to be dropped. Several times after this, Stempel came in to visit Enright, and on one occasion said he was seeing a psychiatrist; he also retained Franklin to advise him on his wardrobe, to arrange for appearances, and to do other public relations for him. Wanting to encourage Stempel, Enright applauded these efforts at self-improvement.

Then on March 1, 1957, according to Enright, Stempel and a friend of his named Bertram Hacken barged into Enright's office, handed him a document, and ordered him to read it. It was a photostat of an affidavit, handwritten and signed by Stempel, which purported to describe in detail how Stempel's appearances on "Twenty-One" were "fixed." Hacken stated that Stempel was responsible for "Twenty-One"'s success and deserved an additional $50,000; if he didn't get it, the affidavit was going to the newspapers. Enright now said he stifled an impulse to report this to the police and stalled, telling Stempel he could do nothing before consulting with Barry, who was out of town.

Enright then called in Franklin, Davis, and Cohen to discuss the situation. Franklin and Davis believed Stempel was basically harmless and could be talked out of his crazy ideas. Calling in the police would simply destroy Stempel, which nobody wanted to do, and the affidavit, no matter how baseless, could hurt "Twenty-One" if it were published. Enright agreed to have Franklin talk sense to Stempel, on the condition that if he failed, they wanted to be able to prove blackmail by surreptitiously tape-recording Stempel in the act.

On two occasions thereafter, according to the story, Franklin managed to have Stempel admit the blackmail attempt, but tape-recording equipment hidden in Franklin's office failed. On a third occasion, a meeting between Stempel and Enright in Enright's office on March 7, 1957, the equipment worked. By this time Franklin's efforts to soothe Stempel had made him contrite. On March 7, according to Enright, Stempel asked him for loans, which Enright firmly refused to make, though he did offer to pay for additional psychotherapy for Stempel and would see about finding him a spot on a new panel quiz, called "High Low," they were preparing to introduce in the summer. On the same occasion, Enright secured from Stempel a handwritten and signed declaration that he had received no assistance on "Twenty-One," a photostat of which Enright now handed over to us:

> I do hereby state and declare to whomever may be now or in the future concerned that Dan Enright, producer of Barry and Enright Productions, has never in any way shape nor form, given

imparted or suggested to me any questions or answers connected with the program *Twenty-One*.

Any questions or answers I gave on the program were entirely my own and no aid or assistance was rendered to me by Mr. Enright nor any of his staff. As a token of this statement and affirming it to be entirely true, I place my signature freely and without any mental or physical duress on the paper below.[4]

Enright also handed over what he said was a copy of the tape recording that proved Stempel had blackmailed him. With this, Worgan turned the group over to me, and I took them to the "tech room" in the offices of our Investigation Bureau, where we kept equipment used for wiretapping and eavesdropping. After Tom Comiskey, the investigator in charge, threaded Enright's tape onto a machine and set it in motion, all we heard was a series of hisses, static, and garbled words. Enright apologized and blamed the tape on faulty copying. The original was in a bank vault; the three-day Labor Day weekend coming up would give them time to make a better copy and type out a transcript, which they could deliver to us first thing Tuesday morning. He also promised to send over the blackmail document Stempel had threatened him with on March 1.

I asked Enright pointedly if he knew of any reason why Stempel thought he might succeed in blackmail. Enright looked me in the eye and said if I meant by that did he give Stempel assistance on "Twenty-One," the answer was absolutely no. McKay pointed out that Stempel eventually did talk to a reporter, who called NBC in September 1957 for comment. At that time Enright showed Stempel's letter to NBC and told them of the existence of the tape. The network was totally satisfied as to Enright's and "Twenty-One"'s integrity. So was the press, McKay added, because nothing was done with the Stempel story until the "Dotto" business and his visit to us.

In view of the fact that Stempel's story was giving the newspapers a field day, Enright wanted our approval to release a statement about their own visit to us. I strongly advised against such a move. We could not consider Enright's complaint—for that was what it amounted to—against Stempel for extortion complete until we heard the tape Enright claimed would clinch the matter. Releasing a statement before we had time to investigate the complaint would create more furor and alert Stempel to take measures to cover his tracks. This was not what the group wanted to hear. Fifteen minutes after they left me, I was called back to Worgan's office, where in front of Enright and the others, he took issue with my telling the group not to make public their visit; it was not the function of the district attorney to advise Enright on the conduct of his public relations.

That afternoon, Donnelly and I questioned Stempel for a third time, not mentioning Enright's blackmail charges but pressing him for proof of his allegations. At this point, Stempel claimed that Enright advanced him considerable amounts of money against his winnings while he was still a contestant. Explaining this, Stempel introduced another angle to his bizarre story, concerning a gambler and small-time hoodlum named Richard Lamme, who had a police record for robbery and bad-check passing and, before Stempel went on "Twenty-One," lived with his wife and infant son in the same building as the Stempels. The couples became acquainted and before long Lamme was regaling Stempel with his exploits as an armed robber and trying to borrow money for various schemes. By the time Stempel was trying out for "Twenty-One," Lamme was pitching an opportunity to double his money by investing in a racing stable syndicate in Florida. After Stempel became a contestant, Lamme increased the pressure through Toby Stempel, in turn flattering and menacing her.

Thus, according to Stempel, on November 17, in the middle of his run on the quiz, he requested from Enright an advance on his winnings, inviting the producer to join in Lamme's investment scheme. Enright declined the offer but gave Stempel a check for $8,500 from the account of Dojo, Inc., a subsidiary of Barry and Enright Productions. In theory, according to the rules of "Twenty-One," Stempel could have lost all of his posted winnings in a single appearance on the show, but, Stempel told us, that hardly mattered in light of his being fixed and of the agreement he had with Enright guaranteeing him $40,000. Stempel turned over the $8,500 advance to Lamme. On November 29 Stempel asked for and received from Enright another advance of $10,000 and gave it to Lamme. Several days after his defeat by Van Doren on December 5, Stempel was given another $10,000 by Enright; then on December 17 he requested from Enright and signed over to Lamme another check for $7,000. Since these sums had been advanced by check, Stempel's new assertions, if they were true, could be easily corroborated.

After the session with Stempel, I had a visit from a colleague, Sheldon Levy, who said a member of his local Democratic party club named Henry Bloomgarden had been a "Twenty-One" contestant and wanted to talk to us about his experience. I called Bloomgarden and suggested he come in for an interview. Bloomgarden said he preferred we meet elsewhere because my office was being besieged by reporters. Ordinarily we did not interview people outside of the office, but I agreed and made an appointment to meet

Bloomgarden at his own office on Fifth Avenue on Saturday, August 30. That morning, the newspapers carried the fruit of Worgan's laissez faire—reports of the Enright visit to the office, which quoted McKay on the baselessness of Stempel's charges and gave excerpts from Stempel's March 7, 1957, statement to Enright.

I rarely if ever had met alone with a witness in an investigation, so when I arrived at his small office accompanied by Donnelly, Stein, and Barrett, Bloomgarden, an upright man in his late twenties, seemed put out by the show of force. Bloomgarden was in the public-relations business and had been champion of "Twenty-One" from March to June 1957, after displacing Vivienne Nearing, a lawyer who had defeated Charles Van Doren. Bloomgarden left the show with $98,500 in winnings. Before "Twenty-One," he told us, he had been briefly a contestant on Barry and Enright's "Tic Tac Dough"; though he won nothing on that show, he was encouraged by its staff producer, Albert Freedman, to take the test for "Twenty-One," which he passed. Interestingly enough, when he was selected as a contestant for "Twenty-One," the same Freedman had become the show's producer, but, Bloomgarden insisted, he received no help from Freedman, Enright, or anyone else. Rather, he owed his success to hard study.

According to Bloomgarden, then, "Twenty-One" was a perfectly legitimate program and Stempel was simply a sore loser. As an investigator and prosecutor I had heard thousands of complaints, but I could not remember anyone going to such lengths as Bloomgarden to provide an unsolicited endorsement of the honesty of a person or activity under investigation by the D.A.'s office. I immediately suspected a whitewash. When I expressed some skepticism, Bloomgarden grew belligerent. I cut the meeting short and advised him to think over his version of events and seek the advice of a lawyer, for we very likely would get back to him.

After spending Saturday afternoon interviewing three friends of Stempel who corroborated his account of what he had told them about upcoming appearances on "Twenty-One," I read in the *Daily Mirror* on the way home Stempel's own explanation to a reporter of the March 1957 statement: "Enright told me if I would sign the letter he would get me a job." He added, "I feel guilty to have been part of the entire situation. I think I was morally wrong—but I was blinded by the glitter and glamor of show business. . . . But 99 out of 100 people would have done the same thing."

On Sunday, August 31, Hogan, in his capacity as a Senate candidate, was the guest on a news-panel television program. He would have preferred discussing issues pertaining to his campaign, but the reporters wanted to know about the quiz scandal. Hogan mentioned the possibility that laws were needed to regulate quiz shows and said that the matter could be brought before a grand jury. To what purpose, he was asked, if, as it now appeared, no laws had been broken? It would be for the grand jury to determine if laws had been broken, Hogan answered; even if there was no basis for indictments, grand juries had the power to probe matters of public concern and to issue reports, known in legal parlance as presentments, which exposed problems and pointed up the need for remedial measures in the form of legislation by appropriate bodies.[5]

On Tuesday morning, September 2, the day after Labor Day, a new copy of Enright's tape and a transcript were delivered to the office as promised. As I immersed myself in the transcript, Barry and Enright held a news conference at the Biltmore Hotel, where they told reporters they had been "pushed beyond all reasonableness of professional and human endurance by the malicious statements" of Stempel. "I was a father image to him," Enright said, "He had to destroy me. I represented authority he had to destroy to be cured."[6] Asked why he had waited a year and a half to report Stempel's blackmail attempt, Enright replied that his press agents had talked him out of it because it would have killed the show. Later in the day, Stempel declared to reporters that the Enright tape was doctored; the simple fact he had been given advances clinched his assertion that "Twenty-One" was fixed.

On September 3 Stempel was back in the office, and we played the tape for him. He admitted the voice was his but repeated the claim he made to the press that the content was altered, spliced together by bits and pieces, a possibility already presented to me by Tom Comiskey. But Stempel did admit the extortion attempt, in effect, conceding he had been foolish to threaten an exposé and blamed Hacken for providing the impetus to do so. Otherwise, he stuck to his story—"Twenty-One" was fixed and Enright had given him advances within the secret guaranteed total of $40,000—then added details in light of the facts revealed by the tape.

As Stempel told it, life after "Twenty-One" was a matter of being mostly broke and increasingly bitter. Taxes would eat up a good part of his $49,500, despite Enright's deferring a large portion of the payment into the new year. On January 8, 1957, Stempel received his last payment from Enright, for $14,000, most of which was earmarked for taxes. Richard Lamme had disappeared, and Stempel was no closer to his dream of financial independence from his wife's family than before he had ever heard of "Twenty-One." Disturbed by the enormous publicity Van Doren was generating for himself on the quiz and his own eclipse as a celebrity, Stempel began seeing a psychiatrist and redoubled his efforts to find work in show business. He retained Franklin for professional advice and public relations at $250 a week. At Franklin's suggestion, he lent $3,500 to a friend of the publicist, who was supposed to place a magazine article about Stempel. But the writer also disappeared, leaving Stempel with a worthless IOU. To top it off, he owed money for payments on a new car, bought in the flush of being on "Twenty-One."

Stempel confided in his friend, Hacken, who had lent him $3,000 to invest in an early Lamme scheme, securing the loan with a chattel mortgage on Stempel's car. According to Stempel, it was Hacken who suggested he write out a kind of confession about "Twenty-One" to sell to a newspaper. They went to see Enright on March 1, 1957, and handed him a photostatted copy of Stempel's confession. Enright read it, then put it in his desk drawer, calling the document lies and blackmail. Stempel dared Enright to call the police, but Hacken intervened, insisting if the game had been played honestly, Stempel, who knew all the answers, would have won much more. Enright asked them to wait outside while he tried to contact Barry. When after fifteen minutes nothing happened, Stempel and Hacken departed.

After a series of calls from Franklin trying to patch things up, Stempel went to Enright's office on March 7, for the meeting which would be, unknown to him, tape-recorded. Stempel did notice, with great annoyance, a blowup of Van Doren's picture as it appeared on the cover of the February 11, 1957, issue of *Time* magazine. The tape-recorded transcript showed Stempel to be contrite from the beginning, telling Enright how badly he felt about their meeting a week before: "Turning on you, when I should have turned toward you." According to the tape, Enright asked Stempel to write down on a piece of paper, in his own words, that questions and answers on the show had not been disclosed to him. Stempel complied and Enright approved the result. Then Enright said, "Herb, I'm going to be very frank and very cold with you in stating certain facts. You are emotionally disturbed. If you were not to recognize that, I think you were to overlook a tremendous factor that governs many things you do."

"I'm not that emotionally disturbed, though."

"Well, let me put it this way. You came in with a blackmail scheme. It was a blackmail scheme—do you agree?"

"Uh, yes."

Expressing his "shock" at the attempt, Enright related how his lawyer had recommended he go to the district attorney, which Franklin told him would destroy Stempel, so he had backed off. "Now as long as you recognize the complete immorality of what you have done—."

"I do most wholeheartedly."

"And as long as you realize that you need help—and the help does not necessarily have to be financial help, but help to reconstruct your emotional self—and you are willing to work an awful lot to help yourself, then you have made tremendous strides."

"Definitely."

When Enright urged him to admit that he lost on "Twenty-One" because he chose the wrong question, Stempel vented his resentment: "I'll admit I flipped, partially, because of the publicity Van Doren received. . . . I just felt that I hadn't gotten to the pinnacle where he had. Aside from that, I have nothing against the guy personally. I don't know him from a hole in the wall. I only met him on an impersonal basis. I mean, how can I have anything against the man. I went on the show; I didn't have shit and I came off with $50,000. It was a hell of a good break, because I could have worked for the rest of my life and never made this much money. Unfortunately I piddled it away through my own stupidity." Stempel then went into a detailed account of money problems and the depredations of Lamme.

Enright listened, then held out the possibility they might be able to use him on a new show, but a decision on this was four or five weeks away and he could make no promises. In the meantime, Enright would underwrite his psychiatric expenses until these could be deducted from whatever salary Stempel might earn from a position with Barry and Enright. "We recognize that part of the problem is that a door was opened for you, you put a foot in the door, and the door was closed," Enright said. "We are in a part responsible for your emotional upsets, because we opened that door for you. While technically and legally, of course, we have no responsibility, emotionally we do have responsibility."

When Stempel again turned to his money troubles, Enright reiterated he would not lend him any money, but was available to Stempel if he ever needed someone to talk to. "When the image of Van Doren looms to the extent that he becomes a bête noire to you, call me up to talk about this thing. You have to talk to someone. And should you ever lie to me, I'd like you a week later to come back and say, 'Look, I lied to you,' and not be ashamed, because I'm not going to whip you and I'm not going to beat you, I'm not going to chastise you."

"You see, this is a holdover from my early days. When my mother used to do these things—"

"Then you don't know me, Herb. I'm not like that."

"I do know you. I know you're not the type of guy who will do these things, and yet there's a certain unconscious fear—" Stempel hesitated.

"Talk to me."

"The whole thing, Dan, in a nutshell. Somehow or other—I feel the following way. I really don't anymore ever since I've been getting it out of my system. Here was a guy that had the fancy name, the Ivy League education, parents all his life, and I had just the opposite—the hard way up, in other words. Here was my sort of own mental delusion, that all this should have been coming to me instead of a guy who had all the breaks. Very frankly and bluntly and openly, that's how the whole thing looks in a nutshell."

"It's understandable, but where the emotionally stable man steps in, the picture takes a different turn, because the emotionally stable man says if there were absolute justice in this world, then Herb Stempel's mother, when he was four years old, would not have to go on relief. But this is the world—a cruel world—and fate plays a bigger part in life than we would like, but this is the way things happen. Over this you have no control. This is what life is. You have to learn to cope with it."

"Somehow, I don't know whether I can cope with life or not. I don't know."

"I don't think you can at this stage, Herb. But I say we have help."

"I'm perfectly willing to need help."

"That's right, and I want to help you."

WHEN HE VISITED Enright the next day, according to Stempel, Enright relented a bit, gave him $800 in cash, then inadvertently threw him another bone. Stempel asked if Enright would help arrange Van Doren's participation in a quiz-show style charity match for CCNY at graduation time. Enright said Van Doren had no more desire to play, but if Van Doren's current opponent, Vivienne Nearing, were still on the show in June, she might be interested in the CCNY event. Stempel deduced from this that the next broadcast was to be Van Doren's last appearance. On March 11 Stempel withdrew $5,000 from his bank and bet it with a bookie against Van Doren at 2–1 odds. That night he became $10,000 richer as he watched Van Doren lose to Nearing. He realized that Van Doren's missing the question—the name of the current king of Belgium—was as ridiculous as his own "ignorance" of *Marty*. The difference was that he became a pariah, while Van Doren would land a job with NBC paying $50,000 a year.

On subsequent visits, as Stempel recounted, Enright was friendly but the specific offers of employment failed to materialize. Each time, Stempel reminded Enright how much he had done for "Twenty-One" and how well he could have done if the game had been played straight, but Enright kept countering with this formulation: "You missed *Marty* because you didn't know the answer, remember that, Herb." Stempel stopped pestering the packager after May, when the Barry and Enright shows were sold to NBC and Enright told Stempel everything was now out of his hands.

SENDING STEMPEL away after telling him to keep himself available for more questioning, Donnelly and I wondered, even if he were telling us the truth as he saw it, where did that take us? If the tape was genuine, it confirmed that cowardice and desperation had driven Stempel to a blackmail attempt, for on it he admitted to having made an oral threat of extortion even if he lacked the grit to carry through the threat and groveled in order to repudiate it. The failure of Enright to produce Stempel's blackmail document seemed like a strange oversight.

Otherwise, his friends' statements to us notwithstanding, the bulk of Stempel's story was uncorroborated and uncorroboratable except by Enright himself. Stempel did hand over canceled checks covering the debts he had paid off with the $800 in cash he claimed Enright gave him the day after the taped meeting. He also gave us four Reno, Nevada, telephone numbers from which Richard Lamme had been calling him recently to demand more money. We sent an investigator to talk to Lamme's mother and tracked down the parents of Lamme's wife, but there was little they could add to what we already knew from Stempel and police records—Lamme was a vicious hoodlum who preyed on the weak. There was nothing we could charge him with in regard to Stempel's money.

Nevertheless, a crucial element was Stempel's assertion that Enright advanced him payments by check against his winnings *while he was a contestant*. Since Stempel did not make the assertion until after Enright's visit to the office, we had had no occasion to ask the producer about it. I put in a call to Enright's lawyer, Irving Cohen, requesting various records, including canceled checks for the period since the debut of "Twenty-One." Cohen promised the records would be in my hands in a day or two.

From the various accounts, including the contents of Enright's tape recording, a few things did seem clear. As Enright and Franklin had put it in Worgan's office, Stempel had severe psychological problems. Yet, if Stempel looked like a patsy and victim reduced to begging, Enright appeared to me as a manipulating showman masquerading as a father figure, employing the manner of the psychiatrist. Enright seemed less interested in prosecuting Stempel than in using the district attorney's office to protect his quiz show enterprise. If Enright had in fact advanced the money to Stempel, it would add a whole new dimension to the affair, for it was hard to imagine a businessman like Enright planning to write off $18,500 if the quiz were honest and Stempel's posted winnings were wiped out by a superior challenger.

The newspapers on Thursday, September 4, carried an admission by Enright that he had indeed paid Stempel advances on his winnings, amounting to $18,500, but only to pacify Stempel when he threatened to leave "Twenty-One" just as he was helping its ratings climb. It was a clever explanation. If advances had been paid only to Stempel, then Enright's excuse was plausible—at a critical moment for the program's success or failure, he took a calculated risk of losing $18,500—and "Twenty-One" could be said on the whole to be on the up and up. But Enright also told the press he had brought in canceled checks for the advances during his visit to us the previous Friday. This was not true; I knew nothing about advances until I heard what Stempel told us right after Enright's visit to the office. Now it was important to ascertain if advances had been given to other contestants, making it all the more urgent for us to see Enright's records.

On Friday, September 5, I received a call from a lawyer by the name of Edwin Slote, whom I didn't know, saying he was representing Barry and Enright in Cohen's place. He apologized for his client's delay in responding to our request for records. Much of the material was with NBC and had to be sorted out, he explained, but it would be sent over as soon as possible. I informed Slote that we wanted to talk to Enright again, and the lawyer promised to arrange a meeting.

CHAPTER THREE

Straws in the Wind

(SEPTEMBER 6–10, 1958)

On Saturday, September 6, the quiz scandal took a new turn when the *Journal-American*, scooping other tabloids, headlined accusations against another show, "The $64,000 Challenge," a spin-off of "The $64,000 Question." The whistle-blower this time was the Reverend Charles "Stoney" Jackson, a Tennessee minister who had been a contestant on both "The $64,000 Question" and "Challenge" as an expert in the category of Great Love Stories. According to the wire-service report, Jackson claimed he was told in advance one of the answers to a four-part question by a "Miss Bernstein," and the question was used on the December 29, 1957, broadcast of the "Challenge." Jackson's opponent, Doll Goostree, the report continued, was defeated in the match because she did not know the answer, but Jackson sent her $300 from the $4,000 he won. Shirley Bernstein, identified as a producer of the "Challenge," was reached at her home in Manhattan by the *Journal-American* and admitted she was the "Miss Bernstein" mentioned by Jackson but denied she had ever fed him or anyone else an answer on the quiz.

On Sunday, other New York papers picked up the story and included comments by Goostree. Confirming that Jackson had sent her $300, she recalled chatting with him just before the "Challenge" broadcast:

> He said, "I guess we'll get the ax tonight," and I said, "I guess we will." We had gotten to feel we were of no importance. . . . It was an intangible feeling that we were slated to get off and we did get off.
>
> They led me to believe that the questioning would deal with Shakespeare. It did not.
>
> I couldn't say there was any dishonesty there, but maybe they felt we didn't have audience appeal. . . . I don't think I got a fair deal, but I can't exactly say why.[1]

Steve Carlin, executive producer of Entertainment Productions, Inc., packager of "The $64,000 Question" and "Challenge," denied to reporters that Jackson had been given the answer, but conceded the possibility of a slip, that the correct answer could have come up accidentally in a conversation between Jackson and Bernstein. Reading these accounts, I recalled from Melvin Stein's recent report of his continuing probe of "Dotto" that the producer, Edward Jurist, had once worked on "The $64,000 Challenge"; moreover, a former "Dotto" contestant interviewed by Stein, named Rochelle Rodney, who had made something of a career of being on quiz shows, hinted that "The Big Surprise"—another property of Entertainment Productions, Inc.—was controlled in a fashion similar to "Dotto."

Early on Monday morning, another one of my associates, Jay Goldberg, a Harvard Law School graduate with a flair for the dramatic, requested assignment to the investigation of "The $64,000 Challenge." Brushing aside my objection that the investigations of "Dotto" and "Twenty-One" were based on formal complaints and that no one had come to us to complain about "The $64,000 Challenge," Goldberg wanted to call Jackson in Tennessee to hear what he had to say. I relented, and later in the day, Goldberg reported that Jackson would confirm only the little he had told a Memphis daily, *The Tennessean*, which the paper had printed on Saturday and the wire services had picked up; he would have to consult a lawyer before talking further to us. I told Goldberg to await word from Jackson before digging deeper.

Goldberg did not have to wait long. Just after I sent him away I turned my attention to the pile of mail already opened and scanned by Hogan and routed to the Complaint Bureau for action. The volume of mail had swelled with the quiz scandal, much of the increase from people who had not succeeded in becoming contestants; the scandal confirmed what they already knew from being rebuffed—the whole thing was fixed. For a much smaller number of would-be whistle-blowers who *had* been contestants, the same logic applied to the fact they hadn't won anything. This morning, however, one letter stood out.

Mailed in an envelope without any indication of the actual sender, it was a mimeographed copy of a circular letter dated several months before, with a Manhattan return address and the mimeographed signature of one Arthur Cohn, Jr. It set out in detail an entirely new allegation concerning Shirley Bernstein and "The $64,000 Challenge." Goldberg wasted no time tracking down Cohn, and at an interview in the office the following day Cohn identified the mimeographed letter as his, then filled in the story it contained.

On CBS since April 1956, following the phenomenal success of its parent quiz, "The $64,000 Challenge" pitted champions from the "Question" against new experts in their categories. On the "Question," the contestants who went all the way to win $64,000 created the most excitement—risking the loss of everything previously won by missing a question at any stage in the double-or-nothing high-stakes quiz—but many contestants "retired" at intermediate stages, preferring to take home lesser amounts rather than risk all on a too difficult question. Such a one was Wilton Springer, a Fuller Brush Company salesman from the Bronx, a contestant on the "Question" in the fall of 1958 in the category of Theater who had won $8,000 before retiring. Because he had not missed answering a question, however, he qualified as a champion in his category, eligible for a stint on the "Challenge."

Cohn, an advertising-space salesman and a theater buff, had been acquainted with George Abrams, the advertising director of Revlon Products Corporation, the cosmetics manufacturer and commercial sponsor of both of the $64,000 quizzes, and it was Abrams who referred Cohn to Entertainment Productions, Inc., better known as EPI, as a possible contestant. Selected to challenge Springer early in 1958, Cohn became friendly with the champion during the weeks they had stood by before their match was scheduled for airing, on March 23, 1958. As Cohn now told it, he and his wife arrived at the CBS studio an hour before the broadcast; then he checked in with Shirley Bernstein, associate producer of the "Challenge," in a dressing room she used as an office before broadcasts.

According to Cohn, on this occasion, Bernstein said he did not appear to be nervous and did not need a warm-up; feeling confident, Cohn agreed. She then asked him to send in Springer. Cohn left the dressing room, found Springer, and directed him to Bernstein. A short while later, Springer reported to Cohn that Bernstein had warmed him up with questions about the names of secondary characters in plays—for example, Maggie Cutler, the secretary in Kaufman and Hart's *The Man Who Came to Dinner*, and Patty O'Neill, the girlfriend in *The Moon Is Blue*. Up to this point, Cohn claimed, he had been studying hard, focusing on performers and playwrights, opening-night dates, and leading actors and actresses and the roles they created, but had not paid attention to secondary characters. He would have been unable to answer the questions Bernstein had used to warm up Springer.

On the air, Cohn and Springer easily answered questions for $1,000 and $2,000, advancing to the "plateau" at which they entered separate isolation booths. Springer was asked to go first. According to the rules of the game, if the first contestant in a round missed the question, the challenger could win by supplying the right answer; if the first contestant was correct, the challenger was asked a different question. Thus the sound was left on in both isolation booths. Cohn listened carefully as the emcee, Ralph Storey, read the question for Springer:

> Romance plays a major part in countless plays. I will name the female member of a romantic team from two different American plays. For $4,000—in each one, first name the play from which the character comes, then name the male half of this theater romance. The first character is Patty O'Neill; the second, Maggie Cutler.

Hearing the names Bernstein had given Springer before the broadcast, Cohn now said, he was tempted to expose the cheating to the public right then and there, but decided to wait till after the program to complain. Springer gave the correct answers. In his turn, Cohn was given the names of two secondary characters, but he could not name the plays in which they appeared and lost the match. In the remaining moments of the broadcast, there was time only for the contestants to leave the booths and be handed dummy checks for their winnings—$4,000 for Springer, $250 in consolation for Cohn. On the way out of the theater, Cohn told his wife in a loud voice that he was going to sue.

Later that night, Cohn telephoned Bernstein at home and confronted her with what Springer had told him before the broadcast. "What an amazing coincidence," she replied but insisted she couldn't understand how the questions could have come into her hands for a warm-up session. Two days later Bernstein called Cohn back, saying she hoped he would not make trouble. He replied that he was reluctant to embark on a lawsuit, but his ego had been badly bruised. His theater expertise was legendary among his friends, and losing so quickly on the "Challenge" could make him a laughingstock, so he would tell his friends what happened.

The morning after this, Cohn was summoned to Revlon by George Abrams, who told him a vice-president of one of Revlon's advertising agencies had overheard his remark about suing. After Cohn told his story, Abrams said he agreed that what happened was more than a coincidence, since EPI was in its third year of producing the $64,000 shows, and there was no excuse for such sloppiness. Rather, it looked more like an apparent fraud. Abrams told Cohn he was going to raise hell over the incident because it could make Revlon look bad. Sensitive to his own position in the advertising business, Cohn assured Abrams he was no publicity hound and had no intention of making trouble; he only wanted to put a humiliating experience behind him.

Eventually he wrote his circular letter, which his wife mimeographed. Some twenty-five copies were made and sent out to various friends, but Cohn had no idea who had passed it along to us.

I believed Cohn's insistence that he had not sent us the letter. In his fifties and currently jobless, he seemed frightened that being mixed up, however innocently, in quiz show hanky-panky could hurt his chances of finding new work in advertising. Our standard assurance that nothing he said in the office would be leaked by us seemed to relieve him. He agreed to let us know immediately if anyone connected with the "Challenge" tried to reach him.

On September 9 Goldberg and I interviewed Wilton Springer. A lean man in his forties whose manner and appearance suggested he had led a hard life, Springer was afraid he might have to give up his winnings from the "Challenge." He quickly denied the substance of Cohn's allegation. He conceded that he had been warmed up by Bernstein with questions about secondary leads in plays and told Cohn as much, but, he insisted, neither he nor Bernstein had mentioned Maggie Cutler or anything else used in the questions on the broadcast. I let Springer go after assuring him that we had no intention of forcing him to return his prize money even if he was the beneficiary of rigging; I asked him to think things over and be ready to come down again for further questioning.

The next day, I received a call from a very agitated Springer. Shortly before, he had been telephoned by Thomas Fisher, the CBS vice-president and general counsel, who wanted him to attend a meeting at the network and tell what happened on the "Challenge." Springer told Fisher he had been down to see us and didn't know whether it was proper for him to go to CBS. Fisher then asked him to call us for approval. I had talked to Fisher at length already, about the events leading up to the demise of "Dotto," in connection with which Fisher had played the leading role for CBS. My guess was that for CBS it was the case of "Dotto" all over again, and the big shots, reacting to the Jackson whistle blowing, were in the throes of endless meetings about the situation, with the fate of the "Challenge" hinging on the outcome. I wondered just how much Fisher knew about Cohn and Springer. If he was summoning contestants to interrogate them about the "Challenge" and they lied to him, they were all the more likely to lie to us when we put our hands on them. Simultaneous investigations by CBS and the D.A. would be confusing and cumbersome; people would hide behind one another; lawyers were sure to jump in and start complaining of harassment by us.

I told Springer to do nothing, then called Fisher and asked him to suspend his interviewing of contestants since we had now opened an investigation of the "Challenge." Fisher agreed, hoping we would keep him informed so that CBS could make the right decisions in the matter. I thanked him for his co-operation but said at this point I could make no promise to tell him anything because we were offering complete confidentiality to potential witnesses.

ON SEPTEMBER 10 Goldberg and I interviewed Shirley Bernstein, who arrived at the office unaccompanied by a lawyer. She was a tall, slender woman of about thirty, cultivated, diffident, and nervous. We explained briefly the na-ture of the investigation, then asked her about her background and profes-sional career. A graduate of Mount Holyoke College, she first came to New York to go on the stage. She had been in the chorus of the hit Broadway musical comedy *On the Town*, composed by her brother Leonard Bernstein, before gravitating to the production side of show business.

In September 1955 she joined EPI, then known as Louis G. Cowan, Inc., named after its founder, a veteran packager who was the creator of "The $64,000 Question." Cowan had come to prominence just before World War II by originating "The Quiz Kids," a popular radio program in which a panel of superbright Chicago-area schoolchildren answered difficult questions sent in by listeners; after the war, Cowan became one of the biggest packagers in the business and produced the most popular radio quiz ever, "Stop the Mu-sic." Not long after launching "The $64,000 Question" in June 1955, Cowan left the day-to-day operation of his company to join CBS as an executive in the development of new programming. In May 1956, when Cowan was pro-moted to CBS vice-president for creative services, his old company changed its name to Entertainment Productions, Inc. In March 1958, Cowan became president of the CBS Television Network Division and severed his last links with EPI by selling his stock to his former associates, principally Steve Carlin, the firm's executive producer, who had hired Bernstein as a researcher shortly after Cowan joined CBS.

By early 1956 Bernstein was an assistant to Merton Koplin, the producer in charge of "The Big Surprise," the first big-money quiz introduced by EPI in the wake of the success of "The $64,000 Question." Contestants on the new show, which debuted on NBC in October 1955, were selected not for great knowledge of a subject but because at some point in their lives they had performed a good deed; on the show they could win as much as $100,000 by answering riddlelike questions that related to their professions, hobbies, and personal histories. Bernstein researched and wrote questions and helped

Koplin evaluate contestants in terms of personality and audience appeal once they were on the show. The "Surprise" had not been well thought out, she said, in the rush to put it on the air following the unexpected success of the "Question." Despite an initially promising performance, the show foundered under complex and cumbersome rules, and in April 1957 it was canceled due to poor ratings.

Still reporting to Koplin, Bernstein then worked on "The $64,000 Challenge" with two other associate producers, Merrill Heater and Edward Jurist. In 1957 production of the "Challenge" was handed over to Jurist. When, late in the year, Jurist was assigned to develop a new quiz, Bernstein took over the "Challenge" as producer in all but name. Because Revlon did not think it suitable for a woman to be credited as sole producer, she retained the title of associate producer.

The producer's job, she told us, was to come up with both contestants and questions. The questions for both $64,000 quizzes were prepared under the supervision of Bergen Evans, a professor of English at Northwestern University in Evanston, Illinois, who had been the moderator of a Cowan panel quiz called "Down You Go," on television from 1951 to 1956. Evans was in charge of writing, verifying for accuracy, and grading for difficulty of questions and answers for the $64,000 shows. Bernstein's job was to compile the many questions and answers provided by Evans and his staff in various categories into the multipart questions used on her program, the "Challenge." Once this was done for an upcoming broadcast, Bernstein submitted her work to Evans for a final check.

As for the contestants, Bernstein explained, at the heart of the concept of the "Challenge" were the champions created by the parent show, and these were a known quantity. Her task was to find people with sufficient knowledge to give the champions a good run for the money. Thus an important part of her job was to make sure the challengers really knew their categories. Thousands of people wrote in to EPI, hoping to become contestants, and claimed to have the requisite knowledge, but very few in fact did, and sorting these out was a stupendous task. Thus she used drill questions both to confirm the genuineness of the challengers' knowledge and, in warm-up sessions before broadcasts, to help contestants relax. Using the drill questions on the air, she insisted, would have made a mockery of all the work that went into the show, and the public would have become quickly aware of any rigging.

At this point, I warned Bernstein that though she was not now under oath, there was the possibility that the quiz matter would be presented to a grand jury, in which case she would be called to testify and placed under oath; if she were then to lie, the penalty would be severe. She nodded her understanding, and I asked her about the allegations of the Reverend Charles Jackson, which she promptly denied.

According to Bernstein, Jackson had been a contestant on the "Question," early in 1957, in the category of Great Love Stories and retired after winning $16,000. He was invited to defend his championship on the "Challenge," and Bernstein first met him several months before he and his challenger, Doll Goostree, began their match on December 22, 1957, when they tied for $2,000 after two rounds of questions. The following week they returned for the next round. Goostree missed, and Jackson answered correctly to win. Since he had been a champion, it was unnecessary to warm him up with drill questions to help him relax. Thus there was not the opportunity to give him an answer in advance, much less the inclination to.

After advising Bernstein to tell the truth, I asked about Wilton Springer, who, it appeared, had needed warming up even though he was a champion. Now Bernstein conceded there were times when the champions were nervous. Since Springer had been very nervous, she asked him a few questions to help him relax, and there was a terrible mix-up. Two of the questions she asked him were used on the show. She called it an awful coincidence, which had never happened before, had not happened since, and could never happen again. Her version now accorded with what Arthur Cohn, Jr., had told us, up to and including her phone calls with Cohn after the broadcast. But, she maintained, it was a mistake and had nothing to do with any plan to make it easier for one or the other of the two men to win. There was no need to make it work that way, since the knowledge of the contestants was always genuine.

AFTER BERNSTEIN'S VISIT, it was clear to me that "The $64,000 Challenge" warranted as much scrutiny as "Dotto" and "Twenty-One," so I gave Goldberg the go-ahead to begin lining up former contestants within reach for interviews; then I answered a summons to Hogan's office to bring him up to date. I stressed the various personnel links we had uncovered between "Dotto" and the EPI quizzes. Stein had already interviewed some fifty people in connection with "Dotto" while I had encountered stalling from Enright's lawyer regarding my requests for "Twenty-One"'s records. Though we were in the dark as to what actually went on behind the scenes of the quizzes, there did seem to be a pattern of questionable practices, if not outright crimes.

This had been pointed up in a September 7 article by the *New York Times* television critic, Jack Gould. According to Gould, the success of "The $64,000 Question" was due to a factor known as "carry-over," whereby contestants made repeated appearances and "became fixed in the public mind and could be exhaustively publicized," imparting "a sense of continuing identity to a show." The importance of carry-over, Gould observed, was acknowledged by Enright in explaining that he had advanced money to Stempel to prevent him from quitting; the longer a winning contestant stayed on a show, the less money the producer paid out in winnings per week; on the other hand, a contestant who knew all the answers but bored the audience would be disastrous for ratings. Given these factors, the producers exercised various "controls," including "the principle of careful casting" in their selection of contestants and the exhaustive testing of prospects, to provide a "fairly complete understanding of a contestant's capabilities, what he could or could not answer." Another cause for skepticism was the practice of using established show-business celebrities as contestants on some quizzes. "Cynics," according to Gould, had argued that celebrities were not apt to risk appearing stupid in public: "If nothing else, astute theatrical agents are not likely to condone a situation where their clients might stand helpless from Maine to California, egg dripping from their unhappy faces."

From our preliminary findings about "Dotto," it seemed that fixing, to the extent that some contestants were favored with assistance at the expense of others, was frequent if not routine. As for "Twenty-One," the burning issue remained one of credibility. In the most recent broadcast of the quiz, on September 9, Jack Barry had made the following statement to the viewing public:

> Before the show starts there is something I must say to all of you. I am talking about the stories that you have read attacking my partner, Dan Enright, and me. All I want to say is: the stories are wholly untrue. I repeat, they are wholly untrue. At no time has any contestant ever been given advance information about any question ever used on this program. It has been a terrible experience to have to combat the unfounded charges that have been flying at us, but we do consider ourselves lucky in one respect. So many of you have expressed your faith in us and our program. A wise man once said, "the truth will out." I know it will for we have not betrayed your trust in us. We never would.[2]

After hearing my review, Hogan was ready to concede that "Dotto" was fixed. But, as for "Twenty-One," Hogan called Stempel "out of left field" with his grudge against Van Doren. All I could reply was that we didn't know all the facts. There were corroborations of parts of Stempel's story by his friends, and Enright had admitted making advance payments to Stempel only after Stempel revealed this to the press. I could not tell whether this was simply an aberration, because Enright's lawyer was stalling in turning over records; we could not question other former contestants until we had their names. At this point, I decided not to tell Hogan about a visit I had two days before from a former colleague and old friend, Jacob Rosenblum, who had served as homicide bureau chief under Dewey and Hogan.

Rosenblum said he had been asked by Edwin Slote, Enright's lawyer, to sound me out about what crimes might have been committed in connection with the quiz shows aside from extortion by Stempel. I replied we were following up complaints but had not yet heard enough to come to definite conclusions about wrongdoing, and we did not yet know whether there was a legal basis for investigating "Twenty-One." When he asked if we had spoken to other contestants, I reminded him that I was not permitted to tell him that. Then he came to the point and confided that it would be good news for certain people to learn that this investigation was going to be dropped. I replied I would take it as far as the evidence would go, all the way if necessary. "I thought so," he said, and when we shook hands, we both knew we had written off a long friendship.

Now Hogan asked if I was really convinced we should continue with the investigation. It was a very serious question. With show business involved, the scandal promised to be a continuing sensation in the press. As such, it offered to an ambitious district attorney—or, for that matter, an ambitious assistant district attorney—considerable temptations. On the other hand, a single mistake could mean being eaten alive by the press and damage to our office's reputation for professionalism. But the can of worms was already open—to drop the investigation could provoke cries of cover-up or special treatment.

With Election Day only weeks away, Hogan was in a delicate position in his campaign for the Senate. The campaign had been in trouble from the start, because of the engineering of his nomination at the state party convention by the Manhattan Democratic party boss, Carmine De Sapio. Hogan and De Sapio were hardly friends—the speculation was that De Sapio's move was an attempt to kick Hogan upstairs by sending him to Washington. Not only did this hand the Republicans a made-to-order issue—"bossism"—it also cooled the relationship of Hogan and the Democrat governor of New York, Averell Harriman, whose own Senate choice had been elbowed aside by De Sapio.

Hogan, who always had been a shoo-in in his reelection campaigns as district attorney, was unused to the rough and tumble of a truly contested race and was eager to campaign on the high road of serious issues, especially civil rights, in which the Republicans, halfway through Dwight Eisenhower's second term, were vulnerable. Hogan was proud of his record of having years before pressured local newspapers into rejecting "hate ads"—discriminatory notices about restrictive real estate and hotel accommodations—and now was eager to make civil rights the centerpiece of his platform. But since the breaking of the quiz scandal, reporters were questioning Hogan about little else.

Just that morning, the New York Times had reported that Judge Samuel Rosenman, the special counsel to CBS who on August 26 had communicated to us the network's official concern about "Dotto," had been named Hogan's campaign manager. Adding to this the fact that the firm of John Cahill, one of Hogan's closest friends, represented NBC, I could see the outline of a set of powerful influences that could make life miserable for the Chief if we bungled the quiz matter.

I told Hogan I believed we had no choice but to follow the investigation through and see whether we were being made fools of or were on the track of a major crime. In that case, he said, he would request Mitchell Schweitzer, the judge presiding that month over Part One of the Court of General Sessions, to convene an extra grand jury to consider the evidence. This was not what I had in mind by following through, however, even though he had mentioned the possibility the first time he discussed the quiz affair with reporters. I told him it was too soon to go to a grand jury; the flexibility and informality of an office investigation were preferable until my associates and I had a better understanding of the broadcasting business and were in a position to determine whether actual crimes had been committed. But Hogan had already made up his mind; he would make an announcement to the press the following day. It was a hasty decision, made under the pressure of his campaign, designed to make him appear resolute and get the reporters off his back by being able to say he could not comment on a matter before a grand jury. Though expedient, it was his decision to make, and since it favored none of the parties to the affair, it was unimpeachable. From my point of view, it meant scrambling harder to prepare for a grand jury presentation, but that at least would strengthen my hand in dealing with witnesses.

After I gave Stein, Donnelly, and Goldberg the news and instructions to begin drawing up lists of prospective grand jury witnesses for my approval, I had an unexpected visitor. Myron Greene was a suave, well-known lawyer, who announced he was now representing Enright. Greene started off by assuring me his client was a fine man, the son of a great Zionist, a family man who lived an unostentatious life, a quiet but generous giver to charity. Then the lawyer launched into a barrage of name-dropping. He had discussed the situation with Bernard Newman, an influential lawyer and the New York County Republican leader, when the two of them dined with Stanley Fuld. Fuld was the distinguished chief judge of the Court of Appeals, whom I knew and admired.

The picture was becoming clear. Enright must have learned I was a Republican and somewhat active in the party, which meant influence could be brought to bear. Someone would have directed him to Newman, who turned him over to Greene. In view of Newman's position as a party leader, he might have been reluctant to handle the matter himself. Greene's name-dropping at this point was meant to inform me that powerful figures were interested in the affair and to signal that, since I was Republican and might someday seek a judgeship, I would be wise to tread carefully. There was nothing new about resourceful individuals involved in investigations lining up well-connected lawyers to represent them via personal contacts in the office, but this elaborate effort to bring influence to bear when there was barely the glimmering of a crime having been committed was unprecedented in my experience.

When Greene advised me not to give credence to the story of a crazy man—Stempel—I replied that I was also investigating his client's own complaint and urged him, for his client's benefit, to provide the records I had already requested. Greene replied that an accountant had been retained for that purpose and I would be hearing from him soon. After Greene's departure, the accountant called and turned out to be Samson Hollander, who not long before had retired as an investigative accountant in the D.A.'s office to go into private practice. He and I had worked together on numerous fraud cases. We made an appointment for early in the evening, when he promised to bring in everything I needed.

When Hollander arrived and handed me a single envelope containing only a few insignificant letters between Enright and Stempel and some other minor "Twenty-One" contestants, I flung the material back and told Hollander he was insulting my intelligence. He pleaded with me—I would be wasting my time with Enright's records and would come up with nothing except embarrassment for his client, who was not afraid of spending money. Seeing the expression on my face, Hollander hastened to clarify: he was speaking simply of "appreciation" for not being bothered anymore by a "nut case who should be in jail." Hurt to be losing another friend as a result of this affair, I sent Hollander away with a warning: if Enright didn't come across with the records we wanted within twenty-four hours, not only would we subpoena the material but I would tell the newspapers the reason—that contrary to his public announcements about cooperation, Enright was stalling.

The next day, September 12, I stood by in Hogan's office as the Chief announced a grand jury probe of the quiz affair to the press: "Charges and countercharges have been made against individuals and businesses and have received a great deal of publicity. All concerned are entitled to as speedy a resolution as possible." The new grand jury, to be called in the following week, would not be a special grand jury in the technical sense, since there was no question of a special prosecutor; rather, it was an extra grand jury, to be impaneled in addition to the First and Second September 1958 grand juries already at work since the beginning of the month. The so-called Third September Grand Jury would investigate the quiz show matter to "determine if the crime of conspiracy or other crimes have been committed." But, Hogan was careful to add, it was "not a fair assumption that we have concluded that there has been wrongdoing."[3]

PART TWO

Diligently Inquire . . .

CHAPTER FOUR

The People against John Doe

(SEPTEMBER 17–23, 1958)

In the five days after Hogan's announcement that the quiz matter would be submitted to a grand jury, there were no startling developments. On Saturday, September 13, the morning newspapers reported the announcement of a decision by the Lorillard Tobacco Company to discontinue sponsorship of "The $64,000 Challenge," though it would continue cosponsorship, with Revlon, of the "Question." The only reason given was that Lorillard was "revising its fall programming strategy."[1] The "Challenge" was to have been broadcast for the last time on CBS on Sunday night, September 14, before moving to NBC on Thursdays—a switch planned before the whistle-blowing of Charles Jackson. But both of these broadcasts were canceled, to be replaced by news specials, and on Monday, September 15, the *New York Times* quoted a network source saying that "these quiz shows are driving us crazy." My guess was that the Cohn-Springer incident, though still unpublicized, added to the Jackson allegation and had doomed the "Challenge."

With Hogan's announcement signaling we meant business, Barry and Enright had begun sending us a trickle of material relating to "Twenty-One," including files on individual broadcasts and contestants. Using these, we began making a complete list of all the contestants on the show, in order of their appearance, the number of points, and the sums of prize money won in each match. In the file on Van Doren, we found a genuine nugget, a canceled check, which showed he had been given an advance against possible winnings of $5,000, in the week following his defeat of Stempel. Another possible nugget was an odd discrepancy. A contestant named Richard Jackman had appeared twice on "Twenty-One" in October 1956, before the advent of Stempel. In his first appearance, Jackman played three games and amassed

$24,500, the largest amount on the program to that time. The following week, Jackman announced on the air he was retiring with his winnings, but a canceled check showed he had been paid only $15,000.

ON THE MORNING of Wednesday, September 17, 1958, some fifty members of the New York County Grand Jury pool answering the call for jury selection sat in the front benches on one side of a large courtroom in the Criminal Courts Building. I sat on the other side, just behind three benches being kept vacant for the jurors who would be selected. The remaining benches were filled with reporters and courtroom buffs. On the other side of the bar that separated the well of the court from the spectators, a clerk, Herbert Roistacker, sat at a table with his back to the empty judge's bench. In front of Roistacker was a large metal drum with a handle. He read off names from a pile of slips and at the answer of "present" put the slips into the drum one by one.

A door behind the bench opened and a tall man in judge's robes moved briskly into the courtroom. The Court of General Sessions, Part One, was in session, the clerk announced, Honorable Mitchell Schweitzer presiding. At age fifty-three, a graduate like Hogan of Columbia Law School, Schweitzer had the reputation of being the hardest-working and most productive judge of General Sessions, the courts that handled felonies in Manhattan. He loved the give and take of plea bargaining and disposed of cases at a ferocious rate with genuine gusto, which made him ideal for Part One, the section of the court dealing with motions, pleas, grand juries, and other matters not involving jury trials. Hogan constantly pressured the Appellate Division, which determined on a monthly rotation basis which judges sat in which parts, to reassign Schweitzer to Part One.

Half an hour after Schweitzer's entrance, twenty-one men, mostly late middle-aged businessmen, and two women—their names drawn from Roistacker's drum—sat on the benches in front of me. The clerk handed their slips up to the judge. Schweitzer asked if any of the selected jurors or their spouses worked in television broadcasting or production or for any advertising firm with clients in the television business. Hearing no answer, he dismissed the other eligibles, then designated two of the selected jurors, Jesse M. Aaron and Louis M. Hacker, as foreman and assistant foreman, respectively. These two were asked to stand and raise their right hands, and were sworn to "diligently inquire and true presentment make" of all matters put before them and to keep their proceedings secret. Following this, the other twenty-one jurors were sworn to the same oath.

Now Schweitzer, in a high staccato voice, charged the jurors. He stressed that though the function of the grand jury was to bring to light crimes, it also served to protect the innocent "against unfounded accusations from whatever source they might originate" and to prevent prosecution "upon accusations which are based on envy, hatred or malice." He introduced me as the person who, along with my associates, would serve as the jury's "legal advisers" in charge of the presentation of evidence. For the past several weeks, Schweitzer explained, the district attorney's office had been investigating the way that certain television quiz programs had been conducted, and allegations, denials, and countercharges had been made that seriously affected the rights and reputations of many people. The district attorney now believed that testimony under oath by complainants and witnesses would help to achieve an early resolution of these complaints. To wait for the regular fall term in October, when four grand juries routinely heard cases, would be an unnecessary delay. Thus this Third September Grand Jury would not be concerned with any other matters.

Schweitzer went on to stress the secrecy of grand jury proceedings—no one besides me and my assistants, the witnesses being questioned, and the stenographer keeping minutes would be allowed into their sessions. No one except the jurors could be present when they discussed the evidence or voted on any matter. The jurors were never to reveal to anybody anything of their discussion or how they voted individually on any matter, and they could not disclose the testimony of any witness except on the order of the court. Finally, Schweitzer summarized the criterion for the jurors' quintessential function: it was their duty to find an indictment when all of the evidence taken together was such, in their judgment, that it would, if unexplained and un-contradicted, warrant a conviction by a trial jury. His charge completed, Schweitzer directed the new jurors to convene for their first session the fol-lowing afternoon.

On Thursday, September 18, the grand jury warden, Harry Blackman, opened the door from the grand jury room and beckoned to me in the so-called witness room, where Donnelly, Stein, and I were waiting, along with Nicholas Barrett and several witnesses scheduled to testify. My associates and I carried several cartons into the spacious room, located on the ninth floor of the Criminal Courts Building, just steps away from our own offices. Twenty of the jurors were seated in comfortable tan leather chairs, arranged in two stepped tiers of ten chairs each, divided by an aisle that mounted to a third tier just below large windows on the back wall. Here, behind a long table in the center, sat Jesse Aaron, the foreman and, next to him, Louis Hacker, the assistant foreman. On his other side sat the juror designated as the secretary, chosen by the jurors themselves as their first order of business.

In what we called "the pit," in front of and below the first row of jurors, was a table where the witness would sit, looking up at the jurors. At one end of the table was a chair where the stenographer would sit facing the witness from the side. The tiers were trimmed with marble, but, aside from this touch, an American flag, a clock on the wall behind the witness, and two brass spittoons on the floor—never-used relics of a bygone era—there was no adornment in the room, not even the slogan "In God We Trust" that graced the walls of courtrooms. An unusual feature this day was the presence of a movie screen and projector.

After introducing my associates, I told the jurors we were investigating the operation of a number of television quiz shows and the relationships among quiz show producers, networks, sponsors, and contestants to determine whether larceny, extortion, commercial bribery, conspiracy, or any other crimes had been committed. We would begin by submitting evidence concerning "Dotto." I pointed out that while the jurors might have read newspaper accounts of allegations by quiz show contestants, none of this had emanated from the D.A.'s office. I said that over the course of the presentation, the press would be hounding us, but no information would be given out. Unlike the custom with trial jurors, I did not tell the grand jurors not to read what the newspapers might write about the case. I added we had no idea how long the presentation would take; we would not meet every working day and would try to schedule sessions as much as possible around their individual needs. It was essential they notify us in advance of absences, since a quorum of sixteen jurors present was required by law for a session to take place.

Now it was time to hear our first witness in the case of *The People of the State of New York against John Doe*, so designated since we had little idea what crimes had been committed, much less who might have committed them. "John Doe" was our fictitious name for the "Dotto" case; presentations of evidence concerning other quiz programs would have similar designations. Stein went to the door and called for the first witness, Terry Laughlin. She came into the jury room followed by one of the grand jury reporters employed by the D.A.'s office, carrying his stenotype machine, which he set up at one end of the witness table. Laughlin was instructed by the foreman to swear to the familiar courtroom oath that the evidence she would give was the truth, the whole truth, and nothing but the truth.

Under questioning by Melvin Stein, in the first grand jury presentation of his career, Laughlin, the "Dotto" production secretary, followed by two CBS executives, repeated what they had already told us in the office about the day-to-day operations of the program and the contractual relations between the producers, the network, and the sponsor. We introduced the broadcast file for May 20, 1958, when Marie Winn defeated Yeffe Slatin on "Dotto." Each of the items from this as well as individual contestant files on Winn and Slatin—including screening test results, release forms, question-and-answer cards—was given a grand jury exhibit number. One of the CBS men was handed a reel of movie film, which he confirmed was a kinescope of the May 20, 1958, broadcast of "Dotto," and this was made a grand jury exhibit. Barrett was called in and testified under oath that he was qualified to operate a movie projector. Once again I saw, in its entirety, the May 20, 1958, broadcast of "Dotto."

Within a week, the grand jury heard the testimony of Edward Hilgemeier, Yeffe Slatin, Marie Winn, and a dozen other former "Dotto" contestants. After a month, the jurors would have heard some forty witnesses concerning "Dotto": contestants, producers, network officials, representatives of Colgate and the Ted Bates advertising agency. These were among scores more interviewed beforehand by Stein in his methodical investigation of the quiz. "Dotto"'s cancelation meant that powerful vested interests, like networks and sponsors, no longer had stakes in concealing the truth. Stein thus was able to pursue the office investigation without potential witnesses refusing to appear for questioning or posturing via the press for public consumption. He had assembled a detailed big picture of "Dotto," clearly showing the extent to which rigging was a routine feature of the program's operation. Absorbing the story in detail of "Dotto"—from its beginnings to its demise—would be the main work of the grand jury in its first weeks of existence.

"DOTTO" was the property of Frank Cooper Associates. Frank Cooper himself was a veteran West Coast talent agent and with Sy Fischer, who had a background in radio and television production, had made the plunge into packaging. Originally called "Magic Money Winner," the "Dotto" concept was pitched by Cooper and Fischer in the middle of 1957 to Richard A. R. Pinkham, a vice-president of the Ted Bates advertising agency in New York and formerly an NBC vice-president in charge of television programming. Liking the concept, Pinkham in turn pitched it to George Laboda, a vice-president and director of television and radio for the Colgate-Palmolive Company, an important Bates client, who was in the market for a replacement for "Strike It Rich," an audience-participation show the company had sponsored in the 11:30 A.M. to noon weekday slot on CBS for seven years.

Colgate's research indicated that a preponderance of middle-aged and older contestants on "Strike It Rich," vying for crutches, artificial limbs, medical treatments, and small sums of cash by answering easy questions, was causing younger viewers to turn their television dials away. After considering other proposals, Colgate chose "Magic Money Winner" to replace "Strike It Rich," and it was somebody at Colgate who came up with the idea of changing the name to "Dotto." In the second half of October 1958, Cooper produced a kinescope pilot, which was shown to Colgate and clinched the deal. Broadcasting was set to begin in January 1958 after the expiration of Colgate's contract with the producers of "Strike It Rich."

At this point, Cooper formed Marjeff, Inc., to produce "Dotto" and broadcast it from New York, and Fischer took charge, hiring the seasoned Jurist, who had worked for EPI on "Quiz Kids," "The Big Surprise," and "The $64,000 Challenge," as the new show's head producer. It was never discussed as such, but there was an implicit understanding between Fischer and Jurist that the latter knew how to handle a show in order to provide a "maximum of entertainment." He would be in day-to-day charge of "Dotto," and whatever specific methods were employed to provide entertainment would be Jurist's responsibility. Jack Narz, previously a spokesman for Colgate products and employed through Bates, was signed to a year's contract as "Dotto"'s emcee. Another quiz veteran, Jerome Schnur, was hired to direct the show from the control room, calling the shots to the cameramen on the set. In New York, Jurist hired, among others, two associate producers, Arthur Henley and Stanley Green, to manage the selection and supervision of contestants; Green had worked several months on Barry and Enright's "Tic Tac Dough." A commercial artist, Eric Lieber, was hired to be in charge of the "Dotto" drawings, and the New York "people getter" Diane Lawson was retained to recruit potential contestants.

Our examination of the records revealed a triangular relationship among the producers, the advertising agency (on behalf of the sponsor), and the network in the mounting of a quiz like "Dotto." The costs of the program had four components: (1) the so-called above-the-line elements were the services provided by the producers—salaries of production staff, writers, and "talent" or on-air performers, as well as the costs of props and building and maintaining the set; (2) "below-the-line" elements were the services provided by the network to the production—studio, dressing rooms, the control room, cameras and other equipment used in the broadcast, camera operators, technicians, and stagehands; (3) the leasing of broadcast time was calculated according to a formula that took into account the number of network affiliates that carried any given broadcast as well as the value of the time slot for advertising purposes; (4) the prize money was budgeted by periods of thirteen weeks, known as "cycles," with a weekly maximum specified.

Under a November 25, 1957, agreement between Bates and Marjeff, the latter supplied "above the line" the services of Jurist, Schnur, and Narz, plus the necessary number of contestants and adequate research and secretarial staff for the screening and interviewing of contestants, and "all other rights, elements, personnel, services, material and equipment necessary and incident" to producing and televising each broadcast. Below-the-line items, including scenery, wardrobe, and rehearsal and production facilities and personnel, from assistant director and lighting director all the way down to cue-card holder, were contracted for under a separate agreement between CBS and Bates.

The term of the Bates-Marjeff contract was for five years, divided into twenty cycles of thirteen weeks each, with Bates, on behalf of Colgate, having the right to terminate at the end of a cycle after proper notice. Marjeff would be paid $9,562.50 a week for the first four cycles, $10,562.50 for the next four, $11,612.50 for the next four, then $12,772.50 a week for the remaining two years of the contract. In addition, the sponsor would provide as prize money for winning contestants the sum of $4,700 per week (raised to $5,500 by the debut of the show), with the express understanding that no less than $3,500 in prizes would be paid out weekly.

Since Colgate, through Bates, was paying for all the costs of "Dotto," there was no direct contractual relationship between Marjeff and CBS. Under the Bates-CBS contract, the network's editorial supervision department would read the texts of advertisements and scripts in advance of broadcast to ensure conformity to its own standards, which were set out in an annex to the contract. Among other things, CBS required that nothing be broadcast "in which the public is unfairly treated," that there be "no ambiguous statements or representations that may be misleading to the audience," and that there be "no advertising matter, announcements, or programs . . . injurious or prejudicial to the interests of the public, CBS, or its affiliates or honest advertising and reputable business in general."[2] The network's "unit supervisors" in the studio before and during all broadcasts would make sure its standards were being observed; likewise, Bates would have a "program supervisor" at the "Dotto" studio to oversee the placement and treatment of the advertising segments of each broadcast. A clause in the Marjeff-Bates agreement provided that Marjeff employees would do nothing to "bring them into public disrepute, scandal or contempt or . . . shock, insult or offend the community or reflect upon or prejudice" Colgate, CBS, or Bates, and that questions used on the program were, like all editorial matter or content, subject to the approval of "an authorized Agency representative." Combing through the contracts, we found nothing in writing that required "Dotto" to be a bona fide contest or that contestants not be given assistance with the questions and answers.

THE KEY PLAYER in the operation of "Dotto" was Jurist, who was paid $750 a week to guide and oversee the show and, most important, make it entertaining. This was accomplished through the selection and management of contestants. Selecting contestants was straightforward—choosing from the thousands of people eager to be on the show a relative handful who met the requirements for lively, attractive, normal-seeming young people. Retained at $150 a week, and given a bonus for each recruit who became a contestant, Lawson was adept at finding likely prospects on the streets of New York. In a typical week, she sent between eight to twelve prospects over, who were interviewed by Jurist and his associates in what was called the "first screening." Five or six of these eventually were used, in addition to people picked directly from the studio audience.

Managing contestants after their selection was a closely held expertise, the quiz producer's stock in trade, and was never discussed by the packager in presenting "Dotto" to the ad agency, the sponsor, or the network. For Jurist, the governing principle was that a quiz had to be "controlled" to make it entertaining. As he put it, the "world of information" was so enormous that even a well-educated person could not answer correctly more than two out of ten random questions concerning general information: "You cannot ask random questions of people and have a show. You simply have failure, failure, failure, and that does not make entertainment."

But, Jurist insisted, controls were designed to avoid having to give contestants the answers in advance. Rather, the idea was to find out what contestants knew, then write questions accordingly, the principle at the heart of the operation of "The $64,000 Question" and "Challenge," he claimed. The $64,000 contestants were extremely knowledgeable in their fields, just as they were presented to the public. In the highly publicized process of "screening" or qualifying prospects, the producers probed them thoroughly to make sure their knowledge was genuine. But that was only part of the purpose of screening, which enabled those carrying it out to determine strong and weak areas within a contestant's field, as hinted in Gould's discussion of controls in the *New York Times* on September 7, 1958. Thus equipped, the producers could tailor questions to the contestant's knowledge, without indicating in advance what they would be. Jurist also admitted to the regular screening of child panelists on the weekly television version of "The Quiz Kids," which he produced for EPI in 1956. Before each broadcast, the children were interviewed individually in their homes, to determine their knowledge in certain areas, and questions to be used on the air were constructed accordingly.

According to Jurist, screening worked well as a control on the $64,000 shows, because there was time to apply it, there was no more than a handful of contestants a week, a good half of them making reappearances, and the questions were limited to specific fields of knowledge. But "Dotto" was a daily show, with a large number of contestants answering questions not limited to special fields of knowledge. There were three classes of "Dotto" contestants: the first was the rarest, the truly knowledgeable, for whom questions could be written according to strong and weak areas. In the second class were contestants with attractive personalities but medium knowledge; for these to keep winning, they had to be "inculcated" with information the producers wanted them to have, in such a way that they were not aware of what was going on. This procedure was the so-called second screening and was carried out by Jurist's associates in private meetings with individual contestants under the guise of extracting personal material from them for "interview" segments. The notes made of these meetings provided raw material for the questions to be used on the show.

The third class of contestants were the majority, the losers, who had to be handled in such a way as not to make them appear foolish or have their feelings hurt, which could reflect badly on the show and sponsor. Thus the screenings served to help write questions designed for contestants to miss as well as to answer correctly. The ideal way to accomplish the former was to ask an intended loser a truly hard question in his or her "strong" area, not something out of left field.

Just as important was what Jurist called, without irony, the "plot." Immediately after every broadcast, he met with his associates, including Eric Lieber, to determine what would happen on the next broadcast—who would win, lose, and tie, and by how much. His decisions were made without waiting for fan mail or polls and ratings, but rather by feel and instinct, keeping an ear open to opinions expressed by the agency and sponsor representatives who attended broadcasts, as well as his own staff. In the "plot," the "Dotto" drawings were a crucial element.

Lieber and several assistants made the drawings on translucent plastic from projections of smaller drawings, made originally from photographs. With a blue pencil, he traced the drawing as lightly as possible on the plastic, then placed fifty dots in black on the blue guidelines. On the reverse side, he numbered the dots in blue, one to fifty. He repeated the process on a second sheet, providing two copies for each celebrity picture to be used. For the broadcast, a sheet was attached to each window of the set with the black dots out, facing each contestant. Lieber and an assistant stood behind the set, using black ink, visible from the front, to follow the numbers and retrace the blue guidelines, connecting the number of dots each correct answer earned a contestant. In the process, the artist shaded in such details as eyebrows and mustaches as called for, as the picture "matured." The use of these details permitted the picture to "break" or become recognizable when desired, a decision made in advance at the plot meetings.

Though he conceded the purpose of controls was to assure that certain contestants won while others lost, Jurist insisted that the case of Winn was an aberration. He had made it clear to his associates that they were "to accomplish what I wanted to accomplish," that is, make sure the designated winners did indeed win, and Winn was a designated winner, but hers was a case of his associates going too far. If they did their jobs properly in the first two screenings, if they "extracted generalities" in conversations with contestants that had more of a "social" than "professional aspect," then a third session right before the broadcast, conducted in the same spirit, merely served as a warm-up for relaxing contestants and overcoming stage fright. But Green and Henley told us that they routinely gave designated winners the answers in warm-ups by burying the questions to be used among others that would not be, relying on the contestants to assume a slip-up occurred. It never occurred to them that somebody would write the questions and answers down.

The stories other contestants told indicated that Winn's experience was unique only to the extent that her indiscretion led to debacle. Daniel Sullivan was recruited in late December 1957 by Lawson to appear in a "brush-up" kinescope rehearsal of "Dotto." He recalled that his opponent failed to recognize a "Dotto" picture even with all the dots connected. This threw the producers, who asked themselves, "What if this happened on the program!" into a tizzy. Later Sullivan was asked by Jurist to be a contestant on the debut broadcast. Beforehand, he was warmed up with twenty or thirty questions, which he was able to answer, and was shown a number of pictures. Just before airtime, Sullivan recalled, he was asked by Jurist to hold off on identifying a picture, already used in the kinescope rehearsal, in order to create a tie. On the third day, when Sullivan had amassed winnings of $420, Jurist paid him $1,000 to let his next opponent win.

The majority of "Dotto" contestants were, in effect, like Slatin, patsies who played, at the most, three or four tie games before losing. Usually selected from the studio audience by Henley and Green, they were tested, then signed up to be standbys. Once scheduled to go on the air, they were interviewed again for material to be turned into jokes for the use of the emcee. In the hour or so before airtime, they were warmed up by Henley or Green with drill questions. Several reported that questions similar to those asked in the warm-up were used on the broadcast early in a game, a standard practice, we learned, to help them relax. The patsies left the show with consolation prizes of $25 for each game they played.

The winners, frequently attractive women like Winn, rarely came from the studio audience and were mostly recruited by Lawson. Contradicting the ideal proclaimed by Jurist, most reported being asked questions and told the answers they didn't know, which then came up on the broadcast. In addition, they were shown the pictures in advance so they could identify them, or at least were asked if they were familiar with certain celebrities. Rochelle Rodney, at the time a high school senior, was a contestant in April 1958 and won $1,487 in two days on "Dotto"; two years before, she had won $2,000 on "The Big Surprise" and also had been a contestant on a musical quiz called "Name That Tune." During her first warm-up session for "Dotto," she was assisted by Green, who asked her to which college team football's famous Four Horsemen had belonged. She didn't know, and Green told her Notre Dame. The question was used on the broadcast, during which Rodney identified the "Dotto" drawing of Louis Armstrong, about whom she had been asked by Green in the warm-up. Rodney was vague about specific help she received on "The Big Surprise," but she compared the screening process in general to a teaching technique known as "pretesting and retesting," whereby a pupil is given a test, told to look up the correct answers to questions missed, then tested on a later occasion with some of the questions that were missed before.

Antoinette DuBarry Hillman, a former reporter from Grand Rapids, Michigan, lived in Manhattan with her husband, a writer for *Time* magazine. She appeared on "Dotto" five times in February 1958, leaving the show with winnings of $1,460. On the first day, Stan Green took her aside and asked her if she would recognize the Danish-born pianist-entertainer Victor Borge, among others. Then, on the broadcast, she connected enough dots to be given the first clue to the drawing—"Danish." At that point the clue meant nothing to her. The game continued and she connected more dots, then received the second clue—"Musician." Now she wondered, how many Danish musicians could one know about? Still, she claimed, she couldn't believe the drawing could actually be of someone Green had mentioned in the warm-up. Some of the questions did sound familiar, too, but she thought the staff were just being kind on her first appearance. But finally she gave in, answered Victor Borge, and won. Offstage she started to thank Green but he hushed her. "From then on we played the whole thing like a solemn minuet, like everybody bowing and smiling and taking you back and forth and pretending nothing at all was going on. We would have these little talks, but we never came clean with each other. We got very cozy." Before her last appearance, Green told Hillman she was going in cold, and there was no warm-up. This time she had no idea as to the "Dotto" drawing, even with twenty-eight dots connected and one clue. As she put it, the drawings were "hopeless unless they did give you a little help." In other words, her services were no longer required.

If the celebrity drawing was "Dotto"'s unique contribution to the quiz genre, both the "plot" strategy and the economics of the show turned on the device of the tie. Ties not only helped "increase drama," as Jurist put it, they also permitted the reappearance of interesting contestants without strain on the budget. A handful of contestants were allowed to defeat opponents and chalk up relatively large winnings, but the dominant pattern was for a new "champion" to win only one or two games after a series of ties as challenger, then face a new challenger in a series of ties before losing. The rules provided only a consolation of $25 for each game played by an eventual loser; therefore, despite the appearance of rapidly mounting stakes, ties kept the actual prize money awarded down.

This subtlety might not have registered on viewers and had been ignored by Bates and Colgate supervisors, but individual contestants knew how to count—at least what they stood to win. Jurist was sensitive enough to see a possible problem here—not with one-time patsies, for whom the small consolation prize and the excitement of being on the show would suffice, but with losers scheduled for an extra day or more of ties. Anxiety on the part of returning contestants could "detract from their performances," Jurist observed, and he dealt with it by frequently dispensing largesse to hard-working patsies in the form of bonuses or "expense" money.

The selection, screening, and inculcating of champions and patsies plus the plotting of the show worked well enough so that a final control that was available was very rarely used. In examining the question cards used by Narz on the air, we found that there was, in addition to three questions in a given category, a fourth, substantially harder question. This was the "killer question," Narz explained, a last resort in a situation where a contestant happened inadvertently to answer a question correctly in a previous round designed for him or her to miss and thus assure a tie. Jurist dropped his keys on the floor of the studio to attract the emcee's attention, then signaled him to use the "killer" by touching his hair. Though he understood its function, Narz insisted he had no say or indication in advance as to which contestants were to be subject to that or any other control. His encounters with contestants were kept to a minimum by design so that his interaction with them would seem all the more spontaneous, and this was confirmed by Jurist.

FROM THE START, the skill, talent, and bag of tricks at Jurist's disposal paid off handsomely; within a short time "Dotto" became the number-one rated daytime television show. This provided little incentive for Bates and Colgate or anyone else not in the know about the specifics to ask questions—it was what Schnur called "a going machine." We interviewed Christie Walsh and James Damon, Bates executives who at different periods served as the agency's production supervisor for "Dotto" and were present for every broadcast. Now and then, Walsh let Jurist know if he liked an individual contestant, and he was dimly aware of the principles of trying to keep especially attractive contestants on the show and not making losers look foolish; he knew that contestants were screened for strong and weak areas of knowledge, but he disclaimed knowledge of specific controls like "inculcating" intended winners. For his part, Damon said it never occurred to him that staying within a prize budget with up- and downside limits meant the operation of controls.

In March 1958, the success of daytime "Dotto" prompted Colgate to exercise the option to mount a prime-time evening version, while continuing the daily version. In preparation for this, Jurist expanded his staff, hiring Robert Van Deventer to be chief question writer. Van Deventer, in his mid-twenties, had been a child panelist on a radio quiz, "Twenty Questions," created and produced by his parents. On "Dotto," he quickly learned the routine, writing questions two or three days in advance of their use, a minimum of thirteen questions a day after discussions with Jurist's associates about the strong and weak areas of upcoming contestants.

Jurist also hired a new assistant, Gilbert Cates, the younger brother of Joseph Cates, another TV quiz veteran who had been the first producer/director of "The $64,000 Question." Gil Cates was a speech and theater graduate of Syracuse University, had worked on a short-lived game show, and understood the importance of gauging the "areas" of contestants' knowledge. Outgoing and energetic, Cates took to the job and soon was promoted to associate producer. That meant increased contact with contestants in the various screenings, then turning over his notes to Van Deventer, who then wrote questions based on them. Cates also attended the daily plotting meetings with Henley, Green, Lieber, and Jurist.

A kinescope pilot of the nighttime version of "Dotto" was produced by Marjeff and shown to NBC, which agreed to lease to Colgate a half-hour at 9:30 on Tuesday nights, from the beginning of July 1958, evicting a faltering detective series. Narz would emcee the new nighttime "Dotto"; Schnur would direct both versions from the control room and take over producing daytime "Dotto," so that Jurist could devote himself entirely to the new show. Jurist made Cates his right-hand man in sole charge of the nighttime contestants, leaving Henley and Green to assist Schnur on the old show.

It was the impending introduction of nighttime "Dotto," as well as the renewal of the daytime version after six months, that dictated the strategy of Jurist and Fischer in handling the crisis created by Hilgemeier. The existence of Winn's notebook page meant something had gone wrong, and Jurist immediately ordered Green to tighten the daytime screening procedures. Hereafter the first screening would be more thorough, to determine as precisely as possible what prospective winners knew so that the questions could be written on that basis; there was to be no more "inculcating" of information from questions prepared beforehand.

As soon as they believed Hilgemeier and Slatin could be appeased with payoffs, Jurist and Fischer turned the matter over to Marjeff's lawyer, Walter Schier, and relaxed. They said nothing of the incident to Bates, Colgate, or even Frank Cooper when he returned from a trip to Europe. By the end of May, Schier reported that Slatin had settled but Hilgemeier was holding out. At a meeting on June 2, Jurist tried to calm Hilgemeier's fears of blacklisting by holding out the possibility of using him on nighttime "Dotto," a promise he had no intention of keeping.

The terms of the agreement covering the new version were negotiated between Marjeff and Bates as addenda to the existing contract. For the above-the-line elements, Colgate would pay $13,050 a week for a term of four cycles. The dot value in the new game would be $100, increasing by $100 in each tie game played; losers would receive $50 for each game played. Marjeff would be provided $7,500 a week for prize money, subject to the usual refund provisions, but Colgate had written into the agreement an understanding that the prize money was not to be limited to the budgeted average; in the event the actual payout exceeded $7,500 a week, Colgate would make up the difference at the end of a cycle. It was testimony to the sponsor's confidence in the new show that Colgate was encouraging "Dotto" to give away more money than its producers believed necessary.

Nighttime "Dotto" debuted on Tuesday evening, July 1, 1958. Behind Narz, a glittering curtain rose to reveal a soft-modern decor, all ovals and arches and at the center an ersatz stained-glass window with a floral design. A "Dotto Girl" escorted contestants on and off and handed Narz the question cards. Off-camera, the studio and control room were crowded with jittery sponsor and agency people, but Jurist was serene in the knowledge that he and Cates had left little to chance, for they had picked their first intended winner with care. David Huschle was a handsome restaurant manager in his late twenties, who early in 1958 had made six appearances on daytime "Dotto," defeating opponents by identifying pictures of celebrities mentioned, Huschle told us, to him by Green in warm-ups, and leaving the show with $3,700 in winnings. His performance had prompted two thousand viewers to write in, saying they liked him.

According to Huschle, at their first meeting for nighttime "Dotto," Cates cautioned he would receive no assistance, but hours before air time, Cates said the pressure to make the debut a success was so great, they needed Huschle's help. Cates proceeded to tell the contestant how many dots to request for each round, the questions he would be asked, and the correct answers, and when to press the buzzer and identify the drawing. On the broadcast, Huschle tied his opponent in the first game, then crushed him in the second, racking up winnings approaching $10,000. A week later, Huschle tied his next opponent, then defeated him, pushing his winnings up to $11,600.

On July 10 Jurist heard again from Hilgemeier, who threatened to go to a newspaper reporter if he wasn't given $4,000, the same amount paid to Slatin. At this point, Jurist and Fischer realized if they called the police, the simple allegation made public by Hilgemeier that something was wrong with "Dotto" would be sufficient for Colgate to cancel the show forthwith. They had no choice but to pay him off. On July 11, when Hilgemeier arrived, Schier and Fischer were prepared with papers drawn up for signature, and $1,500 in cash. After histrionics on both sides, Hilgemeier agreed to the payment, which took place later at Schier's office, with the *New York Post* reporter, Jack O'Grady, waiting outside. When Schier reported back to Fischer and Jurist, he neglected to tell them about O'Grady.

On the same day, July 11, an aspiring model named Connie Hines arrived at the Frank Cooper offices to interview for an opening as a receptionist. Upon seeing her, Jurist and Fischer thought she was an excellent prospect for "Dotto" and sent her to Cates for an interview and tests. When Cates began asking her what she knew and showed her pictures of celebrities, he was not very encouraged by the extent of her knowledge. When he shared his doubts with Jurist, the producer was definite in his reply: "That's not important. She's to win, and be subtle about it." Cates had his orders; in addition to preparing Hines, he informed Huschle that his tenure had been successful but he had to go because of the budget. Huschle did not object, he told us, because Cates had treated him very well. On the next broadcast, after Huschle and Hines answered relatively easy questions, Hines pressed her buzzer and wrote out the correct identification of a picture Cates had previously shown her. Huschle guessed wrong, as instructed by Cates, and left with $11,600; Hines was the new champion.

Selected by Cates and Jurist to challenge Hines was John Ridley, a bearded Englishman, well educated, well traveled, and well read. He had been in the United States for a number of years working as a promoter for a classical-music record distributor. He had been a quiz contestant briefly in England and on a local Chicago show before moving to New York early in 1958. His firm's publicist had given his name to Lawson, describing him as "good TV material." He told us that he agreed to go on "Dotto" with no expectation beyond the consolation prize of $50 and the opportunity to plug his employer on national TV. Ridley had a sense of humor and distinct acting gifts, and in their meetings, Cates frankly explained what was going on. The idea was to build suspense—not knock an opponent off right away but present the illusion of a struggle. One might have the answer right away—as Ridley usually did—but one learned to hesitate, to look baffled, until miraculously the answer would come and everybody could breathe a sigh of relief. Ridley learned that people selected to be "eggheads"—he qualified because of his cultivated speech—could come out with the answer straight off from time to time so that the audience would be impressed by the scope of their knowledge; other contestants, representing the younger generation or the masses, would have a harder time even if they went on to win, to the public's delight.

Ridley played two tie games against Hines on July 22, when she irritated Bates executives by wearing an orchid on her dress, which they found too extravagant and frivolous for somebody who supposedly had been boning up on knowledge. Jurist decided to knock her out in the next broadcast. On July 29 Cates briefed her on the questions but said nothing about the "Dotto" drawings. In the first game, she could not match Ridley's early identification and lost, leaving the show with the $1,400 she had won by defeating Huschle two weeks before. Ridley, now champion, was tied by his first challenger, John Neulin, a management trainee, who told Stein he was not aware of being given any assistance at all.

On August 5, in their session before the broadcast, Cates abandoned all pretense and "went right to it," according to Ridley, telling him all the questions and answers, when he would "dotto," and the identities of the pictures to be used. Ridley defeated Neulin, raising his winnings to $9,800, then met his next challenger, Nina Appel, a third-year student at Columbia Law School. Jurist had already decided to make Appel the new champion the following week. When Cates had first interviewed her, there were "Dotto" drawings of Stan Laurel and Oliver Hardy on the wall of his office that had been used on the daytime show. Thus, since both Ridley and Appel were familiar with Oliver Hardy, the broadcast of the August 5 nighttime "Dotto" ended as the contestants tied with that identification.

NOTHING MORE was heard from Hilgemeier after the payoff on July 11 until August 7, when, with a copy of the affidavit prepared with the help of O'Grady in hand, he appeared at the Colgate offices, told his story, demanded $2,500 to make his settlement equal to that of Slatin, and was told his complaint would be looked into. The following morning, George Laboda of Colgate showed a copy of the affidavit to Richard Pinkham at Bates. For the rest of the day, almost till midnight, Hilgemeier was the subject of nearly continuous meetings, with a shifting cast of characters at both the Bates and Cooper offices. Fischer, Cooper, and Schier were called in, and Fischer admitted to Bates and Colgate executives that Marjeff had paid Hilgemeier $1,500 to keep him quiet, for any allegation made public about "Dotto," no matter how false, would hurt the program. Schier handed over Winn's notebook page, but Fischer denied that Winn had been given answers in advance.

Toward noon, Pinkham called CBS, since the situation concerned daytime "Dotto," and the matter was referred to the network's vice-president and general counsel, Thomas Fisher. Meanwhile, Sy Fischer called Diane Lawson, ordering her to find Winn. Jurist could not be found, but Schnur and Green were called in and told about the rumpus at Bates. Cooper seemed genuinely surprised by the whole business, since he had been out of the country when Winn was a contestant on "Dotto" and had not been told about the affair.

After lunch, Fisher of CBS told a gathering of Bates executives that if "Dotto" was not being played honestly, the network would yank the show. The Bates people repeated Sy Fischer's earlier assurances and promised a full report for the following week. Fisher said he needed answers by Saturday night, then returned to CBS and reported to Louis Cowan, who called Bates to emphasize the seriousness of CBS's concern and said he wanted a network representative at any questioning by Bates of Winn. As far as we could determine, that was the extent of Cowan's action in the matter. A short while later, Fisher was notified that Winn had been located; she and Jurist would be at a meeting scheduled for early evening at the Cooper offices.

By now, Winn was with Lawson in the people getter's office. On the phone, Sy Fischer and Schier, with Cooper, Jurist, and Schnur in the room, discussed with Lawson and Winn what the latter would tell the Bates and CBS representatives later. At that point, according to what Lawson told us, "someone" had the idea that Winn could say she had written down the answers *after* the May 20 broadcast. With this idea planted, Schier still advised Winn to say anything she wanted. When they arrived at the Cooper offices, Lawson left Winn in an outer room to join a meeting in progress at which Cooper, Fischer, Jurist, Schnur, and Schier were present. The upshot of the discussion was for Lawson to tell Winn to answer as truthfully as she could: if she was confused or did not remember, she should simply say so; there was no necessity for her to lie about a warm-up session before the show. In fact, however, the implicit decision, according to Lawson, was that the "truth" Winn should tell was that she had not been given the answers in the warm-up. Indeed, Jurist and the others had all but convinced themselves that this fantasy—that Winn had written down the answers *after* the broadcast—was the truth. If Cooper and his associates were not unanimous as to what Winn's course of action should be, there was also no dissent expressed about the "truth." At 6:30 P.M., the Bates and CBS people arrived.

Fisher recorded an account of what followed in a memo for the files of CBS:

> [Winn] professed not to know what the meeting was all about and . . . considered this an affront to her, that the allegations were not true. She was shown the page from her notebook and she identified the writing as her own. . . . She said that she has a poor memory and that after the show she wrote down what appeared

on the paper because she has a sister in Philadelphia who does not have a television set and she wanted to write to her and describe the show. . . . She could not explain why she had written the names "Bing Crosby" or "Dagwood——Mr. Dithers." She was quite vague about the significance of the entries below the line on the page but she said some of them were answers given to the questions. . . . When asked when she first realized the page from her notebook was missing she said she did not know it until just now. . . . She stated that she had not felt well on May 21 and her doctor advised her not to go on the show that day and that was why she did not appear on the 21st.[3]

Winn and Lawson departed, but the meeting continued as Jurist claimed that Lawson had also informed him that Winn had written down the answers after the broadcast. On May 21, Jurist claimed, he informed his staff meeting there could have been a leak and they would have to be more careful about the security of the "rundown sheets," the form of the script that contained clues to the "Dotto" drawings. For his part, Schier stated that when the Hilgemeier matter was brought to his attention, he believed it was possible that someone had given the answers to Winn, and therefore he recommended a payment to Slatin. Because the Cooper people had decided to keep the matter from Colgate, Schier conceded, they had no choice later but to pay off Hilgemeier, even though he had no valid claim and was simply blackmailing them.

After the meeting, the best Cooper and his associates could hope for was that their and Winn's explanations had sufficed to stop the Hilgemeier matter short of disaster. But, far from satisfied, that night Fisher, bypassing Louis Cowan, telephoned Frank Stanton, the president of CBS, Inc., at home to report on what happened, and, in the memo for the CBS files he wrote later, he concluded that Winn's account was untrue and that she had been fed the answers in advance. For Fisher the problem boiled down to: "(a) Who fed her the information, and (b) whether it was an aberration or in the regular course of the program production."[4]

The next morning, Fisher visited the "Dotto" studio and questioned various staff members, who denied any knowledge of how information might have reached Winn. When asked to explain how she might have received the information otherwise, Schnur replied, "there are a thousand ways." Asked to name two or three, Schnur said Winn could have seen papers lying around in the office; maybe one of the studio hands—or a Bates representative for that matter, Schnur said pointedly—had seen the rundown sheets or question cards and passed along the information. Still not satisfied, Fisher returned to his office and began writing his memos for the CBS files. Matters were not helped when CBS received from the FCC a letter advising the network of Hilgemeier's complaint and asking for a statement in response within fifteen days.

If Fisher was suspicious, Colgate and Bates still had stakes in giving "Dotto" a clean bill of health; they wanted to believe that the allegations and counterallegations of Hilgemeier and Winn amounted to what Richard Pinkham would call a battle of "neurotics" from whom it would be hard to extract the truth.[5] So it was business as usual for Cates, who was meeting in his office with Ridley, preparing for that evening's broadcast, the first since the Hilgemeier matter had become known to Colgate, Bates, and CBS. "Well, John, the time has come," Cates told Ridley, who knew what this meant and was neither surprised nor disappointed. Ridley was instructed to throw the match to Appel by misidentifying the "Dotto" drawing. Cates explained the drawing was made deliberately to look up to a point like either of two celebrities. He held up a sketch. "This man is actually Paul Whiteman, but on this side of the face," he pointed out, "it could look like Khrushchev, so you'll plump for Khrushchev." That night, the Englishman obliged. In addition to winnings of $9,800, he had various offers for new radio and television appearances. Appel racked up $7,200 in becoming the new champion.

The following day, August 13, Thomas Fisher attended a gathering of lawyers at the office of Colgate's general counsel, Walter Reynolds, along with Michael Frothingham, a Bates lawyer, and Ralph Colin, a partner with Samuel Rosenman in the firm that was retained by CBS, Inc. Colin had long been the principal lawyer of CBS's chairman and founder, William S. Paley, indicating that the concern of CBS reached to the very highest level. The lawyers now questioned Hilgemeier at length; he gave an account that tracked fairly well with his affidavit, which CBS had received from the FCC, but Fisher did not tell the others. On August 14, responding to the FCC request, Fisher sketched developments since knowledge of the Hilgemeier allegations had come to him via Colgate and Bates, in order "to make plain that immediately upon learning of this matter last Friday we viewed the allegations in a most serious light and have taken and are continuing to take all steps we believe necessary to reach a conclusion."[6]

At 5 P.M. on August 15 a meeting was convened at Colgate at the request of Cooper, to allow him to plead his side of the story. The usual complement of Colgate, Bates, and CBS executives and lawyers was swelled by the presence of E. H. Little, the chairman of Colgate; Ted Bates, the founder and head of the agency bearing his name; and Frank Stanton of CBS. This was the crunch for Cooper, and he pulled out all the emotional stops in pursuing a strategy of throwing out chunks of the truth in order to maintain the overall deception.

Citing his years of friendly relations with Colgate and CBS in the production of other shows and detailing his efforts to get to the bottom of things, Cooper stressed that no money was stolen from Colgate in the running of "Dotto." He conceded that controls were used, for an audience-participation show required a formula just as mystery and dramatic shows did, and the controls used were "inherited" by the members of his staff who had been hired because of their previous experience. The principal control was favoring contestants for dramatic effect; without this, the show would have become "merely a staring process." After elaborating some more about how the show was run, Cooper conceded that security had been lax, and that approximately 15 people had access to the information before a broadcast. After May 20 the number was reduced, and further tightening occurred after the August 8 interrogation of Winn. Asked if coaching had been ended, Cooper replied that it would continue unless he was ordered to stop it. Finally, the packager said he still did not know how Winn had singled out the specific questions she was to be asked on May 20, for the coaching process was supposed to bury questions that might be asked among many others that would not be. In conclusion, Cooper expressed hope that Colgate and CBS would view things sympathetically and consider his position "as a human being."

Cooper's strategy of candor was doomed. On August 8 he and his staff had insisted, to Fisher, that they had not given answers in advance to Winn or other contestants. But now he admitted that the feeding of answers to contestants was routine; whether or not Winn was given "only" the questions and answers to be used was immaterial. The technique of compartmentalization, which had permitted quiz rigging by limiting the knowledge of it to the producer's inner circle, was now its own undoing. Candor would not work when the big shots had little or no stake in preserving the central deception, especially when they were not implicated themselves. Moreover, Hilgemeier's FCC affidavit was a ticking time bomb. CBS and Colgate had too much to gain by cutting their losses.

The morning following Cooper's last stand, Fisher notified Bates that "Dotto" had failed to conform to the provisions of the agreement between the network and the agency covering the program. Accordingly, the network was exercising its right under the agreement to "refuse to broadcast" the program, effective immediately. Bates's letter to Marjeff on behalf of Colgate was less dry and more to the point, if disingenuous and hyperbolic. Colgate and the agency were, wrote Bates, "deeply concerned by the Hilgemeier incident. . . . If you had told us about this incident in May, as you should have done, Colgate would not have renewed the daytime program and would not have placed the nighttime program on the air." Expressing its "shock" at the revelation of controls, Colgate was withdrawing its sponsorship of both "Dotto"s, an "action . . . necessitated by conduct on the part of your company which has resulted in irreparable damage to Colgate."

Hilgemeier's chances to advance an acting career may have been dashed by peeking into Winn's notebook, but the impulse resulted in bringing "a going machine" crashing down. The district attorney's office and the grand jury now had a detailed picture of the operation of a fixed quiz program; it was a bizarre picture of widespread and systematic deceit, which carried the ominous implication that there was no such thing as an unfixed quiz. But it still remained to be seen whether actual crimes had been committed.

CHAPTER FIVE

The People against Richard Roe

(SEPTEMBER 20–27, 1958)

The grand jury subpoena process not only summoned witnesses, it also filtered out those who had little to offer in the way of useful information, without wasting the D.A. office's effort to seek them out and bring them in on a voluntary basis. We used the list of former "Twenty-One" contestants provided by Barry and Enright to blanket the New York City area with grand jury subpoenas. In a number of cases, people—or their lawyers—called to ask for delays for one reason or another, which we granted in return for their coming in for an informal talk. Most jumped at the chance; those from whom we learned little of interest would have their subpoenas canceled. Others, including those we thought might be hiding something, would be given new subpoenas with obligatory appearance dates. Those we suspected of outright lying were advised to seek legal counsel if they did not already have it, were warned of the consequences of not telling the truth under oath, and were encouraged to call us for another informal office talk if they had a change of mind.

The announcement of the grand jury investigation was also a catalyst, acting beyond the reach of subpoenas, which had no legal force outside of New York State. Within days, a call came in from a Washington, D.C., woman named Rose Leibbrand, who had opposed Stempel briefly on "Twenty-One" and said she would be in New York on business and was anxious to talk to us. We made an appointment for Friday, September 20. In late middle age with a crisp manner, Leibbrand had degrees in foreign languages, had been a schoolteacher, an army officer, and a real estate broker in Missouri before going to Washington in 1956 to become the executive director of the National Federation of Business and Professional Women's Clubs. It was with considerable animus that she told Robert Donnelly and me her story.

In the fall of 1956, at the suggestion of the Federation's public relations firm, Leibbrand applied to become a contestant on "Twenty-One," was tested, and finally interviewed in New York by Barry, Enright, and Albert Freedman, "Twenty-One"'s producer. As a result she was asked to be a standby contestant on November 7, 1956. That afternoon, she met for an hour and a half with Freedman in New York. After a discussion about the mechanics of the show, according to Leibbrand, Freedman picked up a pack of fifty to one hundred file cards and began drilling her with questions so that she wouldn't be embarrassed or ill at ease during the broadcast. He read the questions off the cards, "gave me the points they were worth, seven, eight, nine, or whatever it was," and asked her to answer, without telling her the answers to the very few questions she didn't know. He said the questions used on the air would be "similar but different."

That evening, as Leibbrand stood by, she noted that the questions used when Stempel and his challenger asked for nine, ten, and eleven points did not seem more difficult than those Freedman had drilled her with and to which he had assigned point values of seven, eight, or nine. She was told she would definitely go on the air the following week, and the Federation publicized the fact, alerting its 175,000 members that their executive director would be a contestant on "Twenty-One." The afternoon of November 14, when she met again with Freedman, he drilled her once more with the cards, but didn't ask her questions worth more than six, seven, or eight points. When she asked why, he brushed her off by saying the broadcast would be different. Moments before the broadcast, however, Freedman tapped her on the shoulder and said in a low voice, "You know you're not supposed to bid more than seven or eight." She was speechless, and he repeated, "You're not to bid more than seven, or else."

On the air, after she was introduced and took her place in the isolation booth, she realized it was all a setup, but since the membership of the Federation was watching, she couldn't make a fool of herself. For her first question against Stempel, the category was Fairy Tales. She chose to play it safe and make the best appearance she could, so she requested six points. Barry asked her one of the questions Freedman had drilled her with, and she answered correctly. On the next round, the category was World War I, and she requested seven points. Again the question had been used by Freedman in drilling her. She expected to go another round, but Stempel exercised the option to "knock" and won with seventeen points to her thirteen.

For her trouble, Leibbrand was paid $130, far less than the expenses of her trips to New York, but the Federation was covering these and she turned over her winnings to the organization. Though she was mortified by the experience and afraid of embarrassing her employer, she accepted our assurance of confidentiality and volunteered to testify before the grand jury whenever we wished. Even if her appearance against Stempel was too brief to truly substantiate his story, Leibbrand's account was an important piece of corroboration. If "Twenty-One" was as carefully rigged as Stempel alleged, then somebody had to have been working with patsies like Leibbrand, as well as with the champions. If not Enright, who might have had his hands full with Stempel, why not Freedman, whom Stempel had barely mentioned.

At this point, I called Enright's lawyer, Myron Greene, and said a talk with his client was essential for a detailed picture of how "Twenty-One" worked from the producer's point of view, which would help us sort out conflicting versions of events for a coherent presentation to the grand jury. Greene replied that Enright was not in charge of any of his shows on a day-to-day basis and couldn't provide the kind of detail we wanted. When I asked who could, Greene answered Albert Freedman, the man Leibbrand had just fingered. Greene agreed to set up a meeting between us and Freedman, which was arranged for the afternoon of September 23. Meanwhile, another lawyer, Michael Dontzin, called to say he represented James Snodgrass, who had received a subpoena and wanted to talk to us immediately. Snodgrass had made several appearances on "Twenty-One" in April and May 1957, challenging but losing to the long-reigning champion, Henry Bloomgarden, who had already denied to us any involvement in rigging. I told Dontzin to bring in his client on September 23.

DONNELLY was with me when Greene brought in Freedman, as scheduled. At thirty-seven, Freedman was erect, well dressed, and well mannered; he spoke quickly and articulately as he answered routine background questions. Married, with two children, and currently living in the suburb of New Rochelle, he had been born and raised in Massachusetts, served in the Marines during World War II, and afterward earned a B.A. in motion picture production at the University of Southern California. After spending some time in Paris, he came to New York to make a career as a comedy writer. His first encounter with quiz programs was in 1955, when he joined Barry and Enright and worked on "Life Begins at 80" and "Juvenile Jury," helping in the selection of participants and writing humorous material for them to regurgitate on the air. Late in 1955 he left Barry and Enright to work for Louis G. Cowan, Inc., writing "interview" segments of "The Big Surprise." After a stint as a writer for a short-lived TV situation comedy, he returned to Barry and Enright as the producer of the daytime "Tic Tac Dough" quiz until the end of November 1956, when he became producer of "Twenty-One," two months after the program's debut and while Stempel was champion.

Freedman said he had had nothing to do with the creation of "Tic Tac Dough" and "Twenty-One" and knew nothing of the negotiations and relations among the packager, the sponsors, and the networks, or about the setting of budgets. His job as producer was to make sure his show "got on the air"; he interviewed contestants, managed the writing of questions, handled the commercials, and supervised rehearsals and run-throughs, seeing that the contestants knew what to do on the set, where to stand, how to walk on and off. Assisting Freedman was a staff of four or five, broken down into "research" and "testing" departments. The testing department consisted of two or three young women, known collectively as "Miss York," who handled the thousands of letters coming in weekly from people wanting to be contestants. A tiny percentage of those interesting enough to follow up on were given appointments to take the screening test and be briefly interviewed. Good prospects who scored high enough on the test were scheduled for interviews with Freedman, and if he liked them, they were interviewed by Enright and his executive producer, Robert Noah. Once they passed all these hurdles, prospects were put on standby.

Freedman's research department consisted of a longtime Barry and Enright employee named Glorianne Rader and an assistant, who drafted questions in the one hundred or so categories of knowledge used on the show. The draft questions and answers were submitted to Freedman for approval and then passed on to Noah and Enright. Once cleared for use on the air, they were put in an active file and checked for accuracy by the *Encyclopaedia Britannica* in Chicago, which in return received a "plug" on every broadcast. Once a question was used, it was placed in another file for reference, to avoid any duplication by the writers. When a prospective contestant was selected for standby, his or her screening test score was kept for reference, but the test form itself was destroyed—a practice adopted after a newspaper article speculated on the possibility that, if the individual tests were kept, the producers would know what the contestants knew and didn't know. After their appearances, no records were kept beyond the releases the contestants had signed—promising not to appear on another quiz show for six months—and cards with names, addresses, telephone numbers, scores on the test and show, and winnings.

As for his personal dealings with prospective contestants, Freedman said that he interviewed them to determine, in addition to background and life story, "their strong categories of knowledge and weak ones." This was to avoid using the category of baseball, for example, in a match between a man and a woman. Once contestants were scheduled to go on the air, Freedman dropped into the dressing room before the broadcast to "get them to relax," by chatting about their families and jobs, explaining the rules to new contestants, answering whatever questions they had.

With Leibbrand's story in mind, I asked if he had other meetings with contestants, in the days preceding the broadcast. Freedman's answer was no, except that when returning contestants came in to pick up their fan mail or for a press interview arranged by Barry and Enright, they might drop into his office for an update on their interview segments. Or out-of-town people came in before the broadcast to pick up checks for the travel expenses that Barry and Enright covered.

As Freedman talked, something began to bother me. Greene was Enright's lawyer, and Freedman was Enright's employee, but here was Greene in my office representing Freedman. If it happened that both Enright and Freedman, employer and employee, were involved in wrongdoing, what was Greene doing representing both of them? Presumably, Enright, as employer, was in a better position to pay for Greene's services. If a lawyer's duty was to put his client's interest foremost, how could Greene do this in a case when one client was employed by another? Before I came up with a way of broaching what could be a conflict of interest, my secretary, Marion Hepp, came in unsummoned and signaled me to step outside, and I left Freedman and Greene with Donnelly.

Jay Goldberg was waiting to tell me that former contestant James Snodgrass was ready to blow "Twenty-One" sky high. Snodgrass was claiming that not only had he been given questions and answers—and in advance—but he could also prove it in writing. In Goldberg's office, I met Snodgrass and two young law partners who accompanied him, Michael Dontzin and Burton Shaps. Dontzin said his client was given the scripts for the questions and answers used when he was on "Twenty-One" by Albert Freedman in advance, and they could prove it. He pointed to three envelopes on Goldberg's desk—unopened, registered letters addressed to Mr. James Snodgrass, 221 West 16th

Street, New York, 11, New York. I spent the next half-hour listening to the bare outline of Snodgrass's story; the details would be filled in over the next few days.

SNODGRASS was an artist in his late thirties and a graduate of Cleveland's Western Reserve University. He had tried his hand at scriptwriting in Hollywood before becoming interested in painting and studying art in New York, where he learned the craft of painting and restoring clothing-store mannequins, by which he supplemented his income. In 1954 he was awarded $1,500 for travel study as a promising painter and went to Europe to paint for a couple of years, before running low on money and returning to New York early in March 1957. He was trying to renew his contacts in the mannequin business when a friend, who was impressed by Snodgrass's large fund of general knowledge, told him about "Tic Tac Dough."

After he took the test for "Tic Tac Dough," Snodgrass was notified he had done so well that they also wanted him to take the test for "Twenty-One." Knowing that the consolation prize for "Twenty-One" was $500 and for "Tic Tac Dough" it was a wristwatch, Snodgrass took and passed the harder test, then was interviewed by Freedman and invited to stand by on the broadcast of April 8, 1957. He participated in a dress rehearsal, then watched from the wings as Henry Bloomgarden, the current champion, defeated a challenger from California. A week and a half later, Snodgrass was told by Freedman they had liked the way he looked during the rehearsal and wanted him to go on the air on April 22. After introducing Snodgrass to Enright as the next contestant, Freedman took him back into his own office.

According to Snodgrass, Freedman closed the door, took some papers from his desk drawer, and said, "I want to ask you some questions and see if you can answer them," then read off three or four questions, half of which Snodgrass could answer. These were the questions he would be asked on "Twenty-One," Freedman said: "We want you to be at your ease and not make a fool of yourself the first time on." He gave Snodgrass the correct answers to the questions he had missed and the number of points he was to request before each question, then handed over the slips of paper for Snodgrass to memorize.

Looking at the questions and the points they were worth—four questions in sets of two, each set adding up to twenty-one points—Snodgrass realized that he would play two games and would not lose. Before this, he claimed, he had no idea that "Twenty-One" was rigged, but Freedman's breezy manner suggested that rigging was the accepted practice. In his dressing room before the April 22 broadcast, Snodgrass was visited by Freedman, who used a stopwatch to rehearse him for the interview segment and the questions and answers. The broadcast went according to plan: Snodgrass played two games against Bloomgarden, each a tie at 21–21. He would return to challenge Bloomgarden again during the next broadcast, to play a third game with the stakes accordingly raised to $1,500 a point. Whatever happened then, Snodgrass would wind up with at least $1,500 in consolation prize money for his efforts.

At their next meeting, Snodgrass was told by Freedman that the reaction to his first appearance was so good, they wanted to arrange a series of ties to last several broadcasts, and they had Bloomgarden's approval. Ultimately Bloomgarden would win, but Snodgrass would end up with $2,000 or $3,000, enough money, Freedman pointed out, for him to return to Europe and paint for a couple of years. Snodgrass saw little reason to object, even if Bloomgarden was going to make many times the amount he would in the deal; nevertheless, it occurred to him that someday he might want to be able to prove what was happening.

In his days as an aspiring scriptwriter, Snodgrass told us, he learned the poor man's method of protecting his work against plagiarism—not by paying for a copyright, but by sealing a manuscript in an envelope, sending it to himself by registered mail, and leaving it unopened. After his conference with Freedman, he inserted a sheet of paper and a carbon in his typewriter. At the top he put the date and "To Whom It May Concern," then proceeded to type out the scenario of his part on the next broadcast of "Twenty-One" exactly as Freedman had presented it to him: the categories and their order, the number of points to request in each, the questions he would be asked, and the answers he would give. He put the carbon copy away, signed the original, and sealed it in an envelope addressed to himself, which he took to the post office and sent via registered mail. When he received it a day or so later, he put it away unopened. He had brought the unopened letters with him and now handed us the carbon copies to read, as he continued his story.

All went without a hitch for the next two broadcasts. On May 6, the program was devoted to a single game, going five rounds before ending in a 21–21 tie. The suspense this generated helped the ratings for the next broadcast and kept the stakes for the next game at $500 a point less than they would have been if the usual two games had been played. On May 13 the scenario called for Snodgrass to miss a question in the second game of two and end up with 11 points, presumably to lose—he didn't know for sure and didn't ask. But in the dressing room, Freedman gave him a reprieve, instructing him to answer the question correctly to achieve another tie.

Then, at their next meeting, Freedman told Snodgrass that on May 20 his stint would end in the first game of the evening. With the game being played at stakes of $3,000 a point, Snodgrass would leave with that amount in consolation. Though Snodgrass said nothing, as he studied the questions and answers Freedman handed him, the decision to write him out of "Twenty-One" rankled. On the way home, he stopped off at the library, found a volume of the poetry of Emily Dickinson, and studied one of the poems. The next morning, he typed the following, which he sent to himself via registered mail and which I now read in its carbon copy:

> To Whom It May Concern:
>
> The following are the questions for the first game on the television quiz program to take place at 9 o'clock Monday evening, May 20, 1957.
>
> Round 1: Category "American Literature," 11 points:
>
> Identify the major American poets who wrote the following lines of poetry: "I hear America singing . . . the varied carols" (Walt Whitman); "Fog comes in on little cat feet" (Carl Sandburg); "Hope is a thing with feathers, it whispers to the soul" (Emily Dickinson); "I shot an arrow in the air, where it fell I know not where" (Henry Wadsworth Longfellow).
>
> Round 2: Category "The Armed Forces," 10 points:
>
> Where are the present academies of the following branches of the United States Armed Forces: Army (U.S. Military Academy at West Point, N.Y.); Navy (U.S. Naval Academy at Annapolis, Md.); Coast Guard (The Coast Guard Academy is at New London, Conn.); Merchant Marine (King's Point, Long Island); Air Corps (While the Air Corps Academy is being constructed at Colorado Springs the present academy is in Denver, Colo.).
>
> According to the plan I am to miss the first question, specifically the lines by Emily Dickinson. I've been told to answer Ralph Waldo Emerson. I have decided not to "take the fall" but to answer the question correctly.[1]

On the air on May 20, Barry announced to viewers "the most monumental game in the history of our program," meaning that the longest ever series of ties had raised the stakes to an unprecedented $3,000 a point. If Bloomgarden could win by the maximum—21 to 0—$63,000 would be added to his winnings so far, the largest amount ever chalked up in a single swoop. But, even though Freedman never indicated precisely what Bloomgarden's point selections would be, Snodgrass knew the producers did not intend to add that much to Bloomgarden's winnings. Rather, according to plan, Snodgrass would lose by ten, assuming Bloomgarden answered correctly for twenty-one, meaning the champion's gain would be cut back to $30,000.

In the isolation booth, Snodgrass asked for eleven points in American Literature, and was read lines by four different poets. Disobeying orders, he correctly identified Dickinson, as well as Whitman, Sandburg, and Longfellow. Out of Snodgrass's hearing, but as he learned later and we confirmed after seeing a kinescope of the broadcast, Bloomgarden in his turn requested ten points and correctly identified the authors and titles of three American novels. In the second round, as called for in the scenario, Snodgrass correctly answered the ten-point question about the Armed Forces. Since his total was now twenty-one, Snodgrass was allowed, according to the rules, to listen as Bloomgarden, for eleven points, named the five top U.S. generals and admirals. The game was over and the two men were tied once again at twenty-one.

While the broadcast switched to a commercial, Freedman and Enright both rushed to Snodgrass's booth, opened the door, and asked if he was all right. He said he wanted to continue, and they went to confer briefly with Bloomgarden in his booth. Back on the air, the match resumed, at $3,500 a point, with Snodgrass on his own. The first category was Queens, and Snodgrass asked for ten points. The question concerned several relatives of Marie Antoinette of France. It was a coincidence, since the question was intended for another contestant, but Snodgrass had once written a play about Marie Antoinette and was able to answer correctly.

For his turn, Bloomgarden also asked for ten points and answered the same question correctly. In the second round, the category was Biology. Snodgrass requested eleven points.

BARRY: The bones in our backbone, or vertebrae, are arranged in five groups and named for their positions in the spinal column. Name these five groups. Understand it all right?
SNODGRASS: I imagine the sacrum is part of it.
BARRY: I beg your pardon?
SNODGRASS: The sacrum. S-A-C-R-U-M?
BARRY: I'm sorry to have to call for a ruling on this—
SNODGRASS: Or sacroiliac, it may be also.
BARRY: I'll have to call for a ruling on that, too. One of the groups is called S-A-C-R-A-L. The producers say "no—cannot accept." I'm

sorry, Jim. Sacral is actually the name. . . . All is not lost yet—Hank
still has to answer.[2]

According to the rules, losing the eleven-point question at this point
wiped out the ten points he had won on the first round; Snodgrass's score
stood at zero. Again out of Snodgrass's hearing, but as he learned right after
the broadcast, Bloomgarden requested eleven points and was asked the question about the spinal column:

BLOOMGARDEN: The lumbar.
BARRY: Lumbar is one.
BLOOMGARDEN: The sacral.
BARRY: Two.
BLOOMGARDEN: The—the thoracic.
BARRY: That's correct. You've got three of them. Two more to give
you a victory.
BLOOMGARDEN: The cervical.
BARRY: You need one more for twenty-one points.
BLOOMGARDEN: I'm not sure of the pronunciation of this—I'll spell
it for you—you better pronounce it. Ah, c-o-c-c-y-x—I think it's
cossicks or cocksicks—I'm not sure. c-o-c-c-y-x.
BARRY: I have no idea how to pronounce it, but you're right—you
have twenty-one points![3]

Snodgrass's disobedience had resulted in Bloomgarden's winning, by
21–0, a record $73,500 in a single game, raising his amassed winnings to
$126,000. Snodgrass himself would be leaving with $500 more than if he had
followed orders. According to Snodgrass, when he returned to his dressing
room, he found Freedman on the verge of tears. "You've ruined me," said
Freedman; if Snodgrass had followed the script, only $30,000 would have
been added to Bloomgarden's winnings.

On the way to the NBC press room, as customary after a broadcast, to meet
with reporters, Snodgrass was taken aside by Enright, who whispered to him,
"Something went wrong and we might have to do a rematch." The NBC
switchboard was being flooded with calls from doctors, nurses, and others
protesting that, if Snodgrass's answer to the spinal column question—the
noun form "sacrum" instead of the adjective "sacral"—was wrong, then
Bloomgarden's answer "coccyx," instead of the adjective "coccygeal," should
not have been accepted either.

In the press room, Enright acknowledged that something had gone wrong
and promised a decision in a few days on how to proceed. The next broadcast
of "Twenty-One" would not be for two weeks because of a previously an-

nounced network special preempting the slot. Before the next broadcast, Snodgrass saw nothing of Freedman except in connection with publicity. On May 27 NBC held a press conference to announce the solution arrived at: in the June 3 broadcast, Bloomgarden and Snodgrass would resume their match at the level before the second game of May 20. The stakes would be $3,500 a point. Though Bloomgarden's May 20 winnings of $73,500 would be canceled, he would be guaranteed a minimum total of $52,500, no matter by how much he might lose to Snodgrass in the rematch.

Having had no discussion with Freedman about the broadcast before the evening of June 3, Snodgrass had no opportunity to write himself a registered letter. Only at the last minute, in his dressing room, was Snodgrass given a scenario. Two games would be played: the first was to be another tie; in the second, Snodgrass would lose. Freedman gave Snodgrass all the information for the first. In the first round of the second game, he was told, the category would be Political Leaders. Snodgrass would ask for 11 points and be given a four-part question; Freedman read the questions and the correct answers for two of the parts, then said, "I will not read you the other two parts, because I don't think you can answer them." The producer was taking no chances this time by giving Snodgrass either the answers or the questions themselves that he was to miss, even though Snodgrass had no way of looking them up. In the second round, Snodgrass was to answer correctly a ten-point question, but that would be insufficient to recoup.

On the air, in the first round of the second game, Snodgrass was able to answer one of the two parts Freedman had withheld—identifying Colonel Naguib as the army officer who ousted King Farouk and took over Egypt—but when it came to naming the first prime minister of the newly independent nation of Ghana, Snodgrass failed to come up with the answer, Kwame Nkrumah. The remainder went according to plan: Bloomgarden won, by 21–10, and, at stakes of $4,000 a point, boosted his total winnings to $96,500. Snodgrass was leaving with $4,000. Offstage, Freedman thanked him for his cooperation and pointed out that the mistake of the previous broadcast had worked to everybody's advantage by giving the show excellent, unanticipated publicity. Enright said he had Snodgrass in mind as a panelist on the new "High Low" quiz planned for the summer.

I INTERRUPTED Snodgrass to say I had to leave and proposed he tell all the details to Goldberg now, then return for a grand jury appearance, which we would schedule within days. When Dontzin asked if his client was a target of the investigation and I said he was not, Dontzin advised Snodgrass to proceed. Leaving Snodgrass in Goldberg's hands, I returned to my office and asked Myron Greene to step outside. Out of Freedman's hearing, I informed the lawyer that if he was representing Barry and Enright, then his presence now put him in a conflict of interest. Realizing there was a new development, Greene asked if Freedman was a target. I replied that it was a possibility. Greene understood the implications: if Freedman was a target of our investigation of an affair involving Barry and Enright, then we might be considering a grant of immunity to Freedman in order to have him implicate his employer. For Greene to represent both in this situation would be a conflict because the lawyer's duty was to serve the best interests of every client.

In a brief conference, Greene advised Freedman that he ask for an adjournment of the interview in order to find new counsel. But Freedman told Greene he wanted to continue talking to us. Greene departed and I advised Freedman of the possibility he could be a defendant and he was welcome to find another lawyer before talking further. Freedman shook his head and assured us he had nothing to hide.

I glanced over my list of former "Twenty-One" contestants, then asked Freedman if he gave assistance—meaning did he provide in advance the questions and answers used on "Twenty-One"—to Stempel while he was a contestant. Freedman repeated what he told us already: he joined the show after Stempel became a contestant and had nothing to do with him. Referring again to the list, I asked Freedman if he had assisted any of Stempel's opponents, and I included the name of Rose Leibbrand as casually as I could. He denied giving her assistance. When I asked if he had drilled her with questions and answers, he replied he had, but the questions were from old broadcasts, used only to give her an idea of what to expect. Donnelly and I then went down the list chronologically, asking Freedman about champions who followed Stempel—Van Doren, Nearing, Bloomgarden, Von Nardroff, and others—as well as challengers like Snodgrass. Freedman calmly denied providing assistance to any of them.

I took Donnelly outside and instructed him to make sure Snodgrass was out of the way so we could let Freedman go without the two crossing paths. I returned to Freedman and told him we would shortly decide whether he was to be a target; if so, he would be called before the grand jury and asked to waive immunity before testifying. In that event, he certainly should consult a lawyer. When Donnelly signaled the coast was clear, I sent Freedman away.

Donnelly, Goldberg, Stein, Barrett, and I conferred in my office. Goldberg filled us in with more details from Snodgrass, and in the process introduced a new dimension to Freedman's role in events as they continued to unroll. In the summer of 1957, Enright delivered on his promise to put Snodgrass on the panel of "High Low," the short-lived quiz that was the project Enright had discussed with Stempel in their tape-recorded conversation of March 7, 1957. Snodgrass appeared on several broadcasts, including one with Bloomgarden, and was paid $400 for each appearance. Each time, Snodgrass told Goldberg, he was coached in advance by Freedman.

Subsequently, Snodgrass remained in touch with Freedman, who commissioned him to paint a portrait of the producer's young daughter, for which she sat several times, though the portrait was never completed. Then in August 1958, when Stempel made headlines, Freedman tracked Snodgrass down and invited him to lunch for August 29, the day that Barry and Enright counterattacked Stempel in the press by accusing him of blackmail. Freedman reminded Snodgrass that everything that had passed between them was confidential and asked Snodgrass to tell no one what had happened. Snodgrass replied he had no plans for telling anyone anything; he mentioned nothing about his self-addressed registered letters.

Just after the grand jury announcement, Freedman called Snodgrass, asking him to resume work on his daughter's portrait, and again reminded Snodgrass of his promise of confidentiality. This time Snodgrass replied he would have to answer truthfully if he were called before a grand jury; he would not commit perjury. Freedman asserted it was virtually impossible that Snodgrass would be called to testify. When he brought his daughter over to sit for the portrait, Freedman told Snodgrass he had been advised by a lawyer that testifying under oath was one thing but answering questions in the district attorney's office was another; lying to the D.A. was not perjury.

When Snodgrass received a subpoena, he sought advice from Dontzin and Shaps, and then was telephoned again by Freedman, asking if he had been subpoenaed. According to Snodgrass, Freedman told him he had checked with other former contestants who had been called in, who reported that we questioned them for only ten or fifteen minutes. But, Freedman warned, if Snodgrass did testify under oath and told the truth, he had to be able to back it up. Before Snodgrass could reply, Freedman cut him off, saying they should not be discussing it on the phone; Freedman would come visit him the next day. Snodgrass immediately called his lawyers who advised him to have Freedman meet with him in their office. Snodgrass called Freedman back with that suggestion, to which Freedman agreed, but the next day the producer failed to show up, whereupon Snodgrass's lawyers advised him to make an appointment with us.

Hearing all this, I realized we had to move the "Twenty-One" matter to the grand jury immediately, before Freedman could do more damage. If

Freedman had researched the question of perjury, there was no reason for the D.A.'s office to slouch in that regard; I told Donnelly to begin drafting a memorandum of law on the subject and to get Bloomgarden into the office for another going over.

Donnelly quickly arranged for Bloomgarden to come in on September 26, 1958, and he also set up an interview with Harold Craig, another big-money winner on "Twenty-One." In a large spread in the September 15 issue of *Life* magazine devoted to the "Big Fuss Over TV Quiz Shows," there was a photograph of Craig, a young upstate New York dairy farmer, holding a calf in his arms. Craig had supplanted Bloomgarden as "Twenty-One" champion and had gone on to win $106,000 in eighteen appearances on the quiz. "Controls can fix the show," Craig was quoted in the caption to the *Life* photograph, "They [the shows' producers] can keep you on as long as they want, get rid of you when they are ready." Seeing this, we imagined Craig might have some interesting things to tell us. As a resident of New York State, he was subject to subpoena, but serving one on him where he lived, in a rural area north of Albany, would have been a headache, requiring that we send a process server all the way up from Manhattan. So Donnelly telephoned Craig to suggest he come in voluntarily, at our expense. He agreed to meet with us on Saturday, September 27, when he could find someone to look after his cows.

Meanwhile, on Thursday afternoon, Snodgrass appeared before the grand jury, opening the second case for its scrutiny—*The People against Richard Roe*, our designation for the investigation of "Twenty-One." Snodgrass's three sealed letters were marked and introduced as grand jury exhibits along with the carbon copies he had made. Before they were opened, the letters would be consigned to the police laboratory for testing to make sure that the envelopes had not been tampered with. Then, under oath, Snodgrass retold his story. By now the jurors were well informed about the workings of "Dotto," which few if any of them had heard of before the proceedings began. But, like most people who owned television sets, they had heard of "Twenty-One" and read about Stempel and his allegations. Some of them might have seen Snodgrass on television. Now the former contestant set forth the contrivances in meticulous detail, as he already had in Goldberg's office.

The following day, Friday, September 26, it was Snodgrass who gave press coverage of the quiz scandal a new jolt. The Friday editions of the *New York Post* carried a front page banner blaring, "2nd Star Says '21' Was Fixed!" Inside, the newspaper reported Snodgrass's visit to the grand jury and the existence of the letters. Interviewed after his grand jury appearance, Snodgrass told of assistance on "Twenty-One" but did not name Freedman. Suspecting that Snodgrass's visit to us, like those of Hilgemeier and Stempel, was engineered by the press to create a story, I was in a sour mood when Barrett brought in Bloomgarden, unaccompanied by a lawyer. Before I could say anything, Bloomgarden began upbraiding me for bullying him in our previous encounter at his office.

I informed him that if he did not tell us the truth now, he would not be committing perjury, but before the grand jury, he would be under oath and if he testified falsely, he would open himself up to prosecution. "That's what I mean about your attitude," he interrupted, "Even before you ask me a single question, you're assuming I won't tell the truth and threatening me."

I explained that we were not interested in prosecuting him. He was not a "target" or potential defendant. He would be subpoenaed to appear as a witness before the grand jury and testify under oath; if he lied and we could prove it, he could be prosecuted for perjury. I also explained the law concerning grand jury secrecy and our policy against disclosing to the press statements made by witnesses in office interviews. Witnesses were free to tell anything they wanted to the press even though we recommended their not doing so. We had no intention of embarrassing him, and no information he disclosed to us could be used against him in a civil suit. Our investigation was designed in no way to take away the money he had won on "Twenty-One" or to assist anyone in any civil action that might conceivably be brought against him. He insisted he had not lied to us and he had no intention of doing so.

Asked about his relationship with Freedman, Bloomgarden said he had first dealt with Freedman perfunctorily, when he was a contestant on "Tic Tac Dough," at the time produced by Freedman. He had met Freedman socially, before trying to become a quiz show contestant, and it was a coincidence that, when someone suggested he try out for a quiz show, he went to take the "Tic Tac Dough" test and learned Freedman was the producer. He appeared twice on "Tic Tac Dough" and lost to a small boy, and received a watch as a consolation prize. Early in 1957 Freedman called Bloomgarden and asked him to take the test for "Twenty-One"; then on March 18 he was put on the air and defeated Nearing, who had displaced Van Doren. As Bloomgarden told it, during his four months on "Twenty-One," he never met with Freedman in his office but spoke to him only in the dressing room just before broadcasts.

As for the match with Snodgrass, I asked if Bloomgarden didn't find it unusual that the two of them played thirteen tie games? It was unprecedented, he replied smugly, so it must have been unusual, but that was the way it happened. He denied any advance arrangement for the ties, no matter what Snodgrass alleged. As for the flap over the spinal-column question,

Bloomgarden recounted, after the broadcast Enright offered to guarantee him the $52,500 he had amassed before the advent of Snodgrass if he would agree to a rematch. He thought it was unfair, since he had been declared the winner, but he decided from a public-relations standpoint not to appear to be a "sore winner" for the sake of more money.

Was it just a coincidence that he answered the noun "coccyx" when he answered the other groups with adjectives, and that "coccyx" was also on Barry's answer card? Not at all, he replied: "The coccyx is a group because it is the fused bone." He said this and everything else with a self-important manner, which made it obvious that we were not going to crack him, so I ended the interview; I said he would be sent a subpoena and given a date to appear before the grand jury. By now we had looked at kinescopes of his match with Snodgrass; these plus Snodgrass's letters gave me every reason to believe Bloomgarden was lying. His motive seemed to be to protect his reputation as a publicist in the field of medical research, the importance of which he harped on at every opportunity. Unlike Snodgrass, Bloomgarden had plenty to lose if it came out that his appearances on "Twenty-One" were rigged. Before the end of the day, Snodgrass's letters were handed over to Detective Joseph McNally, the police department's top handwriting expert, who promised a lab report by the following week.

ON SATURDAY, September 27, when I reached the office, Donnelly and Stein had already spent two hours interviewing Harold Craig. After briefing me that Craig was insisting he never received assistance from Freedman or anyone else, Donnelly and Stein brought the former contestant into my office. He seemed frightened and I guessed that my associates had become fed up and begun to play tough with him. Craig listened in silence as I gave him the usual warnings and assurances, then his face turned pale and his lips began to move as if he wanted to speak. He crossed his arms on the edge of my desk and he put his head down on his arms. "I can't lie," he sobbed, "I just can't lie." After a few moments, I urged Craig, for his own sake, to let it all out. He raised his head, apologized for making a scene, then began to tell his story.

NOW TWENTY-EIGHT YEARS OLD, Harold Craig was the third generation of his family to farm dairy cattle on four-hundred acres, near the village of Hebron in upstate Washington County northeast of Albany, a four-hour drive from New York City. He showed precocity since early childhood, and in high school was an above-average student and outstanding in the subject of history. He made a try at Albany State Teachers College, but toward the end of his first semester he had trouble with the required composition course in English and threw in the towel, returning to the family farm.

Though Craig liked farming, it was hard work, and he spent his little spare time reading magazines like *Time* and *Newsweek*, classic novels, the plays of Shakespeare, and books on history. When his mother bought a television set in 1956, Craig watched the one station the set brought in, the NBC affiliate in Schenectady.

On the farm, the main meal of the day, called dinner, was served at 12:30 P.M. most of the year. Just before dinner, there was a little time to relax, and Craig spent it watching "Tic Tac Dough," on from noon to 12:30. Despite his painful encounter with higher education, he still liked to learn things and had an excellent memory, such that he could remember the name, pedigree, and age of each of his 65 cows. He found he was able to answer nearly all the questions asked on "Tic Tac Dough," so one day early in February 1957 he sat down and wrote a letter applying to become a contestant. In reply, he was told he would have to come to New York City at his own expense to take a test. On March 16 he went by train to New York to take the "Tic Tac Dough" test, which he passed, and was interviewed by a producer named Howard Felsher.

According to Craig, Felsher was very interested in his life as a farmer, and promised to be in touch with a decision about using him within a month or two. So it was a surprise when the producer called him ten days later, on March 27, asking him down to be on the show the next day. Arriving at the studio too late for the run-through, he was put on the air cold. He tied with his opponent, an army lieutenant, but lost the following day, and received a wristwatch in consolation.

A few weeks later, Craig was called in from his chores by a phone call from New York City. It was no less than Daniel Enright inviting him down at the show's expense to take the test for "Twenty-One." Craig watched the quiz every week and was very impressed by the current champion, Bloomgarden, but he agreed to try. On April 17 he spent four hours taking the "Twenty-One" test, then was interviewed by Enright, Barry, Robert Noah, and Albert Freedman, who probed him about his background and knowledge, trying out many questions on him, some easy, some hard. Craig was advised to buy some reference books, was given $50 for travel expenses, and told he would be hearing from them.

Back home, Craig began spending two evenings a week studying at the nearest public library, in the town of Granville, but heard nothing more till the middle of June, when Freedman called him back down to take the "Twenty-One" test over again. This time half of the questions were different from the first time, and he finished it in less than three hours. Freedman took him into his office and said they were very interested in having him on "Twenty-One." "If we called you this month, could you come?" the producer asked. When Craig said it was a busy time on the farm and September would be preferable, Freedman was taken aback. "There are thousands of people breaking the doors down here trying to get on and you say you can't come until September? Now, if you came on and had any luck at all, you could make ten or fifteen thousand dollars a week." Craig agreed to be available.

The call came a week later, when Freedman instructed Craig to be at the office at noon on June 24 to go on "Twenty-One" that night. When Craig arrived, Freedman asked him to close the door and sit down. According to Craig, Freedman said: "We want to try something new. I think it will be a lot of fun, but you mustn't tell Mr. Enright or anyone else, because that would spoil it." He picked up a stack of 3 × 5 green cards and explained: there was so much at stake with the program budget that they couldn't afford to take chances with Craig, so he was going to be given the questions he would be asked in advance.

That evening, Freedman informed him, he would play one game against Bloomgarden, in three rounds. Freedman gave Craig the point selections, the questions and answers for each round, for a total of twenty-one points. Freedman then rehearsed him in the way he was to deliver the answers on the air, how long he was to wait before starting them and the pauses he was to make between the various parts. Craig was astonished and asked if Bloomgarden was being given the questions and answers as well. "You just think about what you are doing," Freedman advised, "not to worry a bit about what the other fellow is doing." Since Craig's total was to be twenty-one points, he realized at the least he would tie Bloomgarden.

That was what happened on the broadcast, after Bloomgarden defeated the previous challenger in the first game and Craig was introduced as the next challenger. Craig followed Freedman's instructions, tied the champion, 21–21, in the first of eighteen appearances the farmer from Hebron would make on "Twenty-One." Every Monday morning, after seeing to the cows, Craig went down to New York City and spent an hour in Freedman's office. The producer told Craig the categories and the point selections he was to make that night, then read off the questions from his cards to see how many

Craig could answer on his own, gave him the answers he didn't know, and rehearsed him in the mechanics. After the second or third week, Craig stopped saying whether or not he knew the answers, and Freedman simply provided them. Before each broadcast, Freedman visited Craig briefly in his dressing room and ran through the scenario to see that everything was down pat.

Craig made two return appearances against Bloomgarden, and in the second game on July 15, following Freedman's instructions, he "knocked" with seventeen points, catching Bloomgarden down with only ten. Craig was the new champion, with winnings of $17,500. Leaving "Twenty-One" with $98,500 after months on the show, Bloomgarden seemed to Craig to be more jubilant than disappointed. Craig's triumph made him Washington County's biggest celebrity in living memory. He made appearances on various NBC television shows in New York, and explained to the press that he was picked for "Twenty-One" because the majority of contestants were from New York City, which made the choice of a farmer offbeat. Only on the two nights a week when he put in time studying at the Granville library did his fellow citizens keep a respectful distance.

By the third week in August, he had amassed $84,000 in winnings, and Granville declared his twenty-seventh birthday, August 17, Harold Craig Day. On September 16 he had total winnings of $119,500 when, at the end of the broadcast, there was time only to introduce his next challenger, David Mayer, Ph.D., a New York marketing psychologist. By October 14 Craig and Mayer played five ties, pushing the stakes up to $3,500 a point. That afternoon, at the usual meeting, Freedman had told Craig, "All good things have to come to an end. You're playing against a very smart man. I'm trying to figure out a way so you'll get off the show with as little loss as possible of money."

Craig faced the situation with equanimity. He had followed the TV ratings as closely as anyone else with high stakes in his performance on the medium. The ratings of "Twenty-One" hadn't been spectacular when he made his first appearance, and he might have had something to do with their not sagging even further for awhile, but as his tenure lengthened over the summer, the ratings steadily declined; by the end of the season, "Twenty-One" had fewer viewers than the reruns of "I Love Lucy" on CBS. By now, he also realized, the money he stood to take away from the show was not even half the amount Freedman had hinted he might earn. The total still stood at $119,500, where it had been when Mayer became his opponent; after seventeen appearances, that came out to a cool $7,000 a week.

Moreover, he took into account that when the axe did fall, the final amount would be less, depending on by how much his challenger would win in the final encounter—unless Freedman planned to have him defeat Mayer before losing to another challenger. On the other hand, whatever the final amount, it would be far more cash money than Craig ever imagined he would earn in a lifetime of farming. Under the rules of "Twenty-One," he could have retired with the $119,500 before embarking on a series of ties with Mayer. The possibility occurred to Craig, but he never entertained it seriously.

On October 21 Freedman presented the scenario for that night's broadcast. Craig and Mayer would play a single game. In the first round, Craig would correctly answer a ten-point question. In the second round, the category would be Women, a subject which plausibly would deter him from requesting the hardest question for eleven points. Instead he would ask for eight points and answer correctly. Freedman told him no more, and Craig knew this was the end. That night, following orders, he got eighteen points to Mayer's twenty-one, losing by three and leaving "Twenty-One" with his winnings cut back to $106,000; still, it was the largest amount taken away by a "Twenty-One" contestant since Charles Van Doren's departure with $129,000.

In a studio corridor afterward, Freedman asked Craig if he was upset. When Craig said he was not, Freedman told him, "Well, I don't have to tell you not to say anything to anybody. If anybody says to you I gave you the answers, they won't be telling the truth. They'll just be trying to trip you up." Craig was surprised by this but had no intention of telling anyone the truth. Instead, he fed speculation that he had decided to abdicate after a long, exhausting run to avoid having his amassed winnings trimmed too much in an eventual defeat.

As a farmer with a sharp sense of husbanding resources, Craig was never tempted by schemes for getting richer quicker or the pitches by salesmen of various types. As far as he was concerned, the winnings were still on paper and it never occurred to him to ask for an advance. He told us that out of his winnings, he paid $52,000 in Federal income taxes and $6,600 in New York State income taxes. He gave $5,000 to a brother for working the farm during his absences and $1,000 each to his mother and sister. He spent $4,000 on farm machinery, $3,000 to repair the barn, and $1,500 to have a barn cleaner installed. He bought four cows for $2,000 and a car for $3,000. He donated $2,500 to a hospital, bought an insurance annuity in the amount of $10,000, and deposited $5,000 in his savings account. The remaining $10,400 he put into a mutual fund.

When he had finished, Craig was profoundly relieved to have the story off his chest. It provided an important breakthrough in our investigation of "Twenty-One"; not only was he among the show's top money winners, but since he, unlike Stempel and Snodgrass, seemed to have no personal grievance or axe to grind in coming to us, his testimony before the grand jury would be eminently credible—all the more so if he did not go to the newspapers with the story.

CHAPTER SIX

The Two-Witness Rule

(SEPTEMBER 29–OCTOBER 11, 1958)

On Monday morning, September 29, I was relieved to see that the press had not mentioned Craig's visit to the office and called my associates in for a skull session. I assigned to Stein the task of probing "Tic Tac Dough," which, as Craig's and Bloomgarden's accounts indicated, had served to function for "Twenty-One" as daytime "Dotto" did for the nighttime version, that is, providing a recruiting and training ground for contestants. Then we discussed the investigation in depth and the next steps we would take.

At first blush, there appeared to be no grounds for prosecuting anyone involved in television quiz programs under the laws of New York. Our examination of the contracts between producers and sponsors showed that the programs had not been represented as bona fide contests, therefore larceny by false pretenses had not been committed. Neither did laws against false or misleading advertising seem to apply, because, in New York at least, to make a case of misleading advertising, it had to relate to the merchandise being offered for sale. Although the facts suggested that "Dotto"'s producers might have misled Colgate as to the nature of the package they were selling, the contract between Marjeff and the Ted Bates advertising agency, on behalf of Colgate, specified that if anything about the program put Colgate in a bad light, the sponsor could simply cancel the show, which it had done. If there was a basis for a civil suit by Colgate and Bates against the producers, it wasn't our business. Conceivably, if Edward Jurist was to be believed, Colgate had made more money from "Dotto"'s being fixed than it would have otherwise, because the fixing had made the show "entertaining." Telling in this regard was the fact that so far no sponsor had come to us with a complaint.

But these considerations did not preclude the commission of a crime in the process of fixing a quiz show. Extortion had been alleged, and there was still the possibility that kickbacks were paid by contestants. There were also the discrepancies in the payment by "Twenty-One" to Richard Jackman and the advances to Stempel and Van Doren. A cabal of characters—contestants as well as producers—seemed to be hard at work circling the wagons around "Twenty-One"; what were they trying to hide? Nevertheless, even if we didn't uncover an actual crime in the operation of the quizzes, the grand jury was exercising a legitimate function by investigating a matter of considerable public concern. When he first raised the possibility of submitting the matter of the quizzes to a grand jury, Hogan had mentioned the possibility of a presentment or grand jury report, drawing attention to conditions and making suggestions for reform or legislative action. Our job was to present the facts that would provide the basis for such a report if the grand jury elected to make one.

We agreed Freedman was the key to unlocking the mystery. His knowledge of the workings of the quiz was second only to that of Enright and Barry themselves, and, if Snodgrass was to be believed, Freedman was willing to attempt the subornation of grand jury witnesses. On the other hand, Freedman was little more than a waterboy who had taken over his boss's task of handling contestants that followed Stempel. If there were to be a target of the investigation of "Twenty-One," it was not Freedman but the packagers themselves. Our problem was that the stories of Stempel, Snodgrass, and Craig all indicated that no assistance was given to a contestant when there was a third person present; the likelihood of the existence of any kind of written evidence or corroboration in the form of a memo or a list of questions drawn up for a specific session, aside from Snodgrass's letters, seemed remote. Thus we had no corroboration that Freedman had given assistance to Leibbrand, Snodgrass, or Craig.

To complete the picture of "Twenty-One" meant opening up Freedman, and to accomplish that, we decided to summon him, like the contestants, and require him to testify. We hoped he would tell the truth under these circumstances, but if he lied, we would set about charging him with perjury, which ultimately might loosen his tongue. But it was one thing to know somebody is lying, quite another to prove perjury. Under the law of New York State, a charge of perjury required a number of conditions: (1) the defendant must have sworn under oath to a body that could legally require and administer an oath, such as a court or a grand jury, that he or she would testify truthfully, but then proceeded to testify falsely; (2) the testimony must have been material to the proceeding or inquiry, to bring a felony charge; otherwise, under New York law, the perjury committed was a misdemeanor; and (3) the defendant must have known the testimony was false; if it was given under the mistaken impression it was correct, then there was no crime.[1]

As far as these elements were concerned, we foresaw no difficulty in making a case against Freedman. Our problem was a fourth element: in order to prove the falsity of testimony under oath, it was necessary to have the evidence of two independent witnesses or of one witness and some corroborating evidence in the form of writing, tape recording, legal wiretap, or the like. This requirement was known as the two-witness rule. The testimony of one person to an allegation of perjury without corroboration was not sufficient for conviction—it was simply the word of one person against the word of another.

Leibbrand, Snodgrass, and Craig all were definite about being alone with Freedman in their briefing sessions—and Stempel likewise with Enright. Snodgrass's registered letters, if genuine, were powerful circumstantial evidence that he was given the answers in advance, but they did not mention Freedman by name. There was still only Snodgrass's assertion that Freedman and not somebody else had given him the answers. Even if the letters had named Freedman, they might not have stood up as corroboration in a court of law because they were not *independent* of the sole witness in this instance, Snodgrass himself. Whether or not Enright and company foresaw the possibility of a perjury situation, they seemed to have taken great pains to keep the assistance on a one-to-one basis.

We pondered this apparent absurdity—at least three people would testify they had been given questions and answers in advance by the same producer; but even if we found dozens more who would testify to being fixed, we might not have had a case unless we could find two people to back up a single act. All the producer had to do was deny each allegation. But Donnelly, who had been researching the law of perjury since our first encounter with Freedman, had found a way. Yes, he said, the law did require the testimony of two witnesses, or one witness plus corroborating evidence, to establish the falsity of testimony of another made under oath, but the stress should be not on the falsity of fact X, or instance Y, or event Z—but on the *testimony*, that is, what the defendant *said*. Suppose Freedman were not asked whether he helped Snodgrass or Leibbrand or Craig specifically, but instead whether he helped *anybody*. If he answered no, there were at least three people, Snodgrass, Leibbrand, and Craig, we could depend upon to say he helped somebody, namely each of them. Three witnesses who would contradict— not Freedman's account of X, Y, or Z—but his testimony that he didn't help *anybody*.

Donnelly had found a precedent in a 1943 federal decision in a case where the government prosecuted a ward heeler who, under oath before a federal grand jury, testified he had not paid any person for voting in the general election of 1940. He was indicted for perjury. At the trial, the government produced two witnesses who stated unequivocally that the defendant had paid them separately $2 each for their votes in the election, and he was convicted. On the defendant's appeal, the higher court affirmed, ruling that the fact to be established in the trial was not whether the defendant had paid specific individuals to vote, but whether his assertion he had not paid anyone to vote was false. Since more than one witness testified under oath in the trial to the contrary, then the two-witness rule was satisfied.[2]

Much to my surprise, I had received notification from Edward Levine, an experienced former assistant district attorney in Brooklyn and a well-known appeals lawyer, that he was representing Freedman. I called Levine to inform him that a subpoena was being sent to his office summoning Freedman before the grand jury on October 2. I made it clear to Levine that Freedman was merely a witness, not a "target," and would not be asked to sign a waiver of immunity. Levine knew that if Freedman *had* been a "target," then a different protocol from that used with run-of-the-mill witnesses would have applied.

Not only did the constitution guarantee a person's right against self-incrimination in a matter under investigation by a grand jury, the law all but prohibited a person's inadvertently incriminating him or herself and made the district attorney legally responsible for protecting a witness's legal rights. Therefore we were obliged to inform subpoenaed prospective defendants that they were "targets" and would not be permitted to testify unless they signed a waiver of immunity. If a witness signed, anything to which the person testified under oath could be used against that person at a trial. If the witness declined and the district attorney was anxious to have his or her testimony, then that witness could be brought before the grand jury, with a request that it grant the witness immunity from prosecution, provided that the crime under consideration was among those covered by the immunity statute. Naturally, any witness who testified falsely before a grand jury could be prosecuted for perjury regardless of whether immunity had been waived or granted.

In the interval before Freedman's appearance, Donnelly and I interviewed three more "Twenty-One" champions and a key person on the program's production staff. Two of the former champions—David Mayer and Robert Leicester—were neighbors in Greenwich Village and had known each other even before becoming contestants. Mayer, a psychologist and partner in a consumer research firm, had defeated Craig in October 1957, then retired from the show with $47,500 the following month. Leicester was an assistant director of a private high school in Manhattan. Encouraged by Mayer's experience, Leicester applied early in 1958 and began his run as a contestant in June, challenging the longest-running "Twenty-One" champion, Elfrida Von Nardroff, and defeating her on July 21. The event was noteworthy because she left the show after twenty-one appearances with winnings of $220,500, the highest ever achieved by a contestant on a single program to that date. After defeating two opponents, Leicester himself was displaced on July 28 by a professor of English from Los Angeles, taking home winnings of $43,500. Both Leicester and Mayer denied receiving assistance of any kind.

Mayer told us that, during Van Doren's run, he was urged by friends to try out for the show. After the usual tests and interviews, he was invited to be a standby on the evening when Van Doren lost to Nearing. When Freedman indicated he would be invited at a future date to be a contestant on "Tic Tac Dough" or "Twenty-One," Mayer began watching "Twenty-One" every week and undertook, he claimed, a systematic reading of a Harvard University series of encapsulated textbooks covering political and social history and narrowed down the show's most prevalent categories for study in depth. After he became a contestant, he followed the strategy of requesting ten- or eleven-point questions in what he considered his strong categories, lower-value questions in the others. But he quickly realized he had to change this approach, always taking eleven points in a strong subject, risking all by taking ten in a weak one.

As for a prevalence of 21–21 ties, he said, at first "the ties were no skin off my back. It was Craig's money and it was Craig who was risking practically everything." After defeating Craig, he beat two more opponents in quick succession. Then, on November 4, he met a new opponent named Paul Bain, and the ties began again. Mayer was fearful that if they continued, the winnings he had amassed could go down the drain, since the rules did not permit a champion to retire after a tie. On November 11 he finally defeated Bain and promptly retired. He was firm in denials that he had given any money or gifts to anyone connected with the show. Mayer put on a very good act, but I was convinced by Craig's account that the eight tie games, seven of them 21–21, had to have been engineered. Irked as I was by the possibility that Mayer and Leicester, both well-educated family men, were lying to us despite our assurances, I didn't have to think very hard to fathom their motivations. Mayer was trying to establish himself in the public relations business and Leicester was a school administrator. Like Bloomgarden and unlike Stempel and Snodgrass, they had high professional stakes in not being involved in quiz rigging. We decided to give them stakes in telling the truth by handing them grand jury subpoenas.

The third champion was "Twenty-One"'s biggest money winner, Elfrida Von Nardroff. In her early thirties, Von Nardroff was well-spoken and had a good vocabulary as well as a perpetually quizzical look. The daughter of a professor of physics at Columbia University and of a drama teacher, she grew up in the New York area, attended a private school, then went to Duke University in North Carolina, where she graduated in 1947 with a B.A. in English, after regularly making the dean's list, as she pointed out. Moving to New York City to pursue graduate studies, she worked at a succession of jobs before finding a permanent position in the personnel management field as well as going to night school at Columbia, where she took undergraduate-level courses in the social sciences to fill in the gaps of her Duke education. She had worked for four years as a personnel manager and was earning $500 a month in 1958, when she first appeared on "Twenty-One." She was now studying full time at Columbia and hoped soon to be accepted for matriculation as a graduate student in sociology.

Late in 1956 she saw Van Doren on "Twenty-One," and her roommate of the time urged her to give the show a try, too. She took the "Tic Tac Dough" test in April 1957, then was called back to take the test for "Twenty-One" and passed. On July 15, 1957, she stood by as Craig defeated Bloomgarden. All the while, she claimed, she was studying "Twenty-One," having noted that the categories that came up most frequently could be lumped into three classes—history, geography, and literature. Even the science questions tended to concentrate on names of inventors and dates of discoveries, that is, on the historical aspects of the subject. She began reading heavily, acquiring reference books and haunting the main branch of the New York Public Library during lunch hours, filling notebooks with outlines of what she read. In September 1957 she stood by again on "Twenty-One." Though she was given no definite indication of when she might become a contestant, she continued to study, she claimed. Finally, in February 1958, she became a contestant and reigned as champion until her defeat by Leicester.

According to our tabulation, during her twenty-one appearances, Von Nardroff played some forty separate games, twenty-one of them ties, and gave only five wrong answers to the eighty-two questions she was asked. When we expressed skepticism about that record, she insisted she had accomplished it through hard study. She claimed to have dozens of notebooks to prove how hard she studied, so hard that she had neglected her job. In March 1958 she requested and was given an unpaid leave of absence by her employer to devote full time to "cramming" for "Twenty-One." She had crammed much more than she ever dreamed of doing in college, and attributed her success to study habits and a love of books she acquired as a child. She had written an article, published shortly after she left "Twenty-One," which explained it all, and she would be happy to show it to us.

When we asked about her relationship with Freedman, Von Nardroff claimed he never drilled her with practice questions. They rarely if ever met, only when she went in to the Barry and Enright office to pick up fan mail or for a press interview. She also saw him in the dressing room briefly before each broadcast, but only for small talk or to discuss what she would tell Barry in the interview segments. Beyond that, there was no contact. I thanked Von Nardroff for her visit and suggested she consult with an attorney. Eventually she would be called before the grand jury, I informed her, and it would be useful if at that time she brought in her notebooks for examination by the jurors and us.

ON WEDNESDAY, October 1, 1958, the day of Von Nardroff's visit, we also interviewed Glorianne Rader, Freedman's principal assistant. Rader had studied law briefly before joining Barry and Enright, where she had worked for some five years. Starting as an office manager and bookkeeper, she had moved into assisting the production of "Life Begins at 80," "Juvenile Jury," and a show for children called "Winky Dink and You." When "Tic Tac Dough" was launched in the summer of 1956, with Freedman in charge, Rader helped interview prospective contestants and assisted Howard Felsher, the associate producer in charge of writing questions. Her first involvement with "Twenty-One" was to find contestants for a pilot film. She then interviewed people who scored high enough on the "Twenty-One" test to be considered as contestants for the show. In these interviews, she probed prospects for their strong and weak areas of knowledge, because Barry and Enright were open about their policy not to ask people questions in areas they knew absolutely nothing about.

When Freedman took over "Twenty-One," Rader was promoted to associate producer and chief question writer. Now, for us, she amplified, in stupefying detail, what Freedman had told us previously about the preparation of the questions. For any given broadcast, it was necessary to have on hand at least eleven new questions in each of the one hundred-plus categories of knowledge—Baseball, Bodies of Water, English Literature, Labor, Movie Stars, Mythology, Women, and so on—used on the show, each question rated in value from one to eleven points. Rader and an assistant drafted the questions—mostly in the ten- and eleven-point range, since these were most frequently requested by contestants. Once approved by Freedman and Enright, these were typed on cards and filed for eventual use; copies were also sent to the *Encyclopaedia Britannica* for checking.

In the middle of each week before a broadcast, Enright, Noah, and Freedman met to decide on the categories to be used next. Rader was never present and disclaimed any knowledge of how the decisions were made. She was notified of the selected categories *and their order* for the upcoming broadcast. She then alerted the *Encyclopaedia* to check the questions and answers in the categories on deck for accuracy. The *Encyclopaedia*'s final approval or necessary changes were telephoned to her sometime on Monday before the broadcast. This last-minute checking was by design, to make the questions and answers as timely as possible.

Meanwhile, Rader typed out all the current questions and answers onto a separate 5 × 7 card for each category to be used. This so-called show card was given to Enright, so that he could go over the material with Barry for pronunciation. A carbon-copy card went to Noah for use in the control room during the broadcast and for reference if a "judge's decision" was required. Another carbon sheet was given to Freedman and ended up in the files as part of the record of the specific broadcast.

On Mondays, after hearing from the *Encyclopaedia*, Rader made necessary corrections on the show cards and copies, then locked the show cards into a small box. Approximately fifteen minutes before the broadcast, Rader went to the "Twenty-One" studio, unlocked the box and inserted the cards, *in the prescribed order* for the categories to be used, in a device that would cause them to pop up one at a time for Barry's use on the show.

Rader's job was also to keep track of old questions to ensure they would not be used again on the air. As soon as she received approval for new draft questions to fill up depleted categories, Rader typed out the material on individual 3 × 5 green cards and carbon-copy cards, for two separate file systems. One set was kept in Freedman's office and contained the original green cards arranged alphabetically by category. The set of carbon-copy cards was kept separately. The day after a broadcast, Rader moved the questions just used from a drawer labeled "Available" to one labeled "Used," leaving blank cards with tabs on them in the "Available" drawer to signal the categories that needed replenishment. These she supplied as soon as new questions were written and approved.

Despite her disavowals of rigging, Rader's description made it clear that the system was designed less for security than for the convenience of the producers' access to it. At his finger tips, Freedman had an up-to-date set of all questions available for use—the green cards mentioned by Craig. The key to the system was that Enright, Noah, and Freedman determined in advance which categories would be used and, just as important, what their order would be. The locked box routine functioned to make certain nothing happened to foul up the scenario the producers devised.

ON THURSDAY, October 2, Stein, Donnelly, and I were in the grand jury room when Freedman took the oath and, responding to our questions, briefly recounted his career with Louis Cowan, Inc., then with Barry and Enright, and described his duties as the producer first of "Tic Tac Dough" then "Twenty-One." Keeping our questioning very general, we mentioned no contestants by name. It took no more than fifteen minutes to reach the nub of the proceeding. Now I put to the producer the first of four carefully crafted questions: "Did you reveal to any contestant, prior to his or her appearance on any television broadcast of the program 'Twenty-One,' any questions that later were asked of him or her, for point value, on the program?"

Freedman answered without hesitation that he had never done this at any time. Admonishing him that he was under oath, I repeated the question, and Freedman repeated his answer. I then asked the second question: "Did you reveal to any contestant, prior to his or her appearance on any television broadcast of the program 'Twenty-One,' any *answers* to any of the questions that later were asked of him or her, for point value, on the program?" Freedman said he had not. Then I put to him the same questions substituting "Tic Tac Dough" for "Twenty-One." Again Freedman answered no. I thanked him and said he might step out. He looked both astonished and relieved that the questioning had been so brief.

The following day, Friday, October 3, Louis Hacker—the Third September Grand Jury foreman since September 22, when the originally designated foreman suffered a heart attack and was relieved—and I went to Judge Schweitzer's courtroom. I told the judge that the district attorney, with the consent of the grand jury, was moving to extend the panel's life. Considerable progress had been made in the investigation, but the matter was complex and a great deal more testimony was required. Schweitzer cut me short and asked how much time I wanted. I said three months should do it. "So ordered," said the judge.

EARLY IN THE AFTERNOON of Monday, October 6, I walked into Hogan's working office on the eighth floor to see him for the first time since the empaneling of the grand jury. His Senate campaign had him traveling constantly through the state and he was exhausted, but he gave me his complete attention as I filled him in on our strategy with Freedman. I mentioned the apparently unrelated announcement made by NBC on October 3, the day of Freedman's grand jury appearance, and reported in the newspapers the following day. The network was relieving Barry and Enright of day-to-day "responsibility" for producing the four shows created by the packagers and now owned by NBC: "Twenty-One," "Tic Tac Dough," "Concentration," and "Dough Re Mi." Though Barry would continue to emcee "Twenty-One" and nighttime "Tic Tac Dough," the operation of the shows was being turned over to two executive producers appointed by the network. Calling the move temporary, requested by Barry and Enright themselves so that they could "devote more time to disproving the unfounded charges," NBC quoted the partners:

> We have decided to divorce ourselves from the production and administrative chores involving these shows . . . with the knowledge that our absolute integrity will be clearly and finally established, at which time we will resume our production responsibilities.
>   While we have been unable to uncover any evidence whatsoever of wrong-doing on the program, we realize that the charges and the attendant publicity have raised questions in the minds of many viewers.[3]

Reading between the lines, one realized that the sponsors and the network had questions about the viability of keeping "Twenty-One" on the air. Quite likely the only thing that had kept NBC from canceling the show at the first hint of scandal back in August was the fact that the network owned it; relieving Enright must have been done to appease the sponsors. It was only a matter of time before a new development would scuttle "Twenty-One," and surely the insiders knew it. If so, why had Freedman committed perjury for a sinking ship? The answer had to be, I told Hogan, Enright's concern that any admission that the show was rigged—especially in the period before NBC paid something over $2 million to purchase it and the other Barry and Enright packages in May 1957—could result in action by the network to recover its money.

I turned to our investigations of other programs. Though Jay Goldberg continued to probe the $64,000 shows by questioning numerous contestants, aside from Wilton Springer's concession, at a second interview in the office, that Shirley Bernstein had assisted him on the "Challenge," we had no new revelations of rigging on that show. Charles Jackson, the original whistle-blower, remained out of reach. Goldberg had pursued him with phone calls to Tennessee, but Jackson refused to answer questions unless we paid to bring him and a lawyer to New York.

Among others, Goldberg interviewed two opera experts who had appeared on both the "Question" and the "Challenge"—Michael Della Rocca and Gino Prato. Both heatedly denied receiving assistance. Goldberg asked them many questions about opera he had prepared himself, and they demonstrated that they were genuine experts. We also talked to Redmond O'Hanlon, the New York policeman and expert on Shakespeare who had appeared on the very first broadcast of the "Question" in June 1955 and retired after winning $16,000. In his early forties, O'Hanlon had been a policeman for over ten years and held an M.A. from Fordham University. He had been interested in Shakespeare, as a hobby, since high school. He denied receiving any outright assistance, and I was inclined to believe him. We didn't give up on the $64,000 shows, however, and continued to scatter subpoenas among contestants within reach. As a result, Goldberg had interviews scheduled with, among others, Robert Strom, a teenage science whiz from the Bronx, and Dr. Joyce Brothers, whose appearances as an expert on boxing on the "Question" and "Challenge" had made her the biggest celebrity created by these shows. She had written a book on improving memory and now had her own television show on a local New York station, where she dispensed psychological advice to viewers.

In addition, we had opened an investigation of still another show, as a result of a tip from Roy Cohn, the notorious former associate of Senator Joseph McCarthy and now a high-powered New York lawyer, to my colleague, Harold Birns, a senior assistant D.A. in the Rackets Bureau. According to Cohn, a player for the New York Giants football team named Clifford Livingston had received assistance on the show called "Name That Tune." I did not relish opening another quiz probe, but Cohn could not be ignored; he might be inclined to leak to the press that the D.A. was dawdling if we did not follow up on his tip. Also, I recalled, "Name That Tune" was another client of "Dotto"'s people getter, Diane Lawson.

After clearing it with Jerry Kidder, chief of the Fraud Bureau, I collared Lawrence Bernstein, a junior A.D.A. assigned to Kidder, and asked him to take a look at "Name That Tune." Bernstein arranged with the office of the producer, Harry Salter, to examine his records and tracked Livingston through the Giants organization and scheduled an interview for later in the week.

Finally, I reported to Hogan, knowing it would not add to his peace of mind, that we had arranged an interview with Van Doren for October 10. I guessed Hogan might be having second thoughts about his haste in bringing the quiz matter before a grand jury, because the scandal was still upstaging his Senate campaign. He knew that I was thinking Van Doren might well lie both to me and to the grand jury, but he said nothing beyond telling me to keep him informed.

After lunch on Friday, October 10, Donnelly, Barrett, and I were restive at the prospect of facing the best-known quiz show figure of all. Though our practice was to keep an open mind about witnesses by not delving deeply into their backgrounds before initial interviews, Van Doren was so important that we had viewed kinescopes of his appearances on "Twenty-One" and had prepared a breakdown of all the questions he had been asked on the program; we also had read carefully the February 11, 1957, *Time* magazine cover story on Van Doren, published in the middle of his run as a contestant, a long article that seemed to provide some keys to Van Doren's personality and possible motives.

According to *Time*, Van Doren spent his childhood in a large and loving family of intellectual high-achievers. He was conditioned to excel academically to the plaudits of adoring relatives and a glittering set of family friends. He learned to read at five and from an early age devoured the thousands of books in his family's homes in Greenwich Village and Connecticut.

Van Doren was an excellent student at every school he attended. At the High School of Music and Art in Manhattan, he studied the clarinet and could have had a concert career, but gave up music when he went to St. John's College in Annapolis, Maryland, to pursue a B.A. in a curriculum based on the "great books." Graduating cum laude at age twenty, he went to graduate school at Columbia University to study astrophysics, according to *Time*, "partly because, he now thinks, he wanted to get out of the shadow of his father." Around this time, he played the lead in an amateur production of a play by Connecticut neighbor James Thurber, a performance that so impressed the playwright that some years later—"before Charlie became famous"—Thurber tried to recruit Van Doren to act in a new play he was writing for Broadway. In graduate school, Van Doren switched from astronomy to higher mathematics and took a master's degree with a thesis on inversive geometry. But in the realization that his talent for mathematics "equipped him for nothing more creative than teaching it," he began studying for a Ph.D. in English, his father's field.

In 1951, Columbia granted Van Doren $3,000 in a "traveling fellowship"—the same stipend the university had given his father back in 1919. With it, the younger Van Doren went to Cambridge University in England to do research on his dissertation subject, the eighteenth-century English poet, William Cowper. But before the academic year was over, he left England for the continent and, as *Time* pointed out, owing his Cambridge landlady $62 in rent. In Paris, he took courses at the Sorbonne and started writing a novel, then spent some time hitchhiking around Europe before returning to New York to resume his studies at Columbia, finding a job as an instructor in English at Columbia with a salary of $4,400. To supplement this, he signed on as an assistant editor on family friend Clifton Fadiman's literature anthology, *The American Treasury*. It was not until the fall of 1956, as *Time* presented it, that Van Doren found a "magic billfold" when a friend tipped him off about the money to be made on "Tic Tac Dough" and that the producers found him promising enough for "Twenty-One."

We noted the *Time* reporter's finding:

> Van Doren is the first to admit he is no genius and claims neither a photographic memory nor total recall. Indeed most of his education was in schools that had little interest in memory work or tests, regarded facts as mere accessories in the handling of ideas and the development of taste and reasoning. [Observers] including faculty members of St. John's itself, point out that Van Doren's mind comes through on TV not as a card-index file but as a reasoning instrument that explores a memory clearly imbedded in taste.

That sounded impressive, but I wondered what it meant. Equally puzzling was the writer's assertion that Van Doren's "luck and gambling skill"—in a situation based on a card game known to everybody—were the keys to his success. *Time* quoted a poker friend of Van Doren's when he was an army aviation cadet in the last years of World War II: "He figures the percentage to the last decimal. On the TV show, he follows the old Black Jack rule, 'always hit 16, always stick on 18.' Once on TV when Charlie reached 17, I told my wife that Charlie would call it like Black Jack—and he did." If this was something that *Time* readers could understand, it made no sense to me.

Just thirty-two years old, Van Doren was tall and lanky, well groomed and well dressed. He had come without a lawyer, which surprised me. He listened attentively as I gave him the usual warnings and assurances, showing no outward concern, then said he didn't think he had any information that would be helpful to either the district attorney's office or the grand jury. "Of course I've read Stempel's and Snodgrass's charges in the newspapers," he said, "I played against Stempel on 'Twenty-One,' I met him casually after the broadcast, and yes, I was informed that he was emotionally upset by losing to me, but I was shocked when I heard about his accusations, which are absurd." I told him we would get to that in due course, but first we wanted to know some things about his background. I asked if he had read the *Time* cover story article. He replied that it was substantially correct.

For the record, Van Doren now lived at 91 Central Park West, was married and had a daughter just a few months old. He was employed as an instructor of English at Columbia University at a salary of $4,700 a year. He also received $50,000 a year under a three-year contract with NBC, signed in April 1957. Under the contract, he would soon be appearing on the network's "Today" morning show, every weekday for a five-minute "spot," for which he wrote the script himself. He had completed course work for the Ph.D. degree in English at Columbia but had not yet finished the writing of his dissertation.

I read aloud from the *Time* article the passages that indicated his formal education was not geared primarily to memorizing information. Van Doren agreed but said he had always had an excellent memory. He pointed out passages in the article that referred to his lifelong fondness for reference books, how he had "read" dictionaries as a child, read the Bible straight through in one weekend, and "systematically read his way through the Columbia library stacks on the subject [of English literature], averaging 20 books a week for two years." Before appearing on "Twenty-One," he had stood by a couple of times, and had the opportunity to learn what kinds of questions were being asked and worked very hard studying almanacs, atlases, and other reference books.

As for how he became a contestant, Van Doren recounted that he hadn't owned a television set, but a friend told him in the fall of 1956 she had been on "Tic Tac Dough." She couldn't answer the questions, but her opponent won $900, so she suggested Van Doren give it a try. He paid a call on the producers and was given a written test, which he completed very quickly. The receptionist looked it over and handed him a much longer, harder test to take. "That was a corker," he said, but he completed it and left.

A week later he received a phone call from a woman at Barry and Enright, who told him he had been chosen to be a contestant on "Twenty-One." "I said," Van Doren recalled, "'What is "Twenty-One"?' She said, 'That's our nighttime show.'" He went in and was interviewed by a man whose name he could not recall, who read him a number of questions from cards as examples of the types of things that might be asked on the show. After this, when he was told he would appear as a contestant, he had second thoughts but decided to go through with it. He worried over the fact that some of the hardest questions on the test he had taken could not readily be answered from reference books. "For example," he now told us, "I remember one question they asked: 'What was Shakespeare's first play?' There is scholarly disagreement about this, so there is no real answer."

When he arrived at the NBC studio for the first time, he was ushered into a dressing room, where he remained alone studying a "World Almanac" he had brought in hidden in a newspaper, until he was taken out for makeup and a rehearsal, when he met Freedman and Barry. As it turned out, he stood by for two broadcasts, before making his first appearance on November 21 against Stempel, playing three tie games with the champion. In his dressing room before the broadcast, he met with Freedman, who advised him to be natural and relax, to take his time, not to go off half-cocked, not to give an answer before he was sure of it. But, he insisted, Freedman gave him no instructions about breathing or his voice or facial expressions to use. In the next broadcast, December 5, Van Doren defeated Stempel, then made ten more appearances on "Twenty-One" before being defeated by Vivienne Nearing.

Our calculation showed that in fourteen appearances on "Twenty-One," he played twenty-eight games, fourteen of which were ties. He explained that the large number of ties was not inordinate. Since competing contestants were likely to be striving for twenty-one points in two rounds, if both of them made it, there was a tie. After his initial appearances, he tended to go for twenty-one this way almost every time, taking either a ten- or eleven-point question in each round. "Consequently I either won or was tied."

Now I showed him a Barry and Enright check for $5,000 made out to Charles Van Doren, dated December 19, 1956, and endorsed by him. I said that our examination of the records showed that he had been paid the amount as an advance against his winnings more than two months before he left the show, and asked him to explain.

After his third appearance on "Twenty-One" on December 12, Van Doren had winnings totaling $26,000, more money than he ever imagined he would have in one lump. After each broadcast, he said, he experienced a letdown, and after the third he felt the tension was too much. "I told Mr. Freedman I couldn't stand it and would quit." Freedman didn't want him to stop, but Van Doren said he had a right to. What if they gave him an advance, Freedman asked—say $5,000. Van Doren talked it over with his accountant, who advised him that, for tax purposes, it would be a good idea to take part of his winnings before the end of the year.

When he next talked to Freedman, Van Doren claimed, he was over the letdown of the previous broadcast and felt better about continuing. He told Freedman he would go on and take the advance. In addition to the tax reasons, he wanted to repay his mother $700 he had borrowed from her, and he would have felt foolish about continuing without taking up Freedman's offer. He accepted the check from Enright with the full understanding that it was an advance against his winnings and he would have to pay it back if he lost. At the time he took the advance, it would have required a tie to increase the stakes to $1,000 a point, then losing a game 21–0 to wipe out his amassed winnings after deducting the $5,000. The chances of this happening in one broadcast seemed very small, and even if it did, the $5,000 would have been safe. He played it safer still by not touching what remained of the $5,000 after he repaid what he owed to his mother.

This explanation made sense and I found myself very impressed by Van Doren's performance. But I remembered what Edward Jurist had told us about "the world of information"—"you cannot ask random questions of people and have a show. You simply have failure, failure, failure, and that does not make entertainment." The evidence we had from Stempel, Snodgrass, Leibbrand, and Craig indicated that the producers of "Twenty-One" would not have taken the chance on Van Doren's fumbling and losing a star whose appearances rocketed the show into the top ratings. Despite his supple explanations, then, I was convinced Van Doren was lying and was not about to risk the comfortable niche of celebrity he had achieved. I asked him if he had ever met with Freedman in the latter's office, and he said no. He went to the Barry and Enright offices several times while on the program to pick up the enormous amounts of fan mail he was receiving, which he took home with him in a suitcase. The only times he met with Freedman were in his dressing room before broadcasts.

For form's sake and to show him how serious we were, I asked him directly whether he had received assistance of any kind from the personnel of Barry and Enright—questions, answers, categories, or point-values to request—and he answered firmly he had not. Asked whether anyone asked him to kickback any potential winnings to continue on the show, he replied definitely not. Finally, asked if he ever gave anyone connected with "Twenty-One" gifts of any kind, he answered that at Christmastime on the show he gave a bottle of scotch to Barry, two bottles of champagne to Enright, and a pewter pitcher to Freedman.

Asked if he cared to explain the discrepancies between what Stempel and Snodgrass had told the press and what he was telling us now, Van Doren declined to speculate on the motives of Stempel and Snodgrass; all he could do was speak for himself, he said. After I again stressed the number, range, and difficulty of the questions he answered on the show and he stressed his good memory and the amount of studying he had done, it was obvious he would not budge. I said I did not believe he was telling us the truth and advised that if he doubted any of my assurances, he should see a lawyer. He would hear from us again when we decided on a date for his appearance before the grand jury. On his way out from the interview, Van Doren let himself be stopped by waiting reporters. He felt "surprise and disbelief" at Stempel's accusations, he told the press: "It's silly and distressing to think that people don't have more faith in quiz shows."[4]

CHAPTER SEVEN

The People against Albert Freedman

(OCTOBER 14–27, 1958)

In the first two weeks of October, Melvin Stein compiled a comprehensive history of "Tic Tac Dough" from Barry and Enright records provided in response to our subpoena *duces tecum*. Like "Dotto," "Tic Tac Dough" had begun as a daily show and had been popular enough to spin off a nighttime once-a-week, higher stakes version, but both versions were still on the air. The longer lifetimes of the two "Tic Tac Dough"'s ruled out the vacuum cleaner approach Stein had used with "Dotto." Between fifteen hundred and two thousand contestants had appeared on "Tic Tac Dough" since the debut of the daytime version, and the records filled scores of cartons.

"Tic Tac Dough" had not been packaged for a single sponsor, but was leased directly to NBC, which in turn sold time on it on a "spot" basis. Emceed by Barry, the weekday quiz debuted on July 30, 1956, and quickly became a staple of daytime programming. Its success led the way for the introduction of "Twenty-One" in the following fall season. The central device was a large board, representing the nine spaces to be filled in with x's and o's familiar to everyone as the game of tic tac toe. The difference was that above each of the nine squares was a window showing one of some seventy categories of knowledge, for example, The 1930s, Women, Baseball, Comic Strips, Latin America. Two competing contestants took turns attempting to place x's or o's in squares by answering correctly questions in the categories shown, to complete a row of three in any direction. Each player picked a square by telling Barry the category he or she wanted. Barry pulled a not terribly difficult question in that category from the pigeonholes of a prominent "question box" and read it out loud. Because of the strategic value of the center square, the question in that category was more difficult.

As players of tic-tac-toe quickly learn to stalemate, so did "Tic Tac Dough" contestants play many ties. The initial stakes were small—$100 per game— but a tie added another $100 to the value of the next game and so on. After each tie, the categories remained the same but were redistributed among the squares by spinning the labels in the windows above the squares. When a series of ties was broken, a new contestant was brought in to challenge the winner, and new categories appeared above the squares. The loser received the consolation prize of a wristwatch. In the half hour of the broadcast, four or five games could be completed, and many were stopped in the middle as time ran out; in this case the contestants returned to complete the action on the next broadcast. In theory, a superior contestant could stay on the game indefinitely. The prime-time version debuted in a Thursday night slot in September 1957, with appropriately higher stakes.

Stein narrowed his focus to the two likeliest classes of contestants to have received assistance—children and big winners. According to the Barry and Enright records, the biggest of all was a career army officer, Captain Michael O'Rourke, who, between December 1957 and April 1958, made nineteen appearances on nighttime "Tic Tac Dough," leaving with $108,500 in winnings. An assistant professor of military science and tactics at Western Michigan University at Kalamazoo, O'Rourke was a Korean War veteran, twenty-nine years old, and the father of three. On November 11, 1957—Armistice Day— O'Rourke, wearing his uniform, started as a contestant on daytime "Tic Tac Dough" and defeated three opponents to win $2,500. On the next broadcast, he was defeated himself and left with winnings trimmed to $1,700. Only a few weeks later, on December 5, O'Rourke began appearing on nighttime "Tic Tac Dough" by tying the champion, Timothy Horan, twice, then defeating him the following week. O'Rourke was champion for seventeen additional broadcasts, tying and defeating fifteen opponents before losing to Martin Dowd. Dowd was a twenty-nine-year-old sales manager, who had served in the army in Korea. He previously had appeared on daytime "Tic Tac Dough" late in 1957, winning $3,800.

Attempting to reach O'Rourke, Stein learned the captain had transferred to Fort Sill, Oklahoma, and could not reach him by telephone. Being out of New York State, O'Rourke could not be subpoenaed; for the time being at least, we had to forgo pursuing him. Stein interviewed Horan, a writer who lived in White Plains, New York, and who had won $4,800 on the daytime show at the end of 1956, then appeared on the nighttime version six times in late 1957, leaving with $30,400 when he lost to O'Rourke, but Horan denied receiving any kind of assistance. Stein then turned his attention to Dowd, who after defeating O'Rourke went on to win $19,700 as nighttime champion before losing on May 22, 1958. Dowd lived in New Jersey, but worked in New York. When he declined to come in voluntarily for an interview, we sent a detective, William McCartin, to serve Dowd, at his place of work, with a subpoena to appear forthwith. Dowd drove his own car to the city, with McCartin following in his.

When Stein began questioning him, Dowd blurted out that he had known Howard Felsher, "Tic Tac Dough"'s producer, for several years before becoming a contestant. Needing money for medical bills, Dowd asked Felsher about going on the program and, at Felsher's suggestion, studied for several months, then took the test and was picked to go on. After insisting adamantly that Felsher gave him no assistance, Dowd demanded we let him go to find a lawyer. We told him to return later in the day for a grand jury appearance. At the appointed hour, Dowd showed up with Thomas Sammon, who had been an assistant district attorney in New York County for several years before resigning to go into private practice and Democratic party politics. Sammon asked for a delay so that he could confer with his client, which we granted, handing Dowd a new subpoena for the following afternoon. I then had McCartin tail Dowd. The next morning, McCartin reported that, after conferring with Sammon, Dowd had taken the subway to the station at 103rd Street and Broadway and there met a man with whom he spent the next hour and a half, first in the subway station, then in a car parked on a side street, before Dowd left the man to retrieve his own car and leave the city. The parked car was registered to Howard Felsher.

Presenting Dowd as the first witness in *The People of the State of New York against Harry Doe*, the designation of our probe of "Tic Tac Dough," we hammered away at him. When he persisted in denials of receiving assistance from Felsher, we asked why he had gone to see the producer after our interview. Dowd claimed the meeting was at Felsher's request because of his concern about possible bad publicity. Eventually, Dowd conceded he had been put on the show only days after taking the test but insisted he had studied hard for six months beforehand, reading history books and almanacs and having his wife watch the show at home and write down the questions and answers used. After Dowd denied emphatically that he made kickbacks to Felsher or anyone connected with Barry and Enright, we let him go. I was convinced he was lying, but I was more concerned by what appeared to be Felsher's personal intervention to keep him in line. The producer must have been dispensing a powerful antidote to block the effects of Dowd's brushes with police detectives, subpoenas, district attorneys, and a grand jury. I decided to increase the pressure on Dowd by subpoenaing his bank records.

STEIN made genuine progress when he interviewed two teenagers who were high school students at the time they were "Tic Tac Dough" contestants. One of these, a Cornell University freshman named Frances Li, came in to talk to Stein on October 16. Li had been a senior at the Bronx High School of Science when a Barry and Enright staff member visited the school in search of contestant prospects; during a school break at the end of January and beginning of February 1958, Li was a contestant six times on daytime "Tic Tac Dough" and won $5,700. After she was screened and stood by for one broadcast, Li was told by Felsher they wanted her to be a contestant and he guaranteed she would win $4,000, which would go a long way toward paying for college, so she agreed. Felsher spent the next hour or so going through a stack of pink cards, asking Li approximately thirty questions. When Li was able to answer, Felsher said, "This one will go on." When she was close, he gave her the correct answer and asked her to remember it. When a question completely stumped her, he said, "We won't use this." Appearing on "Tic Tac Dough" four times that week, every morning before the broadcast, she had a session with Felsher and his cards. None of the questions asked on the air surprised her, and she believed they would have liked to keep her on, but she had to return to classes.

Moreover, Li told Stein, Felsher had recently telephoned her at Cornell to say "Tic Tac Dough" was under investigation and her name might come up. He urged her not to say she had been told any questions ahead of time, otherwise there would be "repercussions all over the place." If asked, she should say, in Felsher's words, "I didn't give you any assistance," and he added pointedly, "which I did not do." This made Li wonder if he was recording the conversation, and she took what he said as a kind of veiled threat. "I suppose he felt if I didn't tell you anything," she told Stein, "I wouldn't have to come before a grand jury." As it was, since Li had to return to college, we put her before the grand jury immediately, and the jurors seemed particularly appalled by her story. A week later the jurors would be even more appalled when they heard from another youthful former contestant and her indignant mother.

Kirsten Falke was an aspiring young singer who worked part time at a music store in midtown Manhattan and lived with her mother, Irene Kitzing, a publishing employee. As soon as Stein made contact, they told him that Felsher had anticipated our interest and was repeatedly calling them at home. Falke had been sixteen years old when she went to the Barry and Enright offices in December 1956 in response to a call for musically talented young people to try out for the quiz. She took a test, sang for Enright, then was turned over to Felsher, who sat her down with a box of question-and-answer cards to look through. For three mornings in a row she returned to spend time with the cards, ordered by Felsher to memorize the questions and answers. Then she was told she would appear on the show at least two times, first to tie, then to defeat the then-daytime champion, Timothy Horan, who by now had denied to Stein any knowledge of rigging.

On her first appearance, December 26, 1956, Falke tied Horan, answering questions she had studied on the cards. The second day, before Falke went on, Felsher told her the order of categories to choose in the first game, so as to tie Horan again, then defeat him the following day. According to Falke, Felsher warned her that "some people's careers could be ruined if you don't get it right." As it turned out, Falke mixed up the categories and defeated Horan. A new challenger was brought on and the categories on the board were replaced rather than rearranged, as would have been the case if she had continued to tie Horan. Unprepared in the new categories, she promptly lost and left with $800. She was petrified when Felsher approached her after the broadcast, but he only warned her not to tell anyone about what had happened. Falke obeyed, by joking to her mother and friends that she had been given questions and answers, which made them assume the contrary. Not until the scandal did she seriously admit the truth to her mother. At that time, Felsher called her to say she was going to be questioned by us. We would be tough, he told her, but she shouldn't be scared; she should just tell the "truth"—that she had not been given the answers.

Angry at Felsher, Kitzing permitted us to listen in on their telephone when he called Falke again. Since one of the parties to a phone conversation was consenting to our eavesdropping, it was not wiretapping and required no court order. When Felsher called on October 22, he was unaware that two district attorney's office squad detectives were recording the conversation. Falke reported that she had been questioned by us and subpoenaed for a grand jury appearance the following afternoon. "I'm kind of worried," she said, "because I'll be up there under oath, and, if I'm to tell a fib or something like that, under oath—"

"I don't want you to fib, I want you to tell them the truth, that you never got any help of any kind."

"Yes, but I did."

"No, you didn't, Kirsten," he said, then urged her, before testifying, to go see a lawyer he had retained. Felsher explained he had referred other sub-poenaed contestants to the lawyer, whose name was Sol Gelb. She promised Felsher she would try to see Gelb. She did not, and told her story to the grand jury as scheduled.

When I saw the transcript of this conversation, I decided it was time to haul Felsher before the grand jury. Once more the Barry and Enright opera-tion was resorting to an alumnus of the D.A.'s office for legal counsel, and Gelb was a prize catch. He had started out on the staff of Thomas Dewey when Dewey was a special prosecutor, then followed him to the Manhattan D.A.'s office in 1938, becoming a member of Dewey's inner circle. When Dewey became governor and Hogan succeeded him, Gelb was made Hogan's chief assistant. Gelb left the office in 1945 to go into private practice, and in 1954 was appointed by Dewey to fill a vacancy on the Court of General Ses-sions. When the interim period expired, after little over a year, Gelb returned to private practice but retained the honorific title "judge."

Within hours of service of a subpoena on Felsher, Gelb was on the phone to me. When I told him Felsher was not a target, Gelb declined my invitation to bring in his client for a talk, claiming Felsher was too busy producing "Tic Tac Dough." The subpoena date stood. In the jury room on October 27, Stein spelled out to Felsher his rights in detail, reflecting the fact that we had had no prior discussion with him or his lawyer. Acknowledging he understood, Felsher declined to invoke his privilege to refuse to answer questions on the grounds his answers might incriminate him.

Felsher, at thirty-one, was married with a child on the way. He was a gradu-ate of New York University with a B.A. in journalism and psychology and had worked for Barry and Enright since 1954. He had been associated with "Tic Tac Dough" since its beginning, first as a question writer. When Freedman took over "Twenty-One" in November 1956, Felsher succeeded him as pro-ducer of "Tic Tac Dough," still only a daytime show. At that point, Felsher was earning a salary of $250 a week. When nighttime "Tic Tac Dough" began in September 1957, Felsher became its producer, and Stanley Green was hired to take over the daytime show. When Green left at the end of 1957 (to turn up shortly afterward as an associate producer of "Dotto"), Felsher resumed the daytime duties as well. He was still producing both versions and reported to an NBC executive named Robert Aaron, his superior since September 3, 1958, when Barry and Enright were relieved of the operation of their pro-grams. Felsher currently was paid $450 a week by NBC.

Testifying in a matter-of-fact fashion, enlivened only by his anxiety about the broadcast of "Tic Tac Dough" scheduled for that evening, Felsher explained that his duties included selecting the contestants for the two versions and supervising the question writing. He had a staff who screened prospective contestants, and he made the final choice for the daytime show; his superior—meaning Enright in the old regime—had final approval for nighttime contestants. He and Enright selected knowledge categories to be used on upcoming broadcasts and looked over the questions submitted by his staff a day or two in advance to make sure none had been used too recently before.

The jurors, Stein, and I listened intently as Felsher followed Freedman's steps through a mine field. After twenty minutes, Stein, without mentioning any names, asked Felsher if he had ever revealed to any contestant of "Tic Tac Dough" any questions later used on a broadcast of the show. Felsher answered "no" to this and to a subsequent question concerning "answers" given to contestants. With that we excused Felsher so he could go to his job. While Stein questioned a minor "Tic Tac Dough" winner, I stepped outside to the witness room for a break. To my surprise, Felsher was chatting in low tones with another former contestant waiting to testify. I angrily asked Felsher what he was doing; he said he was waiting for his lawyer to return. I informed him that since he had been excused by the grand jury he had no business in the witness room, that his talking to witnesses scheduled to testify could be construed as interference in the grand jury's work. He apologized and made a hasty departure.

WHILE we put into motion a prosecution of Freedman for perjury, Donnelly and I continued building a complete picture of the operation of "Twenty-One" from its beginnings under Enright's producership. We learned that the contestants in the early phase before Stempel and the advent of Freedman, with one important exception, fell into two categories: patsies who had won nothing beyond consolation prizes, and small winners who stoutly defended "Twenty-One" in general and Enright in particular. Thomas Hendricks, a retired Brooklyn longshoreman, and James Bowser, the managing editor of two pulp detective magazines, freely admitted being in frequent contact with Enright now and were briefing him on what we were asking and what they were telling us. Both insisted they won without assistance from Enright or anyone else. Asked if they had kicked back any of their winnings or given anything to any member of Enright's staff, they replied to the contrary—Enright had given Hendricks a television set when he was in the hospital and Bowser a set of the *Encyclopaedia Britannica* after Bowser inquired whether he could obtain a set at a discount, since "Twenty-One" was plugging it.

The exception to the pre-Stempel pattern was Richard Jackman, whom we had sought since mid-September to explain the discrepancy between his winning $24,500 and receiving payment for only $15,000, according to a canceled check. Barry and Enright's file on Jackman showed an address in Greenwich Village with no telephone, but we could find no trace of him. The back of the check showed Jackman had endorsed the payment to Alma Jackman in Buffalo, New York, who, reached by telephone, said she was the contestant's mother but did not know where he was. Armed with a subpoena, Nicholas Barrett flew to Buffalo to check further but was unable to find Jackman; he left the subpoena with the Buffalo police, who offered to keep an eye on Mrs. Jackman and serve the subpoena if her son turned up.

On Monday, October 13, Burton Shenley, a lawyer I did not know, called to say he was representing the elusive Jackman, and the following day, the two of them appeared in the office. Jackman admitted to knowing we were seeking him but had avoided us because he wanted to keep "clear of the whole business." After Jackman confirmed that the endorsements on the check were his and his mother's, I assured Shenley that Jackman was not a target and at the lawyer's urging, Jackman told in detail a story that did not reveal him to be a great admirer of Enright.

Jackman earned a B.A. in English before going into the army and serving in Germany. After a brief stay in England, where he tried writing for magazines, he moved to New York to pursue his writing ambitions and supported himself by doing odd jobs as a model, a furniture mover, and a railroad worker. In the summer of 1956 he heard about "Tic Tac Dough." Having earned no more than $1,000 in the previous year, he jumped at the chance to take the test and was picked to be a contestant. On his first day he won $500. The following day he added $300 to his total before losing by the same amount, but Freedman, then the show's producer, suggested Jackman try out for "Twenty-One." Jackman did well enough on the test to be introduced to Enright.

Alone with Enright, Jackman was immediately asked to be a contestant on the new show and was shown the pilot film. When Jackman asked Enright how one could determine the relative difficulty of the questions in asking for points, Enright assured him he would get the idea. According to Jackman, Enright said, "I will ask you a lot of questions and mention a lot of categories.

You can select a number, then I will ask you a question." They spent two or three hours together as Enright went through a stack of cards, calling out some twenty to thirty categories. In each, Jackman asked for a certain number of points, depending on how much he felt he knew. Enright then asked a question; if Jackman didn't know the answer, Enright gave it to him. Toward the end of a second session roughly a week later, Jackman believed he was getting the hang of it, but, as far as he knew, it was only a drill. At the end of the second session, Enright announced that Jackman would start on the broadcast of October 3, 1956, then confided, "You are in a position to destroy my career." Asked what he meant, Enright told Jackman he would find out.

Just before the broadcast, Enright visited Jackman in his dressing room and asked him, as a favor, to request specific points in each round against his opponents. In each of three games, he was to stick with a certain number of points. Jackman agreed, beginning to suspect monkey business. But it was only when he was in the isolation booth against his first opponent that he understood he had been primed with the questions and answers in advance. In the game, he amassed 17 points by correctly answering questions he had been asked before by Enright, then "knocked" as instructed. Since his opponent had scored no points, he had won $8,500. He played two more games, against a high school teacher and a New York University professor, following orders and answering questions he had heard in the sessions with Enright. At the end of the show, he had raised his winnings to $24,500.

At a meeting the following day, Jackman claimed, he told Enright he didn't want to cast aspersions on the way the packager was running "Twenty-One," but participating in it was just not his cup of tea. Enright asked him to think it over, saying that Jackman's appearance had noticeably boosted "Twenty-One"'s rating; if he would continue for four or five weeks, they could guarantee him the equivalent—if wisely invested—of $100 a week for the rest of his life. But Jackman said his mind was made up; he wanted to have no more to do with the deception, adding that he had no moral right to the $24,500.

Whereupon, according to Jackman, Enright explained that at this point the show's budget would be hard put to come up with the entire $24,500; if Jackman would accept $15,000, they could have a check for him in a couple of weeks. Jackman decided to accept. Enright said that no one else in his organization knew about their sessions together before the broadcast, and no one else would know about their financial arrangement; it would jeopardize Enright's career if Jackman talked about it to anyone. Jackman agreed to announce his retirement on the air, and did so on October 10, a week before Stempel's first appearance on "Twenty-One."

If Jackman's motivation in not wanting to play along was murky, his account seemed to provide a dramatic corroboration of Stempel's accusations regarding Enright's personal and pivotal role in the rigging. And that was not all Jackman had for us. Asked about further contacts with Enright, Jackman said he returned a few times to the packager's offices that fall, to pick up fan mail as well as the check for $15,000 and to introduce a friend of his as a possibility for "Tic Tac Dough." Returning from Europe, where he had spent the summer of 1957, Jackman visited Enright for help in finding work as a reader for movie companies, but Enright could do nothing for him. In early September 1958, when Jackman returned from another trip to Europe, he found a message from Freedman asking him to call.

Now aware of the quiz scandal, Jackman met Enright on September 8, and the two men spent five minutes walking up and down on a balcony outside Enright's office. According to Jackman, Enright said that "some madman" had brought charges which he was trying to refute through legal action, and that the D.A. had been calling in "Twenty-One" contestants for questioning. He asked Jackman what he would do if he were called. "Remember," Enright said, "you and I are the only ones who know about it." Jackman replied he wanted to stay away from the whole business, but if required to testify, he would have to tell the truth. Three days later, Jackman told the same thing to Freedman when they met at Freedman's request. Two days after this, when Jackman learned we were looking for him, he called Shenley, then fled to Buffalo. He happened to be away from his mother's house when Barrett went there looking for him.

The puzzling thing about Jackman—why, after being so elusive, he had become so forthcoming—was cleared up when, after he was finished, Shenley stated that since his client had cooperated with us, it was our turn to cooperate by giving them a photostat of the canceled Barry and Enright check. It seemed that Enright, in giving the payment to Jackman, had neglected to have him sign a release waiving any further claim. Now Jackman had just filed a law suit against Barry and Enright for $9,500, the difference between what he had been paid and what he had won on "Twenty-One." Shenley wanted a copy of the check in our possession for use in the lawsuit. I told Shenley that he should have known I could not hand out a copy of a document in our custody without the authorization of its owner.

Two days after the Jackman interview, in the afternoon of October 16, a three-week lull in newspaper coverage of the scandal was broken. The *New York Post* carried a huge front-page headline: "'21' is DYING; Tonight's Show the Last?" On the show that night, Elizabeth Anderson, a housewife from Illinois, won $66,000 by defeating Wilson Valentine, a Baltimore college instructor. The next day, the papers confirmed the cancelation of "Twenty-One" on their front pages. According to the reports, "Twenty-One"'s ratings had plummeted to the point where the show had to be replaced. From a peak Trendex rating of 54.7 percent of "television homes" watching when polled—during Van Doren's appearances—"Twenty-One" had already declined to 21 percent by the time Von Nardroff was defeated. By October 5, 1958, six weeks after the eruption of the scandal, the show was down to a dismal 10.3 percent. In the Nielsen ranking of the most popular television programs, "Twenty-One" was down from a peak position of sixth to thirty-fifth.

Both NBC and Pharmaceuticals, Inc., the sponsor of "Twenty-One," issued strong statements of support for Barry and Enright. Calling the packagers "two ethical businessmen," a spokesman for the sponsor said, "We can only repeat what we said before about Barry and Enright. They are above reproach. In our investigation of the charges, we haven't found a thing that would personally implicate these two fellows in any wrongdoing."[1] "Twenty-One" was being replaced by a prime-time version of the popular Barry and Enright daytime game show, "Concentration," on which contestants tried to remember series of numbers, not for cash but for prizes of merchandise and trips. The demise of "Dotto" had removed most if not all incentive for its creators to lie to us, but the replacement of "Twenty-One" by another of its creators' properties indicated that the cancelation would change little as far as Barry and Enright and we were concerned.

THOUGH the two-witness rule made perjury difficult to prove, the prosecution of it was not without its uses. It could act to shake the tree to see if any apples would fall, or as a lever to pry away a vulnerable defendant from a main pack of conspirators. This was our strategy in seeking to indict Freedman for perjury. A more immediate goal was to put out the word to all concerned that we meant business and would not tolerate efforts to suborn prospective grand jury witnesses. There was no legal bar to moving against Freedman before the Third September Grand Jury itself, but our policy was to present such a case before another grand jury, especially when the original grand jury was exclusively engaged in investigating the matter to which the alleged perjury pertained.

I reserved several blocks of time, starting on October 17 and spread over the following week, before the Fourth October Grand Jury, sitting since the beginning of the month. Our presentation of the case of *The People of the State of New York against Albert Freedman, Defendant* began with the formality of establishing that the Third September Grand Jury was legally constituted to administer the oath to Freedman. After this, Freedman's October 2 testimony was read out loud. In the following week, we went to the next phase, presenting evidence to prove the falsity of Freedman's testimony.

Our first witness was Leibbrand, who repeated what she had told us in the office on September 19. The fact that she was the first to come forward and tell us of being handled by Freedman on "Twenty-One," and her willingness to travel from Washington to testify, plus her indignation at her treatment by Freedman impressed the jurors. Likewise, the second witness, Craig, had credibility for having shunned publicity and for acting out of a guilty conscience. Moreover, Craig provided a detailed account of the months he spent as a "Twenty-One" champion when the rigging had become routine.

Next we presented Joseph McNally of the police laboratory, who told the jurors in detail how he was able to determine that the post office seals on Snodgrass's three registered letters were intact and the envelopes had not been opened or tampered with. These were now passed among the jurors who looked them over with intense curiosity. McNally was followed directly by Snodgrass, who again told his story. He was handed the letter postmarked May 17, 1957, and, at my request, tore open the envelope and read the contents aloud. This was the scenario for the first part of the May 20 broadcast, in which he was to take a fall to Bloomgarden by deliberately mistaking a line of verse by Emily Dickinson. At this point, we projected for the jurors the kinescope of the May 20, 1957, broadcast, which unrolled as Snodgrass had written in his letter. This was as dramatic as testimony could be, and probably sufficient to make the case against Freedman as far as the jurors were concerned.

But there remained a recital of the law and its requirements. I reminded the jurors that the mandate of the Third September Grand Jury included inquiring as to whether the quiz shows represented themselves as true contests, which made the issue of whether questions and answers were given to contestants in advance a crucial one; this in turn made Freedman's testimony on providing questions and answers to contestants material. His testimony that he had not regularly met with long-running contestants in his office several days before broadcasts, for example, would not directly or even circumstantially determine whether he had given the questions and answers in advance (he could have done it on the phone, in the dressing room, on the street, wherever), and therefore was immaterial.

Since three former contestants had testified to being given questions and answers in advance by Freedman, I told the jurors, the two-witness rule was satisfied. I then repeated the criterion stated at their impaneling: their duty was to find an indictment when all the evidence taken together would, if uncontradicted, warrant a conviction by a trial jury. This was a far less rigorous standard than for trials. A defendant who had been arrested or a person who was the target of an investigation had no right to appear before a grand jury without having first waived immunity and could not cross-examine witnesses, and therefore had little opportunity to raise a reasonable doubt against a well-presented case by the district attorney.

Five minutes after completing my presentation and leaving the Fourth October jurors to deliberate, the buzzer sounded for me to return. The jury secretary handed a slip of paper to the warden; he looked at it, then said to me, "The jury voted a true bill." I thanked the jurors for their attention, then went to my office and began drafting the text of the indictment.

NOVEMBER 4 was Election Day and the television quiz grand jury was given a week off from its labors. It was the moment of truth for Hogan's Senate campaign. Though the Democrats were in the ascendancy in the country as a whole, halfway through the second term of Dwight Eisenhower, in New York State the gubernatorial campaign of Nelson Rockefeller against a sclerotic Democratic statehouse regime amounted to a steamroller. In the election, Rockefeller defeated the incumbent Averell Harriman by more than a half-million votes; Kenneth Keating, the Republican candidate for the Senate, beat Hogan by 160,000 votes in the total of some 5.5 million cast.

On the day following the election, newspapers carried reports that "The $64,000 Question," the first, the longest-running, and the most successful ever of the big-money TV quiz shows, had been canceled by CBS, effective immediately. Back on October 16, when the demise of "Twenty-One" had made headlines, the reports mentioned the travails of the "Question," as well, which, despite an absence of specific allegations of rigging concerning the show, was tottering in the ratings. Now the axe had fallen, and the "Question" was being replaced in its Sunday night slot on CBS by a comedy game show.

After Freedman's indictment, signed by the Fourth October Grand Jury foreman, was handed up to the presiding judge, a bench warrant was issued and delivered to us for action. I called Edward Levine and suggested he bring in Freedman to be arrested. Levine asked about bail, reminding me Freedman was a family man, a veteran with a good war record. Freedman was not the type to flee prosecution, but he had been out of a job since the cancelation of "Twenty-One," and that was sufficient justification for imposing some bail, which I told Levine would be nominal. We agreed on a time on Friday morning, November 7, for Freedman to come to the detectives' squad room on the ninth floor, where Barrett would be waiting with the warrant. I then called Hogan to bring him up to date. He said he would schedule a press conference for the afternoon of the arrest and instructed me to be there.

On Friday, Freedman and Levine kept their appointment with Barrett, who followed regulations and put handcuffs on Freedman, to the producer's consternation. Barrett took Freedman downstairs, onto Leonard Street, through a mob of reporters, to the Fifth Police Precinct on Elizabeth Street in Chinatown, for booking as flashbulbs popped. While Freedman's fingerprints were being checked to see whether he had a previous criminal record, I joined Hogan in the ceremonial office, jammed with reporters. Hogan made a statement setting forth the charges against Freedman and read out verbatim the salient questions asked of the producer before the grand jury as well as his answers, which formed the basis of the charges. Each of the two counts, Hogan added, was punishable by up to five years in prison and a fine of $5,000. After I provided some background details on Freedman, Hogan took the reporters' questions. Freedman "knowingly lied when he gave the answers," the Chief replied in response to one: "He had in fact revealed both questions and answers to the contestants prior to their appearances on the show." Hogan refused to confirm or deny when reporters shouted out the names of Stempel and Snodgrass. That information, Hogan said, was in the nature of evidence, which would be revealed at the proper time. How many contestants did Freedman help? "Plural," replied the Chief, "I'll stick to plural." [2]

At 2:30 P.M., Freedman was arraigned before Mitchell Schweitzer, again presiding over Part I, for the month of November, just begun. It was simply coincidence that Schweitzer, presiding over Part I in September, had impaneled the grand jury before which Freedman had testified. Schweitzer informed Freedman of the charges and Freedman pleaded "not guilty." Donnelly, representing the people, moved for bail to be set at $1,500. Schweitzer concurred, and Levine promptly posted the amount. Freedman was now free to go. He and Levine were mobbed by reporters outside the Criminal Courts Building. "Everything I told the grand jury was true," said Freedman. "The charges are ridiculous," chimed in Levine, "They set him up like a clay pigeon." [3]

Late in the afternoon, the Barry and Enright organization issued a brief public statement concerning Freedman: "We have complete faith in his integrity and we are confident of his ultimate vindication." For its part, the National Broadcasting Company was quick to point out: "Albert Freedman is not an employee of NBC."[4]

CHAPTER EIGHT

The $64,000 Empire

(OCTOBER–NOVEMBER 1958)

A few days after Freedman's indictment and following upon the cancelation of "The $64,000 Question," I received a visit from a former colleague, John McAvinue, who had served in the office for fourteen years before leaving in 1956 for private practice. We had worked together in the Fraud Bureau and trusted each other; now he was representing Entertainment Productions, Inc., and wanted to know why we were breathing down their former contestants' necks.

It was Jay Goldberg's relentless zeal in office interviews of former $64,000 contestants, seeing how they fared by asking them the same questions they answered on the air, that prompted McAvinue's complaint. A month before, on October 8, I had sat in as Goldberg interviewed the person who was second only to Van Doren in gaining prominence as a result of quiz appearances—Dr. Joyce Brothers. Nearly three years before, on December 3, 1955, Brothers had been the first woman to win the top prize on "The $64,000 Question," as an expert on boxing, then made several appearances on "The $64,000 Challenge," bringing her total winnings on the shows to $132,000. As a result of this exposure, she had gone on to become a television personality, with her own program on the New York NBC station, and, along with Edward Eagan, a former amateur boxing champion and a well-connected New York lawyer, had written a book on improving memory. Eagan was the expert whom Brothers had taken into the isolation booth with her, as permitted by the rules of the "Question," to consult at the final "plateau."

Now thirty years old, short and slight, Brothers had steely blue eyes and a stern pedantic manner. The daughter of two New York attorneys, she earned a B.A. from Cornell in the field of home economics, then took her M.A. and Ph.D. in experimental psychology at Columbia, and taught at New York's Hunter College and Columbia for six years; she was married to a New York physician and had one child. She told us that when she first saw a broadcast of "The $64,000 Question" in the summer of 1955, she wrote in to inquire about becoming a contestant. Near the end of September, she was reached by Ben Kagan, an associate producer for Louis Cowan, Inc., and was asked in for an interview. According to Brothers, when she told him that her category would be psychology, Kagan turned her down, saying they did not take contestants in their own professions. She then suggested boxing, because her husband was a boxing fan and she knew something about the subject. Kagan called this a "cute idea" and promised to be in touch.

As Brothers recounted it, she immediately gathered the few reference books available on boxing, including one called *Ring Facts*, written by Nat Fleischer, the editor of *Ring* magazine and a friend of her father's. She borrowed five years' worth of back issues of Fleischer's magazine and put her hands on a set of films called *Great Fights of the Century*. After a few weeks of memorizing every fact and statistic about boxing that she could find, she called Kagan to remind him of her "cute idea." In October she stood by on two broadcasts of the "Question" before beginning her appearances in November and going on to win $64,000 in December, only the second contestant to do so.

In May 1956 she made her first appearance on the "The $64,000 Challenge" and won $4,000 after defeating a challenger in the third round of questions. Late in 1957 she was invited again to defend her championship against a squad of seven former professional boxers. The boxers took turns facing Brothers over five broadcasts, which ended with her defeating them all and winning a full $64,000; her opponents each received $1,000 in consolation money. Despite the appearance of this formidable challenge, her studying for the "Challenge" was easier than for the "Question," she said, because the scope of material to be covered in each upcoming broadcast was publicly announced and narrowed to a certain area, for example, middleweights.

Brothers explained that she was able to become an expert on boxing in a matter of weeks, by simply "absorbing" facts and figures, making lists, tearing them up, making new lists, over and over again until she knew the material. She looked at the films repeatedly, memorizing odd details that stood out. But the key was, she insisted, to memorize only what she wanted to know; when she felt she no longer needed certain facts, she banished them from her memory to make room for more. "I dismiss everything I possibly can," she explained, "the more you try to hold in mind, the less you can learn." This was why, she claimed, when Goldberg asked the questions she had answered correctly on the air, she could not remember what she had studied and regurgitated three years before.

She was adamant in her insistence that she never received help of any kind. She did meet frequently with people like Kagan, Merton Koplin, and Shirley Bernstein, on the production staff of the programs. But the meetings, she claimed, were solely to update the "interview" segments for the emcees. There was never any indication of what to study beyond what was publicly announced on the air. In fact, she insisted, she was never screened for her knowledge before receiving the green light to appear on the "Question." The producers simply accepted her assurance that she had mastered the subject of boxing and were satisfied with her knowledge when she started on the show.

Hearing this account, I first thought it preposterous that, memory tricks notwithstanding, one could become an overnight expert in anything. On the other hand, the recorded history of professional boxing was not extensive; it involved the feats of no more than a few hundred individuals and had little of the complexity of a sport like baseball, with its thousands of participants and obsessive record keeping. Conceivably then, what there was to know about boxing filled only a handful of books, and someone as intelligent and methodical as Brothers could have mastered it all in a matter of weeks.

Goldberg, a boxing fan himself, called in several of the boxers Brothers defeated on the "Challenge." One of them, Tiger Jones, reported that some of the EPI staff told him that all the information needed to answer the questions was in Fleischer's *Ring Facts*. Given the advance public hint that the next broadcast's questions would concern, say, middleweights, it was not an insurmountable task to memorize the several pages in *Ring Facts* concerning middleweights. This corroborated the general tenor of Brothers's account, but the fact that Fleischer was a friend of her father's was food for thought and meant new questions for Brothers when the time would come for her to appear before the grand jury.

In October, Goldberg had also talked to another of the top $64,000 winners, a twelve-year-old ninth grader from the Bronx named Robert Strom, who was accompanied to the office by his father, a public-school teacher. A year and half before, in the spring of 1957, the young Strom had won $64,000 on the "Question" by answering elaborate questions in science, then returned to answer questions for additional "plateaus" introduced by the producers in response to the winnings being posted in the same period by Van Doren on "Twenty-One." By the end of April, Strom boosted his winnings to a total of $192,000; then, a few months later, he appeared on the "Challenge," playing to finally tie with his opponent and dividing $64,000. This brought Strom's total on the shows to $224,000, an amount not matched by another quiz show contestant until Von Nardroff in July 1958. It did not take much questioning to determine that Strom was truly a science genius.

Two days after our interview of Strom, on October 12, 1958, a story appeared in the *New York Post* headlined: "Dad Terms DA's Call of Boy Quiz Whiz 'a Shame.'" Strom's father was complaining that those who had "no unfortunate experience on quiz shows should be subject to the investigation." Not surprisingly, Hogan called me in to ask if it was necessary to interrogate children. He didn't have to mention his concern over the innuendo of the *Post* story, that is, that the D.A. was badgering children, and its possible effect on the Senate campaign just three weeks before the election. I replied that these children were much brighter and more self-possessed than normal; the grand jury had heard from several young "Dotto" and "Tic Tac Dough" contestants without any fuss being made. Moreover, their testimony raised the question whether the quiz producers had impaired the morals of children, an aspect of the matter we had to probe. This sufficed for Hogan.

In the following week, Goldberg interviewed the Spanish-born bandleader, Xavier Cugat, a celebrity contestant who appeared on "The $64,000 Challenge" against the singer and writer, Lillian Roth, in June 1958. In their appearances, Cugat and Roth answered questions in the category of Tin Pan Alley, reaching the $16,000 level; at that plateau, Cugat answered his questions correctly, but Roth missed parts of hers, ending the match and winning him the $16,000. According to Cugat, his appearance on the "Challenge" had been arranged by his publicity man to plug a New York engagement for the Cugat band. Likewise, Roth's appearance on the show would publicize a book she had written. Cugat said he first agreed to go on in the category of his own field, Latin American Music, or his hobby, Latin American Art. But the producers thought these too obvious and decided to make the category Tin Pan Alley, that is, American popular music. Cugat knew something about this but not as much as he would have liked to, he told Goldberg, so he spent some time studying, perusing songbooks, listening to records, and having his brother drill him with questions. When asked if he had been given assistance by the producers, Cugat replied indignantly, "Music is my business and life. Why should I need help?" Goldberg then read off the questions Cugat had answered correctly on the air, and the bandleader was unable to answer any of them. Flustered, he made excuses about the time elapsed since his appearances on the show (some five months), his busy professional life, and so on, then was excused by the skeptical Goldberg.

Mindful of the criticism of our questioning child contestants, I sat in on October 20 as Goldberg interviewed an eleven-year-old professional actress, Patty Duke, and her manager, John Ross. Duke was a contestant on "The $64,000 Challenge" from February to April 1958, appearing against another child actor, Eddie Hodges, in the category of Popular Music. The two had gone all the way, to win and divide $64,000. Ross now did most of the talking, first explaining how Duke had been picked to be a contestant. She had been under his managership for several years and had begun landing small parts in television commercials and dramas. Irving Harris, an EPI staff people getter, happened to have introduced Ross to the Duke family, and he called Ross to say they were seeking child contestants and Duke might be suitable. After Duke was accepted, Ross proceeded systematically to prepare her, as he would for any other job, he claimed, helping her study up on popular music, which Duke enjoyed as much as any other child her age. As her personal manager, Ross received 15 percent of all her earnings. He claimed he had started Duke out in show business, paying all the expenses required—private schooling, clothing, pictures, and publicity—then collected his percentage when she began earning money, and that included her winnings on the "Challenge."

When the appearances began, Ross accompanied Duke to the studio before the broadcasts, where she met with Shirley Bernstein for drill sessions. Ross was convinced, he said, that Duke was given no assistance, and Duke herself now said no one had helped her except Ross. When Goldberg went through the questions Duke was asked on the show, she was able to answer most of them still, but then she said that some of the questions she was asked had come up in drills with Bernstein. When Goldberg all but accused Ross of being given the "Challenge" questions and answers by Harris and relaying them to Duke, Ross vehemently denied it, as much as he denied giving anything in the way of a kickback to Harris.

Goldberg also talked to Eddie Hodges, accompanied to the office by his father. At the time, Hodges was better known than Duke; he was the juvenile star of a hit musical, *The Music Man*, which opened on Broadway in December 1957. Several months before that he had been a contestant on "Name That Tune" and had won that program's grand prize of $25,000, which he divided with his partner on the show, a marine aviator named John Glenn. As a result of his appearances on "Name That Tune," Hodges was signed for the part in *The Music Man*. Thus he had been picked for the "Challenge" as a youthful "champion" in popular music, and Duke was found to challenge him. Hodges's knowledge seemed genuine, and he was able to remember the answers to most of the questions he had been asked.

After several more interviews, we realized that direct fixes like Wilton Springer would be difficult to find. For one thing, the $64,000 producers had placed a premium on contestants who lived outside of New York, to give their shows more appeal to a nationwide audience; this limited us to a relative handful of prospective witnesses within immediate reach, without resorting to legal proceedings to extradite people from other states. More important, EPI had relied on contestants with genuine knowledge of their subjects, and determined this by careful screening.

This factor made for the significant difference between the $64,000 shows and other quizzes—only in emergencies did the producers need the contestants' direct collusion in order to rig the outcomes. In essence, the shows were less complicated, therefore easier to pull off than "Dotto" and "Twenty-One." EPI made no secret of its screening practices, because they wanted the public to know the great lengths they went to in order to find genuine experts. But it was the screenings that enabled the producers to tailor their questions to the contestants' knowledge and set things up so that the people they wanted would continue to win without the necessity of collusion—the ideal already enunciated to us by Edward Jurist. Presumably these techniques had worked well enough with all but a small handful, when for one reason or another, as in the case of Springer, situations arose requiring the producers to break their own rules.

NEVERTHELESS, as I told John McAvinue when he visited me in November to complain of harassment, there were sufficient discrepancies in the accounts of certain individuals to justify our probe of the $64,000 shows. If these accounts were repeated under oath, then somebody would be committing perjury. The indictment of Freedman was meant as a warning to McAvinue's clients, as much as anyone else, that they should not try to interfere with former contestants or influence what they would tell us, and rabble-rousing in the press about how we were treating children might make matters worse as far as the grand jury was concerned. After expressing his clients' fears of bad publicity and hearing my assurances in that regard, McAvinue asked about immunity. I answered that we were flexible; immunity could be arranged for contestants and subordinates like Bernstein, for example, but not for Steve Carlin and Harry Fleischman who, as the principal stockholders and directors of EPI after the departure of Louis Cowan, were ultimately responsible for what had happened.

It wasn't long before McAvinue brought in, for a second visit, Shirley Bernstein, who now apparently realized she had nothing to gain from lying to us. Through the good offices of McAvinue, Bernstein was followed by Merton Koplin, formerly of EPI, and George Abrams, the marketing manager of Revlon. The word had spread so by the time we brought Patty Duke's manager in for another talk, he was singing a different tune. Goldberg also found Mel Braverman, Xavier Cugat's publicity manager, who told a story significantly different from that of his client. When the band leader returned to New York, we gave him another chance to talk.

In the first week of December, we began presenting testimony concerning "The $64,000 Question" and "Challenge," under the case title of *The People against Richard Poe*. We brought before the jurors several former contestants to set the stage before the Christmas season began. While the jury was given a vacation during the last two weeks of 1958, we put together a behind-the-scenes history of the operation of the $64,000 programs, the most successful of the quiz show enterprises. Most helpful were Koplin and Abrams, who seemed eager to cooperate; I sensed they had their own personal reasons for doing so, aside from the fact that they no longer had financial stakes in the now-defunct shows.

Koplin was an intense man in his late thirties, with an alert, animated face behind thick-lensed glasses. At the University of Wisconsin, Koplin switched from a prelaw course to speech and drama, but joined the army in 1942 before graduating, working first as a radio operator and ending up in public relations. After the war he went to New York and worked for five years in radio, producing a daily children's show, working on an NBC experimental news project, and producing for the network a fairly successful comedy show. He was hired by Louis Cowan to work on the "Question" because of his comedy experience as well as his evident skills with people. Having joined the "Question" after its debut, Koplin disclaimed any knowledge of the role Cowan played personally in selecting and managing the show's first contestants. Koplin reported to Steve Carlin and had little direct contact with Cowan, though his own role quickly became pivotal. More than anyone else he could make or break a contestant, because he not only screened prospects but also prepared the questions to be used.

His first job was to handle the torrent of mail from would-be contestants pouring in as a result of the instant success of the program. He supervised twenty employees in processing ten to twenty thousand letters arriving every week from aspirants, out of which ultimately four or five would be brought into the Cowan offices for personal interviews. This process yielded several early contestants who helped make the "Question" the number-one rated television show in 1955—notably Gino Prato, who quit the show with $32,000 on August 9. This decision prompted newspapers to point out in detail the relative risks involved in continuing. Prato would keep roughly $21,600 after taxes on $32,000; if he had gone on for the top prize and won, he would have netted an additional $13,480 after taxes. If he had lost, he would have taken home only the consolation prize of a Cadillac car, valued at $7,500.

Though the contestant selection process was well publicized, the question-writing process was kept under wraps, particularly the fact that the chief screener, Koplin, was also the chief question writer. Bergen Evans, the professor of English mentioned to us by Bernstein, received screen credit for "supervising" the questions, but, according to Koplin, Evans only provided bits and pieces of knowledge, which Koplin himself assembled into the multipart questions posed to the contestants. Koplin turned to outside experts for the bits and pieces in categories, like sports, in which Evans was weak.

Once composed by Koplin, the questions were stored in the vault of the Manufacturers Trust Bank until the evening of the broadcast, when they were brought to the studio under guard. The impression given was that no one had read the questions until Ben Fite, a bank officer, handed them over to the emcee, Hal March, on the air. An effort was made to follow this procedure in the early weeks, Koplin claimed, but it became impractical to maintain full sets of questions for all listed categories in the vault, especially when visual devices were employed in such categories as Art and Movies to make them more interesting for the audience. In addition, March had to be made familiar with the questions simply to be able to pronounce unusual words and names correctly. Thus the bank vault routine was followed for only the questions needed for the next broadcast, depending on the progress of scheduled contestants. The gimmick of the bank teller on stage could not be abandoned, because it had become a trademark of the show. Often the questions were rushed to the bank vault just hours before a broadcast, and Fite continued to bring them to the stage, presumably unaware that he was only going through the motions.

By August 1955, more than two months after the "Question"'s debut, no contestant had made a try at the top prize, a fact being made light of by the newspapers. It was at this point that Koplin read a letter from a twenty-eight-year-old marine officer and ROTC instructor from Ohio whose hobby was food and cooking. When Koplin brought the writer, Captain Richard Mc-Cutcheon, to New York for an interview and asked him some two hundred questions about cooking, McCutcheon was able to answer all but fifteen correctly. Handsome and appealing, with an expertise that provided the most charming paradox conceivable to his profession, McCutcheon was the ideal contestant. As a marine with combat experience, he could be expected to ignore the tax angle and go for the top prize.

On September 13, 1955, with the biggest television audience in history—some fifty-five million Americans—watching, McCutcheon was the first contestant to say he would try for the $64,000 question. The question was in seven parts: "Identify five dishes and two wines on the now famous menu of a royal banquet given in 1939 by King George VI for French President Albert LeBrun." After consulting with his father, a retired navy captain whom McCutcheon had taken with him into the isolation booth, he gave the answer: "Consommé quenelles, filet de truite saumonée, petits pois à la française, sauce maltaise, corbeille," for the courses and "Château d'Yquem and Madeira Sercial" for the wines. McCutcheon's feat made the front pages of the *New York Times* and newspapers around the world.

In fact, as Koplin described to me, this triumph had been carefully engineered, employing the controls available to quiz producers. In the case of genuine experts like McCutcheon, the principal control was determining the depth and extent of their knowledge. This Koplin called "playback." The two hundred questions he asked McCutcheon in their first interview functioned to "play back" McCutcheon's knowledge of cooking. Thus Koplin knew what McCutcheon knew. After McCutcheon's first appearance on the show, answering easy questions in his subject, Revlon's reaction was enthusiastic; therefore Koplin wrote only questions he knew McCutcheon could answer.

For Koplin, the real challenge of the quizmaster was to avoid using a specific question for the show that he had used in the screening; to allay suspicion on the part of contestants, Koplin did not give them correct answers to questions they missed in the screenings. Instead, he relied on the logic of inference. Thus, if a contestant in the category of American History, in playback, knew the names of all the presidents in order, Koplin inferred the contestant could give the year in which any one president had been elected; likewise, in the category of the Civil War, if a contestant could provide minute details about the Battle of the Wilderness, Koplin assumed the contestant could answer difficult questions about the better-known Battle of Gettysburg.

For McCutcheon's second appearance, Koplin wrote questions based on the playback in the initial interview. Thereafter, before each broadcast, Koplin took McCutcheon aside to give him a warm-up, supposedly to ease his tension. This provided new playback material for use in composing the questions for the following broadcasts. Though he acknowledged that he rigged the outcome, in effect, Koplin insisted he gave no assurance of the outcome directly to McCutcheon, who in turn made no indication that he realized the questions were tailored to his knowledge.

While Koplin managed the contestant selection and question writing, he was not the final arbiter of the fate of contestants once they started on the air. In this and other respects, George Abrams of Revlon was closer to the center of power. Relaxed and courteous when I interviewed him, the forty-year-old Abrams had been in advertising and marketing all his professional life, formulating successful product ideas ever since the age of twenty-two when, working for the National Biscuit Company, he came up with the idea of the chocolate chip cookie, which, he claimed, ultimately made his employer some $200 million in sales. By the time he joined Revlon in 1955, shortly after the debut of "The $64,000 Question," Abrams had spent some eight years as advertising director of the Bloch Drug Company and was responsible by his own count for some fifty successful products, including Breakfast Power, a cornflake cereal with caffeine added. A true believer that the power of advertising makes life better for all, Abrams was no fool, and outspoken about the foolishness of others.

After the end of the summer of 1955, when Cowan left to join CBS, the overall direction of "The $64,000 Question" passed to the office of Martin Revson, Abrams's superior as executive vice-president and second in command at Revlon. At weekly meetings chaired by Revson and sporadically attended by his brother Charles, a flamboyant playboy and the compulsively tyrannical head of Revlon, every aspect of the most recent and upcoming broadcasts was evaluated. With the slightest upturn or dip in the ratings setting the tone, the discussion involved detailed critiques of each contestant's performance and how this was reflected in the ratings and in newspaper coverage and viewers' response in the form of telephone calls and letters to the network, local stations, Revlon, and EPI. The regular participants were Fleischman, Carlin, and Joseph Cates, the "Question"'s first producer-director (and older brother of "Dotto" associate producer Gilbert Cates), as well as representatives of Revlon's advertising agencies who were most heavily involved in the "Question," in addition to Abrams.

Abrams conceded that this degree of personal involvement by a sponsor's top executives in the so-called creative control of a program was unusual, but the Revsons were unusual and the program was a gold mine. Its impact on Revlon's sales and earnings was instantaneous and phenomenal. In 1954 the company had earned $1,298,000 after taxes on sales of $33,604,000. In the first two quarters of 1955, sales grew modestly, totaling $17,533,000 for the period. In the third quarter, coinciding with the introduction of "The $64,000 Question," sales jumped to $11,831,000. In the fourth quarter, sales *doubled* the third quarter amount to reach $22,283,000, making for a 1955 total of $51,647,000, an increase of 154 percent over 1954. This translated into after-tax earnings of $3,656,000, an increase of 281 percent over 1954.

Though Koplin did not attend the Revlon meetings, he, Bernstein, and others at EPI were acutely aware of their importance, as Carlin and Cates relayed the decisions made at them. An early example was the directive that a young woman contestant be found. As Koplin told it, it was his wife who spotted Joyce Brothers's inquiry, and it was he who explained to Brothers the paradox requirement. As for the subject of psychology, he explained to us, even if she had not been pursuing it as a profession, it would not have been suitable, because, like philosophy, for example, it was insufficiently concrete for the audience to understand when a contestant would be right or wrong in answering questions about it. When Brothers asked for examples of a suitably paradoxical subject for her, Koplin answered, "Lacrosse, wrestling, boxing"; several weeks later, Brothers was back as a boxing expert. He termed her a "synthetic" expert, one who could absorb an entire body of knowledge in just a matter of weeks by dint of concentration and hard work.

But after Brothers's first appearance on the "Question," Martin Revson made it known that he not only disliked her personality, looks, and taste in clothing, but found her expertise in boxing simply not believable, and Koplin was ordered to knock her off the show. He turned to Nat Fleischer, the boxing writer, for help in devising the hardest questions possible, but Brothers seemed to know the subject too well to be stumped. Koplin claimed he did not know until after she left the "Question" that Fleischer had helped her become an expert.

Abrams and Koplin agreed that it was Revlon's desire to capitalize on the success of the "Question" that led to the creation of "The $64,000 Challenge." Koplin was again in charge, finding that the new show meant much more work, for the knowledge of competing experts had to be played back in long sessions with each. Still, he insisted, he succeeded to the extent that he received no overt indication from anyone he handled that they were aware of what was going on. The most remarkable "Challenge" contestant was a St. Louis warehouse clerk named Ted Nadler, who knew everything there was to know about English kings and queens, baseball, the American Revolution, the Civil War, movies, and classical music. Though Nadler had not gone beyond the eighth grade in school, he had a genuine photographic memory that recalled literally everything he had read in books up until his teens. In screening Nadler, Koplin claimed, his task was simply to determine the outline of Nadler's "areas." Once that was done, it was unnecessary to play back Nadler's knowledge in detail and construct questions by inference. At the end of July 1956, Nadler was introduced on the "Challenge" in the category of Total Board, referring to the twelve diverse categories listed at the beginning of the broadcasts. (The public was not aware that the categories happened to be Nadler's specialties.) The public responded well, and in September 1956, when Joseph Cates resigned from the organization, Koplin was rewarded with the title of producer for both the "Question" and the "Challenge," and began regular attendance at the Revlon meetings.

But when the "Challenge"'s ratings slipped in late 1956, coinciding with the introduction of "Twenty-One" on NBC, the Revsons increased the pressure on EPI. Expressing dissatisfaction at contestants, categories, and even the questions, they played on the inherent fear of the producers that Revlon might not exercise its options to renew the shows when the time came. Revlon also used its leverage to "steal" broadcast time to lengthen commercials beyond what CBS guidelines permitted. The device of introducing new contestants at the end of broadcasts, too late for actual matches to begin, gave the producers and sponsor extra leeway in gauging audience reactions to new faces before determining whether these would be winners (and thus continue to return to the show) or not. The need for losers as well as winners, to prevent the audience from thinking all was a foregone conclusion, combined with the sponsor's opinions and Koplin's own assessments, translated into using playback on occasion to oust contestants at early stages by simply asking them questions he knew they could not answer.

The appearances of Herbert Stempel on "Twenty-One" caused a stir at Revlon. At one of the weekly meetings, Martin Revson gave his opinion that the new show must have been fixed. Koplin and his colleagues were acutely aware of the difficulty of securing genuine experts in a single field, and had earlier turned to making contestants of already established celebrities, like the movie stars Edward G. Robinson and Vincent Price, who were art experts. The idea of experts in "everything" seemed preposterous, so the EPI producers concurred that "Twenty-One" must have been fixed and hastily assured Revlon that no such hanky-panky could happen on their programs. EPI nevertheless had the problem that, despite all its experience in people getting, it could find no one as popular with the public as Stempel's successor, Charles Van Doren.

A crisis of a different sort occurred when Dale Logue, a former contestant on "The Big Surprise," filed suit in the U.S. District Court in New York against EPI and the program's sponsors, claiming she had been treated unfairly and deprived of possible winnings of $10,000. Carlin was summoned to a pretrial hearing and questioned about the warm-up procedures on "The Big Surprise" as well as the possibility of guaranteed payments to celebrities appearing on the show, which he denied. Carlin repeated his denials to the press and assured Revlon that the staffs of the "Surprise" and the $64,000 shows were separate. In April 1957 "The Big Surprise" was quietly canceled after a year and a half on the air.

In the midst of Van Doren's run, Revlon and EPI attempted to counter "Twenty-One"'s openended format by introducing additional big-money "plateaus" to the "Question." While Robert Strom was climbing these, Nadler was brought back to the "Challenge" to hold off challengers in several categories simultaneously, piling up winnings of $152,000 by April 1957. The frenzy of ever higher stakes drew renewed press attention as even the *New York Times* was reporting the results weekly, but the coverage was becoming more critical. In the April 22, 1957, issue of *Time*, an article titled "The $60 Million Question," a reference to the sums being spent on TV quiz shows by producers, networks, and sponsors, cited various techniques of posing questions to retain or remove contestants for "psychological"—that is, ratings—reasons. It was observed that McCutcheon earned his winnings "in French cuisine not in Cantonese or Neapolitan"; likewise, Prato "got his tough questions on Italian opera." Responding to this criticism, EPI would admit that Prato's category was indeed "Italian opera" and the sign "opera" on the show at the beginning of Prato's run was a mistake but they felt it would cause confusion to change it.

In a series of articles in the *New York World Telegram & Sun*, Harriet Van Horne described controls that enabled the producers to ease off the shows contestants whose personalities did not appeal to viewers. Contestants interviewed by Van Horne told of hours of warm-ups and how questions used in these could turn up on broadcasts. Joseph Cates, the former producer-director of both $64,000 shows, told Van Horne bluntly: "The questions are controlled. . . . The men who assess the contestant's field of knowledge are usually the men who mark out the field from which the question is to be drawn."[1]

To the Revsons, Carlin called Cates a disgruntled former employee and denied active collusion with contestants, though he did concede that EPI had the option of using hard or easy questions. Having purposely distanced themselves from knowledge of the procedures employed for question writing, Abrams and the Revsons were of the mindset to accept EPI's excuses. They were further mollified when Strom's and Nadler's record winnings in April boosted the ratings of both shows. Moreover, the Revsons did not complain when contestants they did not like were defeated. Al Ward, an advertising agency executive who attended the meetings, wrote confidential minutes for distribution to the participants. After one meeting, Ward made the mistake of writing up too explicitly the announcement by EPI that a "Challenge" match was slated to end on the following broadcast, meaning its outcome was predetermined. When Martin Revson read his copy of the memo, he did not admonish EPI but simply ordered the end of minutes-taking.

At the beginning of the summer of 1957, "Giant Step," an EPI attempt to combine the concepts of "Quiz Kids" and the $64,000 shows, using children as contestants, was launched but quickly flopped. Its producer, Edward Jurist, was put in charge of the "Challenge" so that Koplin could concentrate on finding new faces for the "Question," still the flagship of EPI. In the fall, when Jurist left EPI to work on the development of "Dotto," Shirley Bernstein was given full charge of the "Challenge." It was under Bernstein's control of the program that Joyce Brothers faced her challenge by the team of professional boxers. At the end of 1957 Bernstein also managed the appearance of the Reverend Charles Jackson, and now in my office, Bernstein and Koplin both described in detail their dealings with Jackson.

According to Koplin, Jackson wrote to EPI several times in 1956, representing himself as an expert, first on the movies, then on great love stories. The latter, for a Tennessee minister, was paradoxical enough for Koplin to bring Jackson to New York for an interview, then to schedule him for the "Question" starting in January 1957. When, before the contestant's first appearance, Koplin asked him how much money he would be satisfied with, Jackson, who made no secret of being in debt, answered $16,000, and Koplin told him he knew enough to win that amount. In two appearances, Jackson advanced to and won $16,000; at his next appearance, he announced he would take the money and retire. After the broadcast, Koplin thanked Jackson and said they would consider him for a run on the "Challenge" in the future.

At the end of 1957 this came about, and it was Bernstein's turn to work with Jackson, but she was given the word via Carlin from the Revlon meeting that the Jackson-Goostree match was not to go beyond the $4,000 level. Meeting with Jackson for a drill session several days before the broadcast, she covered the material he would be asked, as well the material Doll Goostree would be asked; thus equipped, Jackson was able to challenge a wrong answer by Goostree and win their match at the level desired by EPI. Bernstein could not recall precisely if Jackson had been able to answer all the questions in the drill, but she made it clear to us that if he didn't know the answers they wanted him to know, she would have indicated that he should find out. As for Goostree, Bernstein conceded pointedly that if she or any other contestant missed a question, it probably hadn't been covered in the drills.

As for the Duke-Hodges match in early 1958, Bernstein showed us a fierce side in exposing the controls employed when it came to child contestants. Only after Eddie Hodges and Patty Duke were accepted for the "Challenge" was the category of Popular Music selected, since Hodges obviously knew the subject. In the case of children, not only was the paradox requirement relaxed, but another rule operated. As Bernstein put it, "No one wants children to lose. If they missed they would be hurt at school with their playmates, their parents. If you were going to have children on the show—all I handled had good to superior knowledge—they must not be hurt in any way." Asked if that was the policy of EPI, she snapped, "It was my policy and I was never contradicted in it."

Duke and Hodges were separately interviewed by Bernstein in numerous sessions. In conversation about school and their friends, Bernstein gently imbedded questions about popular music as she played back their knowledge. After these sessions, Bernstein informed Hodges's father and Duke's manager, John Ross, of specific areas within the category to be covered. This way the children were required to work fairly hard for their appearances, and, Bernstein claimed, she never received any indication from them of awareness they were being helped. But Duke was a talented actress, and it was hard to believe she didn't know what was going on in light of what Ross himself admitted at his second interview by us. Whenever he took Duke to Bernstein's office for a session, a day or two before the upcoming broadcast, he made sure she always had a paper and pencil with her to take notes. When she was through, she told him what Bernstein had covered, and this guided him in his drilling of her for the next broadcast.

Bernstein now made no bones about what happened in the Cohn-Springer match. In the session with Wilton Springer just before the March 23, 1958, broadcast, she was frightened by his nervousness. Since he was "the poor little man with the small job" who adored the theater, he was the underdog and the preferred contestant, so she had to do something, with no time to consult with her superiors. She simply drilled him with questions she knew would be used on the air, never dreaming he would tell his opponent. She stressed the extraordinariness of this emergency—nothing so dire ever happened before or after. For his part, Abrams confirmed hearing of Arthur Cohn's complaint, whereupon he called Carlin to say Cohn was upset about "something," then reported to the Revsons with Carlin's assurance that the incident was an aberration. Since this was the first concrete allegation against the shows since their debut, the Revsons let it pass.

From Koplin we also had an account of the Cugat-Roth match in the summer of 1958, the one occasion, he insisted, when the proper application of the controls eluded him. Before Bernstein went off to England for two months, to serve as a consultant to the British commercial TV network's version of "Twenty-One," she had scheduled what promised to be an attractive celebrity match. Lillian Roth had previously offered herself as a "Question" prospect in the category of Great Religions of the World. Koplin, upon examining her, found she didn't know the subject well enough to qualify, but had referred her to Bernstein as a prospect, and it was arranged for her to face Xavier Cugat in the category of Tin Pan Alley. But when Koplin first interviewed Cugat, he discovered to his dismay that Cugat thought in Spanish. The mental process Cugat went through to answer drill questions—in effect translating the question into Spanish, finding an answer, then translating that into English—was too laborious to work with in the ordinary sense of playback. Koplin assigned an EPI staff member to research Cugat's background, focusing on his relationships and acquaintances with show-business figures in the course of his long career, to help devise questions to be used.

Like other celebrities, Cugat believed a big-money quiz show appearance was good publicity, but he didn't want to make a fool of himself by losing on the air. According to Mel Braverman and Cugat himself, when we brought him back into the office for a second talk, there was a tacit assurance from EPI that at the early stages he would be asked easy questions. The day before his first scheduled appearance, Cugat panicked and demanded from Braverman a guarantee he would not be humiliated. Braverman alerted Koplin, who agreed to meet with Cugat to calm him down. As soon as he saw Cugat, Koplin realized that the contestant had not studied his subject and was unprepared. For Koplin, the "horror hour" had arrived and he resorted to the "direct" method, asking Cugat questions, some of which the bandleader could answer, others of which he could not. For these, Koplin supplied the answers. Among them were questions used on the broadcast the following night.

Roth also proved difficult. She was too busy to study and to give Koplin enough time to put a true fix on her knowledge, so he had to write questions based only on what he guessed she knew. In the case of Cugat, Koplin visited the bandleader the day before each of the next two broadcasts and simply told him the questions and answers that were coming up, as well as what Roth would be asked, so that Cugat would know enough to challenge her answers if necessary. After June 22, when the pair reached the $8,000 level, Koplin decided to end the match in Cugat's favor, since Cugat had been the more cooperative.

FROM Koplin and Abrams we also learned the details of the demise of the $64,000 shows, following upon Jackson's allegations against the "Challenge." At the beginning of the summer of 1958, as a result of a rift between the brothers, Martin had quit Revlon, leaving Charles in sole control. Revlon also announced the end of its cosponsorship of "The $64,000 Challenge," which would continue during the summer sponsored solely by Lorillard; it was to be replaced in the fall in the Sunday night CBS slot by the "Question," which was taking a summer vacation, the first since its debut. Upon its return in the fall, the "Question" would be cosponsored by Revlon and Lorillard. If Lorillard did not find a cosponsor with a slot to take on the "Challenge" in the fall, the program was doomed. In August, Nadler was brought back and gave the show enough of a lift for NBC to agree to schedule it in a slot on Thursday nights, beginning in September. Lorillard would be the sole sponsor until NBC could find a cosponsor.

In the second week of August, when CBS was informed of the rigging of "Dotto," an order went out to the producers of the network's quizzes to investigate their shows for irregularities and report back. When the cancelation of "Dotto" was made public on August 16, Fleischman and Carlin stated to Hubbell Robinson, Jr., executive vice-president of the CBS Television Network Division, that there was no rigging of EPI shows: even if, as they now acknowledged, screening could reveal strong and weak areas in contestants' knowledge, this did not amount to rigging; contestants whose "areas" had been determined by deep probing had lost on the shows, while others, not so deeply probed, had won. Carlin and Fleischman were ordered to follow up with a written report.

Meanwhile, the breaking of the "Dotto" scandal prompted Cohn to write his circular letter explaining what happened on the "Challenge." When a copy reached Abrams, he showed it to Charles Revson. Though Revlon had cut the "Challenge" loose, it still had an interest in the "Question" and was still heavily identified with the former show as well, so once more Fleischman and Carlin were called in to explain. They adamantly repeated their previous denial of wrongdoing in connection with the Cohn-Springer match. Within days, Stempel's allegations about "Twenty-One" made headlines, but, since the Revsons and EPI had long privately shared the opinion that "Twenty-One" was rigged, Charles Revson was still inclined to accept EPI's assurances. Nevertheless, Revson dreamed up the idea of creating a "czar" for the quiz shows, that is, appointing somebody with impeccable credentials to head an independent office, financed by an association of producers, sponsors, and broadcasters, to supervise and control the questions used on all quizzes. Abrams was ordered to talk up this idea to his fellow members of the Association of National Advertisers, while Revson presented the idea to no less than Cowan at CBS. Cowan expressed support in principle but said the network could not be part of a "czar" setup. Revson then had Abrams formally present the proposal to EPI. The producers were strongly opposed, saying that to acquiesce in such a scheme was tantamount to admitting they had done something wrong.

On the morning of September 6, all came unglued as the news of Jackson's allegations spread. While Carlin and Bernstein made denials to reporters, CBS was alerted, and a meeting was called by Thomas Fisher, the CBS lawyer. Koplin was called in, as were Bernstein and Carlin; they were joined by lawyers from Revlon and Lorillard. A decision whether or not to cancel the following evening's broadcast of the "Challenge" was riding on the outcome. Much of the time was spent by Fisher on the phone to Jackson in Tennessee, as Carlin listened in. Unable to resolve the contradictions, Fisher felt he had to give the benefit of the doubt to EPI. Over the objections of Revlon but with the approval of Lorillard—the sole sponsor of the "Challenge" at this point— Fisher advised CBS not to cancel. When the Revlon lawyer handed Fisher a copy of Cohn's letter, Fisher said he would look into it, but the "Challenge" went on as scheduled. On September 8 Fisher tried to set up a meeting with both Cohn and Springer. Abrams claimed to us that he urged Cohn to attend, but the whistle-blower, reluctant to risk his chances of finding further work in advertising, refused. Springer, for his part, told Fisher he had already been called in by us, with the result that we requested Fisher to halt CBS's questioning of former contestants on the grounds this might complicate our investigation. I unwittingly had done CBS a favor.

On September 12, hours after our announcement of the grand jury investigation, Lorillard notified both CBS and NBC that it was dropping sponsorship of "The $64,000 Challenge." With the show's cancelation, Bernstein was out of a job, but Koplin was preparing the return of the "Question" to the air on October 5. During the summer he had found several strong contestants who were able to perform adequately without further screening or even warm-ups before broadcasts, he claimed. Every aspect of the production was now carried out under the scrutiny of nervous CBS production supervisors, and EPI staff were not permitted to be alone with contestants. Despite the precautions, the "Question"'s ratings sagged immediately, and its credibility was not helped by the travails of "Twenty-One," as NBC assumed direct control of the Barry and Enright operation and hired Joseph Cates to be in charge of "Twenty-One." Even before the axe fell on "Twenty-One" on October 16, the ratings collapse of the "Question" was making news on its own.

Revlon's problem was that it and Lorillard had another twenty-six-week contractual commitment to the "Question." Since there were no specific charges of rigging against the show, the sponsors could not cancel it for cause and would be stuck if EPI did not play ball. By the end of October, Lorillard was seeking similar relief. After a series of meetings, a settlement was reached. EPI was to be paid $255,000 by Revlon, $90,000 by Lorillard, and $75,000 by CBS in return for agreeing to cancel. The announcement, made by CBS on November 4, did not mention these figures. Commenting on the cancelation, Hubbell Robinson declared: "Although the integrity of the first . . . big quiz show was not an issue in the replacement, 'The $64,000 Question' has nevertheless become a victim of declining quiz show audiences."[2] No one we were able to talk to knew or admitted any knowledge as to what role Louis Cowan, the president of CBS Television, played in the network's investigation of the rigging of its quizzes.

... and True Presentment Make

CHAPTER NINE

Shaking the Tree

(NOVEMBER 1958–JANUARY 1959)

While delving into the operations of the $64,000 quizzes, we did not wait for the indictment of Albert Freedman to shake apples off the Barry and Enright tree. Howard Felsher had been given the opportunity to tell the truth but stepped into the same trap as Freedman by denying under oath that he gave assistance to contestants. We had the testimony of the two teenagers, Frances Li and Kirsten Falke, to the contrary, but wanted corroboration by adults before proceeding, if Felsher did not come in on his own to recant. In addition, we wanted to present the same quandary to Enright if we ever had the opportunity to take the packager's sworn testimony.

With that in mind, we brought Richard Jackman and Herbert Stempel before the jurors in the first two weeks of November. Since Enright had brought a complaint to us against Stempel for blackmail, the former contestant was still a target of our inquiry and could not be granted immunity, which he waived with alacrity. Before the jurors, he added to his previous account the story of his efforts to expose "Twenty-One." Even before his blackmail attempt, Stempel was in touch with reporters from two newspapers—David Gelman of the *Post* and Jack Horan of the *Journal-American*. After the meeting of March 7, 1957, tape-recorded by Enright, Stempel believed himself reconciled with the producer and did not follow through on his threats. But later in the spring, after Enright said there was nothing more he could do about providing Stempel with a job since NBC now owned the business, Stempel resumed pressing Horan to print his story.

Bertram Hacken and several others were hailed before the grand jury and testified about how Stempel had told them in advance the questions he would be asked and the answers he would give on the air. These at least served to corroborate this part of Stempel's testimony and to establish beyond any reasonable doubt the fact of his receiving assistance. We faced squarely the fact of Stempel's blackmail attempt and used it to show that indeed there had been something for Enright to be blackmailed about.

We read to the jurors a complete transcript of Enright's 1957 tape recording, and explored for them the strange circumstances surrounding it. Alfred Stettner, the business manager of Production Services, Inc., the Barry and Enright entity employed by NBC to carry out the day-to-day operations of "Twenty-One" and the other programs after their purchase by the network, testified on November 12 and 13, 1958. His story of assisting Enright in several attempts to tape conversations with Stempel showed the lengths to which Enright went to secure self-incriminating evidence from Stempel; it also alerted us to the pivotal role of Arthur Franklin, Enright's publicity man, who operated as a confidant to both Stempel and Enright. Franklin and his partner, Alfred Davis, meanwhile made themselves scarce and managed to elude the service of subpoenas.

ON NOVEMBER 12 Elfrida Von Nardroff arrived in the jury room carrying a shopping bag, containing the study notes she had cited as the key to her record-breaking success on "Twenty-One," which she had described to me in the office as filling "dozens of notebooks." Now she turned over a total of four, as well as a copy of *This Week* magazine with her picture on the cover and an article about her inside. Many of her notes had been on loose sheets of paper, she explained, and were lost in the times she had moved since the beginning of her involvement with "Twenty-One."

The magazine article was a first-person account of how Von Nardroff had become a contestant and what enabled her to win. In it, she wrote that her schooling had been "erratic," that she had been an underachiever, and that after two years at Duke University she was suspended from college. But this taught her a lesson; when she returned, she spent "the next two years studying hard—and here, for the first time my lifetime reading habit came to my rescue. I found out I could not only read and absorb my textbooks—but I could enjoy them . . . managing to achieve some pretty good grades. I even made the Dean's list." The gist was that during her long period as a standby she had the opportunity to study the program and determine what categories to study in detail. The bulk of questions concerned history, geography, and literature, Von Nardroff observed, so she "devoured almanacs, drowned myself in a sea of encyclopedias, spun globes and pored over atlases. I haunted the New York Public Library to such an extent that one day a librarian asked me if I was triplets."[1]

Each of the four notebooks she brought in contained fifty-five pages, but the pages were mostly blank. In one notebook, for example, eighteen pages were marked. On them, Von Nardroff had outlined the following subjects: the French Revolution, Kings of Europe, Napoleon, Chemistry, World War I, Women's Suffrage, Boxing, Music, TV Plays, Shakespeare, and Opera. In another, the six marked pages covered World Political Leaders and World History. Given this small effort, I had no reason to revise my previous skeptical impression of Von Nardroff, as she repeated, under oath, her denials of receiving assistance. I decided then to give her the full treatment—an examination of her bank accounts, telephone calls, and school records; we would send detectives to the 42nd Street library to check on her story of all the time she had put in there.

After Von Nardroff, the best-known woman to appear on "Twenty-One" was Vivienne Nearing, notable not for a long run or large winnings but for dethroning Van Doren. She had stalled from the first time we tried to talk to her, so that when she finally answered a subpoena on November 25, we put her directly before the grand jury without a preliminary interview. Attractive and self-assured, Nearing had studied economics and law at Columbia. She clerked two years for Arthur Vanderbilt, the chief justice of the New Jersey Supreme Court, was a statistician, a social worker, an editor for the monthly *Journal of Taxation*, and a trial lawyer for the Legal Aid Society, before joining the legal staff of Warner Brothers in 1956, working in the movie studio's New York offices.

Nearing testified that she and her husband, Victor, also a lawyer, both took the test for "Tic Tac Dough," scoring high enough to be considered for "Twenty-One." Victor Nearing appeared briefly on "Twenty-One," losing to Van Doren on January 21, 1957. When it was her turn, she met with Freedman only for warm-up sessions, she claimed, just before each of her five appearances. The first of these was on February 18, 1957, when Van Doren had amassed winnings of $143,000 and she tied him in the second match of the broadcast. The following week, she tied Van Doren again in two games. Skipping a week when "Twenty-One" was preempted for a network special, Nearing and Van Doren met for the third time on March 12, playing at stakes of $2,000 a point.

In the first game, Nearing decided to knock with seventeen points after two rounds. Van Doren in the first round failed to name Baudouin as the current king of Belgium, missing a question worth ten points. Thus, though he recouped with ten points in the second round, Nearing's knocking caught him down by seven points, ended his championship, and won her $14,000. This amount, subtracted from Van Doren's previous total, trimmed his final take to $129,000. On the same broadcast, the new champion met and was tied by the next contestant, Henry Bloomgarden. Nearing and Bloomgarden played a series of ties until March 26, when she lost. The $14,000 Nearing had won from Van Doren was reduced to $5,500.

But a canceled Barry and Enright check showed that Nearing was paid the sum of $10,000, a week after her defeat. Her explanation was that she told Freedman she wanted to retire as soon as possible, but he pleaded with her to stay because the simple fact that she had defeated Van Doren made her interesting to the public. He offered to guarantee her $10,000 if she would continue to play until she lost, to which she agreed. When that came about, Freedman lived up to his end of the bargain. But we had Stempel's testimony that in March 1957 Enright inadvertently signaled to him that Van Doren would be losing to Nearing in their next encounter. Though we did not share this with Nearing, we pressed her, but she stuck to her guns and denied assistance. She also denied being told in advance she would defeat Van Doren or lose to Bloomgarden.

SIMILARLY, the two biggest "Tic Tac Dough" winners within reach—Timothy Horan and Michael Truppin—insisted both in the office and before the jurors that they were not helped. I realized that this reflected how effectively Felsher and his lawyer, Sol Gelb, were working against us, after hearing from many former "Tic Tac Dough" contestants we interviewed that they had been instructed by Felsher to tell us the "truth," that is, they had not been given assistance on the program, and, equally important, to avoid saying anything to the press, because any kind of publicity connecting the D.A. to "Tic Tac Dough" could hurt the show.

One important "Tic Tac Dough" contestant who had not gone to Gelb became the first big apple to fall from the tree. In the second week of December, Thomas Sammon, Martin Dowd's lawyer, called to say he would bring his client back in if we gave our assurance that Dowd had nothing to fear if he now told the truth. At this point, there was no bar to Dowd's correcting his previous testimony because the grand jury was still in existence and there was no *legal* evidence that what Dowd had previously told the grand jury was not true. Even if such evidence existed, he could still recant, unless we could prove he had knowledge of the evidence. Given neither of these conditions, in the eyes of the law, he would be making a good faith effort to set the record straight.

Once again, Dowd told us his story. In the week before Thanksgiving in

1957, Felsher informed him he had passed the "Tic Tac Dough" test and they wanted to put him on immediately in order to defeat James Friedlander, the current champion, who was winning too much money. When Dowd said he was confident he could do well, Felsher, according to Dowd, shook his head and said, "You don't understand. This guy is *very* good." He explained that Dowd would be assisted with questions and answers in advance, which was a common procedure, done by other producers.

When Dowd realized Felsher could just as well find somebody else, he agreed, and the two men spent several hours over the next two days alone in Felsher's office. Felsher ran through a box of some 150 index cards, asking questions in nine categories of knowledge; after providing the answers Dowd didn't know and encouraging him to write them down, Felsher had Dowd study the cards by himself. His job was to memorize all the questions and answers that could come up in the nine categories on the "Tic Tac Dough" board, to tie Friedlander a number of times to raise the stakes sufficiently to cut back his previous winnings to the level of $3,000, and then defeat him. Creating a series of ties was easy, Dowd learned, when you knew all the questions and answers: if your opponent made a mistake, you simply missed on purpose in your next turn. On November 26 and 27, Dowd followed instructions and tied Friedlander for six games, then defeated him, cutting his winnings from $8,800 down to $2,800. Meanwhile, Dowd studied another 150 cards after working hours at Felsher's office, covering nine new categories. He spent two more days on the show, pushing his winnings up to $6,500, tying another challenger, then following instructions to deliberately miss and lose. He left "Tic Tac Dough" with winnings of $3,800.

Felsher thanked Dowd for his great favor, and indicated they probably would ask him to play on prime-time "Tic Tac Dough." According to Dowd, Felsher backed away from his original assurance concerning assistance that "everybody did it," saying his bosses did not know that he had worked with Dowd and if they found out, he would be fired. In February 1958 Felsher invited Dowd to challenge the current nighttime champion, Captain Michael O'Rourke, who, according to Felsher, was very popular with viewers but was being pressured by his army superiors to leave the show. Dowd did not like the situation: if he lost to O'Rourke he would win only the consolation prize of $300 per game played on the nighttime show; if he defeated O'Rourke, it might seem that the game was fixed. But after a pep talk by Felsher, Dowd agreed to play along. Again the two men set to work, meeting twice a week, often in Felsher's parked car, where Dowd memorized the index cards Felsher brought along.

By the time Dowd made his first appearance on nighttime "Tic Tac

Dough" on March 20, 1958, O'Rourke had amassed some $140,000 since December. Following Felsher's instructions, Dowd tied the captain nine times in their first three encounters. Then Felsher announced the ties were beginning to bore the audience and something had to give. If O'Rourke won, he would retire and take not only his previously posted winnings of $140,300 but an additional $25,000 that had accumulated as a result of the ties. So the decision had been made for Dowd to defeat O'Rourke on April 10. All went according to plan, as O'Rourke and Dowd played two more tie games, increasing the match stakes to $29,500. In the third game, O'Rourke gave the wrong answer to a baseball question and lost. He departed with winnings trimmed back to $108,000. With Dowd the new champion, the arrangement continued through the rest of April. He defeated his first four challengers, raising his posted winnings to $47,500 before meeting Dr. Michael Truppin on May 1. According to Dowd, Felsher's plan was for him to leave the show with winnings in the range of $10–12,000; Dowd thus realized that Truppin was his nemesis and the tie games were intended to scale back his winnings. Though he was not in such desperate need for money as when he first played on the daytime show, his wife had become pregnant and he was nervous about that as well as his situation on the show. He had not shared with her the secret of his success, but it was no secret to anyone but the most casual viewer that a champion's winnings were threatened by long series of ties. When he told Felsher his wife was pestering him to quit, the producer pleaded for him to continue, saying he would lose his job if Dowd won too much money.

But the pressure became too much for Dowd. On May 22, before his ninth game with Truppin, Dowd told Felsher he would deliberately miss a question and throw the match. According to Dowd, Felsher exploded in anger and called Dowd a thief, but Dowd's mind was made up. On the broadcast, he played two more ties with Truppin, then deliberately lost. His posted total was reduced by $28,000, and he left "Tic Tac Dough" with $19,700.

Dowd continued to watch "Tic Tac Dough" out of curiosity but had no contact with Felsher until the quiz scandal broke and the producer called to say the district attorney had requested certain records, including names and addresses of contestants. According to Dowd, Felsher intended to tell us he had given no assistance, but he was concerned that other former contestants might tell us otherwise. Though for Dowd this was the first concrete indication that he was not the only one helped on the show, the shoe was now on the other foot: he could not let his old friend down. He agreed to a meeting with Felsher in person to discuss the situation. It was a shock to Dowd when

1   The "Dotto" set. [Howard Frank Archives, Personality Photos, Inc.]

2   Page torn from Marie Winn's notebook, showing some of the answers to questions she was asked as a contestant on the May 20, 1958 broadcast of "Dotto." [Author's collection]

3   Marie Winn on "Dotto," May 20, 1958. [Author's collection]

4   "Twenty-One" emcee Jack Barry (*left*) with contestant Herbert Stempel in the isolation booth. [Culver Pictures]

5   Barry, with contestant Charles Van Doren in isolation booth. [Culver Pictures]

6   Van Doren and Stempel, in split-screen video shot, during their last match on "Twenty-One," December 5, 1956. [Author's collection]

7   Daniel Enright (*left*) and Jack Barry, with tape recorder, at a press conference after the quiz scandal broke in September 1958. Barry holds a copy of letter in which Stempel declared he did not receive assistance on "Twenty-One." [AP/Wide World Photos]

8   Front and back of a sealed registered letter sent by "Twenty-One" contestant James Snodgrass to himself in advance of a broadcast of the quiz, detailing questions and answers that would be used. [Author's collection]

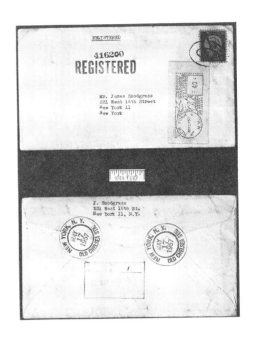

9   Snodgrass (*left*), Barry, and contestant Henry Bloomgarden on "Twenty-One," May 20, 1957. [Author's collection]

10   Production and studio staff of "The $64,000 Question." Behind emcee Hal March, foreground, stand EPI executives Steve Carlin and Harry Fleischman, and to their left Joseph Cates, producer-director. In the very rear, third from left, stands Merton Koplin, associate producer. [Howard Frank Archives, Personality Photos, Inc.]

11   "Question" champions gather for a publicity photo to launch "The $64,000 Challenge" in 1956. Sitting, opera expert Gino Prato has his arm around boxing expert Joyce Brothers; standing on the right is Shakespeare expert Redmond O'Hanlon. [Author's collection]

12   The first $64,000 winner and the food and cooking expert Marine Capt. Richard McCutcheon, in uniform, cuts cake for the "Question"'s first birthday. [Howard Frank Archives, Personality Photos, Inc.]

14   Albert Freedman, former "Twenty-One" producer (*left*), escorted by Detective Nicholas Barrett after Freedman's arrest on charges of perjury, November 7, 1958. [AP/Wide World Photos]

13   Shirley Bernstein, associate producer of "The $64,000 Challenge." [AP/Wide World Photos]

15 Howard Felsher, former "Tic Tac Dough" producer, at Washington quiz hearings, October 1959. [AP/Wide World Photos]

16 Charles Van Doren and his lawyer, Carl Rubino (*left*), at Washington quiz hearings, November 2, 1959. [AP/Wide World Photos]

17 Panoramic view of crowded Washington hearing room as Van Doren takes the oath; Joseph Stone can be barely made out, sitting at the dais in the background, ninth from the left, wearing glasses and looking to his right. [Photo by *U.S. News & World Report*]

18   Former "$64,000 Challenge"
contestant Patty Duke, accompanied
by her manager, John Ross (*right*),
and lawyer, Martin Leonard (*left*), after their testimony at the quiz hearings, November 3, 1959. [AP/Wide
World Photos]

19   Manhattan District Attorney Frank Hogan (*left*) and Assistant District Attorney Joseph Stone inspect grand jury minutes from the quiz investigation, early
1960. [Photo courtesy of *Broadcasting* magazine]

a detective showed up at his office the morning before his date with Felsher to haul him down to Manhattan. Frightened by the belligerence of Melvin Stein, Dowd decided he needed a lawyer and was lucky enough to find Sammon available on extremely short notice. Sammon explained to him the grand jury procedure and urged him to tell the truth, since there was no indication he was a target of the investigation and he had nothing to fear unless he lied under oath. Dowd did not tell the lawyer what the truth was. At that point, he now told us, he still had not told his wife what actually happened on "Tic Tac Dough."

At their rendezvous that night, according to Dowd, Felsher said he was trying to save "Tic Tac Dough" and the jobs of other people as well as his own career. He demanded that Dowd tell the grand jury he was not given assistance and to deny meetings while he was a contestant because that would create an "area of suspicion," and the D.A. would want to know their purpose. As for their meeting that night, Dowd should say Felsher called it in order to urge his cooperation with the investigation. By the end of their talk, Dowd was ready to do the producer's bidding, and Felsher solemnly promised, if something happened to Dowd, his family would be taken care of. The following morning, October 15, Dowd received a call from Felsher, who was in the office of Sol Gelb. Felsher put the lawyer on the phone, who said he wanted to see Dowd. Dowd replied he already had a lawyer and gave Gelb Sammon's name. That afternoon, when Dowd met Sammon outside the jury room, the lawyer reported receiving a call from Gelb, then told Dowd under no circumstances was he to have any further contact with Gelb or Felsher. In the jury room, when we focused on his meeting with Felsher just the night before, Dowd realized we didn't believe his denials of rigging, but he still didn't confide in Sammon; the following day, on his return to the grand jury, he believed he was in too deep to change his story.

Over the next few weeks, the enormity of what he had done weighed heavily on Dowd, particularly after the indictment of Freedman. When he learned from his bank that his records had been subpoenaed and turned over to us, he realized he was in the middle of a nightmare. He had lied to his lawyer and to a grand jury, and he couldn't even tell his wife. His situation was worse than simply living a lie, which he had done while he was on "Tic Tac Dough"—now he had broken the law and could go to jail for it. He finally decided his first duty was to himself and his family, not loyalty to a friend who had duped him and now was hiding behind him. Dowd made an appointment with Sammon and spilled the whole story.

In his third grand jury appearance, on December 17, 1958, Dowd apologized to the jurors and recanted his previous testimony. This marked another watershed in the investigation. The jurors now had a detailed picture of the operation of "Dotto," "Twenty-One," and "Tic Tac Dough," and my associates and I were preparing presentations to cover "Name That Tune" and the $64,000 shows. The chances of uncovering actual crimes in the operations of the quizzes were slim, even though, as Dowd now had made obvious, people were willing to commit perjury to conceal their involvement in rigging. But it was just as clear that the quiz shows involved a pattern of chicanery as disturbing as any kind of bribery or fraud on the books, in light of the fact that millions of people were taken in by them. For this reason, the jurors—led by Louis Hacker—my associates, and I committed ourselves to preparing a presentment or official report on the quiz shows, which would contain recommendations for legislation to correct the abuses; this was a possibility mentioned by Hogan at the beginning of the probe. Without indictments or a report, the enormous effort expended by the jurors would go to waste, a matter of vital importance would remain unexposed, and the public interest would not be served.

ONE DAY shortly before the grand jury recessed for the Christmas holiday period, I reached the end of my patience with Enright's lawyer, Myron Greene, who was in my office impugning the credibility of Stempel while assuring me of Enright's eagerness to cooperate when his busy schedule permitted. When I said I doubted Enright's intentions, the normally placid Greene became enraged and accused me of making political capital of the quiz investigation and destroying innocent people in the process. Telling Greene it was time he peddled his influence elsewhere, I ordered him out of my office, saying I wouldn't see him again except in the company of his client. I had already received a call from another lawyer, an old acquaintance named Hyman Zoloto, who boasted that he and his partner, Arthur Karger, a highly respected legal scholar, were being consulted by Enright. Any minute then I expected Zoloto to arrive in person to fill the vacuum left by Greene. Instead, in walked Thomas Gilchrist, Jr., to announce he was representing Enright. Gilchrist was a former assistant district attorney and had preceded me by a number of years as chief of the Complaint Bureau before leaving to join his father's Wall Street firm.

When Gilchrist expressed concern over our effort to "destroy" Freedman by giving credence to Stempel and Snodgrass, I pointed out that Stempel had nothing to do with Freedman. As for Snodgrass, Gilchrist knew very well that the law required more than one person's testimony to bring a perjury charge. The lawyer looked at me eagerly as if I might tell him who else had testified against Freedman. When that was not forthcoming, Gilchrist announced he was assembling affidavits signed by all former "Twenty-One" contestants stating they had at no time received assistance or information of any kind from anyone. I reminded him that such affidavits would have no legal weight, since lying in a sworn affidavit, in which the oath was not required by law, was not a prosecutable offense. I guessed Enright was using these to prop up the morale of the contestants and to have something to trot out for the delectation of the press at the appropriate time.

Though he argued with apparent conviction, Gilchrist was playing the same game as Greene—sniping at Stempel and Snodgrass while simultaneously stalling and trying to pump me. I told Gilchrist what I had told Greene—it behooved Enright to come in and tell me everything himself, otherwise his original complaint of blackmail could not be pursued. Gilchrist hastened to assure me he would set up a meeting just as soon as Enright's busy schedule permitted. Once more the stall was on.

Gilchrist might have thought that Stempel was the only witness I had against Enright personally; otherwise I would have subpoenaed Enright and put his feet to the fire as we had done with Freedman. With Jackman's story in hand, however, I had no need to bluff, but before I called Enright's bluff by hailing him and Barry before the grand jury, I wanted to corroborate Stempel's story from the inside and show the grand jurors that Enright's manipulation of Stempel after his contestancy had stemmed from the deal with NBC for the purchase of Enright's shows. The keys were Arthur Franklin and Alfred Davis, Enright's public relations men, who had served as go-betweens in Enright's efforts to keep Stempel quiet, according to the latter. Franklin and Davis, who had been in Enright's entourage when the packager came to the office to lodge his original complaint, were now making themselves scarce, which fed our suspicion that they had important things to reveal. By the middle of December we had process servers regularly visiting their office on East 62nd Street, but the two partners were staying away. By the end of December we maintained constant surveillance on the site during working hours.

Finally, in the first week of January 1959, a subpoena was served on Davis's wife at their home in Queens, and in the morning of January 8, detectives caught Franklin at his office and served him with a subpoena forthwith. In the office, the detectives found another man, Peter Yolde, and, taking no chances, served him as well, then brought both men down. Davis, meanwhile, came in under his own steam and volunteered to talk. After a few hours' questioning, we handed him a new subpoena for later in the month. Since Franklin and Yolde refused to talk in the office, we put them before the grand jury that afternoon. Yolde testified that he was working with Franklin to promote a treasure hunt expedition to the Indian Ocean, which would be filmed. Swept up in the dragnet we had put out for Franklin, Yolde by coincidence had a contribution to make to our knowledge of the quiz show affair, but his involvement came at the tail end of the stories Franklin and Davis would tell.

Franklin and Davis had been partners for some eight years and numbered among their half-dozen principal clients, in addition to Barry and Enright, the singers Kate Smith, Roy Hamilton, and Martha Wright. Franklin had been working for Barry and Enright for ten years, first doing personal publicity for Barry, then publicizing the packager's television programs and giving advice on all manner of corporate-style public relations. Franklin and Davis were retained for a basic annual fee of $25,000, payable at $500 a week, plus bonuses, which had pushed their total 1958 earnings from Barry and Enright to the level of $40,000. Before and after the debut of "Twenty-One," Franklin and Davis gave Enright their opinions on prospective contestants, including Stempel. They believed Stempel's offbeat personality, combined with his fantastic knowledge, just might work on TV, so they recommended in his favor. It was soon clear the choice had paid off by helping "Twenty-One" overcome its early shakiness. Davis became friendly with Stempel, who took to dropping by Franklin and Davis's offices. Franklin pegged Stempel as a bizarre combination of insecurity and ambitions out of focus with reality, but he didn't have the heart to disabuse Stempel of his hopeless ambitions to be an actor.

Before long, according to Davis, Stempel was telling him "Twenty-One" was rigged. Davis shared this with Franklin, but they dismissed it, until December 4, 1956, when Stempel came to Davis with the "rundown" script of the next broadcast, with questions and answers added, and said he was being set up to lose to Van Doren. Franklin went to Enright and expressed his alarm at the dangers of alienating Stempel, but Enright equivocated. After his defeat, Stempel retained Franklin to manage his career as an entertainer; while Franklin gave Stempel tips on how to dress and comport himself, he urged Stempel to see a psychiatrist. At this point, Stempel confided to Davis that Enright had given him advances on his winnings, that he had been giving money to a hoodlum who was threatening him with violence, and that Enright had promised him a job. While doing their best to mollify Stempel,

Franklin and Davis derailed an attempt by Stempel to tell his story to David Gelman of the *New York Post* by prevailing upon Paul Sann, the executive editor of the *Post*, to spike the story because of Stempel's mental condition.

On March 1, 1957, when Franklin and Davis were summoned to an urgent meeting at Enright's office, they knew Barry and Enright were in the midst of negotiations with NBC to sell their shows to the network for several million dollars while staying on as producers on a salaried basis. Franklin and Davis now filled in for us an account of the meeting already provided to us by another participant, Enright's administrative assistant, Fred Stettner. Convinced that Enright had in fact rigged Stempel's appearances, the PR men realized that they had to come up with a solution to keep the lid on Stempel so that the deal with NBC would not explode.

Enright agreed to Franklin's talking sense to Stempel but wanted to catch Stempel in the act of blackmailing as an insurance policy. After an abortive attempt in Franklin's office, when the recording equipment failed, the meeting of March 7 was set up at Enright's office and this time was successfully recorded. With Stempel apparently taken care of, there arose no obstacles to the NBC deal, which was consummated on May 2, 1957. While Davis continued to handle the Barry and Enright account day to day, Franklin made plans to leave the business and write a play.

According to both Franklin and Davis, late in the summer Enright received a tip that the *Journal-American* was preparing an article based on Stempel's story. The same source informed the office of Sidney Eiges, the NBC vice-president in charge of press relations. Enright summoned Franklin and Davis to a meeting with himself and Eiges. Asking "What can be done with this Stempel?" the NBC man seemed to take it for granted that Stempel had lied to the *Journal-American*, especially after Enright made it known he had a statement signed by Stempel that he had never been given assistance. As Franklin recalled, Eiges was eager to be reassured, "as if a husband suspected his wife but loved her too much to really want to know" the truth. All agreed on the goal of keeping Stempel's story from being published.

At Eiges's request, Enright met with NBC's general counsel, Thomas Ervin, and explained that Stempel had been under psychiatric care after his appearances on the show, then showed Stempel's statement of March 7, offering to make available to Ervin the tape recording and a transcript, which were being kept in a safe at his office. When the *Journal-American* informed Eiges that it had insufficient backup evidence to run the Stempel article, NBC dropped the matter without listening to the tape or asking Stempel himself about his charges. As a result, there was no further investigation of "Twenty-One" by

its new owner, and the management of the show by Barry and Enright—
under the new corporate name of Production Services, Inc.—was not altered.
As Franklin put it, "NBC really loved 'Twenty-One' in those days."

Franklin and Davis heard little of Stempel until nearly a year later when,
following upon newspaper stories about the fixing of "Dotto," the *New York
World-Telegram* identified Stempel as the former "Twenty-One" contestant
who had made charges to the district attorney. An urgent meeting was called
at NBC, attended by Eiges, Ervin, Enright, Franklin, Davis, and Enright's lawyer,
Irving Cohen. The main business was preparing a press release in response
to the *World-Telegram* story. Enright once again repeated his denials of
Stempel's charges without demurrer from Franklin and Davis, who were
acutely aware of the consequences if NBC did not stoutly defend Barry and
Enright. Enright wanted to release Stempel's written statement and the tape
recording, but Ervin said these should be turned over to the D.A. before
being made public. Ervin then had Lawrence McKay, a senior partner of NBC's
main outside law firm, arrange an appointment with us for the following day.
When Cohen said he would file a lawsuit against the *World-Telegram* and
asked NBC to join, Ervin temporized, pending the outcome of the visit to the
D.A. After playing the March 7, 1957, tape for reporters the following week
and emphasizing Stempel's poor credibility, Barry and Enright outwardly
seemed to weather the storm. But behind the scenes, as we pressed for Barry
and Enright's records, Cohen found he was out of his depth. Franklin therefore introduced his own lawyer, Edwin Slote, to Enright.

Slote, who knew his way around show business as well as around legal
and Democratic party circles, seemed at first to move with energy and effect.
He quickly brought in Jacob Rosenblum, a former assistant district attorney,
to help deal with us, telling Franklin and Davis that Rosenblum had me "in
his hip pocket." When the grand jury investigation was announced, Slote
pooh-poohed the development to Franklin, saying there would never be indictments; according to Franklin, Slote boasted he knew the judge in charge,
who would keep him apprised of developments. If Slote's boasting at first
reassured Franklin, the situation deteriorated on September 26, when the
New York Post published the allegations of Snodgrass. This time, in addition
to the usual press release, NBC demanded a sworn statement from Enright.
Franklin, recalling previous assurances that Stempel was the only possible
troublemaker, now realized Enright had kept him in the dark. Enright turned
over to Ervin affidavits signed by himself, Barry, Freedman, and others of his
staff who had dealt with Snodgrass, stating flatly that at no time had they
provided questions or answers to him.

But NBC decided to take direct control of the Barry and Enright programs.

An agreement was quickly reached by which Enright was relieved, though his employees, from producers on down, were retained, as were the services of Franklin and Davis. The new arrangement was announced on October 5 but did not halt the ratings collapse of "Twenty-One," and the show was canceled after the broadcast of October 16. Slote now told Franklin and Davis that what they knew could be very damaging, especially the fact Stempel had shown them the script of the December 5, 1956, broadcast in advance. Enright told Franklin and Davis that if he and Barry were called, they would testify that they knew nothing about giving Stempel assistance, and Slote suggested that Franklin and Davis simply "forget about the paper" Stempel had shown them.

Yolde, the treasure-hunt promoter, happened to be at Franklin and Davis's office when Enright and Slote arrived for a meeting and was asked to wait in a back room of the suite, across an air shaft from the main office. Because it was a warm evening, the windows were open, and Yolde overheard much of the conversation, as Slote grilled Franklin about what he would tell the grand jury if called. It was an attempt to make what Franklin would have to say jibe with what Enright intended to tell the D.A. when and if the occasion presented itself. Franklin replied that his reputation as a PR man would suffer if the newspapers learned he was involved in Enright's cover-up of what had happened with Stempel. Hearing this, Slote changed tack and said if Franklin didn't want to testify, he could make himself scarce. "For crying out loud," the lawyer said, "you are only a cog in the machine, you should get going—get away, leave the country." Franklin rejected this advice but agreed to avoid being subpoenaed as long as possible.

On a later occasion, Slote cautioned Franklin and Davis that if they told the truth under oath and everyone else lied, *they* would be the ones indicted for perjury. Realizing they were being set up as sacrificial lambs, they cut off their relations with Slote. But for Franklin the paramount consideration remained being on the NBC payroll as long as possible, so he played ball to the extent that he avoided being served with a subpoena by, in his words, "drinking in different saloons."

WITH Franklin and Davis now corroborating key parts of Stempel's testimony, we were sufficiently prepared to confront Enright directly, but, before that, we decided to give the two star "Twenty-One" contestants the opportunity to come clean. In the week of January 12, 1959, Von Nardroff, in a return appearance, and Van Doren testified.

Since Von Nardroff's previous testimony, we had given her life intense

scrutiny by securing her school records, bank accounts, even telephone records for the period she was a contestant. Now in the jury room, we went
over the discrepancies with her between what we had learned in the interim
and the persona presented in the *This Week* magazine cover story she had
shown us before. In the article, she claimed she was on the dean's list at Duke
University, but the school's records showed no such thing. After hemming
and hawing, she conceded that her academic career had not been as successful as the article indicated, but, she claimed, there was an "unofficial" dean's
list at Duke, which one could make with a B average.

Our investigators had interviewed staff members of the New York Public
Library but found no one who recognized Von Nardroff's picture. Her reply
to this was that she had taken books out of the circulation department and
spent little time in the library building itself. "Actually," she characterized *This
Week*'s presentation, "the article is sort of impressionistically true." She had
approved it because "the general feeling was right."

On a more pertinent plane, we asked her about the large number of
phone calls made to Freedman in her last weeks as a contestant, from her
summer home in East Hampton to his office and home. She defended these
as legitimate, necessary to keep him posted on her whereabouts. Since her
departure from "Twenty-One," she had met with Freedman once, when they
had lunch after her receipt of a subpoena, but they did not discuss what she
would tell the grand jury. After that he had called her once, asking her to sign
an affidavit to the effect that she had received no assistance as a contestant.
This she had referred to a lawyer, but no action was taken. The last time she
had spoken to Freedman was soon after his indictment, when she called him
to express her sympathy.

After being referred to a caveat in the *This Week* article to would-be quiz
show contestants that the IRS would take most of their winnings, Von Nardroff
admitted she paid out little of her winnings in taxes because she had invested
the lion's share in an oil-depletion venture as a tax shelter. The recipient was
a lawyer-accountant named Norman Gluss, to whom she had been referred
by Van Doren in March 1958, when her winnings stood at over $70,000. At
that time, Gluss told her he was handling the prize money of Bloomgarden
and Horan, as well as Van Doren, in addition to managing some investments
for Enright and Barry themselves. When Von Nardroff received her winnings
of $220,500, she handed the check over to Gluss. Of the amount, Gluss sank
$150,000 into the tax shelter, returned $10,000 to Von Nardroff for her personal use, and put the remainder into special accounts after deducting a fee
of $28,000.

Van Doren appeared before the jury twice, on January 13 and 15, bracketing Von Nardroff's return. By this time he had retained Carl Rubino, a highly skilled and competent attorney, who once had been my superior in the D.A.'s office. He had taken an active part in Hogan's campaign for the Senate and was a good friend of Lawrence McKay, whose firm represented NBC. Van Doren now was confident and earnest, as he repeated under oath what he had told us in the office: there was no rigging whatsoever of his appearances on "Twenty-One." However, he revealed that he had met Freedman before being picked to be on the show, at parties in Greenwich Village where both men resided at the time. While a contestant, Van Doren visited Freedman in his office many times, to arrange things like press interviews and picture-taking sessions. He also was invited to Freedman's home for dinner on several occasions but, Van Doren insisted, "Twenty-One" was never discussed.

Questioned about Norman Gluss, Van Doren answered that Gluss's brother had been handling his tax returns since 1954, so he had known Gluss before striking it rich on "Twenty-One." After his departure from the show, Van Doren deposited his final check of $124,250 in a special bank account nominated to Gluss, authorizing him to invest $100,000 in oil exploration and drilling ventures. Out of his winnings, Van Doren paid $6,000 in federal taxes, $250 to New York State. Van Doren confirmed he had steered Von Nardroff, as well as Bloomgarden, to Gluss. He did not receive a finder's fee for the references, but Gluss charged him less on his account after he brought in Bloomgarden.

Wanting the jurors to see how Van Doren might have fared as a contestant, we put to him eight sets of questions he was asked on "Twenty-One," six of which he had answered correctly. The performance was not stunning: he again missed the questions he had missed on the air. Of the six he had answered correctly, he now missed parts of half of them. He gave correct answers concerning Nobel prize-winning novelists, baseball, and the United Nations, but missed questions in U.S. history, women's suffragists, and dogs. On the last, he showed he knew next to nothing about dogs and admitted as much. As for being able to answer the question on "Twenty-One," he claimed because he had missed a question about dogs in an earlier game, he studied up on the subject, but now had forgotten what he learned.

ON JANUARY 20, 1959, Alfred Davis was testifying before the grand jury when word arrived that Enright, Barry, and their executive producer, Robert Noah, were outside, responding to subpoenas sent to Myron Greene. I requested a recess, and Donnelly took Davis out through the jury cloakroom so that he could not be seen—to my office, where he was told to wait.

We had already choreographed what was to happen next. The jurors had heard Stempel's side of the story—in great detail, from a number of witnesses. Now Enright, the other principal in the affair, had arrived, presumably to tell his side of the story. In my role as their legal adviser, I previously had told the jurors that even if Enright was a complainant in the matter of the extortion attempt by Stempel, he, Barry, and Noah had become targets of the investigation. It was the jurors' decision to make, but I was advising them to have Enright, Barry, and Noah sign waivers of immunity before they would be heard, as Stempel himself had been required to do. I further advised the jurors that, according to the law, if Enright and company testified without waiving immunity, two things could happen: if they lied they would not be subject to perjury prosecution because, in the eyes of the law, as targets they would not have been legally sworn even though they took the oath; at the same time, they would be immune to prosecution for any wrongdoing they might admit to before the jury that came within the scope of the investigation. And so, at my request, the jury already had voted not to hear Enright, Barry, and Noah unless they signed waivers of immunity.

I went out to the waiting room and, in addition to Greene, found Jacob Rosenblum, whom I hadn't seen since September, when he tried to soften me up and pump me for information about the investigation. Enright, Barry, and Noah, the last a slight, intense man with glasses, stood apart in a group. Only Rosenblum, an old hand, was relaxed.

I informed the gathering that the grand jury was investigating possible conspiracy, larceny, commercial bribery, and extortion charges in connection with the operation of television quiz programs; in view of the connection of Enright, Barry, and Noah with such programs and the indication they had made in statements to us that they were anxious to cooperate with the investigation, they would be given the opportunity to do so by appearing before the grand jury. However, I added, neither the district attorney nor the grand jury was prepared to offer them immunity from possible prosecution in return for their testimony. Rosenblum replied that his clients were happy to testify but could not sign waivers. I went in and told the jurors what they must have known would happen, then returned to inform Enright and company that the jurors would not hear their testimony at this time. There was no further discussion; the quiz men and their lawyers trooped out, and I sent for Davis to resume his testimony.

The familiar figure of Barry entering the building earlier must have alerted the press, because a throng of reporters was waiting outside when Barry and Enright emerged. The following day, January 30, the *New York Times* reported that Barry was asked, "How do you think the public will react to your refusal to sign a waiver of immunity? Do you think it will hurt you professionally?" According to the *Times*, the emcee smiled and replied, "That depends on how you write the story. I acted on the advice of my lawyer."

CHAPTER TEN

The People against Peter Poe

(JANUARY 1959)

Between Van Doren's grand jury appearances and Enright's refusal to waive immunity and testify, we completed the presentation of testimony regarding another quiz program with the appearance of its owner and originator. On January 15, 1959, Harry Salter waived immunity in order to tell us everything we wanted to know about the CBS quiz, "Name That Tune." If nothing else, this venerable showman demonstrated how a quiz producer could handle allegations of rigging with a minimum of publicity and survive with his reputation intact and his show still on the air. For, instead of name-calling, stonewalling, and legal finagling, Salter had turned to two law partners and former assistant district attorneys, Samuel Cantor and Wyllis S. Newcomb, who urged him to give us complete cooperation.

When we began our investigation of "Name That Tune" in early October 1958, after a tip that Clifford Livingston, a professional football player, had been given assistance as a contestant, we found that the program, on television since 1953, was more a guessing game than a quiz show, with a simple core concept despite rules that seemed complex. In the first of three separate phases, two contestants raced each other some fifty feet to pull a cord on a bell and identify a familiar tune being played by a small orchestra, conducted by Salter. The winner had the option to go on alone or invite his or her competitor to join in as a partner in the next phase, which was to correctly identify seven tunes in the space of thirty seconds of listening time. If successful, the contestant or pair was invited to return to join in partnership with the "write-in" contestant, that is, the person who had sent in the list of tunes identified in phase two, for a stab at the "Golden Medley Marathon."

In this third phase, the new team raced a thirty-second clock to identify five more difficult tunes selected around a theme. This was repeated in subsequent weeks for increasingly higher stakes until a fifth and final round. If successful to the very end, the winners divided a total prize of $25,000. In practice, a broadcast allowed time for no more than three or four contests in the various phases by different teams. Aside from commercials, the rest of the show was given over to extensive banter and interview segments conducted by the emcee, George DeWitt.

Given the long history of "Name That Tune" and a huge number of former contestants, my associate Larry Bernstein had issued subpoenas only to a few New Yorkers who had gone all the way to win or share in the grand prize. After talking to Livingston and several others, we decided the grand jurors should hear their stories and began presenting witnesses to them before the Christmas break, under the case title of *The People against Peter Poe*.

Contestants for "Name That Tune" were picked at mass screening sessions of prospects, many of them recruited by Diane Lawson, "Dotto"'s people getter. After brief interviews, prospects were taken aside in small groups to listen to tunes played on a piano and to write down their guesses. Those who passed were invited to stand by on one or two broadcasts of the program. Most of the contestants we questioned freely admitted receiving some kind of assistance, and it was clear that knowledge of music on the part of a contestant was less important to the producers than "personality"—a combination of being folksy, extroverted, and lovable. Not that musical knowledge hurt, especially if one could sing or play an instrument on the air. This added to the "fun" and meant less time spent on the contests and ultimately less prize money given away.

Once selected to go on the air, each contestant had a private session with Harvey Bacall, the show's musical arranger. He would hum or play tunes and ask the contestants to identify them, noting their responses. The contestants we interviewed at first assumed this was merely for practice; not until they were on the air did they realize that the tunes being used had been played or hummed to them by Bacall. Bacall was a show-business old-timer whose function was summed up in the philosophy Salter himself would enunciate to the grand jury: "We like to have winners." By the time contestants reached Bacall, he told the jurors, they had been "ordained" by Salter as having "personality." Bacall's job was to determine their precise musical strengths and weaknesses and select the tunes to be used on the air accordingly; this way, Bacall asserted, contestants would not embarrass themselves and the audience.

In effect, Bacall employed Merton Koplin's techniques of playback and inference; the difference was that he took few pains to hide from the contestants what was going on. Bacall's practice was not to provide the titles of tunes to contestants who could not identify them; if they asked, he told them but made sure these were not on the final list to be used on the air. All contestants were nervous when it came to going on, Bacall said, to the extent that many would be shaking visibly. Part of his job was to determine how to give them a good start such that they would relax and perform well once the program was under way. If a contestant seemed to be the type who would freeze up, Bacall made sure the first two or three tunes played would be ones he, Bacall, had hummed and the contestant had identified in their previous session. A strict rule was never to program a tune that Bacall believed the contestant could not identify. Under these circumstances, Bacall was asked, how could anyone lose? He replied that he wasn't foolproof. Sometimes he inferred too much, and occasionally contestants did freeze up and simply forgot what they knew. For this reason, a final warm-up just before the broadcast was useful.

Taking his turn before the grand jury, Salter was as candid as Bacall, though more inclined to dress up his presentation with a homespun entertainment philosophy: "We have found it's good business not to give Mr. Rockefeller another oil well. So you try to get people who can be helped and whose lives will be changed for the better." It was Salter, conductor of the orchestra for the popular 1930s radio show "Your Hit Parade," who introduced music to the quiz genre in 1937, with his "Melody Puzzles," a short-lived effort in which contestants tried to guess song titles from clues hidden in skits performed on the show. After World War II, during which he was a musical consultant to the Pentagon, Salter returned to radio. His idea for "Stop the Music" was packaged by Louis Cowan in the late 1940s and became the most successful radio quiz ever. With Salter's orchestra providing the music, the show offered huge prizes for the times—up to $30,000—to the lucky people at home who answered the phone and were asked to identify a "Mystery Melody." "Stop the Music" showed that top ratings could be earned by shows with production budgets—despite the appearance of big-money prizes—sharply lower than productions starring big names whose salaries alone could be as much as $30,000 a week.

Though Salter repeatedly emphasized that there were no real losers on "Name That Tune," in fact only one in sixteen contestants went all the way to share in the top prize; yet from the beginning, people won money, none of which was risked by losing at a more advanced phase. Or, as Salter put it, "Nobody loses on the show. You just stop winning." Thus, if a team failed to win at the final phase of the Marathon, the partners still went home dividing

$20,000. As for financing the prize-money budget, the sponsor provided $5,700 a week, plus $2,000 for the costs of the screenings; an airline plug on the show brought in another $650 a week. Salter's company threw in the difference to make a total prize budget of $10,000 a week.

Salter claimed that, rather than hiding his screening techniques from the sponsor and network, he simply never discussed it because they never asked him. But when CBS learned we were looking into his show, Salter took a daringly simple step to contain the damage. From December 22, 1958, on, each broadcast of the weekly quiz opened with the following announcement:

> This is a game that everybody can play. We play tunes drawn from the types of music the contestants are most familiar with. Some of the tunes have previously been identified for us by our contestants. But you don't have to be an expert to win. All our tunes are songs you've heard and sung all your life.[1]

If the public had felt deceived prior to the use of this proviso, it didn't show it. The ratings remained high, as 12.1 million homes, with 30 million viewers, continued to tune in. Salter contrasted this to the time when the clock that contestants raced against skipped a second, and "I had a couple of million letters." Putting in the announcement had prompted some 35,000 letters, but not a single one said, in Salter's words, "You have misrepresented, we are not going to look at you now, we don't love you anymore."

IN SHARP CONTRAST to the situation regarding the $64,000 quizzes but in the pattern that prevailed with "Dotto," the sponsors of "Name That Tune" were happy to leave "creative control" in the hands of Salter and his staff. One of the two agencies that handled the show for its primary sponsor, the Whitehall Pharmicals Company, was Ted Bates of "Dotto" fame. James Seaborne, a Bates executive, downplayed his firm's role, testifying that "Name That Tune" had been a vehicle for Whitehall products—Aerowax, Anacin, BiSoDol, and Liquid Heet—long before Bates's involvement with the sponsor. Bates simply conducted a "traffic operation," purchasing the station lineup for "Name That Tune" and other programs sponsored by Whitehall on CBS and other networks.

The "producing agency" of "Name That Tune" was the small firm of Sullivan, Stauffer, which had leased the show for Whitehall back in 1953. Philip

Cohen, the agency's vice-president for radio and television, said Whitehall had been attracted to the concept of "Name That Tune" for TV because of its previous success on radio. He characterized it as a contest of two partners against a clock, less a matter of skill than an opportunity for anyone to join in the fun and perhaps win some money. After some vacillation, the ad man conceded that "prompting" of contestants would have violated the spirit of the Whitehall-Salter contract and the understanding by the client as to the nature of the program. Nevertheless, he insisted, there simply had been no reason not to accept at face value the appearance of spontaneity on the show, especially since they were dealing with a producer like Salter, who had a formidable track record in broadcasting.

Walter Seldon, a program supervisor for Sullivan, Stauffer, echoed Cohen on the importance of trusting the judgment of people with track records, repeating the now-familiar credo that since there were never any complaints about the show, there was no reason to believe anything was wrong. When pushed, however, Seldon admitted that the show was presented as essentially a contest and viewers were led to believe that no prompting was involved; if, in fact, contestants had been "corrupted," then it could be argued that the client had been defrauded by the producer, but Seldon was not ready to acknowledge this as the case. Whether the producers were simply lucky in never becoming entangled with a whistle-blower like Hilgemeier or Stempel was unclear, but it was clear that the sponsor's and agencies' attitude was one of hands off until somebody rocked the boat, which had never occurred.

AT THE END of January 1959, two weeks after Salter's testimony and a week after Enright, Barry, and Noah declined to waive immunity, we presented to the jurors the story of "Twenty-One" from the points of view of the NBC network and "Twenty-One"'s sponsor up to its demise. Three NBC officials and Edward Kletter, vice-president and advertising director of Pharmaceuticals, Inc., the manufacturer of Geritol and other products advertised on "Twenty-One," testified from their various perspectives and confirmed the laissez-faire attitude reigning at their end of the quiz business.

Kletter had marketed over-the-counter drugs most of his working life and, after 1953, was president of his own company, handling TV advertising for Pharmaceuticals and others. He recounted at length the relationship between Pharmaceuticals and Barry and Enright, which predated the creation of "Twenty-One," as well as the history of the sponsor's involvement in the show. Although Kletter and Matthew Rosenhouse, the head of Pharmaceuti-cals, were consulted at every stage of the development of the show, time and time again they told the producers, "This is your baby. You produce the pro-gram the way you see fit." If the show was produced badly and it failed in the ratings, it would be dropped as soon as permitted by the contract, which contained the usual clauses spelling out the rights of the sponsor and net-work to cancel under various circumstances. But nowhere, Kletter conceded, was there a written assurance that "Twenty-One" would be operated as a bona fide contest; nobody ever gave it any thought.

When "Twenty-One" debuted, Hugh Brannigan of NBC had day-to-day su-pervisory responsibility for it and "Tic Tac Dough." Since he worked for the NBC business department, Brannigan's main job was to keep track of the shows' below-the-line costs, making sure that the producers' use of the studio facilities and personnel remained within budget. Since prize money was an above-the-line element, it was no concern of his. Brannigan's job also was to make sure his programs adhered to the network's broadcasting standards, codified into a leaflet back in radio days in 1934 and unchanged since. In essence, the standards required that nothing be broadcast that could offend any significant group of listeners and reflect badly on commercial sponsors; nothing in the code dealt specifically with quiz programs. Robert Lewine, Brannigan's superior as the NBC vice-president responsible for all program-ming except the news, summed up his own job as seeing to it that programs got on and off the air on time. Since Barry and Enright were veteran produc-ers and Brannigan never reported any irregularities, Lewine never had the occasion to hear of any problems concerning "Twenty-One."

Be that as it may, Pharmaceuticals provided the prize money, so we con-fronted Kletter with copies of Barry and Enright memos to the sponsor re-garding the advances to some contestants as well as discrepancies in final payments to others. Kletter said since he had no idea there was any problem with "Twenty-One," it never registered on him or anyone at Pharmaceuticals that Richard Jackman had won $24,500 yet was paid only $15,000. More to the point was that Vivienne Nearing won only $5,500, yet was paid $10,000, a transaction that was duly reported but set off no alarm bells in the accounting department. Being told of the Nearing payment now before the grand jury, Kletter claimed, was the first he had heard of it. He shrugged off the discrep-ancies as academic, since Barry and Enright had to pay for prize moneys expended beyond the budgeted amount.

On the other hand, Kletter admitted, he had approved Enright's request for advances to both Stempel and Van Doren, and he defended the action. He was told Van Doren wanted the money to buy a car, and he was sure Van Doren would have returned the money if it had come to that. Again, Pharmaceuticals had risked nothing. Besides, there was "nothing unkosher" about an advance; his own company occasionally gave advances to employees. But Stempel and Van Doren were not his employees, we pointed out, asking if the advances were not in fact loans made without collateral. Again Kletter shrugged; his concern had been that Barry and Enright stay within budget, which they had.

But in retrospect, Kletter conceded, the fact of advances might have indicated that some kind of controls were in effect, though it never occurred to him. That Enright was able to keep within the budget was not cause for suspicion; to the contrary, it meant that Enright knew his business. As it turned out, when accounts were settled, with the sale of the shows to NBC, Barry and Enright refunded $3,000, the difference between what Pharmaceuticals had paid for prizes and what Barry and Enright had actually disbursed since the beginning of the show; by contrast, in the fall 1958 season, with rigging suspended because of the scandal, "Twenty-One" hemorrhaged, disbursing $60,000 more in prize money than budgeted in less than two months up to its cancelation. This was NBC's problem, not Pharmaceuticals'.

As for creative control, Kletter claimed that, like everyone in the business, he paid attention to ratings but, unlike the Revsons, he did not attach great importance to weekly ups and downs. It was the overall performance that counted. In addition to "Twenty-One," the company sponsored in prime time "To Tell the Truth," a celebrity panel guessing-game show, and two musical variety shows. He would not affirm that "Twenty-One" had done more for his product, Geritol, than these. Nevertheless, Van Doren made "Twenty-One" an unexpected sensation, prompting CBS to approach Pharmaceuticals with the idea of moving the show, which prompted NBC's preemptive move to buy the property from Barry and Enright. As a result, Pharmaceuticals received $750,000 from the network, representing the value of the discounts on airtime CBS had offered Pharmaceuticals to bring "Twenty-One" over. Otherwise, the involvement of Pharmaceuticals was unchanged, except that it was no longer dealing with an independent packager. Now Pharmaceuticals was paying the network its $25,000 a week for production and prize money, as well as the weekly broadcasting charge now averaging over $50,000 a week, which had more than doubled when the show was moved to the earlier-evening Monday slot, with a larger hookup of affiliate stations, hence more viewers, than the late-evening Thursday slot where it debuted.

At this rate, Pharmaceuticals was paying some $3.5 million a year simply to sponsor one television show. In 1956, when Pharmaceuticals sponsored "Twenty-One" for only three months, the company sold some $10,782,000 worth of Geritol, the main product advertised by the company on its shows. This mixture of vitamins, minerals, and alcohol, promoted as a cure for "tired blood," retailed at $2.95 for a twelve-ounce bottle, as compared to an identical formula sold under different brand names by discount vitamin packagers at $1.39 for the same quantity.[2] In 1957, when the company sponsored "Twenty-One" for an entire year, sales of Geritol totaled some $13,975,000, with most of the increase registering in the first six months of the year, when the popularity of "Twenty-One" was at its peak. For the year 1958, when the quiz scandal hit and "Twenty-One" disappeared, Geritol sales slipped to $12,379,000. With total annual company sales of some $25,000,000 for all its products, Pharmaceuticals had done very well with Geritol.

In a business where up to 40 percent of a manufacturer's revenues was routinely spent on advertising and promotion, Pharmaceuticals had little to complain about regarding "Twenty-One" until the scandal hit and the ratings tumbled. For November 1958, the month after its cancelation, Geritol sales fell to a mere $609,000, the lowest monthly figure since 1955.[3] Kletter would not acknowledge a direct link, though he did concede "a temporary end" to Geritol's previously healthy sales growth. Even if, strictly speaking, these figures were not the grand jury's concern, they provided an idea of the stakes on the table in March 1957, when Stempel walked into Enright's office and threatened to blow the whistle on "Twenty-One."

Negotiations for the sale of the Barry and Enright quizzes began in earnest in February 1957 with a meeting that included Thomas Ervin, the NBC general counsel; Robert Kintner, then NBC's executive vice-president; and Robert Sarnoff, NBC's president; and on the other side were Barry and Enright's agents David "Sonny" Werblin and Herbert Rosen. Handling the details for NBC thereafter was James Denning, a lawyer and NBC vice-president for talent and program administration, whose job was negotiating the finer points of NBC acquisitions and supervising the writing of final contracts. In his grand jury testimony, Denning stressed the informality of the three-way NBC–Barry and Enright–Pharmaceuticals deal, despite numerous meetings and the complexity of contracts signed, approaching one hundred pages each in length. This, Denning said, reflected the nature of the broadcasting business, where programs were put on the air on a trial basis under oral agreements before anything was put into writing. Thus it was that the NBC–Barry and Enright agreement was effective March 18, 1957, coinciding with the end of the first phase of the original Pharmaceuticals–Barry and Enright contract, though not "consummated" until May 2. Likewise, the new contract between Pharmaceuticals and NBC for sponsorship of "Twenty-One" was not dated until June 21, 1957, though in effect from March 18. Again, the smooth running of the business was based on, in Denning's words, "reliance on the integrity and record of the people involved."

The May 2, 1957, employment contract between NBC and Jack Barry and Daniel Enright ran to one hundred pages and designated the two partners as the "artist." A "public morals clause" specified various kinds of private or professional conduct that were grounds for termination by the employer; these included: "If Artist (despite Artist's legal right to do so) refuses to testify before any Court, Congressional or other legislative committee, administrative board or any other duly constituted federal, state or municipal authority that may be investigating possibly subversive activities or activities possibly contrary to the best interests of the United States of America...." But there was no assurance by Barry and Enright that their quizzes were honest contests. Though this was now considered an oversight by witnesses like Kletter and Denning, before the scandal no one had ever thought of bringing up the issue.

THIS TRUSTING ATTITUDE dovetailed neatly with the attitudes expressed by sponsors, advertising men, and network people involved with figures like Salter and Cowan and his successors, and which Frank Cooper had tried appealing to in his last stand on behalf of "Dotto." At the beginning of the scandal, Kletter said, he asked Barry and Enright point-blank, "Is there anything to this thing?" "Absolutely not," was the answer he received. Having dealt with these "two fine gentlemen," Kletter accepted their characterization of Stempel's mental condition and sought no independent confirmation. Not surprisingly, the earlier attempts by Stempel to publicize his story, known to NBC officials as early as September 1957, were not shared with Kletter by Barry and Enright or by NBC. Not until Snodgrass's letters had been publicized did Kletter's trust begin to erode. Even now Kletter refused to entertain the possibility he had been defrauded. Had he known of any rigging, he would have canceled the show, he said, not because he was defrauded but because he would have lost faith in its "integrity." It would have been a fraud for Pharmaceuticals knowingly to accept "consideration" from NBC for a rigged show, but had there been such knowledge, there wouldn't have been a sale, because there would have been no show.

WITH THE APPEARANCES of Koplin and Shirley Bernstein on January 29, 1959, the presentation of witnesses before the grand jury slowed to a trickle. The jurors were deeply concerned by the breadth and scope of the deceptions practiced by the quiz producers and the complacency, if not compliance, of the sponsors and broadcasters. Particularly rankling were the concluding remarks of Koplin, following upon Bernstein's self-righteous defense of the use of children as contestants. Asked if he thought the public would have watched if it had known the contestants were being helped, Koplin said he could not answer, but he was certain that his shows had entertained, stimulated, and challenged the public while avoiding violence and bloodshed. He cited the letters of praise and appreciation EPI had received from educational institutions whose enrollments had increased and teachers whose students were working harder, in direct response to the shows. "Deceitful?" he asked back. "Not at all. This was great entertainment for all."

In a final statement, Koplin defended the use on "The $64,000 Question" of "legitimate, real people." The show was unique in the way it provided entertainment—its primary function—to more people than any other program had done, he claimed. But more than any of the other jurors, Louis Hacker, a lifelong educator, was appalled, considering the attitude of Koplin a corruption of educational values. If Cowan and his successors had considered the $64,000 shows a "crusade," Hacker was embarking on a crusade of his own, to use the grand jury's presentment power to expose the quizzes as a hoax, even if their operation had not violated the law.

Hacker was eager to subpoena Cowan as well as William Paley and Frank Stanton, the chairman and president, respectively, of CBS, and Robert Sarnoff and Robert Kintner, the top men at NBC. I strongly disagreed. We had no evidence that Cowan was personally involved in rigging the "Question" and "Challenge"; even if there was something phoney about Cowan's public stance over the years about what he tried to accomplish with his shows, there was nothing remotely illegal about it. I imagined he and the other broadcasting chiefs would simply present a combination of denial, hand wringing, and high-mindedness, which would be a waste of time to all concerned. Not that we didn't make an effort to reach Cowan as well as the Revson brothers for interviews to see what matters of substance they could contribute, but they managed to be out of town or otherwise unavailable. Fatigue on the part of the jurors was a factor as well, and when he brought it up with his fellow jurors, Hacker could not martial enough votes to overcome my objections to issuing subpoenas for the bigshots.

On January 29, the jurors decided to suspend hearing testimony while a committee of seven volunteers under Hacker and the assistant foreman, Richard Mangano, began drafting the presentment, a move that appeased everybody. The majority could now resume their normal lives, remaining on call to convene when necessary, while Hacker and other zealots transferred their outrage to paper. Meanwhile, since the extension of the grand jury's life, granted back in October, would expire with the month of January, I went to see Judge Schweitzer in his chambers.

Like Hogan, Schweitzer was a native of Connecticut, a graduate of Columbia College and Columbia Law School. There the resemblance ended. Unlike the shy and aloof Hogan, who had built his reputation on a meticulous adherence to the rules, the mercurial Schweitzer was a master of cutting corners and making deals. Active in the Democratic party, Schweitzer was elected in 1944 as a municipal court judge and served two terms before being elected to the Court of General Sessions in 1954 for a term of fourteen years. Here his talents for expediting things had made him one of Hogan's favorite judges. When I told the judge I was requesting another extension for the quiz jury, I explained there were few witnesses left to be called, but the jurors needed time to prepare a presentment concerning what they had heard. Even though we had come up with nothing as a basis for indictments, the jurors had labored hard to get to the bottom of a very rotten business, something that at least one man, Freedman, had committed perjury to cover up, and, I assured Schweitzer, Freedman wasn't the only one to do so.

Making no comment on the presentment, Schweitzer asked if we planned to proceed against other perjurers. I replied that we preferred to have them tell the truth, under oath, which the grand jury could help accomplish if it were kept alive. If we simply folded up the investigation, the quiz people as well as the public would think we hadn't been serious. We had the goods on another producer (Felsher) and could indict him for perjury whenever we wished; but if we kept the pressure of an investigation up, he would try to recant, and then Freedman himself would probably come around. The people who lied had been scared into it and bought the bad advice that they could get away with it. If they saw they couldn't, my hunch was they would be so frightened by the possibility of open trials that they would sing like birds. Schweitzer did not seem impressed by my arguments, but he granted one month's extension.

CHAPTER ELEVEN

Recantations

(FEBRUARY–JUNE 1959)

The constitution and the Code of Criminal Procedure of the State of New York gave grand juries the explicit power, besides indicting for crimes, to investigate three other areas: the detention of prisoners held in county jails, the management of penal institutions, and the misconduct of public officials. In addition to the powers granted by statute, the grand jury had the power to "present" or report its findings and recommendations to the court on matters of public concern in circumstances where there was insufficient evidence to indict individuals. The power of presentment, even in the absence of indictable crimes, had its roots in English common law and was part of the law of New York before the adoption of a state constitution in 1777.

Before the year 1869, the records were sketchy, but from that year till 1959, according to the records of New York's Court of General Sessions, nearly five hundred grand jury presentments were filed and made public, including twenty during the terms of District Attorneys Dewey and Hogan. Although the majority of these concerned public agencies or officials, a large number dealt with conditions in nonofficial fields that smacked of fraud, racketeering, and crime, covering such diverse matters as professional boxing, automobile thefts, accident claims, courthouse construction, bucket shops, securities advertising, public auctions, ice dealers, pushcarts, the disappearance of the legendary Judge Crater, various forms of gambling, dancing in hotels and restaurants, carbon monoxide deaths, tax lien sales, grounds in divorce actions, even the black market sale of Salk polio vaccine. These presentments served to bring to public attention conditions warranting action by appropriate authorities or remedial legislation.

Louis Hacker, an experienced writer with an instinct for the jugular, honed by his experience of various academic wars and controversies, and I began work on separate rough drafts of a presentment of the quiz grand jury's findings. We did not publicize the effort, but the word soon spread, giving rise to rumors that the jurors and I were out for blood. Hyman Zoloto, latest in the succession of lawyers retained by Enright, called for an appointment. He was not a former assistant district attorney, but at forty-five, polished and manicured, he was a high-powered and well-connected criminal lawyer. As he had on occasion over the years, he went through the ritual of inviting me to leave the district attorney's office for an opulent career in private practice with him. Then he got down to business, accusing me of using the presentment to drag his client through the mud because he had broken no law and could not be indicted. I could not comment on the presentment directly, but I pointed out hypothetically that a presentment did not preclude additional indictments and added that Freedman was not the only one to have lied to the grand jury. This veiled reference to Felsher was not designed to go over Zoloto's head.

Soon after this, Samuel Cantor called to pick a bone on behalf of his client, Harry Salter, saying "Name That Tune" could be destroyed if a grand jury report named the program. Since "Name That Tune" was a harmless venture devoid of chicanery and Salter had cooperated fully with us and been courageous enough to tell the public precisely how his show worked, Cantor maintained, it would not be fair or serve the public interest for the show to be ruined by the action of the grand jury. I told Cantor that I could not dictate what went into a report except as the law required, but I recommended that he set out his grievance in a formal request to Hogan. If it was not prejudicial to the investigation, then some kind of representation on behalf of "Name That Tune" could be made directly to the jurors.

AT THE END of February I requested a second extension of the grand jury's term, telling Schweitzer we had additional testimony to hear (notably that of the $64,000 shows' executive producer, Steve Carlin, who had agreed to testify under a waiver of immunity). Schweitzer now expressed doubts about the advisability of a presentment, echoing the complaints of Zoloto and Cantor that a presentment could smear people against whom indictments could not be brought. When I assured him no names would be used, he grudgingly granted another month's extension.

Before long, two former daytime "Tic Tac Dough" contestants came in to tell us of receiving assistance on the program, one a lawyer who now wanted to amend his previous grand jury testimony, made in November 1958, when he denied assistance. Both now admitted to contacts with Felsher after the investigation began and consulting, at Felsher's behest, with the lawyer, Sol

Gelb, who advised them in essence that there was no case against Felsher, therefore it did not matter what they told us about "Tic Tac Dough," the implication being that it would not matter if they lied to us. We were happy to give both of them subpoenas for new grand jury appearances, hoping they would inform Felsher and thus add to the pressure on him. In the second week of March, Zoloto called to say he had a present for me—Howard Felsher. We set up an appointment, and on March 16 Felsher came in accompanied by both Zoloto and Gelb.

Technically, it was too late for Felsher to recant and wipe out the perjury of his previous testimony. According to New York law, a recantation was acceptable only "if and when it is done promptly before the body conducting the inquiry has been deceived or misled to the harm and prejudice of its investigation, and *when no likelihood exists that the witness has learned that his perjury is known or may become known* to the authorities."[1] It had to take place in good faith, not when the testifier had reasonable grounds for knowing that the jury had evidence he was lying. Not only did we have legal evidence that he had perjured himself the first time, but Felsher admitted to us right off that he knew Dowd, Falke, and the two former contestants we had most recently heard had testified against him. Thus he could only "correct" his previous testimony in the hope that the jury and D.A. would take this into account in considering the disposition of his case. But for all practical purposes, there was now an understanding between us and Felsher and his lawyers that we would exercise prosecutorial discretion and let him off the hook in return for the truth. For us it was a good deal: in long sessions we had with Felsher over the next three weeks we extracted a complete account of the rigging of "Tic Tac Dough." It would be only a matter of time before Freedman approached us for similar relief in return for the truth about "Twenty-One."

As Felsher now told us, in November 1956, when he took over "Tic Tac Dough" from Freedman, his main task was to make the show entertaining. He was bothered that many attractive contestants were losing, not because they didn't know the answers to the fairly easy questions, but because they were playing badly. Once on the air, many people forgot the basic tactics of blocking opponents and blurted out answers instead of pausing to think as advised. If the contestants knew the answers in advance, Felsher reasoned, they could relax and pay attention to what they were doing. After he met at a party a knowledgeable physician named Michael Truppin, who expressed interest in "Tic Tac Dough," Felsher told Enright he had a good prospect, but since he wasn't sure how long Truppin could last on his own, he wanted to give him questions and answers. According to Felsher, Enright consented so long as Truppin could be trusted to keep quiet. Though he had never discussed this sort of thing with Enright before, Felsher claimed he was not surprised to be given the green light; there had been a great deal of skepticism in the television business about the ability of contestants on "The $64,000 Question" to answer the complex questions being used, and it was "a common understanding" that these contestants were being fed answers.

Starting with Truppin, and over the next two months, Felsher provided questions and answers to twelve contestants, covering nearly every broadcast of "Tic Tac Dough" in the period and clearing each with Enright in advance. With handpicked champions on the show for three or four broadcasts each, winning in the range of $500 to $1,000 a day, Felsher kept easily within the prize money budget of $6,500 a week. By the time Frances Li was a contestant at the end of January 1957, "Tic Tac Dough" had passed an important hurdle and was strong enough in the ratings, after six months on the air, for its sponsors to renew their commitment, and plans were made for a weekly prime-time version beginning in the fall. Felsher had helped make "Tic Tac Dough" an attractive part of the package being sold to NBC by Barry and Enright along with "Twenty-One."

After Li, "Tic Tac Dough" was allowed to coast without the constant assisting of contestants. Up to the debut of nighttime "Tic Tac Dough" on September 12, 1957, Felsher claimed, he gave assistance only to three more people, when he felt the ratings needed a nudge, and always with the approval of Enright. One of the three was the lawyer who had recently recanted his previous grand jury testimony. Handing over the daytime show to his associate, Stanley Green, Felsher devoted his energies to the nighttime show, which occupied the Thursday 7:30 P.M. slot on NBC. For the first two broadcasts, no one was assisted, with dismal results; contestants beat one another in quick succession without ties to build excitement. Enright quickly approved of Felsher's assisting a contestant, who accepted help for two weeks, then refused it in the third week and retired with $16,000. Starting with the broadcast of October 17, Felsher established a daytime alumnus, then challenged him with another daytime alumnus; both had been rigged in their daytime stints. Controlling both contestants enabled Felsher to have as many tie games as he wanted; after a few weeks, they were succeeded by Timothy Horan, another rigged daytime alumnus, who, with Felsher's assistance, was nighttime champion for nearly two months. Horan had denied to the grand jury that he received assistance.

In the middle of November 1957, Green reported that daytime "Tic Tac

Dough" was in trouble—way over budget—two-thirds of the way through a thirteen-week cycle. Green suggested bringing in a friend and giving him the questions and answers. Enright turned down the idea, instructing Green simply to slow down the game. This was tried for several days, as Felsher watched from the control room. More time was devoted to chatter, and Barry slowed the pace in asking questions. When this had no effect, Felsher asked Enright for approval to put in a controlled contestant, which Enright gave on the condition that Green be kept out of it, because they knew he was looking for another job (he would join the new "Dotto" at the beginning of 1958). This was when Felsher turned to Dowd for the first time; after Dowd, Felsher brought in another friend who left the show after three days with a mere $500, which represented a significant easing on the budget.

Meanwhile on the nighttime show, Horan had met a new challenger, Captain Michael O'Rourke. Felsher explained to O'Rourke that the public was tiring of Horan, hence the show's ratings were slipping and someone was needed to help boost the ratings long enough for the show to be renewed after six months. Since he was the kind of contestant the public would take to its heart, Felsher told O'Rourke, they wanted to ensure his being able to last on the program by giving him the questions and answers. According to Felsher, O'Rourke blanched and asked for time to think it over, but an hour or so later, he returned to Felsher and said he would do it. After O'Rourke defeated Horan on January 9, 1958, everybody was happy: Horan left with $30,500, the public responded with enthusiasm to the brilliant, earnest Korean War veteran, and the show's ratings rose. Felsher brought in Virginia Nance, whom he had assisted on the daytime show, to challenge O'Rourke, and the two played a series of fourteen ties lasting till the middle of February, when Nance lost and departed, apparently happy with a consolation prize totaling $4,200.

The only person not happy was O'Rourke's commanding officer, so Felsher had to plan for the captain's retreat, which led the producer back to Dowd. While Dowd held the fort on the nighttime show, Felsher turned his attention to a new assault on the daytime budget, caused by another military man, Lieutenant Philip Petty, a dull contestant who was winning without assistance. After using a friend to knock out Petty, Felsher found another military man willing to accept assistance, Navy Captain Charles Gilliam. Gilliam was the daytime champion for three weeks in April 1958, before going down to prearranged defeat and leaving with winnings of $16,800. The battle of the daytime budget had been won.

By the end of April, Dowd's posted nighttime winnings had risen above

$40,000, and the contestant let it be known he wanted to take home more than the $10,000 Felsher had promised. Felsher's problem was that the promised amount was all the budget could manage. He turned again to Truppin and prepared him to challenge Dowd, hoping Dowd wouldn't go off the deep end in the meantime. Truppin started on the nighttime show on May 1; he and Dowd played ties until May 22, when Dowd double-crossed Felsher, threw the match, and left the show with winnings almost twice what Felsher planned to let him have. Truppin then played a long series of ties against Patricia Sullivan, also assisted by Felsher. As choreographed by Felsher, Truppin lost to Sullivan on June 19, leaving the show with $12,700 after eight appearances. Sullivan reigned as champion into July, when she met another daytime alumnus, Captain Gilliam, again controlled by Felsher. Sullivan and Gilliam played a series of ties until August 21, when Sullivan lost and took only $14,300 after two and a half months of appearances.

By this point, the quiz scandal had erupted and Hilgemeier's revelations were followed by Stempel's allegations against Enright. Felsher and Enright agreed to stop giving assistance, and Gilliam was so informed; after two more broadcasts, on September 25, an unassisted Gilliam was simply beaten by another unassisted contestant. Since this occurred abruptly, Gilliam's posted winnings were not trimmed back; he left the show with $58,300 after nine appearances, three times more than Sullivan had won for twelve appearances, and four and a half times more than Truppin for eight appearances. This budget-busting continued, as Enright was removed as executive producer in the wake of Snodgrass's revelations. Felsher continued to produce both "Tic Tac Dough"'s, under the direct supervision of NBC executives, but all controls were dropped. When it was canceled in late fall 1958, the nighttime show, which in the period of controls never had more than $3,000 in deficit in a cycle, was tens of thousands of dollars in the red.

AFTER our last office session with Felsher on March 25, 1959, I went to Schweitzer for a third extension of the grand jury, reporting that an important witness had buckled and was providing a complete behind-the-scenes account of rigging, meaning significant new material for the presentment. Schweitzer granted the extension, but his grumbling about the presentment escalated to threats to block it. Even if names were not used, he pointed out, the knowledge was widespread of which programs were under scrutiny and who worked for them. I assured the judge that every precaution would be taken to make sure nothing improper was in the report. He turned down my offer to show it to him in advance.

Schweitzer's objections to a document he had not seen were disturbing. Not that he had problems with presentments per se, for as recently as March 11 he had accepted and released to the public a report from another grand jury, dealing with the failure of the police to crack down on the numbers racket flourishing in Harlem. Harry Salter's lawyer had written a long letter to Hogan on behalf of "Name That Tune," expressing concern about the presentment, and I wondered if there was similar importuning, behind the scenes, to Schweitzer himself. As if on cue, Zoloto called and claimed that he knew all about Schweitzer's objections to the presentment. He proposed that his partner, Arthur Karger, "assist" us in writing the report so that it would pass Schweitzer's approval and make everybody concerned—his client, the judge, the grand jury, and the district attorney's office—happy. It was vintage Zoloto and totally outrageous.

ON APRIL 2, a quorum of grand jurors gathered for the first time in two weeks. Before presenting Felsher, I recited the law in regard to correcting testimony and advised the jurors that Felsher's appearance would not expunge the fact he had previously lied; in addition to perjury, he could be liable to prosecution for suborning perjury by others and for conspiring to do so. But his cooperation now would be taken into consideration in the ultimate disposition of his case. Called in and put under oath, Felsher stated that he understood the circumstances under which he was being permitted to appear and admitted that his previous testimony about giving assistance to contestants was "not truthful at all." He had lied for two reasons—to keep "Tic Tac Dough" on the air and to form a united front with the others he had encouraged to lie after promising he would tell the district attorney that he had never given help of any kind. He had assumed also that some contestants could be hurt professionally if they admitted cheating on a quiz.

The jurors listened attentively as Felsher repeated what he had covered in the office, in the same detail. At the end, he averred there had never been any money kickbacks to him by contestants. Aside from being taken out to dinner once or twice, there was the single instance of a contestant, whom he had not assisted, who worked for a men's clothing manufacturer and was allowed to plug his employer on the air. For this, Felsher received the gift of a sport jacket.

Not only did Felsher's testimony reinforce what the jurors had already learned from "Dotto"—that quiz rigging was frequent, routine, even necessary—it introduced a new element, the extent of the compliance of the contestants in rigging and their willingness to break the law in consequence, by lying under oath. According to Felsher, not one of the people to whom he proposed assistance turned him down. Out of twenty-six contestants named by Felsher as receiving assistance, fifteen had testified. Of these, eleven—more than two-thirds—had denied receiving assistance. Two had returned in good faith to amend their testimony. That left only four out of fifteen who had testified truthfully to start with. The jurors had every reason to believe the ratio was similar for the twenty former contestants who had testified in connection with "Twenty-One."

When I reported these developments to Hogan, he was in his seventeenth year as Manhattan district attorney, the longest anyone had ever held the post, and arguably the most experienced, certainly the most respected, prosecutor in the United States. He had never heard of any investigation in which so many people who were not actually targeted as criminals had lied before a grand jury. He expressed his support for the presentment despite Schweitzer's threats, but I detected anxiety in Hogan at the implications of the situation for Van Doren and, by extension, the reputation of Columbia University, where Van Doren continued to teach.

OUR HARD WORK was not the sole cause for Felsher's knuckling under. Rather, a new scenario was being played out by Enright and his lawyers, with the aim of cutting their losses, averting an indictment of Felsher, who continued to produce daytime "Tic Tac Dough" for NBC, and to save "Concentration," the other Barry and Enright creation still on the air. It was in line with this new scenario that, a few days after Felsher's testimony, Gelb came in to announce he had been retained by Freedman, who wished to go before the grand jury and recant. Gelb knew that a recantation could not of itself wipe out Freedman's perjury indictment and the jurors had to agree to hear him again, but he also knew we would gobble up the opportunity. He was right, and the jurors needed no arm-twisting. Real testimony from the producer of the most elaborately rigged of the quizzes would round out the presentment and be the culmination of eight months of work.

On April 24, Donnelly and I received Freedman and Gelb in my office, the first of a number of meetings over the following two weeks. After he listened to a summary of the legal issues concerning his reappearance, Freedman launched into a bitter tirade against the manner of his arraignment, being handcuffed and hauled into a police station for booking as flashbulbs popped. After I apologized for a police department procedure I hadn't known about, I went down a chronological list of the contestants and their appearances on "Twenty-One." Freedman admitted to giving assistance to all the major winners after Stempel: Van Doren, Bloomgarden, Snodgrass, Craig, Mayer, and Von Nardroff. He denied assisting Nearing and Leicester. But he admitted assisting some twenty small-time players who reigned briefly as champions or were defeated as challengers. Three of these had appeared before the grand jury and denied receiving assistance: Ruth Miller, an opponent of Van Doren; Richard Klein, an opponent of Craig; and Paul Bain, a small winner after Mayer late in 1957.

As he told it, Freedman's career in quiz rigging began during the half-year he worked as a writer on EPI's "The Big Surprise." On occasion, he was asked by Merton Koplin to visit contestants before airtime in their dressing rooms to warm them up with drill questions; he told them the answers they didn't know but didn't tell them that some of the questions would be used on the broadcast. As producer of daytime "Tic Tac Dough" when it debuted, he selected contestants and decided which ones to "help" or not, subject to the approval of Enright in each case. Among those he assisted in this period were a sixteen-year-old boy and an elderly former foreign correspondent for the *New York Times*, who had a bad memory. The man was ill and needed an operation; with Freedman's help, he won $8,000, a large amount for the show at the time.

Taking over "Twenty-One" in November 1956 was an opportunity for Freedman to make his mark in the television business. The short-term aim was to increase the ratings enough to move the show from the late-night slot to one earlier in the evening when more stations would carry it and more people could watch it. In his view, the immediate problem was Stempel, not the ideal contestant. He assumed Enright was giving Stempel assistance but was never told anything about it. Freedman bided his time, learning the ropes by working with Stempel's challengers. One of these, Rose Leibbrand, was interested in publicity for her employer and seemed willing to lend herself to manipulation in order to obtain it. This was an important lesson, and Freedman, we now learned, would use the lure of something beyond mere cash more than once to seduce contestants. After a chance meeting with Van Doren, the producer thought the Columbia English instructor was ideal for replacing Stempel. When Freedman shared his opinion with Enright, he was given the go-ahead, on the understanding that Van Doren was an exceptional prospect; it would be a waste to have him simply appear on the show and go down to defeat at the hands of Stempel.

Freedman called Van Doren to his office and asked what he would do if he won several thousand dollars. Van Doren replied he wanted to write a book and do more research for his doctorate. Freedman then confided that they wanted Van Doren's help in removing Stempel; if Van Doren would accept assistance, he could win. Van Doren replied that he wanted to go on without assistance but agreed to think it over. At another meeting several days later, Freedman wheeled out the higher lure: by going on "Twenty-One," Van Doren could take the spotlight off crime and violence on television; he would show people that teachers were "regular guys"; he would be entertaining the public while helping himself and his profession. According to Freedman, Van Doren thought it over a few minutes, then said he would try it for a couple of weeks.

At their next meeting, after coordinating with Enright, Freedman asked Van Doren how many points he would request in various categories of knowledge. With this information in hand, Freedman had questions written to match the point selections. Freedman then tried these out on Van Doren, but did not provide the correct answers to those Van Doren missed, because the contestant wanted to look them up himself. After standing by several times, Van Doren went on against Stempel, and everything went according to plan.

After ousting Stempel, Van Doren told Freedman he needed the $20,000 he had won, but agreed to take an advance of $5,000 and continue. From this point on, Van Doren was told how many points to select in a category, though he continued to look up for himself the answers he missed in the first re-hearsal sessions. Over the next two months, despite the cajolery of increasing guarantees of winnings, Van Doren begged to be released. Freedman and Enright finally relented and arranged a series of ties with Nearing, so that Van Doren's exit could be accomplished dramatically.

Freedman claimed that Nearing did not need direct help. He merely questioned her on a number of subjects, then wrote questions he knew she could answer. She wanted to quit immediately after beating Van Doren and take her $14,000 in winnings, but Freedman prevailed on her to continue, guaranteeing her $10,000. Her cool and aloof manner depressed the ratings, however, and Freedman lined up an old acquaintance, Bloomgarden, to replace her. Bloomgarden was the first former "Tic Tac Dough" contestant to be recruited to "Twenty-One," but was not assisted on the former show.

Aware of Bloomgarden's efforts to gain a public relations foothold in medical research, Freedman snared him with the higher lure. As a contestant Van Doren had done a great deal for the teaching profession, Freedman told Bloomgarden; now he could do the same thing to get his message across about medical research. This had the desired effect. With Bloomgarden, Freedman dropped the charade of having the contestant look up answers, and adopted the routine described to us by Stempel, Snodgrass, and Craig, telling the contestant everything, rehearsing every utterance and gesture.

Freedman corroborated Snodgrass's account point for point, including his own subsequent meetings with the artist and attempts to appease him. In addition, Freedman revealed, after the flap over the answers "coccyx" and "sacral" on the May 20, 1957, broadcast, Bloomgarden could very well have sued NBC for the $126,000 he chalked up on the air that evening, instead of agreeing to a rematch. But Bloomgarden cooperated because he wanted to work in TV to further his career. By early June 1957, Bloomgarden had been on long enough and was replaced by Craig, whose account Freedman also corroborated.

In the middle of October 1957, Craig was replaced, after a series of rigged ties, by David Mayer. Since Mayer had invested in a firm connected with advertising and was heavily in debt, no higher lure was needed; he took assistance until the end of November, when he retired. A small winner, Paul Bain, followed and also accepted assistance. From November 20, 1957, to January 6, 1958, Dr. Richard Wall, a chemist and professor at Fordham University, was champion, but, according to Freedman, without assistance. Freedman claimed they let the show go on its own while they looked for a new prospect. Deciding, for the first time since Nearing, to have a woman as champion, they turned to Von Nardroff.

Von Nardroff had passed the tests for "Twenty-One" as early as spring 1957 and had been a longtime standby. When he proposed to her the usual arrangement, she was at first reluctant, but then agreed and reigned as champion until July 8, 1958, receiving assistance all along, which Freedman rendered not only in his office but in her Brooklyn apartment and in a Manhattan hotel room when she sublet her apartment and moved to Long Island for the summer. By the time she retired, "Twenty-One" was far down in the ratings; the last big-winning contestant, Elizabeth Anderson, on the show for seven weeks—after the scandal broke and the investigation began—was given no assistance, according to Freedman, and she left the program with $66,000.

Freedman could not recall any prospective contestant who flatly turned down assistance; he offered it to relatively few people and these had been "extremely screened," in his words. Testing determined intelligence and knowledgeability and satisfied a major criterion—that the contestants' ability to answer many difficult questions be plausible, not only to viewers but also to the contestants' own families, friends, and acquaintances. The screening proper, or interviewing, of candidates by him and then by Enright, usually with the help of Noah, functioned to evaluate prospects in terms of other requirements—that they come across as attractive on television and their specific need of money be for crucial yet worthy ends. Just as important was the hard-learned lesson of Stempel—that contestants should have a professional or social standing that gave them a stake in keeping their mouths shut, as well as the psychological capacity to do so.

As for why he had committed perjury, Freedman said that the first time he appeared in the office, he believed if he told the truth, it would have leaked out and the publicity would have ruined the contestants. He had given them his word of honor that what they did would never be revealed, and they had made the same promise to him. These were good citizens, he claimed, who would have been devastated if it became public that they had been assisted on the program. But, he asserted, he never asked them to keep quiet; they asked him. After his first appearance before the grand jury, he met with Van Doren, who said the impact of exposure would be disastrous—it would destroy his family, might even kill his father. Now it was with anguish that Freedman said he had told none of the contestants of his intention to recant. He lied the first time, he said, because he had not understood the secrecy of grand jury proceedings and feared leaks that would jeopardize the show and his career. Now by telling the truth, he hoped the indictment would be dismissed and he might again be employed in broadcasting. Freedman acknowledged that Enright was providing him with financial help and knew he was now cooperating with us. He insisted that his perjury was the result of his own initiative, not at the behest of Enright.

Aside from the substance of Freedman's revelations, I welcomed the fact that he was not holding out and forcing us to take him to trial. Our case would have been less than ideal, even with the testimony of three witnesses against him. Leibbrand had little to say; Snodgrass's motives were murky; and our best witness, Craig, might have balked at taking the stand and exposing himself to the public. On the other hand, Freedman's confession, like Felsher's, underscored the fact that dozens if not scores of people had committed perjury. To prosecute them as they deserved would be a nightmare and probably impossible—since in each case there would be only one witness,

Felsher or Freedman, and our formula for indicting Freedman could not work in reverse. Enright's techniques in isolating the contestants had made sure of that.

AT THE END of April, when Schweitzer granted another month's extension, he called the committee of the eight jurors in charge of writing the presentment to his chambers. He had come to the conclusion, he announced, that the presentment would not be legal, therefore he could not accept it for filing and publication. When Hacker assured him that the report would not name individuals, television programs, or corporations, Schweitzer countered that the law limited reports to conditions in prisons and the conduct of public officials and agencies, citing as a proper example the report concerning the police department he had approved earlier in the year. I had heard all this before, but it was the first formal expression of Schweitzer's attitude to the jurors, who were furious at the prospect of having the fruit of their long labor plucked from them. They saw no good reason for this judge, better known as a mechanic who kept the wheels of justice moving than as a guardian of the rights of citizens, to be suddenly climbing on a high horse.

On May 11, 1959, the full grand jury convened to hear Freedman under oath, the last witness it would hear. Using our charts of the various contestants and game results, revised with Freedman's help, Donnelly and I took Freedman through his recital. A sticking point for the jurors was the assertion that he had not directly helped Nearing. Freedman denied he was protecting her because she was a lawyer and a perjury conviction could mean her disbarment. When asked if somebody else could have helped her, he replied he had no way of knowing. He toadied a bit by praising the salutary effect of the investigation in ridding the airways of rigged quizzes. Still, he recommended, prize money in the future should be kept low, and he followed this with a suggestion for the creation of a kind of Hays Office for quiz shows—a central agency to prepare and guard all the questions used on all broadcast quizzes.

Hacker and the jury committee, armed with Freedman's corrected testimony, embarked on the final rewriting of the presentment, which in the last week of May was ready for the full jury to hear and approve. Running to some twelve thousand words, the report had four parts. The first was a brief history of the life of the grand jury and a statement that the jury, despite the absence of violations of the New York Penal Law, was obliged to report to the citizens of the state that in their midst the jury had discovered a situation of grave concern involving harmful and corrupt influences.

Part 2 contained the main substance of the report. Without naming names, it spelled out the specifics employed by packagers and producers to deceive the public as well as quiz show contestants who were not involved in rigging. The different types of contestants, from "experts" to patsies and children, were described as well as the criteria for their selection and manipulation—in terms of paradox, plausibility, and personal appeal. The various methods of assisting contestants—the "direct," "playback," "test and retest"—were set out, along with the other controls, such as the "killer" question and suspenseful ties. Also described were budgetary control and "creative" control by sponsors, that is, the use of guarantees to some contestants and the payment of advances to others, as well as the fakery of "safeguarding" the questions and answers.

Parts 3 and 4 vented the outrage of Hacker and the jurors, skewering the rationalizations of the producers that the shows were harmless ventures in mass entertainment on the one hand and had promoted the importance of education to the public on the other. Just as the public would not tolerate the fixing of sports events, so it could not condone the rigging of a quiz show. When it believed the shows were genuine, the public was fascinated by them; as soon as the shows were revealed as fake, the public deserted them in droves. The claim of the educational value of the quizzes was dismissed as preposterous. The acquisition of a miscellany of unrelated and frequently unimportant facts had nothing to do with the systematic acquisition of knowledge toward a real understanding of the world. Education consisted in the inculcation of habits of virtue and civic responsibility, whereas the quizzes were profoundly antisocial enterprises based on fraud and deceit, entailing the moral seduction of the contestants who were assisted. Not only had the producers preyed on the very young and naive, blunting their sense of right and wrong and rendering them incapable of proper judgment, they had fostered a situation in which some of their victims had been manipulated and still refused to admit it. The characters of these people had been permanently twisted; thus they would live with a secret lie for the rest of their days.

Pulling together these strands in the final section, the report noted the juridical vacuum in which the quiz producers had operated. The Federal Communications Act of 1934, which provided for the licensing of broadcasting stations, did not extend the statutory obligation of stations to operate in the public interest to networks or programming suppliers, nor did it regulate the content of programming. Not only had no laws of New York State been violated, but it was unlikely the state had any power at all to legislate in this field. Nevertheless, such practices violated social codes and it was up to the broadcasters to regulate themselves; until they took clear action to do so, quiz programs would always be suspect.

INFORMED that the jury had heard its last witnesses and was winding up its work, Schweitzer set the date of June 10 for formally discharging the jury. On June 3 he once more summoned Hacker and the committee of eight for a conference, which I attended along with Richard Denzer, chief of the Appeals Bureau and our resident legal expert. In two hours of acrimony, Schweitzer all but ordered the jury to end its existence without a report, repeating his threats to expunge. Hacker, Denzer, and I doggedly demurred; our research revealed that in the long history of presentments in New York County, only one had been expunged and the action upheld on appeal. In that case, a grand jury used a presentment to censure a prosecutor appearing before it; the appeals court held that the jury had no right to express its displeasure in a public report impugning the conduct and motives of an individual without an opportunity to defend his name and reputation.[2] Denzer and I argued that anyone aggrieved could move to set portions or the whole presentment aside after it had been received, filed, and made public.

Dismissing the jurors, Schweitzer turned his guns on me, and once more we went through the arguments. I said there was nothing unfair about the report, which described conditions and made recommendations for rectifying a situation of crucial public concern, not simply the private affairs of businessmen. Finally Schweitzer asked to see the report. Although it was not yet in its very final form, I was happy to demonstrate to the judge that it was not unfair for any reason and handed him a copy of the draft. Several hours later, it was returned to my office without comment from Schweitzer.

After working hours, two days before the scheduled public presentation of the report, Hogan came to my office unannounced, asked to see the presentment, and read it through. He asked if Hacker and the jurors were satisfied, and I answered yes. He said he expected the newspapers would have questions for him about it; now he would be ready for them. "Good work," he said, then left without another word. I took the unprecedented gesture of Hogan's coming to my office as a symbol of his backing. Sharing Hacker's suspicion that pressure was being brought to bear on Schweitzer from the producers through their lawyers, I was all but certain that the judge would seal the presentment even though, having seen it, he knew it was basically harmless. I was now counting on Hogan's support in a battle royal with Schweitzer.

SCHWEITZER'S courtroom was jammed at 10 A.M. on Wednesday, June 10, when the judge entered and Hacker, Richard Mangano, the assistant grand jury foreman, and I approached the bench. I opened the proceeding by stating that the panel had heard over two-hundred witnesses in fifty-nine sessions of testimony and was ready to submit a report before being discharged. "The community owes the grand jury a vote of gratitude," I said. "It has uprooted a tawdry hoax which was perpetrated on the American public. It is hopeful that its report will have a salutary effect on certain segments of the television industry." Hacker handed up the report to the judge.

Without glancing at the document, Schweitzer said: "The court's right to accept and make public this report has been challenged. Pending determination of the court's power to accept it, it is ordered impounded and sealed." Schweitzer was delivering on his threat, but his announcement of a formal challenge to the presentment was a bombshell. "I can direct that the presentment be filed and have it expunged, or reserve decision," Schweitzer continued, "I certainly don't believe in accepting a document which may be prima facie expungeable. I will give the District Attorney an opportunity to submit any law on my power to accept this report."[3]

Anticipating Schweitzer's action, Hacker had prepared a statement. He noted that neither the judge nor the district attorney had attempted to place limits on the investigation, nor had the judge charged the jury that it could not make a presentment. The jury had carried out its work "having in mind . . . the latitude" provided by "the long and honorable tradition of the grand jury as an important Anglo-Saxon institution." The jury's report was "on a matter that has attracted universal attention" and reflected an important public interest in two ways. First, moral questions, if not legal ones, were involved in the manipulation of quiz programs; second, the quiz shows originated in New York and had a national audience. "With this sense of responsibility, we have worked long, carefully and soberly, and we are hoping therefore that we shall be heard—and that our presentment shall be accepted."[4]

Replying that he did not indicate that the grand jury was not empowered to make a report but was primarily concerned with felonies, such as larceny and extortion, Schweitzer discharged the jurors with the thanks of the court, ending the existence of the Third September 1958 Grand Jury. He then ordered the district attorney to be ready to argue the merits of its position on the presentment before him on June 26.

In the corridor, mobbed by reporters, Hacker called Schweitzer's action all but a betrayal by the judge. "Even though we're discharged," Hacker said, "we cannot discuss the contents because we're still under the jurisdiction of the court . . . . if the judge quashes the report, there is no basis for public action unless the investigation starts all over again."[5]

Asked if he knew who had challenged the presentment, Hacker answered, "The members of the grand jury knew that our business is super-secret—that nobody is supposed to know what a grand jury is going to do. Ask Judge Schweitzer who challenged the presentment and who knew it was to be handed up."[6]

Later in the day, a reporter managed to put Hacker's two questions to Schweitzer, who refused to identify the presentment's challengers; as for who could have known about the presentment in advance, the judge said, "I don't place any significance in that at all. I don't know what Mr. Hacker is talking about."[7]

PART FOUR

National Fraud

CHAPTER TWELVE

Congress in the Act

(JUNE–OCTOBER 1959)

Schweitzer's decision to seal the grand jury presentment catapulted the quiz affair back onto newspaper front pages for the first time in six months. While my colleague, Richard Denzer, and I began work on a memorandum of law on behalf of releasing the presentment, Hacker and other former jurors spoke out to the press, emphasizing that the presentment had been carefully crafted to protect the contestants who testified truthfully. Its impounding by Schweitzer under the guise of protecting the innocent, Hacker predicted, would lead to action by other authorities, with dire results, especially to "the young, naive, and unmatured"; their testimony in public "would ruin them for life." [1]

At Hacker's urging, the Grand Jury Association of New York County, to which all members of the Manhattan grand jury pool belonged, announced it would file an amicus curiae brief on the matter with Schweitzer. As a result, the Association received and forwarded to us a letter from Columbus, Ohio, written by Richard McCutcheon, the first $64,000 winner, offering his testimony and citing "personal feelings of shame."

Since Merton Koplin had insisted that McCutcheon, among others, was unaware that the questions he answered were tailored to his knowledge, I decided to talk to the former contestant. After several attempts to reach him by telephone and telegram, I flew to Columbus on July 5 and found him the next day at the office where, now a civilian, he worked as service manager for an imported car distributorship. The story he told me of his experience as a celebrated quiz contestant was in great contrast to the sparkling image created by the media.

Now thirty-three years old, McCutcheon had joined the marines in 1949, after graduating from college and marrying a classmate. One of his first assignments was the marine guard detachment at the U.S. Embassy in Paris, where he gained his knowledge of French cooking. After a tour in Korea, where he experienced combat, he was assigned to teach military history and science at Ohio State University. By this time he had three small daughters and his marine pay could not keep him out of debt. When "The $64,000 Question" started in the summer of 1955, McCutcheon wrote to the producers, and Koplin quickly responded. At their first meeting in New York, Koplin invited him to begin as a contestant immediately.

During his first two appearances, McCutcheon claimed, he was asked no questions on the air that he had been asked in the screening, but prior to the third appearance he was called into Koplin's office for a warm-up to help him relax. As in the first screening, McCutcheon was able to answer the bulk of the drill questions easily, and he was not told the answers to the few he missed. But inside the isolation booth during the broadcast, he was shocked when parts of the question used were items he had just answered correctly in the warm-up.

Confused and upset, McCutcheon consulted his wife and mother-in-law, who encouraged him to continue, pointing out he was not defrauding or hurting anyone since he actually knew the answers to the questions, and it was his need to make money that made him continue. The warm-ups with Koplin were repeated for his three remaining appearances, and the questions asked on the air included material covered in the warm-ups. After McCutcheon won $64,000 on September 13, newspaper reports noted that during the thirty seconds he was given to think about the multipart question before starting his answer, he seemed calm; he now told me he had already answered the question in a session with Koplin.

When he discussed it later with Koplin, the producer tried to reassure him that he had hurt no one; on the contrary, he had been a source of wholesome entertainment for tens of millions of people. Late in spring 1956, Koplin invited McCutcheon to appear on the "$64,000 Challenge." Since rumors of the invitation were being spread, McCutcheon thought he had to accept, given what people might think if he turned it down. On June 24 he made his first appearance as a defending champion, facing a New York hotel chef. Before this and three subsequent broadcasts, McCutcheon was warmed up by Koplin, either in his office or at the television studio, but now he knew what to expect. McCutcheon won the match at the $16,000 level.

Despite his affluence, life did not go well for McCutcheon; he left the Marine Corps and separated from his wife in 1957. For all his intelligence, talent, good looks, and energy, it seemed that he had gained little or nothing from being a quiz star. A moralistic streak and a profound fear of being exposed had induced deep feelings of shame and anxiety in him. To me he called the quiz shows destructive of decency and of an orderly society; the producers' claim that no one was hurt was simply a lie. He felt responsible for having been part of a hoax and now wanted to atone for letting himself be used. He authorized me to use his letter and account in any way the office saw fit in order to bring about the release of the presentment.

BACK IN NEW YORK, I turned my attention to the memorandum of law we would file above Hogan's signature on behalf of the presentment. Since we had to make a case for the validity of the presentment under an edict of secrecy on its contents, we focused on the unprecedented nature of the judge's action. Hitherto, the procedure invariably followed was that the court received and disclosed the contents of a presentment. Anyone who desired to have the report quashed moved in court for expungement of the offending part or whole, and the court then made a decision. But Schweitzer had sealed the quiz presentment before anyone with a possible objection had the opportunity to read it.

Noting that the presentment did not name or mention any individual, program, agency, company, or entity connected with the quiz business and that it recommended that copies be sent to "certain official agencies, the functions of which are relevant to the conditions discovered," the memorandum laid out the legal arguments for a main point: the presentment was proper and valid and it dealt with a matter of urgent public concern. The historical fact was that the overwhelming majority of presentments had been made public by judges who followed accepted practice and did not have to justify their actions in formal opinions. It was only in the tiny minority of instances in which motions to expunge presentments were granted that judges explained their reasons in writing. The underlying principle of these was that, despite the public interest being served by releasing the report, expungement was equitable because of possible injury to designated individuals who had no opportunity to test the accuracy of the report. Thus a cornerstone of our motion was that the quiz presentment named no names.

The other main argument in favor of expungement was that grand jury reports should be limited to the activities of public officials, not private individuals. To this, we wrote:

A presentment dealing with the inefficiency of a village dog-catcher could hardly be deemed of greater public significance than one exposing fraudulent labor union practices resulting in unemployment of thousands of people. To accept and publicize the former as a boon to the community because of the dogcatcher's official status, and to reject or expunge the latter because labor unions are not government agencies, obviously would be the acme of absurdity. Such action would become even more ludicrous, if possible, in the light of further facts that the "dogcatcher" presentment criticized a specific person while the labor union report mentioned no individual but spoke in terms of conditions and practices.[2]

Because a wrinkle in New York law made lower-court rulings on such matters as presentments unappealable, we had to look for precedents in the judicial opinions of other states. We found one in a 1957 New Jersey Supreme Court reversal of a lower-court judge's decision not to accept and file a report critical of the widespread retailing of pornography in the county on the grounds it had no relation to official misconduct. The high court ruled that the judge erred in concealing constructive endeavors of the grand jury in matters affecting the public interest, writing: "To impugn such laudatory efforts . . . is not only unfair but would have a tendency to deter subsequent panels from similar endeavors, although there might be a great need for the moral stimulant of a grand jury directive."[3]

Thus we held that no sound reason could be advanced for expunging a report, which, without mentioning individuals, directed its criticism more generally to official agencies, to commercial entities of one sort or another in connection with unsalutory conditions savoring of fraud, racketeering, and crime, or to conditions in an area of great public concern. The popularity of the quizzes with millions of viewers made the matter an important one to the public, for the fact was that the viewers had had many hours of their time stolen. The basic immorality involved could not be sloughed off by protestations that the only deprivation was that of the viewing public's leisure time and that, in return, the public received "entertainment."

Television quiz shows, we pointed out, were not comparable to professional wrestling, which, in New York at least, was officially stamped an "exhibition" as distinguished from a "match" or "contest." The very essence of the quiz program's appeal lay in its implied representation of honesty. Had it been common knowledge that the programs were not honest tests of the contestants' knowledge and intellectual skills, they would have been flops. The time spent by viewers watching a program and its commercials was the consideration rendered for the entertainment provided, and that consideration constituted money on a large scale. Thus misrepresentation of the entertainment offered was a fraud emanating from the most venal of motives. Apart from the public's right to know the extent to which it had been duped and cheated, there was little doubt that the reaction of the public to the conditions described in the presentment would lead to legislation and regulation designed to prevent a recurrence of such fraud. We cited the example of the report of a 1947 Manhattan grand jury dealing with an investigation into professional boxing. That presentment—not directed against any public official or agency—resulted in legislation that had since produced indictments and convictions.

We also cited a decision of Federal Judge Edward Weinfeld in which he thundered against presentments that were "foul blows" against individuals who could not be indicted. But in the opinion, Weinfeld explicitly exempted from his concern "reports of a general nature touching on conditions in the community," which "may serve a valuable function," and in concurring in the practice of state courts that have "countenanced general reports which do not single out individuals."[4] The closest the quiz presentment came to singling anyone out was to say that the practices of "six of the most popular television quiz programs" had been examined, without naming them. Any damage to reputations had to stem from the fact that prior newspaper coverage had made known the identity of some programs involved, their producers could be identified, and therefore the identities of some individuals referred to in the presentment might be surmised. But prior publicity and speculation did not change the presentment's nonspecific character. It would "exceed the limits of proper judicial concern" to suppress the report for "the mere fact that the investigation was accompanied by public speculation."[5]

ON JULY 13, 1959, we filed the memorandum with Schweitzer's clerk, and the judge passed the word that he would reach a decision on the matter sometime in August. Hogan held a press conference and released the text of the memorandum, which ran to twenty pages, almost the length of the presentment itself. On July 17 NBC, responding to press coverage and editorials, announced that it never tried to suppress the presentment and would welcome its release. We noted no move, however, by NBC lawyers to file a brief with Schweitzer along those lines.

On July 29 I was on vacation when Hogan received a letter from Senator Warren Magnuson, chairman of the Senate Interstate and Foreign Commerce Committee, asking what steps he should take to obtain a copy of the presentment. Hogan responded that the senator had to apply to Schweitzer. On July 30 Magnuson and his counterpart in the House of Representatives, Congressman Oren Harris, chairman of the House Interstate and Foreign Commerce Committee, announced they planned to investigate the quiz shows, bearing out the prediction of Hacker. Harris said he had information indicating that certain contestants were coached "in order to enhance their audience appeal," which, if true, meant that the American public had been "defrauded on a large scale."[6] On July 31 Harris announced that his committee's Subcommittee on Legislative Oversight would investigate the quizzes, which he called a "national" problem and "a proper concern of the federal government." The purpose of the investigation would be to ensure that "effective enforcement measures" were taken by government regulatory agencies subject to his committee's jurisdiction and to assess "adequacy of existing laws." If these were found to be lacking, new legislation would be recommended. "The subcommittee will exercise extreme care so that innocent persons will not be exposed to public ridicule or castigation," Harris said in concluding his statement.[7]

Meanwhile, Robert Lishman, the chief counsel of Harris's subcommittee, had drafted an affidavit requesting the minutes of the testimony taken by the quiz grand jury. On July 30 Lishman and Richard Goodwin, a subcommittee staff lawyer, slipped into New York and called on Hogan to ask for his cooperation by not interposing any objection when the subcommittee moved in court to examine the minutes. Hogan ordered that I be summoned back from vacation and called in Denzer, who confirmed that there were strong precedents for giving congressional investigators access to grand jury testimony. In 1950, in the course of Senator Estes Kefauver's special committee investigation of organized crime, Hogan had turned over minutes of grand jury testimony by Frank Costello and other crime figures pursuant to court orders.

Given the precedents, Hogan informed Lishman and Goodwin that the office would pose no objection to the Oversight subcommittee's motion. On July 31, 1959, Lishman's affidavit, which spelled out in proper legal form the essentials of Harris's July 30 press statement, was presented in open court to Judge Irwin Davidson of the Court of General Sessions, in lieu of Schweitzer, who was on vacation. Making the motion for the subcommittee was Goodwin. Davidson said he would refer the matter to Schweitzer.

Unfortunately Hogan made his decision not to interpose before I was able to return to the office to advise against it. From the beginning, I had confidently assured former contestants that if they came clean, their testimony would be sacrosanct except in the event of a public trial of criminal charges. It never occurred to me that Congress would investigate the quiz shows. On August 3 a meeting was held in Schweitzer's chambers. Present were the judge, interrupting his vacation, Lishman and Goodwin, with me acting as the D.A.'s representative. Hogan had given me permission to try to persuade Schweitzer, more or less on my own behalf, not to release the minutes. This was not an official interposition of an objection by the D.A. to the congressional request, however, and we would be bound by Schweitzer's decision.

Lishman, a soft-spoken New Yorker in his late fifties, and Goodwin, a bright, aggressive young man from the Boston area, restated their position on behalf of securing the grand jury minutes, while I argued against it, not unmindful of the ironic reversal of my position vis-à-vis Schweitzer. If Schweitzer gave the nod to the congressional request he would be contradicting everything he had stated as grounds for declaring the presentment "prima facie expungeable." Lishman and Goodwin argued that the minutes could help them screen out and spare the innocent from being dragged in all over again; if their investigators could review the testimony, which they would keep *secret*, then they would have to ask only certain people to appear *voluntarily* at public hearings.

Schweitzer said he would reserve a decision on this until he decided upon the question of the presentment itself. He had already announced another delay in ruling on the presentment until September, in response to a request by the New York chapter of the Federal Bar Association, so that it too could file an amicus curiae brief on the matter. This indicated that a decision on Lishman's motion would not be made until September. Later in the day, Schweitzer said the same thing to newspaper reporters. But it was only the following day, August 4, when a late edition of the morning *Daily News* and the afternoon papers reported that Schweitzer had agreed to the Harris subcommittee's request. The judge had "reread" the affidavit, "detected urgency" in it, and changed his mind. He granted the request forthwith and ordered the transcription of the minutes by the stenographers from their notes, which might take weeks to complete. For its part, the subcommittee had assured

Schweitzer that even though it planned open hearings as part of its investigation, it would keep the minutes secret.

CARRYING OUT Schweitzer's order was a Herculean project. Except for what had been transcribed for use in the perjury proceeding against Freedman, the testimony remained in stenographic form, much of it in the shorthand of grand jury reporters, all but unintelligible to anyone else. We had to hunt down several grand jury reporters on vacation, plus one or two who had left the office, and set them to work typing the minutes of the testimony of roughly two hundred witnesses. As the transcriptions dribbled in, I went over them for accuracy, as the assurances of secrecy I had made to the witnesses who had cooperated weighed on me. By now my associates in the quiz investigation had left the Complaint Bureau for assignments in other bureaus, but they remained within reach for consultation. In one meeting, we came up with the idea of selecting only highlights to convey to Harris and asking Schweitzer to amend his order accordingly; this way we thought we could screen out the testimony of Dowd, Craig, and others. But Hogan vetoed the scheme, on the grounds that a selection would cause a rumpus with the congressmen and that the people we wanted to protect were named in the testimony of Felsher and Freedman, which we could not sanitize.

When we began turning transcribed minutes over to the subcommittee in batches, I had no idea what direction the congressional investigation was taking. I had occasional calls from the mercurial Goodwin, asking for addresses and phone numbers of former contestants and others. Goodwin was spending a great deal of time in New York but did not share his findings with me. When I heard no complaints of harassment, I hoped it meant that Goodwin was adhering to the tacit agreement not to turn the public spotlight on the former contestants who had cooperated with us.

At the beginning of September, Harris, in a series of letters to Hogan, requested my services as a special consultant to the subcommittee, which Hogan approved, and set out the official basis for his investigation as "ascertaining the adequacy of the Federal Communications Commission and Federal Trade Commission enabling statutes and of their enforcement so far as they pertain to the representation of fixed exhibitions as honest contests of skill." He stated his staff was "developing information that competing products which were not involved in this type of advertising campaign suffered sales losses and did not keep up competitively." This sounded promising, an area of inquiry quite outside the purview of the Manhattan district attorney.

In the third week of September, I went to Washington as the D.A.'s liaison, carrying with me the charts we had made, minutely plotting the progress of the contestants on the scandal shows, as well as kinescopes of a number of key broadcasts, and I met Oren Harris for the first time. He was a powerful conservative Southern Democrat from Arkansas and aloof in his dealings with me. Not until I learned something of the history of the subcommittee did I grasp the nature of the chairman's attitude toward me. Created in a post–World War II reorganization of the committees of Congress in 1946, to conduct a general investigation of the federal regulatory agencies under the jurisdiction of its parent, the House Interstate and Foreign Commerce Committee, the Special Subcommittee on Legislative Oversight first came into public notice in late 1957.

A New York University law professor named Bernard Schwartz was hired as chief counsel, to head the subcommittee's staff and probe the regulatory agencies anew, notably the Federal Trade Commission, the Federal Communications Commission, and the Securities and Exchange Commission.[8] Schwartz soon uncovered massive evidence of very cozy relations among various commissioners, figures in the industries they regulated, and the congressmen who supposedly oversaw the regulation. By the end of 1957 Schwartz not only exposed wrongdoing by two FCC commissioners, including the chairman, John Doerfer, but he also embarrassed Oren Harris, forcing him to sell the interest he owned in an Arkansas television station. In early 1958 Harris and a majority of the Oversight subcommittee voted to dismiss Schwartz on trumped-up charges of misusing travel expenses. To deflect the bad publicity engendered, Harris and the subcommittee, using evidence developed by Schwartz, turned to a more convenient target—Sherman Adams, a former congressman and governor of New Hampshire and since 1953 President Eisenhower's White House chief of staff. The subcommittee aired Adams's intervention with top FTC and SEC officials on behalf of a Boston textile manufacturer named Bernard Goldfine after receiving hospitality and gifts from Goldfine, notably a rug and a vicuna coat, which became the symbol of the scandal. At the end of the summer of 1958, with the midterm elections approaching, Adams resigned. The affair contributed to the Democratic party sweep in the elections that fall and helped transform the image of Harris and his Oversight subcommittee into one of fearless investigators.

My sense was that Harris saw the quiz affair as another opportunity for grandstanding, but I also sensed, after meeting with him, that he was wary of New York investigator types. I assumed he knew of my opposition to the transfer of the grand jury minutes, but he did not mention it; instead he launched into a tirade against Louis Hacker, all but calling him a Communist. Harris was familiar with the fact that Hacker had spoken up for academic freedom during the McCarthy era, and the congressman did not like the innuendo in Hacker's criticism that his quiz investigation smacked of McCarthyism. I wondered what had prompted Harris's request for my services if he saw me as somehow in league with Hacker, especially now that he had, in the form of the minutes, an excellent scenario for his hearings.

After meeting with Lishman, who had succeeded Schwartz as chief counsel to the subcommittee, and others on the staff, I was taken under the wing of Goodwin, the special consultant to the subcommittee. Goodwin had been first in his class at Harvard Law School and editor of the law review, then served a year as law secretary to Supreme Court Justice Felix Frankfurter before joining the subcommittee staff at the beginning of the summer. Not waiting for the minutes to be transcribed, Goodwin had assumed what amounted to carte blanche authority as a congressional investigator.

Goodwin boasted how he had terrorized producers, advertising men, former contestants, and others by brandishing blank subpoenas signed by Harris. Enright and Felsher, among others, had been subpoenaed, and Freedman was being brought in from Mexico, where, unemployable in the U.S., he had moved at the beginning of the summer, hoping to write a novel while he planned how to make a comeback in show business. Goodwin told me how his strong-arm method had worked with Freedman. When Freedman ignored his telephone calls, Goodwin passed the word through a contact in the U.S. Embassy in Mexico City that if Freedman didn't come back to testify, he should consider never returning to the U.S. Freedman decided to cooperate, and was coming to Washington at government expense. But Goodwin's boasting and the questions the subcommittee staff asked me, mostly concerning the credibility of various people, gave no hint of what material the subcommittee intended to develop in the public-hearings phase of its investigation.

On Friday, October 2, four days before the Washington hearings opened, the Enright deception, maintained through thick and thin well over a year, began a denouement as NBC, seeking to distance itself from the revelations to come, announced termination of all contractual relations with Barry and Enright. The following day, newspapers reported that negotiations had been underway since February to dissolve the individual contracts between the network and the two partners. Signed at the time of the acquisition by NBC of the Barry and Enright shows in May 1957, the contracts still had some three years to run. Only in the last two weeks had the negotiations been resumed in earnest; now an agreement had been reached, with a cash settlement indicated but not spelled out.

ON OCTOBER 2 I received a phone call from Henry Bloomgarden, and I agreed to meet him Monday morning, October 5, before my departure for Washington. After an impassioned apology for lying to me and the grand jury, he spent two hours spilling a story that corroborated Freedman's corrected testimony in his regard. He also revealed in detail what had led him to lie to us and the grand jury and described what appeared to be a lame, belated attempt by Enright to derail the congressional hearings.

Bloomgarden confirmed that he was lured by Freedman into rigging by the prospect of enhancing his career as a publicist in the field of medical research. Several times while on "Twenty-One," he was tempted to retire but decided not to cross Freedman and Enright for fear that it might hurt his career. This was the consideration that made him accept a compromise following the "coccyx-sacral" incident, when he could have insisted on taking the $126,000 he won that night. He looked forward to following in Van Doren's footsteps as a celebrity, but it did not happen. After "Twenty-One," he slowly built up his public relations business, finding that his brief renown had helped little. In fact, he had to overcome initial resistance from the Consumers Union to retain him, because the organization did not approve of Geritol. Nevertheless, he wrote a book about the crisis in medical research, public health, and education,[9] then began research for a series of biographical essays on women social reformers.

When Stempel's allegations were made public, Bloomgarden was in the midst of negotiating with Van Doren for an article for *Consumer Reports*. Bloomgarden took Stempel for a sorehead, remembering that Enright long ago had warned him that Stempel was trying to smear "Twenty-One." Now that the attempt was succeeding, Bloomgarden realized the black eye the program was receiving could hurt him as well. Knowing that Sheldon Levy, a member of his Democratic party club, was a Manhattan assistant district attorney, Bloomgarden decided to use Levy to give a clean bill of health to "Twenty-One." He called Freedman to report his move, and it was Freedman who suggested Bloomgarden see us in his own office to avoid being spotted by reporters.

Several days after first meeting with us, Bloomgarden reported the en-counter to Freedman and Enright, who made light of the investigation, saying Hogan was interested in headlines because he was running for the Senate. At a meeting with Barry and Noah, Bloomgarden was introduced to the lawyer Thomas Gilchrist, who, Enright explained, had good connections with the D.A. and would attempt to have the investigation dropped, but he needed to know that Enright had told him the truth, that the quizzes had not been rigged. Bloomgarden repeated to Gilchrist what he had told us.

At lunch on September 24, 1958, Freedman informed Bloomgarden he had been at the D.A.'s office the previous day and expected to be called be-fore the grand jury but would stick to the story that he had not helped Bloom-garden or any other contestant. Bloomgarden realized Freedman expected the same from him and understood Freedman's urgency when newspapers reported the revelations of Snodgrass; Bloomgarden kept his end of the bar-gain in his second session with us on September 26. Between Freedman's grand jury appearance and his indictment on November 8, Bloomgarden met with Freedman several times; on these occasions, Freedman denounced Snodgrass as a bitter, greedy trickster whose "sealed" letters were a hoax and assured Bloomgarden that Van Doren and other former contestants were pre-pared to deny rigging. According to the legal advice he had received, the producer insisted, if he continued to deny that he had helped contestants, there was no way that contestants could open themselves to perjury charges by denying being helped by him. After the cancelation of "Twenty-One" put Freedman out of a job, Bloomgarden called the producer to express his sym-pathy. Freedman said he would do all right; he had some savings and Enright was undertaking to pay his legal fees. This was their last conversation. When it came time for Bloomgarden to testify before the grand jury, on December 18, 1958, he stuck to his guns and denied he had been assisted in any way by Freedman.

As the quiz affair faded from public attention in early 1959, Bloomgarden was grateful that "Twenty-One" had not made him a celebrity, as he contin-ued building his business through new contacts in Washington and Boston. The sealing of the grand jury presentment in June seemed to be the end of the affair. But in September 1959 he received a letter from Mexico, in which Freedman revealed that he had purged himself before the grand jury and admitted he had given assistance to Bloomgarden and others. A short time later, Bloomgarden received a phone call from Enright asking him to drop by his office, where he was introduced to Zoloto.

According to Bloomgarden, Enright stressed the damage the upcoming congressional hearings could cause, then urged him to visit a contact Bloomgarden had in Washington, Senator John O. Pastore of Rhode Island, the second-ranking Democrat on the Interstate and Foreign Commerce Committee, the Senate's counterpart of Harris's own committee, and suggest Pastore's committee intervene and head off the Harris hearings. When Bloomgarden said this would be impossible, Enright suggested he leave the country for a few months and avoid a subpoena. Astonished, Bloomgarden said he didn't have the money to do this, it would destroy the momentum of his career, and the timing—if he were to leave just as the hearings began—would be obvious and disastrous. Zoloto then interposed that if Bloomgarden couldn't leave the country, he should go to Pastore, adding, according to Bloomgarden, "You can feel free to offer up to $15,000 to Pastore if that will help." Thinking Enright had lost his mind, Bloomgarden made excuses and departed. A day or two later, Enright called to smooth things over, saying he didn't believe Bloomgarden would be subpoenaed.

At this point, Bloomgarden had reached a delicate stage in negotiations for a consulting job involving the Harvard Medical School, and the seriousness of what might happen in Washington dawned on him. A week before the hearings were to open, he was visited in his office by Goodwin, who pulled papers from his pocket and began reading from Freedman's grand jury testimony regarding Bloomgarden. When Goodwin asked if the statements were true, Bloomgarden knew he was trapped and had no choice but to come clean. When he admitted the truth of Freedman's statements as well as the fact he had lied to the grand jury, Goodwin asked him to volunteer to testify in Washington. Bloomgarden pleaded that appearing at a public hearing would destroy him. Goodwin conceded Bloomgarden probably would not be called against his will, but strongly urged him for his own sake to go back to the district attorney and tell all.

Bloomgarden now realized he had fooled himself all along with a misplaced sense of loyalty. Freedman had let him down by not bothering to tell him he had recanted, robbing Bloomgarden of the opportunity to correct his own testimony. As for Enright, in their most recent encounter, he simply stood by while his lawyer encouraged Bloomgarden to attempt the bribe of a U.S. senator. Assuming that Goodwin and I were working together, Bloomgarden panicked, and did not even think of consulting a lawyer before calling me. When he finished his story, I asked him to wait in my office, then I went to brief Hogan.

As far as we were concerned, Bloomgarden's confession was anticlimactic, but it was a straw in the wind for a new turn in the affair, since, for the first time, a major "Twenty-One" contestant had admitted to perjury. If the hearings were to provide no factual surprises, they could spotlight others who had lied under oath, possibly stampeding them back in to tell us the truth. Hogan instructed me to have Bloomgarden repeat the story with a stenographer taking it down as a formal statement for signature. Back in my office, I explained to Bloomgarden the technicalities that ruled out purging himself of perjury; his cooperation could be taken into account but it would be no bar to prosecution. He said he understood this; the important thing was to get the truth off his chest, and he eagerly repeated his story for the stenographer.

CHAPTER THIRTEEN

Washington Circus

(OCTOBER 6–12, 1959)

On Tuesday morning, October 6, I took my assigned place at one end of the dais in the huge pilastered Caucus Room of the Old House Office Building near the Capitol. Officially there only to observe, I sat to the side of the congressmen, above and in full view of the audience. A witness table, below and facing the dais, formed the top of a T with a long table, with places for the counsel and other subcommittee staff. The witnesses' chair would be looking up at me as well as Oren Harris and the eight other Legislative Oversight subcommittee members, half Democrats, half Republicans.

Calling the proceeding to order, Harris entered into the record the rules of procedures for such hearings, which provided for executive, or closed, sessions if witnesses requested them on the grounds that their testimony might "tend to defame, degrade, or incriminate any person." Once such testimony was taken, however, it could be released to the public upon the simple vote of the subcommittee members. Citing the testimony and evidence gathered by the New York grand jury, Harris announced that the subcommittee was bound not to disclose information from the grand jury minutes except if testimony given by a witness in the hearings conflicted with that given by the same witness before the grand jury. I realized my presence would be a visible reminder of the subcommittee's ability to confront witnesses with their previous sworn testimony.

Declaring the subcommittee could accomplish its business in a week of hearings, including evening sessions, Harris announced that the testimony of Albert Freedman and Daniel Enright would be taken in executive session at their request. This was the first indication to me that the quiz hearings would be a three-ring circus. In the center ring would be the performances of those testifying in the open. In a side ring, obscured from the public as it happened but revealed later, when the subcommittee released the bulk of the testimony involved, would be a series of closed sessions, stage-managed in great part by Enright. In the third ring, revealed only in glimpses at first, was the show that would most intrigue the public—the drama of the fate of Charles Van Doren. The entire production would consist of two acts—a week of public hearings at the beginning of October, and a second week of hearings in November. In between would be a month's intermission, during which the drama of Van Doren would move to New York, before returning to Washington for a spectacular climax.

For Herbert Stempel, the lead-off witness, the occasion was an hour in the sun. He grinned for the photographers, who were granted half a minute for picture-taking before witnesses were sworn in. Otherwise, cameras were barred from the proceedings. Ironically, given their subject matter, the hearings were not televised, unlike the celebrated Army-McCarthy and Kefauver crime hearings conducted by Senate committees in previous years. Television cameras had never been permitted into House hearings, because of the strong personal aversion to television of the Speaker of the House, Sam Rayburn.

After an explanation, by Lishman, of how "Twenty-One" was played and a projection of the kinescope of the November 28, 1956, broadcast, in which Stempel and Van Doren played two tie games in their second encounter, Stempel testified. Questioned by Lishman, he retold his story with relish, but he was not asked about being swindled out of the bulk of his winnings or about his attempt to blackmail Enright. He conceded he had no personal evidence that Van Doren had also been given the questions, answers, and point selections in advance, but the implication was clear. Congressman John E. Moss of California, the most astute member of the subcommittee and the last to question Stempel, inquired pointedly about Stempel's last game. Was it fair to assume, Moss asked, that because Van Doren "knocked" at three points shy of twenty-one, he must have had some information about the outcome? "That is right," replied Stempel, "I would say that was a very, very good assumption."[1]

In the first two days of public hearings, Stempel was followed in the center ring by a familiar cast: the contestants, James Snodgrass, Rose Leibbrand, and Richard Jackman; Enright's public relations men, Alfred Davis and Arthur Franklin; and the Pharmaceuticals executive, Edward Kletter. They added little to what I already knew, but for the public the revelations were stunning, making headlines across the country. It must have been a bitter pill for Stempel to see the coverage of his appearance accompanied by bigger file photographs of Van Doren than any taken of him as testifier, for what made his testimony a big story were the implications it carried for Van Doren. Newspapers reported that Van Doren had not been subpoenaed but had been interviewed previously by subcommittee investigators and denied any involvement in fixing. Van Doren himself could not be reached for comment, and NBC referred reporters to statements it had made earlier, adding that its representative would testify before the subcommittee.

That occurred late in the afternoon on October 7, the second day of hearings. Thomas Ervin, the NBC lawyer, with whom I had had several talks during the early stages of our investigation, was the first subcommittee witness not to have testified before the grand jury. He read a brief statement stressing NBC's cooperation with the authorities at various stages of the investigation, its action in relieving Barry and Enright of control over the programs and instituting a review of its own internal security procedures, and its avowed support for release of the grand jury presentment. His statement concluded with praise for the subcommittee's undertaking to place the "true facts" before the public.

The true fact was that Ervin had the public relations task of justifying NBC's failure to investigate seriously on its own, especially in the light of Davis and Franklin's testimony that NBC all but panicked at crucial junctures. Ervin rationalized NBC's failure to question Stempel directly when it first had wind of his allegations, on the basis of its excellent relations with Barry and Enright over the years, the plausibility of Enright's characterization of Stempel as a disturbed person, and the fact of Stempel's own signed statement that he had not received assistance. Even after the scandal broke, NBC did not undertake to question former contestants because, Ervin asserted, we in the D.A.'s office requested this not be done.

Instead, NBC permitted Barry to defend "Twenty-One" on the air and accepted at face value Van Doren's own public denial of participating in rigging—on the Dave Garroway show days after Stempel's story made headlines. In addition to securing affidavits from "Twenty-One" personnel who had come in direct contact with Snodgrass when he was a contestant, the network hired the management consultants, Arthur Young & Co., to evaluate its other quizzes. In January 1959 the Young organization reported back with recommendations for tightening the security of questions but apparently found no evidence of rigging of other NBC quizzes.

When asked if "Tic Tac Dough," still on the air, was fixed, Ervin replied that he had learned from Howard Felsher a week before that he had been subpoenaed by the subcommittee. At that point, Ervin recounted, he asked Felsher to declare in an affidavit whether or not he had ever given questions and answers to contestants. Felsher declined and was fired, an event that had not been announced to the public. Now Ervin revealed that NBC had only recently learned that Felsher had appeared before the New York grand jury, still insisting that it was awaiting the outcome of the public investigations before making its own probe. The congressmen did not ask Ervin if the network would have been so cautious if "Tic Tac Dough" were still the property of an independent packager.

Asked if, in light of Stempel's subcommittee testimony, he believed Van Doren was given assistance and lied about it, Ervin sidestepped, repeating that no NBC investigation had been made of Van Doren and none was in prospect. Van Doren had not been asked to sign an affidavit but, as Ervin understood it and now revealed, Van Doren had sent a telegram to the committee, volunteering to testify.

At 7:30 P.M. the congressmen were through with Ervin, but their day's work was not done. At noon, a telegram from Van Doren had reached the subcommittee, which Lishman acknowledged to reporters without releasing its text. In reply, Harris telegraphed an invitation to Van Doren to appear later in the week, asking him to advise of a time when he could be expected. At 8:30 P.M. the subcommittee reconvened in a smaller room in the New House Office Building to take its first testimony in executive session, from which I was barred. The witnesses were Freedman and Enright; the session would last until just before 1 A.M.

Up to the eve of the hearings, the subcommittee was in a quandary, reflecting Freedman's recanted grand jury testimony that nearly all the "Twenty-One" winners had been fixed and the fact that many had testified to the contrary under oath. As soon as they understood the testimony's significance, Goodwin and Lishman had requested of Schweitzer that he permit its release word for word into the record of the upcoming hearings, since Freedman was in Mexico, out of reach of a subpoena. When Schweitzer refused, the subcommittee wrote to Freedman asking him to return to testify or submit to interrogation by a subcommittee staff member in Mexico. When Freedman did not reply, the subcommittee made a formal motion before Schweitzer to enlarge the original order; this time Hogan—without informing me—was roped into the effort and personally urged Schweitzer to relent, but the judge still refused.

The subcommittee's problem was whether or not to call and take testimony from people like Van Doren and Von Nardroff when their denials of complicity before the grand jury had not been submitted to further probing by the district attorney. Lishman and Goodwin were acutely aware of court decisions denying to Congress the power to expose private citizens for the simple sake of exposure, following upon the excesses of the McCarthy era. The subcommittee therefore decided not to compel testimony by former contestants against their will but to turn the spotlight on the quiz producers. They served subpoenas on Enright, Barry, and associates like Felsher, Robert Noah, and Glorianne Rader. Yet the subcommittee had no stomach for conducting a witch-hunt that might explode in its face, a possibility if Enright and others were to take the Fifth Amendment. Thus the situation had given Enright leverage that he would use to maximum advantage. Freedman slipped back into the United States, and Enright offered a deal to the subcommittee. He would deliver himself as well as Freedman and Felsher, in return for the cancelation of subpoenas on Noah, Rader, and Barry.

Subcommittee investigators scoured New York for Freedman, but he eluded them. With the opening of hearings fast approaching and the prospect that Enright and the others would take the Fifth if no deal was made, the subcommittee accepted the advice of Lishman and agreed, the day before the hearings opened, to the conditions proposed by Enright's lawyer, Myron Greene: Enright, Felsher, and Freedman would testify in closed hearings and corroborate the open-hearing testimony of Stempel and Snodgrass; Freedman and Felsher would not be required to name other contestants. The subcommittee also agreed not to call Barry unless new evidence was uncovered that would link him directly to the rigging. Enright's goal seemed to be to save daytime "Tic Tac Dough" and "Concentration," and to protect Barry's reputation and ability to make money in show business.

On Wednesday, October 7, hours before the scheduled executive-session testimony of Freedman and Enright, the delicate deal nearly came unglued. Enright had brought Freedman to Washington but kept him hidden until the last minute for fear the subcommittee would renege and simply subpoena him to ask any questions it pleased, but Freedman then balked at facing another interrogation. In the event of a hitch, Enright had a fall-back plan: he, Felsher, and Noah would take the Fifth before the subcommittee. But another hitch developed when Noah announced he could not take the Fifth Amendment and would break ranks by telling all and naming new names if called. At this point, Freedman gritted his teeth and decided to keep his end up. The deal was on; Noah, Rader, and Barry would not be called.

Enright and Freedman were accompanied at the witness table by an able Washington lawyer, Charles Murphy, though Greene was present in the room. Freedman testified first in a proceeding that went by fits and starts with frequent discussions off the record as to which questions were proper under the ground rules agreed to. Under questioning, Freedman covered the same ground he had during his return appearance to the grand jury, with the difference that he now mentioned no names beyond Snodgrass's. Freedman claimed that Enright never suggested what he should say if called to the grand jury, but Enright did discuss with Freedman his "feelings" about keeping the shows on the air and protecting the contestants. Freedman was never advised by any lawyer that he should testify to the grand jury that the shows were not fixed, but he didn't recall the lawyers telling him and Enright that if they told the truth to the grand jury there would be no criminal liability under state or federal law. Freedman also revealed that Enright had lent him some $15,000 since November 1958. Before he was excused, Freedman was ordered to remain within reach for the remainder of the week's hearings.

Enright was next and played his part with appropriate deference but no false regret. Asked by Lishman if he was the one who instructed Freedman to rig the contestants, Enright charitably assumed responsibility if not blame:

> Well, this has been a subject of debate or discussion between Mr. Freedman and me for the past six months, as to who initiated the idea between us. And frankly, none of us have a recollection. To me it doesn't matter. For the sake of the record, and just to minimize time, I will assume responsibility for it.[2]

He acknowledged furnishing questions and answers in advance to Stempel, Jackman, and one other person whom he did not name. His style was neither to contradict nor to confirm the testimony of those already heard in the open hearings. Enright "did not recall" or had "no recollection" of many things, but he did not deny them, and on occasion when he did confirm something he qualified it by saying that he was not sure it was his memory or the influence of the others' testimony. On the matter of meetings with NBC that were prompted by attempts of Stempel to take his story to the newspapers, Enright confirmed Davis's account that the network's prime concern was "how to avoid having the story," irrespective of its truth.[3]

Likewise, when Enright met with Ervin and others of NBC after Stempel's story surfaced, no one asked him directly whether he had given questions and answers in advance to Stempel, but "in all fairness" to Ervin, the NBC attorney could have deduced from Enright's conduct that Stempel was lying. Last of all, asked if NBC executives knew controls were used on "Twenty-One," Enright replied that he could only go on assumption:

I think, being in an industry for 20 or 25 years, you would have to be very unsophisticated or very naive not to understand that certain controls have to be exercised. Now, the extent of controls is something else. As to what NBC knew, I cannot testify to first-hand. I would assume that certainly the sophisticated employees in their program department would realize that some controls have to be exercised.[4]

On the morning of Thursday, October 8, newspapers headlined the firing of Felsher by NBC the week before and Van Doren's communicating to the subcommittee his willingness to testify. A reporter had cornered Van Doren at Columbia University and asked him to comment on Kletter's testimony concerning the $5,000 advance. Van Doren replied that he had explained this to the grand jury, but would not now elaborate on this or anything else.

At the opening of the day's public hearing, Harris announced for the record that Enright and Freedman had testified in executive session and a decision on releasing their testimony would be made at a later date. Now the congressmen turned their attention to "Dotto," as two contestants who had testified before the grand jury, David Huschle and Antoinette DuBarry Hillman, presented the "entertainment defense" for their own willing collusion in rigging. In an attempt to explain the difference between quiz rigging and the fixing of sports events like boxing or basketball, Huschle contended that since he was not the equivalent of a professional athlete, by winning some money, then taking a dive, he did not really "lose," and neither did his opponents nor the viewers who were entertained by the presentation. Hillman's stance was lighthearted: it never occurred to her that rigging was fraudulent or immoral; rather, the audience was "having a happy time; so was I. Everybody was."[5]

A less carefree perspective was provided by Edward Hilgemeier, the original whistle-blower. The affidavit signed by him and filed with the Federal Communications Commission and a photostat of Marie Winn's notebook page were made part of the hearing record; then the kinescope of the May 20, 1958, broadcast was projected. After recounting his bumbling attempts at extortion, Hilgemeier told of his difficulties securing employment as an entertainer since the scandal. When he announced he was suing the TV talk show host Jack Paar for libel, because a "$64,000 Question" and "Challenge" champion, Billy Pearson, had accused him of blackmail on Paar's show, Hilgemeier was hastily excused with the subcommittee's thanks. Harris noted for the record that Winn was in Europe and, therefore, beyond the jurisdiction of the committee. But he was "authorized" to state that she had appeared before the grand jury in New York, where she corroborated Hilgemeier's testimony by stating that she had received assistance on "Dotto."[6]

During a lunchtime recess, the subcommittee reconvened in a closed session to hear first Martin Dowd, then Edward Jurist. Dowd justified his request for a closed session with the assertion that testifying openly could result in his losing his job, and the fact that he had lied in his first grand jury appearance might tend to incriminate him. It was not clear whether he had been subpoenaed or had volunteered to appear, but he was warned that his testimony could be released in the future. Dowd then revealed how prize-money budget considerations determined his tenure on "Tic Tac Dough" as champion and described in detail the use of ties to trim back champions' winnings before their displacement. Yet Dowd clung to the belief that the champion he had displaced after many ties, Michael O'Rourke, himself had not been rigged.

Jurist, now a resident of Beverly Hills, had also requested an executive session on professional grounds—a Hollywood studio was considering the purchase of a pilot film he had produced, which would be "dynamited," he told the congressmen, if his name appeared in the paper in connection with the hearings. Under questioning, he acknowledged "Dotto" was controlled in every way precisely to avoid having to give questions and answers to contestants in order to achieve "entertainment," but he claimed to be unaware of the cruder techniques resorted to by his associate producers. Questioned on the moral aspects of the operation, Jurist stressed that they were out to give the contestants something:

> If they were lucky they won a lot of money; if they were not so lucky they won a little money. They were not injured or maimed. All they had was a lot of fun. . . . I don't consider that immoral, particularly if you have grown up in the entertainment business as I have.[7]

When Jurist claimed the public kept watching even though every viewer must have suspected at one time or another the show was fixed, Congressman Moss, who had been absent from the questioning of Freedman and Enright the night before, thundered:

> I have two small daughters. They were very ardent fans of these programs. These youngsters now know that those were just as

phony as they could be. . . . I say it is rotten, right down to the ground . . . . you have created problems for every youngster who watched them and who had confidence in them. I think it is symptomatic of some far more basic problems in this whole industry with you people in a mad rush to develop something which is salable, which will draw a greater dollar, without any regard to a public obligation.[8]

In this vein, Steven Derounian, a New York Republican, pursued Jurist about his earlier experience of producing "Quiz Kids" and "Giant Step," asking whether the same techniques were used. Jurist replied, "Kids are much closer to information than adults. They are going through the acquiring of information. We are forgetting it. You had to find out what they knew."[9] He conceded that the producers talked to the children to find out what they knew so they could be asked about that on the programs, and they suggested to them what areas to study. The possibility that the children's parents knew what was going on was not taken up.

Reconvening in open session late in the day, Harris announced that both Dowd and Jurist had testified in executive session. This dismayed and baffled me, because Dowd was one person I had made it my mission to protect from exposure, and I simply could not believe he had now volunteered to testify. What Harris had to say next, however, sent the reporters rushing for the telephones. In his telegram to the subcommittee, Van Doren had included a statement that he wished to be inserted in the record of the hearings, which was not appropriate at this point, Harris said, but he had wired Van Doren in return, inviting him to appear this afternoon or the following morning, Friday, October 9. But, Harris added ominously, no reply had been received from Van Doren.

The next public witness, the former "Tic Tac Dough" contestant, Kirsten Falke, retold briefly her experience, giving Congressman Moss the opportunity to blame the television industry for aggravating the "problem of the ethics of the juvenile population of this country."[10] Then it was the turn of Sy Fischer, the former executive producer of "Dotto" and Jurist's boss. Though I had talked with Fischer in the office at the beginning of the investigation, he had balked at waiving immunity to testify before the grand jury (as partner of Frank Cooper and co-owner of the "Dotto" package, he had qualified as a target of our investigation). Now he asked that he be heard in executive session, on the grounds his testimony might tend to defame, degrade, or incriminate another person. I was struck by the fact that he was compelled to go through the motions of this procedure in public, while others had made the arrangements behind the scenes. In the evening executive session that followed, Fischer irritated the congressmen by revealing nothing incriminating or defamatory. Admitting "Dotto" was "controlled" because the format required it for successful entertainment, Fischer claimed he had been insulated from the details and could not answer as to such specifics as whether questions and answers had been given to contestants in advance, or even if the emcee Jack Narz had been aware of controls.

ON THE MORNING of October 9, Richard A. R. Pinkham, a vice-president of the Ted Bates agency and former NBC vice-president in charge of all network programming, puzzled the congressmen with his claim that until the "Dotto" business he had no idea that any quiz shows had been rigged. Congressman John Flynt of Georgia pointed out that other witnesses had characterized rigging as common knowledge spread "by a process of osmosis if nothing else" among people in the producing end; if so, why had that knowledge not seeped over into the "industry part." Pinkham answered he had been "living in a dream world" until Hilgemeier. As for what he might have known of NBC's early concern about Stempel, Pinkham commented: "This is not the sort of information that a network is eager to tell its advertising agency customers."[11]

The next witness was Felsher—the first Barry and Enright associate to testify publicly. After projection of the April 10, 1958, broadcast of nighttime "Tic Tac Dough," showing Dowd defeating O'Rourke, Felsher retold his story in matter-of-fact fashion, without naming contestants. Since Felsher had survived in his job until being subpoenaed for the hearings, the congressmen wondered how the rigging could have been carried on so long with so many people knowing about it. Felsher answered that he had supposed one day it would come out, but he had been more concerned with putting on a good show. When the scandal erupted, self-preservation became an element but was secondary, he claimed, to the goal of protecting the contestants. This prompted him to encourage them to lie, saying he would do so himself; Enright had not advised him to do this but he had acted out of panic. Intrigued by Felsher's assertion that after the rigging of the daytime show was stopped, the number of ties continued as high as before, Moss asked Felsher to explain how the ties worked in the Dowd-O'Rourke match projected earlier. The producer requested that he not be compelled to answer because he might damage the reputation of an innocent person. Harris agreed to post-pone further questioning of Felsher until an executive session.

Thomas K. Fisher, the CBS general counsel, in a prepared statement, briefly narrated the network's actions in connection with "Dotto," "The $64,000 Challenge," "Name That Tune," and "For Love or Money." The last was a new one to me, since no complaint had ever been filed with us against it. In this program, which debuted as late as June 1958, competing contestants played a kind of roulette for prizes of merchandise or cash. The retail price of a piece of merchandise, say $50, was posted on a machine visible to the audi-ence but not the contestants. The decimal point began jumping among the digits in this figure. A contestant who first thought he or she had the answer to an easy question pressed a buzzer, stopping the "dancing decimal point." Upon correctly answering the question, the contestant had the choice of tak-ing the merchandise or gambling on where the dancing decimal had stopped and winning the cash indicated—5 cents, 50 cents, $5, $50, $500, or $5,000.

According to Fisher, the decimal machine was controlled from backstage by a network employee acting on the orders of the producer. If the decimal point was in a position to push the cash prize into the $1,000 range when the contestant's buzzer was heard, the stagehand had standing orders to throw a lever that gave the decimal point one last jump, lowering the cash value of the prize. This precaution helped the producers stay within their prize-money budget. As a result of its investigation, Fisher told the subcommittee, CBS had canceled "For Love or Money" in January.

Recounting the network's moves in the wake of Charles Jackson's allega-tion against "The $64,000 Challenge," Fisher could not answer why CBS was not aware of rigging yet made a half-hearted attempt to defend certain "con-trols." If screening to keep drunks off the air was proper, there was also nothing wrong with screening for interesting as opposed to dull personali-ties. Likewise,

> I would suppose, you gentlemen may appear on television and they probably tell you to wear the blue shirt and maybe make up your face. I can't see we are really misleading . . . . if a man comes in and says "I am an expert in wars of all kinds, ancient, modern and so forth," . . . it would be profitable and necessary for the producer to find out whether he was just saying that in order to get on the air. . . . When the producer is determining that, he neces-sarily is finding out some things that are in that man's head. . . . I would not suppose that to be improper, to find out that he is what he represents himself to be, an expert in a given field.[12]

Fisher stressed that CBS had not produced its quiz shows and had taken steps to prevent future rigging, through amendments to standard contracts with agencies that spelled out such procedures as the selection of contestants and the conduct of "surveillance" by the network's editing department. "The fact that representatives of the editing department drop in on the program is the same idea as the policeman on the beat. By now these producers know that when X comes in that he comes in for a certain purpose," but Fisher added, in a pointed reference to the competition, even as he tacitly conceded, as had Ervin of NBC, that no amount of supervision could be a 100 percent guarantee of honesty; nothing could "prevent a producer from jumping in a car and driving out to a man's home." [13]

The target of Fisher's barb was the next public witness, Enright. Deprived of questioning Enright myself before the grand jury, I was to be further disappointed when, right off, Lishman announced that the questions in this open session would be limited to "Tic Tac Dough." Enright confirmed Felsher's previous testimony without being specific, conceding his wrongdoing as well as providing excuses—even when it came to the possibility of suborning grand jury witnesses. "What was condoned, obviously, is not condonable," he said, "but all I ask you to do is try to understand that terror and panic had besieged us in those days." Asked what measures might be taken to prevent future rigging, he answered:

> While it might be somewhat ironic that this suggestion comes from me . . . I think the best regulation that can be obtained is through industry control rather than through legislation, as has been evidenced in other industries. . . . A commission can be established either by the industry or by each individual network, which is solely responsible for the propounding of questions. . . . All the security measures [would be] conducted by this unit, so as to minimize contact between researchers and contestants . . . as long as you have questions being prepared in the same office which produces a program, the likelihood [of rigging] is greater than ever. [14]

After some hedging, Enright conceded that screening contestants amounted to the same thing as directly giving questions and answers. "When it started, I don't know," he said, "I do know that when I became actively involved in radio programs, it was talked about around that several panel shows were under control." Without being asked to be specific, Enright made analogies to news interview programs described as "spontaneous and unrehearsed" in which, beforehand, the subject already had been interviewed by the reporters. Not that deception was necessarily harmful, he pointed out: "Deception is practiced in everyday life. . . . The magician or the mindreader who says 'I can read your mind,' he is inflicting deception. I think it must be measured by the hurt he inflicts on people." Yet Enright didn't want to give the impression that all quiz and panel shows were "controlled": "Tic Tac Dough" had not been rigged for the last year and a half. As for "Concentration," which he had created for NBC and which was currently the number-one rated daytime show on the network, Enright claimed:

> I decided that there was to be no controls on that show. Not for any moral reasons but simply I felt that the factors and essentials of this particular show were so strong that the show could ride without any of the artificial excitement interjected. It has happened. It is terribly strong programwise and did not require any injection of artificial stimulants.[15]

Calling Pinkham's expression of shock at learning of quiz rigging naive, Enright went on to say: "With this I am sure I cannot be restored to the television industry after what has happened—what I am going to say . . . will seal any possibility in the future of returning to television." He then turned the tables on the congressmen, asking if they themselves ever had wondered about the shows before the scandal. When one obliged by saying he had been suspicious, Enright countered by asking might not then network executives have had the same suspicion? Enright had made himself the interrogator briefly and scored a subtle point. But pressed on the issue of network officials, given the fact that rigging techniques spread like osmosis among producers, Enright came up with a complicated way of saying the network people simply looked the other way. That is, the situation depended on the competence of the producer in "inverse ratio": the more competent and successful the producer, the less likely he was to draw the attention of network officials and others to the details of the operation of his shows.

The day's open session ended at 6 P.M., with Harris announcing that the hearings would continue the next day, Saturday, October 10, with the appearance of FCC chairman John Doerfer, to be followed on Monday by Earl Kintner, chairman of the FTC. Harris then ordered the room cleared for an executive session, in which Felsher admitted the rigging of O'Rourke on nighttime "Tic Tac Dough." When Felsher pointed out that O'Rourke carried shrapnel in his body from wounds received in Korea, Harris acknowledged the country's debt to O'Rourke, but said that gave him no license to "commit fraud" on the American people. Moss added that he was all the more disturbed by O'Rourke's participation in rigging because of his being in the army: "He might be General O'Rourke someday with responsibility for very large sums of money. If he is corruptible, it is well that we find it out."[16]

After Felsher, the congressmen had more questions for Freedman, prompted by information conveyed to the subcommittee in an affidavit from an NBC executive, James Stabile, concerning a conversation with Van Doren in New York the evening following the Washington testimony of Stempel. According to Stabile, Van Doren continued to insist he had not been given assistance on "Twenty-One" but was claiming that Freedman had asked him for a loan while he was a contestant. Freedman now heatedly called this a lie, but remained unwilling to go on record as to whether he had given Van Doren assistance.

ON SATURDAY MORNING, October 10, the newspapers headlined Enright's statement that quiz fixing was a standard practice. The fact that his testimony had not included the names of "Twenty-One" contestants merely added to anticipation of the fate of Van Doren, who had dropped from sight. When Harris declined to tell reporters whether a subpoena would be issued for Van Doren, they correctly assumed it was in the works. On Friday evening the subcommittee had voted to subpoena Van Doren and sent Goodwin to New York to serve the summons.

John Doerfer was flanked by the general counsel of the FCC and the chief of its broadcast bureau. The chairman's task was analogous to that of the chief legal officers who had already appeared for CBS and NBC. But since the FCC was a creature of Congress, the elected representatives of the people were prepared for a field day. Doerfer was already under a cloud, because of revelations early in 1958 of his acceptance of honoraria from a broadcasting industry association and of entertainment by a prominent broadcaster, making his situation now all the more precarious.

In a lengthy opening statement, Doerfer revealed that the FCC's action in the "Dotto" matter amounted to no more than soliciting and receiving from the networks assurances that they had been ignorant of what went on and would do their best to see that it didn't happen again. In Doerfer's view, the FCC had no real power in the circumstances, for a number of reasons: the legislation that created the FCC, the Communications Act of 1934, provided that in return for their licences, which were granted without fees, broadcasters were required to serve the public interest; but it was up to licensees to determine that their programming met the criteria. With a staff of six people to investigate the renewal requests submitted every three years by some thirteen-thousand radio and television stations, the FCC did not monitor broadcasting but depended upon complaints to point out irregularities.

But when Doerfer added to these certain constitutional constraints, Lishman countered that preventing the deception of the public had nothing to do with censorship, citing the U.S. Code of Criminal Procedure, which set criminal penalties for devising "any scheme or artifice to defraud, or for obtaining money or property by means of false or fraudulent pretenses, representations, or promises" and for transmitting "by means of wire, radio, or television communication in interstate or foreign commerce, any writing, signs, signals, pictures, or sounds for the purpose of executing such scheme or artifice."[17] Lishman also cited a long-standing FCC regulation that prohibited the broadcasting of mechanical reproductions, recorded music, or films without announcing the fact, precisely to prevent the deception of the public as to their nature.

In response, Doerfer stressed the difficulty of applying what he called "legal deception," that is, the legal concept of deception, to dramatic expression, which would amount to the FCC's invading the area of programming. Moreover, the broadcasters had acted themselves in this case by canceling the rigged quizzes. Doerfer said he preferred to use the licensing power to encourage broadcasters to weed out deceit and misrepresentation rather than lay down rigid rules. The latter would "detract from the enjoyment of the public or the entertainment value" by requiring "somebody to stand up before the screen and say, raising his hand, 'we solemnly represent to the public that this program is exactly what it purports to be and there is no deceit involved.' If you do that every hour or every half hour, it just becomes ridiculous."[18] Doerfer was justifying his agency's passivity by reducing to absurdity the consequences of action.

If the FCC could do nothing to prohibit reprehensible and immoral practices, Doerfer was asked, why had he not reported the situation to Congress so that it might be remedied? Doerfer replied that it was not until the hearings began that there was proof anything reprehensible had happened. At any rate, he was not prepared to suggest legislation, for that would "intimate to the American people that [the FCC] can deal with a subject which is beyond its powers [which would be] just as much a deceit as what has been going on. . . . To tamper with our cherished freedom of speech is not a simple matter. It takes a good deal of study."[19] Finally, Doerfer reiterated, in the wake of the scandal, the networks could be trusted, with their broadcasting licences at stake, to exercise more control in the future over the material they broadcast.

ON OCTOBER 12, the subcommittee convened for the last scheduled witness, Earl W. Kintner, chairman of the Federal Trade Commission, accompanied by a phalanx of six underlings. A past president of the Federal Bar Association and a part-time professor at New York University Law School, Kintner was widely respected; his name had never come up in connection with any charges of influence peddling.

Determined to present a better picture than his FCC counterpart, on the level of substance Kintner had little different to offer. In his opening statement, he said that Section 5 of the Federal Trade Commission Act, which prohibited "unfair methods of competition in commerce and unfair or deceptive acts or practices in commerce," gave the commission the power to proceed against false and deceptive advertising. But this power did not extend to the quizzes, which he described as a form of "deceptive entertainment" constituting "the surrounding circumstances during which nondeceptive advertisements were made [and] not an intricate part of the sale and [did] not [themselves] exploit customers who are unable to protect themselves."[20] If the commission's jurisdiction were to extend to "entertainment," Kintner asserted, it "would not stop at 'deceptive entertainment.' . . . I do not believe that by enactment of the Federal Trade Commission Act the Congress intended the Commission to become censors of television entertainment."[21]

Kintner outlined, without naming her, the matter of "The Big Surprise" contestant Dale Logue in 1957, the only specific complaint ever filed with the FTC in relation to TV quiz shows. Since the program went off the air not long after the complaint and the producers agreed not to represent that their programs were spontaneous and unrehearsed when such was not the case, the FTC closed the case without taking action; it had come to Kintner's attention only after a combing of the files by his staff in preparation for the hearings.

Under questioning, however, Kintner conceded there had been informal feelers from lawyers "dropping by" in the period 1955–57 to ask on behalf of unnamed clients whether there was anything illegal about the new quiz shows their clients were "up against." But, since at the time there was no assumption that the quizzes were not honest—the question was rather whether they presented unfair competition—Kintner's staff decided there was no way to recommend initiating a proceeding that had as its objective the "abatement" of the quizzes.[22] No documentation of these goings-on was offered now, nor was any requested by the subcommittee.

Asked if the FTC was taking the same position as the FCC—that it had to wait for complaints or for others to take action—Kintner, cannier than Doerfer, replied that the FTC was prevented by its mandate and court decisions from initiating proceedings in doubtful areas. Such a gray area was the possibility that the sponsors of rigged quiz shows increased their sales unfairly at the expense of competitors who did not sponsor such shows, an aspect previously touted by Harris as an important focus of the subcommittee's investigation. For even its legally mandated tasks, the FTC was woefully understaffed, insisted Kintner, slyly making the point that if Congress wanted to expand the powers of the commissions it would have to provide the wherewithal. Making quiz rigging a crime would be helpful, he said, as would broader rule-making authority for the commissions; but any increased authority concerning television should properly be given to the FCC.

Kintner sounded perhaps the most important theme of the hearings, reflecting the ethos behind the government regulation of business, by deploring the tendency of a "predatory business class" to, on the one hand, "justify any illegal practice they might engage in on the grounds that their competitors are doing it or would if they had been smart enough to think of it first," and, on the other, if victimized themselves, to be the first to "look to the Federal Trade Commission as the only lighthouse on a stormy sea." Kintner admonished businessmen that

> their responsibilities not only extend toward obedience to the laws on the books, but also extend toward protecting the good name of their industry. . . . Businessmen should not sit supinely by until the government is forced to intervene in a moral situation. Men of conscience . . . the great majority of the American businessmen, should find a point where they are willing to say "no" to any [immoral] practice that is growing up.[23]

But Lishman read out loud from the FTC's own 1958 annual report to Congress, under the rubric "Types of unfair methods and practices" within the commission's jurisdiction: "Using a merchandising scheme based on lot or chance or on a pretended contest of skill." As recently as the spring of 1959, the FTC had issued a cease and desist order against a complicated marketing scheme involving use of misleading claims to promote the sale of advertising time to merchants as sponsors of essay-writing contests on local radio stations. Here Kintner was forced to acknowledge his ignorance of the fine points at stake, promising to follow up his appearance with a statement on the case for the record.

If the networks and sponsors were unaware of the fixing, Lishman asked, would not misrepresentations by the producers when they leased their programs have brought the matter within the jurisdiction of the FTC? Here ensued a lengthy argument over whether a television program was a "product" in the sense that would bring it within the FTC's purview, or a "service," which presumably would not. For Lishman the essence of the quiz show scheme was the selling of the product of the sponsor, who had bought the entire program, not simply the time during which the commercial was being aired, the idea being to create in the mind of the viewer an "indication that their product was of the same high quality [as] the program they were viewing."[24] Invoking the example of wrestling, Kintner said in effect that deceptive means legally could be used to get people to watch a commercial that in itself was not deceptive. If the commercial itself was deceptive, it could be stopped; the means of attracting people, if it were not a commercial, could not be stopped, no matter how deceptive, on the grounds of free speech.

During a luncheon recess of Kintner's daylong testimony, the subcommittee met in a hastily called executive session, prompted by a report by Drew Pearson in the morning papers that Freedman, in his previous closed-hearing testimony, had fingered Van Doren. According to Pearson, Freedman and Enright "had reached agreement that Enright would handle Herbert Stempel" on "Twenty-One," "and Freedman would handle his opposite number, Van Doren. Under this arrangement, Freedman said, he supplied Van Doren with the questions in advance, but did not supply him with the answers."[25]

Called back to clarify this and other matters, Enright now confirmed that in more than half the broadcasts of "Twenty-One" results had been planned in advance with his own approval. He deplored the leak to Pearson, saying, "This obviates the extent and all our efforts in the last few days because we had only one intention, that regardless of what hurt might be heaped on us, one of our main purposes was to avoid hurt of other people." Enright denied knowledge in advance of Van Doren's telegram to the subcommittee, which "again obviated what we were trying to effect."[26] Finally he told Harris he did not know where Van Doren was. Harris then said the hearings would be adjourned for three weeks, until November 2, and Enright should be prepared to return.

Back in the Caucus Room, after the end of Kintner's testimony, Harris announced the new round of hearings, then read out loud Van Doren's October 7 telegram:

> Respectfully request you read following statement into the record of the proceedings before your committee, quote:
> "Mr. Van Doren has made himself available to members of the committee staff. He has advised them that at no time was he supplied any questions or answers with respect to his appearances on *Twenty-One*. He was never assisted in any form and he has no knowledge of any assistance having been given the other contestant. He further stated that he voluntarily appeared before the New York County grand jury and told that body under oath that he never received any assistance in any form from any person at any time. Mr. Van Doren has advised that he is available to this committee to reiterate what he has told the New York County grand jury under oath and to the members of this committee's staff." Unquote.[27]

No further word had been heard from Van Doren, Harris added, and a subpoena was issued which Van Doren had "purposely avoided." Concluding the proceedings, Harris paid tribute to Hogan and the district attorney's office. Then I spoke a few words, briefly summarizing the work of the grand jury and repeating what we had said on behalf of the presentment—that it would lead to legislation and regulation designed to prevent recurrence of the quiz hoax, the extent of which the hearings had dramatically demonstrated. Outside the Caucus Room, when asked by reporters if the D.A. would be opening a new probe of the quizzes, I answered that we would have to study the matter.

CHAPTER FOURTEEN

Intermission

(OCTOBER 13–NOVEMBER 1, 1959)

"WHERE'S CHARLIE?" screamed a banner headline of the *Journal-American* when I returned to New York midday on Tuesday, October 13. With Harris publicly throwing down the gauntlet, the drama of Van Doren took center stage and his whereabouts became the question of the hour. Behind the scenes, fate had been closing in on Van Doren even before the hearings opened, as I would learn later from various sources, including Van Doren himself.

At the outset of the subcommittee's investigation during the summer, Goodwin, like many others, had given Van Doren the benefit of the doubt, despite the plausibility of Stempel's account. But reading Freedman's recanted grand jury testimony changed Goodwin's mind. In a meeting at Van Doren's Greenwich Village townhouse, with Van Doren's lawyer, Carl Rubino, present, Goodwin read excerpts of Freedman's testimony out loud. Van Doren denied everything, saying Freedman himself had lied to the district attorney and grand jury. He confided to Goodwin that someday the reasons would come out why Freedman and company were smearing him. Soon after this, Goodwin invited Van Doren to Washington for a heart-to-heart talk, telling him, "Charlie, I know you are lying."[1] When Van Doren simply shook his head, Goodwin warned that even though the subcommittee had decided not to subpoena any contestants, he would have to keep his mouth shut. Any public proclamation of his innocence at this point would amount to a challenge of the subcommittee, which then would be forced to summon him. Goodwin apparently did not share with Van Doren the reason for the subcommittee's forbearance—to secure the cooperation of Enright in providing the producers' side of the story.

On October 6, reading the early account in the afternoon newspapers of Stempel's Washington testimony that morning, NBC chairman Robert Sarnoff

summoned to his office Robert Kintner, the president of NBC (and no relation to the FTC chairman, Earl Kintner), and several others, including David
Levy, the network's head of programming; James Stabile, director of talent
negotiations; and Lawrence McKay, the lawyer who had arranged Enright's
first meeting in the district attorney's office at the beginning of the scandal.
Kintner instructed Levy and Stabile to suggest to Van Doren that he volunteer
to testify before the subcommittee, or otherwise be suspended by NBC.

For several hours of discussion that night between Stabile, Levy, and
McKay, on the one side, and Van Doren and Rubino, on the other, Van Doren
denied any involvement in fixing but claimed he had been offered assistance
by Freedman and turned him down; in addition, Van Doren told the gathering, Freedman had tried to borrow $5,000 from him while he was a contes-
tant. Around midnight, Stabile reported to Kintner by phone that Van Doren
had agreed to make himself available to the subcommittee. The following
morning Van Doren sent his telegram to Harris.

After Stabile drafted the gist of what Van Doren had told him into an affidavit, Van Doren and Rubino were summoned to a meeting with Kintner and
Sarnoff for a personal explanation. When Van Doren, on the advice of Rubino,
declined to answer questions, he was suspended from the NBC network
pending a resolution of the allegations. Later, Kintner directed that a copy of
Stabile's affidavit be sent to the subcommittee; Van Doren asked Columbia
University to provide a substitute for his regular class the following morning,
then dropped out of sight.

Nothing more was heard of Van Doren's whereabouts for nearly a week
until Tuesday afternoon, October 13, when Rubino denied to reporters that
Van Doren was ducking service of the subpoena. Explaining his client's disappearance, the lawyer said: "He was disturbed and just went off. He phoned
me last night and I told him that allegedly there was a subpoena out for him.
I had heard it over TV."[2] Rubino added he would be meeting with Van Doren
later in the day to discuss the subpoena before they made themselves available for its service. In Washington, meanwhile, Harris told reporters that
Rubino had been informed of the subpoena as early as Saturday, October 10.

ON OCTOBER 14, Charles Jackson resurfaced to embroider his original allegations, in an article by Drew Pearson. Jackson now claimed that he first pro-
voked interest on the part of "The $64,000 Question" by writing to the
producers that he was suspicious of the show and wondered whether it was

necessary to go through a talent agent to be picked as a contestant. Invited to New York for a personal interview, Jackson continued, he was immediately tapped to be a contestant and treated so well that he "felt like a hog in 10 acres of slop." They did not give him the answers, but he was never asked a question he hadn't been able to answer in the screening. When he had won $16,000, however, the producers' attitude cooled and he realized that he was through: "They knew the questions I couldn't answer. And when they want you off the show they feed you questions 16 college professors couldn't answer. So I took my $16,000 and went home." The rest of Jackson's story, his appearance on "The $64,000 Challenge," was as he had told it previously, and he summed up his experience for Pearson: "The trouble is that these people in television get someone who looks stupid, like me, and they make human pawns out of you. One producer in New York told me: 'The biggest temptation in this industry is to play God.'"[3]

Asked to comment, other $64,000 contestants like Ted Nadler and Joyce Brothers denied to reporters that they received any assistance. Louis Cowan issued a statement, declaring that he was "in a position to comment on the actual production of *The $64,000 Question* only for the seven-week period I was at the production company. During that period there was no rigging of the program, so far as I know and if there had been, I think I would have known about it."[4] Meanwhile, Lishman in Washington conceded to reporters the Harris subcommittee now had "some information that *The $64,000 Question* program was rigged" and it would be the subject of testimony when the hearings resumed.[5]

On Wednesday afternoon, October 14, reporters were informed by the U.S. marshal's office in New York that a congressional subpoena had been served on Van Doren at the Roosevelt Hotel, where they found Rubino and Van Doren ready to meet the press. Declining to answer questions, Van Doren read a three-hundred-word prepared statement, in which he said he had not avoided a subpoena but, distressed by his suspension by NBC, had arranged a leave of absence from Columbia and traveled with his wife to New England to enjoy the fall foliage. He said he had great respect for Congress, and his appearance before the subcommittee would be the proper time and place to answer questions. "To do otherwise," he said, "would be disrespectful."[6] He again dropped from sight, not to reemerge for another week.

Ripples from the news that the subcommittee was investigating the $64,000 shows quickly spread. Drew Pearson followed up his Jackson story with charges that Charles Revson had used wiretaps to steal trade secrets from his arch-competitor Raymond Spector, owner of the Hazel Bishop Co.; these included the sponsorship of "The $64,000 Question," which, according to Pearson, Spector had been on the verge of signing up when it was snatched away by Revlon. Pearson also noted that the Harris subcommittee had in its files copies of memoranda from Revson instructing the Batten, Barton, Durstine and Osborne advertising agency to keep certain contestants on the "Question" and to remove others.

On October 15, the *New York Times* reported a statement by the Manufacturers Trust Company, the bank that had stored the $64,000 shows' questions in its vault: "We accepted the assurance given us by the program producers and so stated on the telecast, that no one, except for the editors, had seen the questions before they were placed in the vault." The following day, the man credited on the air as the editor, Professor Bergen Evans, was quoted as saying "The $64,000 Question" had been honest and its producers were "all honorable men": "It doesn't seem reasonable that the producers would spend that kind of money—and they spent a lot through me—to provide those accurate questions if the show was rigged."[7]

On Thursday, October 16, Frank Stanton made a speech in New Orleans, acknowledging CBS's failure to "meet our duty" with regard to quiz shows; in the process "millions of Americans were duped," and broadcasting had "lost a degree of public trust." The task facing CBS was "to make certain that we are the masters of our own house."[8] The eventual termination of the three big-money quiz shows remaining on the network—"Name That Tune," "Top Dollar," and "The Big Payoff"—was announced. But two days later, NBC stated it was keeping its quizzes, saying "we do not believe amputation . . . is the answer to television's current difficulties"; rather, the "primary task" would be to implement "effective safeguards."[9]

On Monday, October 19, Van Doren resumed teaching at Columbia, while CBS announced an end to all "deceits" used on its TV programs. The network's new rules would ban the giving of advance looks at questions to guests appearing on interview shows like Edward R. Murrow's "Person to Person," even the use of canned laughter on comedy shows. Overlooked by the reporters the following day was the fact that Louis Cowan entered New York City's Presbyterian Hospital suffering from thrombophlebitis in the left leg. Concealed from reporters was the additional fact that Rubino called Hogan to make an appointment for Van Doren to see the district attorney.

It was at this time that I received a telephone call from Martin Revson saying he wanted to set the record straight about his involvement with the $64,000 quizzes. Several months before the quiz scandal, after a long history of dramatic and highly publicized ruptures, Martin Revson had broken finally with his brother; now in my office, a well-groomed, plain-spoken, and self-important man, he freely expressed his resentment and told how, before the final split, the two had a violent quarrel. Martin stormed out of the Revlon offices, and it took several days for his wrath to subside enough for him to return and try to make peace. Arriving at Revlon headquarters, he found that his office had simply disappeared. The walls had been moved, new furnishings and decorations were installed, and all physical traces of Martin's presence were eliminated.

Revson contradicted down the line the grand jury testimony of his former sales manager, George Abrams, as well as of Merton Koplin and Steve Carlin of the Cowan organization, concerning his own participation in the weekly meetings at Revlon. Though he was the senior Revlon executive responsible for the quizzes and chaired the meetings, Revson claimed he knew nothing of rigging and denied any knowledge of any question or answer before it was used on the air or that any contestant was fed information in advance. It was his understanding that the questions were prepared by Evans, whom he called an incorruptible scholar, and their integrity was protected by the Manufacturers Trust bank.

Though Revson admitted to having opinions pro and con about various contestants, he denied ever expressing preferences with the expectation that the producers would act on them. As far as he had known, the producers could not throw a contestant off the air; he certainly had wanted hard questions to be used, because the winners had to *deserve* to win the big prizes, but not in order to remove an unwanted contestant. During the time he was involved, some three hundred contestants had appeared on the shows, but he never received a complaint from any of them. He would have had nothing to do with a dishonest show because an investment of millions of dollars a year could have been wiped out at the slightest hint of dishonesty. Moreover, the operation of the shows was entirely in the hands of EPI, which had made it abundantly clear that they did not need Revlon because other sponsors were lined up at their door.

Soon after talking to Revson, I learned from Hogan that Simon Rifkind, a former federal judge and senior partner of one of the most prestigious law firms in Manhattan, had called to say his client, Charles Revson, wanted to make a statement to us. Since Martin Revson's statements were of no use, I told the Chief there was no real need; all indications were, from the testimony of Abrams, Carlin, and Koplin, that Charles Revson had not been responsible for what happened on the quizzes. But Hogan made it clear I was not to brush off the influential Rifkind, so I arranged a meeting with Revson in his apartment in the Pierre Hotel.

Charles Revson, at fifty-one, was tall, thin, and fragile-looking. Apparently annoyed that Hogan had sent an underling in his place, Rifkind haughtily explained that his client was concerned about the adverse publicity Revlon had received during the various investigations. Even though it had long ago canceled its sponsorship of the shows, the company feared that criticism of it was contained in the grand jury presentment. Mr. Revson now wanted it made clear that neither he nor anyone else at Revlon had been responsible for any dishonest techniques involved in the operation of the quizzes. After Rifkind's speech, Revson went to work on me. It was now obvious, he insisted, that the $64,000 producers wanted to shift responsibility for any abuses to the sponsor by accusing Revlon of pressuring them. Revson then digressed to relate the history of the fantastic growth of Revlon through the manufacture of outstanding cosmetics. He had long known Cowan, for whom he had great respect. It was precisely Cowan's reputation for showmanship and integrity that had prompted Revson to sponsor the "Question." Like millions of television viewers, Revson personally had been a fan of the program; would that have been the case if he knew it was rigged? He rarely attended the weekly meetings, at which Revlon was well represented by his brother and Abrams. Certainly everyone concerned wanted the programs to improve; of course they were interested in the variety and quality of the contestants; they had wanted the categories of knowledge used on the programs expanded. But at no time was it ever suggested that a particular contestant win or lose.

When Revson finished his diatribe, the meeting was over; I did not ask any questions nor did Revson and Rifkind seem to expect any. Nothing Revson said altered what I had already known about the quizzes and his participation in them; if the grand jury presentment were ever released, Revson would see how he had been wasting his time as well as mine. I knew Goodwin was again running around New York with his sheaf of blank subpoenas; the chances were he had confronted the Revsons, so the cosmetics tycoons wanted to be in the position, when the time came to be questioned in public about the quizzes, to say they had cooperated with the district attorney.

Before long, Abrams, who had recently become the president of the Richard Hudnut cosmetics division of the Warner-Lambert Pharmaceuticals Corporation, came to me to complain that Goodwin had the minutes of his grand jury testimony and was threatening him with a subpoena. I refereed a meeting between the two, at which, in return for not being required to testify in person in Washington, Abrams agreed to the preparation of an affidavit based on his grand jury testimony. Goodwin drafted a statement, focusing on the weekly meetings held at Revlon during the heyday of the $64,000 shows. Goodwin was also talking to Martin Revson, who apparently provided a different perspective on the Revlon meetings. Goodwin did not share with me what Revson had told him, but, guessing from what Revson had told me, I realized one of them—Revson or Abrams—had not given Goodwin the whole truth.

ON FRIDAY, October 23, the morning papers carried reports that President Eisenhower, when asked at a press conference about the quiz scandal, said, "Fixing TV shows was a terrible thing to do to the public." The president had directed the attorney general, William Rogers, a former colleague of Hogan's from the Dewey era, to investigate the matter and report back to him. At 11 A.M., as arranged, I met alone in my office with Van Doren and Rubino. Before he could say anything, I warned Van Doren that since he was not obliged to come in at this point, under no circumstances could I make any promises that he might not be prosecuted if he told me the truth now.

Van Doren volunteered that the biggest mistake he had made was not having a lawyer like Mr. Rubino, who would have advised him to tell the truth in the first place. Beyond that, there was no discussion of perjury. He was, he said, taking the opportunity to apologize for not telling the truth to me and to the grand jury. Then it was true, I asked, that while he was a contestant, Freedman had provided him with all the questions and answers in advance? All the questions, yes, Van Doren answered, but on a number of occasions he had looked up the answers on his own. But, as for the point values he was to request, the questions he would miss in order to achieve ties with opponents, even the gestures he would use in the isolation booth—all this was arranged in advance.

There was more to ask Van Doren, but this was not the time; he was preparing a statement for his appearance before the subcommittee when it resumed its hearings, and he would tell the whole story at that time. I would be there again as an observer, I told him; after that, we would probably call him back for a more complete interrogation. He and Rubino left for a brief meeting with Hogan. That, I imagined, would be painful for all concerned, since the Chief's worst fears were being realized—the young man who in the last several years had brought so much publicity to Columbia University (of which Hogan, at the beginning of October, had been named a trustee) would reveal himself as a fraud.

After that meeting, which Hogan did not discuss with me, he called in reporters to tell them he had seen Van Doren but was not at liberty to reveal what was said—beyond the fact that Van Doren had confirmed he had not been completely truthful on previous occasions—because the matter was being considered by Congress. When asked about the possibility of a perjury indictment, Hogan would not comment except to say that the determination of whether perjury should be submitted before a grand jury was his responsibility. As to whether Van Doren would be called before another grand jury after the congressional hearings, Hogan said: "That is a question we will have to decide. It requires some reflection and whether it would serve any useful purpose. . . . There might be any number of persons who might wish to correct statements made in this office which may cause me to reflect on their grand jury testimony." [10]

On the way out of the building after their meetings with us, Van Doren and Henry Bloomgarden, who had come in to sign his statement made to me on October 5, were photographed by the press. Van Doren did not stop to answer questions, saying he was in a hurry to go to his class at Columbia. Almost overlooked by the press among the events of the day was the announcement by NBC of the cancelation of daytime "Tic Tac Dough," the very last of the scandal-touched quiz shows to bite the dust.

IN THE LAST WEEK of October, newspaper accounts of Van Doren's visit to the office and Hogan's comments upon it prompted telephone feelers from the lawyers of several other former "Twenty-One" contestants, including David Mayer. Mayer's lawyer, Frank Brenner, another former assistant district attorney, now a successful criminal lawyer, wanted to bring in his client immediately, and I agreed to a meeting for October 30. Now Mayer, prompted by the surmise that Freedman and Enright had told all in Washington, was eager to tell the truth—he had been provided all the questions and answers in advance and, moreover, had been enlisted into lying to us by Freedman on assurances that nothing would ever get out. Mayer was full of bitterness at what he took to be Freedman's betrayal; he now felt he had no choice but to try to save himself, especially after Hogan's invitation to those who lied to come in and set the record straight.

Finally, on Sunday, November 1, one day before the hearings were scheduled to reopen, the *New York Times* carried on page 1 what was for us the first genuine revelation about the quizzes since the sealing of the grand jury presentment. An Allentown, Pennsylvania, department store owner named Max Hess had paid $10,000 to production personnel of "The $64,000 Question" to place one of Hess's employees as a contestant and thereby "plug" the store on national television. If the sketchy *Times* account was accurate, there was the possibility that an actual crime had been committed in connection with the operation of the quiz shows, a possibility that had eluded us throughout our investigation.

That afternoon I flew to Washington to resume my role as Hogan's emissary at the second round of hearings. I had an invitation from Goodwin for dinner at his home that evening. To my amazement, I found among the other guests: Charles Van Doren; his wife, Geraldine; his father, Mark Van Doren; and Rubino. Goodwin and his wife, Sandra, were genial hosts and kept the drinks and conversation flowing, but for me the situation was as awkward as could be. Since Van Doren had admitted to me in person that he had committed perjury, I would have to grapple with the problem of whether to prosecute him for it. As his potential prosecutor, I had no business socializing with him. I kept my mouth shut, and Charles Van Doren had little to say. It was Mark Van Doren who rose to the occasion and told anecdotes from a vast storehouse of wisdom. A trim man with iron gray hair and a craggy face, he appeared completely at ease. With his perceptive eyes and gentle manner of speaking, he seemed to be telling us that he had come to terms with the tragedy that had befallen his errant son and had forgiven him.

CHAPTER FIFTEEN

Second Round

(NOVEMBER 2–6, 1959)

On the morning of November 2, 1959, when I took my place on the dais, the Caucus Room was jammed with some one thousand spectators, including those standing four deep at the back and along the sides of the room. In a section reserved for special guests sat Herbert Stempel, ignored by a horde of reporters and photographers focusing on Geraldine and Mark Van Doren, seated behind the witness table where Charles Van Doren would sit.

Shortly before 10, a door behind the dais opened; flashbulbs popped as Van Doren and Carl Rubino moved into the room and passed in front of me. Rubino paused to shake my hand, and Van Doren did likewise. As they took their places at the witness table, there was a last spasm of picture taking before Oren Harris gaveled the hearing to order. Without preliminaries Harris swore in Van Doren, who began with a well-crafted, prepared statement, which took him some ten minutes to read, without the gestures of hesitation and mental strain that had made him famous. The only signs of nervousness were a jiggling foot and almost constant smoking.

"I would give almost anything I have to reverse the course of my life in the last three years. . . ," he began, easily heard in the absolutely hushed room:

> I have learned a lot in those three years, especially in the last three weeks. I've learned about life. I've learned about myself, and about the responsibilities any man has to his fellow men. I've learned a lot about good and evil. They are not always what they appear to be. I was involved, deeply involved, in a deception. The fact that I, too, was very much deceived cannot keep me from being the principal victim of that deception, because I was its principal symbol.[1]

These opening words sent a number of reporters rushing from the room to put out the word that Van Doren finally was admitting participation in quiz rigging. "I have deceived my friends, and I had millions of them. Whatever their feeling for me now, my affection for them is stronger today than ever before," Van Doren continued. One man I supposed he would not count among his friends—Stempel—was wearing a very wide grin. Van Doren said he had told his family the truth on October 16, then came to tell Hogan and me, and now was prepared to tell the public the whole truth.

Going back to the beginning, he recounted being steered to "Tic Tac Dough" by a friend, encountering Freedman, whom he had met previously on social occasions, then being selected to go directly on "Twenty-One." When asked by Freedman as a personal favor to help defeat Stempel, he asked in return to be allowed to go on without assistance, but Freedman ruled that out because Stempel was too knowledgeable. Freedman told him:

> The show was merely entertainment and giving help to quiz contestants was a common practice and merely a part of show business. . . . He also stressed the fact that by appearing on a nationally televised program I would be doing a great service to the intellectual life, to teachers, and to education in general, by increasing public respect for the work of the mind through my appearances. In fact, I think I have done a great disservice to all of them. . . . Whenever I hesitated or expressed uneasiness . . . , the same sort of discussion ensued, and foolishly and wrongly, I persuaded myself it was all true. Freedman guaranteed me $1,000 if I would appear for one night.[2]

After the first appearance, Freedman raised the guarantee to $8,000, and so it went for the next twelve broadcasts as Freedman continued to raise the guarantee.

But this kind of fame was troubling, Van Doren said. He realized he was giving a wrong impression about education; he wrote articles to correct it, but few people paid attention. Sharing his misgivings with Freedman, Van Doren pleaded to be released, but Freedman said that had to be done in a "dramatic manner," which was finally arranged for March 11, 1957, when Van Doren would lose to Vivienne Nearing. When, just before the broadcast began, Enright told him to go to his dressing room, not the press room, after he was off, Van Doren had the first concrete indication that Enright knew what was going on.

Under the contract given him by NBC, Van Doren welcomed the opportunity to do daily segments on the network's morning show, speaking about science, history, poetry, and famous people.

At least once a week during my five minutes I read poetry and talked about it as I would do to a Columbia class. I think I may be the only person who ever read 17th century poetry on a network television program—a far cry from the usual diet of mayhem, murder, and rape. I hoped that television viewers would . . . forget my role on *Twenty-One*.[3]

But, in August 1958, upon hearing the news of Stempel's allegations, Van Doren was "horror-struck." Feeling that he carried "the whole burden of the honor" of the teaching profession, he "made a statement on the Garroway program . . . to the effect I knew of no improper activities on *Twenty-One* and that I had received no assistance. I knew that most people would believe me. Most people did."[4] After being interviewed by me in October 1958, Van Doren engaged Rubino, but did not tell him the truth. Before testifying in the grand jury, he assured Freedman he would not tell the truth. Freedman assured him in turn he had nothing to fear: "They can break my legs," the producer swore, according to Van Doren. Enright also promised that everyone in his organization would "die" for him.

Moving forward to August 1959, Van Doren said that when the subcommittee investigators first interviewed him, they pointed out there was grand jury testimony conflicting with his own, without specifying whose. Not until the end of September, in the week before the first round of hearings, did he learn of Freedman's reappearance before the grand jury. Up to this point, Van Doren seemed to be telling the truth, but I recalled that the *New York Herald Tribune*, as early as the first week of August 1959, reported that Freedman had returned to the grand jury after his indictment, had begun to cooperate, and was expected to be a willing witness in the upcoming hearings. It was difficult to believe that Van Doren had overlooked this information.

After the grilling by NBC on the night of October 6, Van Doren hoped that the wording of the telegram to Harris would satisfy the network and he would not appear to be defying the subcommittee. By the time Harris replied with an invitation to appear, Van Doren had told all to Rubino, who concluded that Freedman and Enright had spilled the beans to the subcommittee; at the same time, NBC had relayed to the subcommittee the partial information he had provided about the rigging of "Twenty-One." All this, plus his suspension by NBC and reporters outside his door, made Van Doren panic:

I simply ran away. . . . Most of all, I was running from myself. I realized that I had been doing it for a long time. I had to find a place where I could think, in peace and quiet. . . . My wife and I drove up into New England. I drove aimlessly from one town to another, trying to come to some conclusion. But I still could not face up to what I had done.

When he returned to New York and accepted service of the subpoena on October 14, he was still looking for a way out. It was a letter from a stranger, a fan who had seen him on the Garroway show, that finally set him on the right course, Van Doren claimed:

> She told me that the only way I could ever live with myself, and make up for what I had done—of course, she, too, did not know exactly what that was—was to admit it, clearly, openly, truly.
>
> Suddenly, I knew she was right. And this way, which had seemed for so long the worst of all possible alternatives, suddenly became the only one. Whatever the personal consequences, and I knew they would be severe, this was the only way. In the morning I telephoned my attorney and told him my decision. . . . He said "God bless you."[5]

With these words, Van Doren concluded his statement. Mark Van Doren was ashen; Stempel was beaming. Harris complimented Van Doren on his candor, and Lishman said he had no questions. Congressman Walter Rogers called Van Doren's statement "the most soul-searching confession" he had heard in a long time, adding that "the American people are against corruption but they are for forgiveness when a man comes in and tells the truth. . . . It took a long time to get you to do it, but when you did, I don't think you left any stones unturned."[6]

The congressmen's questions focused on Van Doren's relations with NBC, how much of the truth he revealed to the network, and at what stages. After Stempel's charges were first aired in 1958, Van Doren told NBC executive Robert Lewine that he had received a $5,000 advance while on "Twenty-One" but had not been involved in anything improper. Van Doren had been friendly with Sidney Eiges, the NBC public relations vice-president involved in the fall 1957 crisis caused by the threat of Stempel's story surfacing in the press, and he occasionally dined with him, but Eiges never questioned him about "Twenty-One." Not until the night of October 6, 1959, was he seriously confronted by NBC; now he described his attempt to counter what he took to be the fact that Freedman had already implicated him, telling Stabile this was the reason he was reluctant to go to Washington. When

Stabile asked him whether Freedman had ever asked him for any money, Van Doren now testified:

> I recalled and told them that at one time . . . Mr. Freedman told me that I was going to be the first contestant to win more than a hundred thousand dollars. . . . He said to me, I think these are almost his exact words, "Charlie, I think I ought to have $5,000 of that money."
>
> I am very sorry I ever mentioned this, and this is not because I am trying to hide anything from anybody. It is simply that I don't believe that Mr. Freedman meant that in the way it sounds. He never mentioned it again. Nothing was ever done about it.[7]

Steven Derounian of New York broke ranks, saying he could not commend Van Doren for telling the truth, "because I don't think an adult of your intelligence should be commended for telling the truth." After several terse questions about Van Doren's various statements to the press about the subpoena, Derounian summed up his skepticism by asking if Van Doren had done what he did for money. "That was not the only reason," Van Doren replied, but "of course, that was a reason." In a brief speech of his own, Harris told Van Doren they had not meant to single him out, but his wire, contradicting the testimony of former contestants and others who had volunteered to testify, had made it "absolutely necessary" to call him to "unravel this whole picture and get at the true facts."

> You have been duped into a certain situation, even though at your age you should and did know better, as you have revealed here today. . . . [A]nyone, regardless of how it hurts, who comes to tell the whole truth in a matter so important to the American people and the public interest is to be highly complimented. . . . I could end this session with you by saying what your attorney did say to you the other day; that is, "God bless you."[8]

When Harris gaveled a recess, the reporters mobbed Van Doren and Rubino, who handed out copies of the statement. Stempel came over to me and launched on a diatribe against the professors at the City College of New York who had turned down his Ph.D. thesis proposal. Out of the corner of his eyes he watched the swarm of people around Van Doren, who inched his way out of the room to the corridor where newsreel cameras were waiting. Even in confession and public shame, Van Doren had again triumphed over Stempel; he had done it with finesse and on the grand scale. Posterity would recall Van Doren as the symbol of a tawdry hoax that shook the nation, while Stempel would be lost in the shuffle.

WHEN THE SUBCOMMITTEE reconvened, it turned to the $64,000 quizzes, and for the remainder of the hearings, the action took place in public; closed sessions were few and sporadic. The Reverend Charles Jackson was the first to testify. In his late thirties, thin, with a crewcut, Jackson was not unconvincing in his presentation as a befuddled country boy out of his element. This was the quality that made him attractive to EPI, because, he guessed, they needed some contrast to the "suave-looking gentlemen" predominating among their contestants. The producers had turned to him as a rough diamond to be deployed for effect, then finding him untelegenic if not irascible, decided to cut him off. But in puffing up his ego before deflating it, they created bitterness and resentment, and possibly a thirst for revenge. Even if his motivations were murky, his folksy manner and homespun tale served as a dramatic introduction to an airing of the rigging of the $64,000 quizzes. More significant, Jackson was the first to impeach publicly the integrity of "The $64,000 Question," which Koplin had fought valiantly to defend before the grand jury.

In 1948, early in his career as a Protestant minister, Jackson established a foundation to give awards to talented young athletes who were outstanding Christians. This led to the idea of a football game called the Christian Bowl, as a way to raise money to publicize Christianity in sports and to build and maintain a Boys Town–type home in Tennessee. After organizing three Christian Bowls with high-school athletes, Jackson attempted to promote a college all-star version, but the effort failed, leaving him $25,000 in debt, which prompted his efforts to become a quiz contestant.

Less than two weeks after an interview with Koplin in New York, at the end of January 1957, he was called back and asked some fifty to one hundred questions by the producer, some of which he could answer, many of which he could not. On his first appearance, Jackson won $8,000; all eight questions had been asked him previously by Koplin, or their answers could be inferred from material covered in the screening. At his next meeting with Koplin, he was asked how far he expected to go. When he said that he hoped for $16,000, Koplin said he believed Jackson knew enough to try for that much. On the next broadcast, he correctly answered the $16,000 question. Though he was invited to remain in New York at EPI's expense till the following broadcast, he found the cordiality cooling. A young producer's assistant described to him what happened to a contestant, a truck driver whose category was Geography, who indicated to the producers that he would quit at $32,000 but then went ahead and tried to answer the $64,000 question. He lost and went home with a Cadillac, worth only five or six thousand.

According to Jackson, Koplin pressed him for a decision in advance as to whether he would retire or continue, assuring him that he was eligible for the "Challenge" as a champion in his category. Jackson took the hint and informed Koplin he would retire. Eventually Jackson appeared on the "Challenge," as previously described by him to the press and by Shirley Bernstein to the grand jury. Describing his experience at being asked on the air a question whose answer had been given to him before the broadcast, he now told the congressmen:

> My first reaction was to say, "No,—yes, I know this answer but I got it on a screening," and I could see visions not only of six cases of apoplexy there, but I could see my bullet-riddled body as I passed an alley somewhere. I decided against that plan and when I got out off the stage I even considered in my mind saying, "Well, I don't think I ought to take this check."[9]

In fact, he gave the right answer and won $4,000. His moral reservations about accepting the money were overcome, he said, when he queried the IRS and was informed he would have been liable for taxes on the amount even if he turned it down.

Jackson was followed to the witness table by Arthur Cohn, who testified about his experience on "The $64,000 Challenge," and an affidavit by his opponent, Wilton Springer, now recuperating from a heart attack, was read into the record. Ending the day's session, Harris announced that, because of illness, Louis Cowan would not be called before the subcommittee. This development was barely noted in the newspapers on Monday evening and the following morning amid the torrent of coverage of Van Doren. Under headlines like "Charlie Tells All," even the tabloids carried full versions of Van Doren's statement, and all the papers editorialized on it. The run-of-the-mill commentary was forgiving in tone, stressing that no public good would be served by hounding Van Doren further.

More high-minded writers found Van Doren's tragedy symptomatic of a "disease" of radio and television in general, which, in the words of a *New*

York Times editorial on November 3, "permits things to be represented not quite as they are. . . . The industry will have to undergo drastic reform to regain the confidence of the American public." And the *Herald-Tribune* the same day asked: "What price may eventually have to be paid for the current debasement of taste and deterioration of all standards except the fast sell? The quiz shows may well represent only the first installment of the bill, and not the largest one."

In addition, Hogan was grappling with the implications of Van Doren's testimony for the office. Answering questions from reporters about whether Van Doren would have to face charges of perjury, Hogan stalled. "It's a matter that will have to be considered and not in terms of one contestant. . . . The hearings are not over yet." Manhattan grand juries had the power to bring new investigations without waiting for the district attorney to initiate action, and the grand jury might want to know the "degree of contrition" shown by a prospective perjury defendant before deciding whether to ask Hogan to submit evidence.[10]

Hogan also told reporters, to my surprise, that Rubino personally had taken a copy of Van Doren's statement as early as the previous Friday evening, three days before Van Doren testified, to Hogan. The Chief had failed to share it with me. On Monday, Hogan participated in his first monthly meeting as a Columbia University trustee, which considered the resignation previously submitted by Van Doren, in light of his testimony in the morning, already printed by the afternoon papers. Around 6 P.M., the university announced that the trustees had accepted Van Doren's resignation.

ON THE SECOND DAY of hearings, the congressmen heard two more former "Challenge" contestants who had testified before the grand jury, Xavier Cugat and Patty Duke. Cugat told of accepting assistance from Koplin on the grounds that "as an entertainer, sometimes I am called to play a part that I am not, in show business. So, I felt I was doing the same thing then." Asked why he had quit at the $16,000 level, Cugat earned a big laugh when he answered: "I didn't quit. They quit me"—that is, they asked his opponent a question they knew she couldn't answer, making him the winner and stopping the match short of the highest prize level.[11]

Duke, now twelve years old, had become a genuine celebrity since her grand jury appearance. Less than two weeks before the congressional hearings resumed, a play called *The Miracle Worker* had opened on Broadway, with Duke starring in the role of Helen Keller as a child. The critics had raved about Duke's performance, so the press was back in the Caucus Room in force to cover her appearance before Congress. She was accompanied by her manager, John Ross, and their New York lawyer, Martin Leonard. Ross was sworn in first and immediately requested an executive session.

The Caucus Room was cleared, and under questioning Ross asserted that only in the last three days had he learned from Duke herself that she had been given the questions and answers for each broadcast of the "Challenge" by Shirley Bernstein in the last warm-up just before the show. Thus, according to Ross, all the studying by Duke he had supervised was unnecessary, since EPI had determined she would win. Ross's explanation for his belated knowledge was that, at the time of our investigation, Leonard advised him not to discuss the matter with Duke at all, in order not to unduly influence her conduct in whatever proceedings might ensue.

Leonard then tried to persuade the congressmen not to release Ross's testimony and that of Duke to follow, not on the grounds that Duke might be defamed, though it could have a harmful effect on her career; rather, it would defame Irving Harris, the EPI staff member who had recruited Duke for the "Challenge" and to whom Ross later gave $1,000 in cash, a fact that Ross admitted to the grand jury. But since Ross insisted the payment was not a bribe but a gift, as Congressman Charles Bennett observed sarcastically, its disclosure was neither defamatory nor incriminating; therefore, it did not warrant a closed hearing. In her testimony, Duke admitted that in the final warm-up before each broadcast, Bernstein had narrowed the material to no more than four possibilities and rehearsed Duke in these; when she faltered, Bernstein supplied the correct answers.[12] After Duke's appearance, the subcommittee voted to release all the executive-session testimony taken up to that point, with the exception of that of Frances Li, who was fifteen when she was a contestant on "Tic Tac Dough," and Duke's.

WITH THE CONTESTANTS out of the way, the congressmen turned their attention to Koplin and Carlin. Koplin, presenting himself as a meticulous professional who had taken seriously the task of finding qualified contestants for the programs, admitted that "The $64,000 Question," "Challenge," and "The Big Surprise" all had been controlled to the degree that, when desired, contestants could continue to win about 80 percent of the time. But he insisted on his principal aim of keeping contestants unaware of what went on; even with the language barrier Cugat presented, Koplin claimed, he struggled to avoid giving the bandleader the answers outright. Instead of confronting Koplin about his handling of Jackson, the subcommittee questioning focused on better-known contestants like Nadler and Brothers. Koplin repeated what he had told the grand jury: Nadler was a phenomenon who had absolutely encyclopedic knowledge of his categories.

Brothers, on the other hand, was the "synthetic expert" whose ability to absorb every available fact about boxing defied attempts to oust her, even after Revlon expressed doubts about her credibility. But Koplin had a little surprise for me. In preparing questions for Brothers, he had consulted with Nat Fleischer, the boxing writer. Only after Brothers won the top prize on the "Question" did Koplin learn, he now claimed, that Fleischer was a friend of her father's and had helped her prepare for the broadcasts. For this reason, Koplin said, he did not consult Fleischer when it came to preparing questions for her appearances on the "Challenge." During our investigation we had tried to bring in Fleischer but he managed to elude us by being out of the country, involved in preparations for the 1960 Olympic Games.

With the nature and extent of the controls established, the questioning turned to the relationship between the producers and sponsor, and Koplin and Carlin pointed the finger at Revlon for its obsessive attention to detail and ratings. Their testimony, as well as excerpts introduced in evidence from memos of the weekly meetings written by an advertising-agency participant, demonstrated the degree to which Revlon made it clear which contestants it wanted and didn't want on the shows.

Read into the record of the hearings was a sworn interrogation of Bernstein, carried out by Goodwin, just before the first round of hearings, in Los Angeles, where Bernstein had moved. No explanation was provided as to why Bernstein was not called to appear in person. Corroborating the accounts of Koplin and Carlin regarding the extent and pervasiveness of controls on the "Challenge," without referring to specific contestants or broadcasts, she asserted: "I did nothing of any importance without Steve Carlin knowing of it, and much of what I did was at his direction."[13] While the play-back method was employed roughly two-thirds of the time, some 20 percent of the time she resorted to the more extreme method of asking questions in screenings virtually identical to those to be used on a broadcast, "either because the contestant was very nervous or the sponsor had requested a particular outcome of a match."[14] In the latter case, it was Carlin who relayed the sponsor's wish. In her opinion, it was safe to assume that the use of controls was generally known by producers, advertising agencies, and networks.

Carlin himself now testified that Revlon expected the decisions on contestants to be carried out; when they were not, the reaction was one of extreme displeasure. Nevertheless, according to Carlin, the parties were able to agree 75 percent of the time on such matters as new knowledge categories, contestants, and details of format. As Carlin, less articulate but more sardonic than Koplin, told it, a more frequent problem than disagreement was when an agreed-upon change did not work out as hoped and produced a down-tick in the ratings. He went on to explain:

> There is a tradition in television . . . of trying to please the client. If you have a client whom you see once in 13 weeks, pleasing becomes a relatively simple matter. But if you have a client whom you see each week, a very persuasive client, pleasing him becomes more difficult. You have to please him every week, not every 13 weeks. We were willing to please the client.[15]

But asked if the high overall ratings of the "Question" didn't mean that another, less demanding client could have been found, Carlin admitted they had been "foolishly nervous" in the belief that, with Revlon sponsoring both $64,000 quizzes, in the public mind the sponsor had become so identified with the shows that a sale to another sponsor would have been impossible.

Both Koplin and Carlin were asked what steps CBS took to investigate after the Cohn and then the Jackson complaints, as well as approaches made by such authorities as the FCC and FTC. The chain of command had insulated Koplin from any such contacts, but Carlin reviewed the flurry of meetings between himself and CBS officials at the outbreak of the scandal, adding nothing to my own previous knowledge of these. There was no mention by Carlin—neither was he asked—about what personal role Cowan, as CBS Television president, might have assumed at the time in the network's probe of the quizzes he had created. Both Koplin and Carlin spared the congressmen speeches extolling the high-minded impulse behind the creation of the "Question," but they explicitly exonerated Cowan from any involvement in "controls."

ON NOVEMBER 4, the morning newspapers gave more attention to Cugat and Duke than to Koplin and Carlin, but the big story was the dismissal of Van Doren by NBC, without a cash settlement for the remaining term of his contract. In a statement, NBC cited Van Doren's having denied the truth about his involvement with "Twenty-One" "to the press, the New York City District Attorney, the grand jury, the viewing public, and to his employers at NBC."[16] Particularly galling had been the use of the "Today" show for his denials in 1958. Now on that show, host Dave Garroway unburdened himself; he was, he proclaimed in a choking voice,

> still a friend of Charles Van Doren. . . . I can only say I am heart-broken. He was one of our family. We are a little family on this show, strange as it may seem. . . . Whatever Charles did was wrong of course. I cannot condone or defend it. But we will never forget the non-Euclidean geometry essays or the poetry of Sir John Suckley which Charles left us with.[17]

Later it was learned that Garroway's outburst, though genuine, was taped several hours before its broadcast.

Of greater concern to me was an announcement by Hogan that he expected other contestants who "told less than the truth" to the grand jury to come in and correct their testimony. Only then would the matter be evaluated and a decision made about possible perjury prosecutions. This "we'll see" attitude was not characteristic of Hogan, who usually kept his mouth shut on matters where his own discretion was an issue. Finally, the *New York Times*, in its coverage of the previous day's happenings, mentioned that Judge Schweitzer had indicated he would be making known his decision on the release of the grand jury presentment in two weeks.

ON NOVEMBER 4, the first witness was Martin Revson, who, unaccompanied by a lawyer, expressed dismay at Koplin's testimony and launched a spirited counterattack on behalf of the company in which he retained substantial stock holdings. In a prepared statement, echoing what he had told me two weeks before, Revson stressed the stake Revlon had in the integrity of the shows and the damage it could have suffered in terms of reputation and consumer goodwill, emphasizing that the shows were EPI's property, not Revlon's. The weekly meetings simply provided a forum for suggestions—about details like lighting and wardrobes and how to make the shows more interesting and entertaining. This entailed criticizing contestants and suggesting ideas for better contestants and categories, and making questions harder so that winners would deserve the high prizes awarded, but in all these matters EPI had the final say.

The problem with Revson's position was that the shows had been fixed, with the result of boosting the earnings of Revlon into the stratosphere. His task now was to counter not only the testimony of Koplin and Carlin but the cumulative record, especially in the memos written by an advertising man, Albert Ward, of Revson's own role in the management of the shows. Trying to brush off the memos, Revson was hard put to explain ordering their discontinuance after one memo bluntly listed the steps determining the outcome of an upcoming broadcast. He couldn't remember that memo but he recalled others that could be interpreted in a favorable light. At this point the sworn statement procured by Goodwin from George Abrams in my office the week before was read into the record, confirming the understanding by Revlon that the "destiny of a contestant" could be controlled by employing tough or easy questions. "If a contestant or match did not come out as we had suggested," said Abrams, "the sponsor and the agency representatives would be upset and expressed displeasure often in a very heated fashion."[18]

Disagreeing with the term "destiny," Revson conceded the meetings were devoted to "how we could get more picturesque, more interesting contestants" and that it was to Revlon's advantage in terms of ratings and sales to have "picturesque" contestants continue. But he was boxed in by Abrams's affidavit, the testimony of others, and the memos, of which he was reduced to sputtering, "The ones I said are true, are true; the things I said are not true, are not true."[19] Congressman Derounian said he hoped the attorney general would look into this testimony, "because somebody is not telling the truth,"[20] and Harris was asked to call Abrams to appear in person.

Martin Revson was followed to the witness table by his brother Charles, accompanied by the eminent Washington lawyer and political insider, Clark Clifford. In a lengthy statement, Charles Revson insisted that he personally never heard anything to impeach the integrity of the shows until the summer of 1958, and took the tack that he had been the victim of deceit by EPI and of indifference by EPI and CBS to his proposal for a quiz show "czar." Moreover, when he finally decided to drop the "Question" in the fall of 1958, Revlon had to pay EPI to be released from its contract.

Accepting the evidence of Charles Revson's limited personal role in the Revlon meetings, the congressmen limited themselves at first to scoring debating points. In the view of Rogers of Texas, the Revsons were presenting themselves, along with the public, as victims of deceit on the part of the producers and contestants, yet they had profited the most from the deceit. "I am wondering," said Rogers, "what is in your mind and the mind of the Revlon Co., to try to make restitution or correction of a wrong which you admit occurred." He had never given any thought to it, Revson replied:

> In view of the circumstances, we went along for the several years in sponsoring the show. We did not realize what it was. It is the same as any other commercial company that would earn something because of something—a network or producer or contestant and so forth. I don't know how to answer it. It is something that is past. It is part of a business experience.[21]

Asked if federal regulation should be adopted to protect responsible businessmen as well as the general public from deceitful TV producers, Revson said the affair had taught all concerned to be much more careful, implying that regulation should not be necessary.

By the end of the questioning, the importance of the shows to Revlon's profits plus Charles Revson's renowned attention to detail weighed heavily against his credibility as he left the witness table. Two advertising executives, from separate firms working for Revlon, followed and echoed Revson's characterizations of the meetings and of the nature of Revlon's input into the quizzes. Their testimony lost weight when it was revealed that their participation in the meetings came after Ward had been ordered to stop writing his memos. One of them, James Webb of C. J. LaRoche & Co., also admitted he had been asked to testify by Revlon and had discussed his upcoming appearance with Revlon's lawyer, Simon Rifkind. I wondered why the subcommittee didn't ask Ward himself to testify.

The following morning, Thursday, November 5, Abrams came before the subcommittee in person, attempting to downplay the apparent contradictions between his earlier affidavit and the testimony of Martin Revson. By contrast to his appearance before the grand jury, Abrams, in the limelight, was concerned not to appear to be betraying his old bosses. Stressing ratings as the determining factor in everything, Abrams claimed that the word "control" never came up at meetings, and the possibility of contestants receiving questions and answers in advance never arose before Cohn's complaint, which was why Revlon accepted EPI's explanation in that instance. Only at the time of Jackson did he realize "that the producers might have been using a technique other than tough or easy questions to control the future of the contestants."[22] Abrams also seconded Martin Revson's interpretation of the significance of Ward's memos; such reports, he asserted, were often used as vehicles by agencies for making a point or editorializing to clients.

Abrams now characterized the controlling of the shows as an "act of desperation" on the part of EPI dictated by a steady ratings decline, after attempts to shore them up with higher dollar prizes and the use of celebrities as contestants: "[T]he producers felt this pressure and resorted to rigging and fixing to save their property and satisfy the sponsor. . . . They were living between the mixed values of show business and the advertising business, and moral values were lost sight of in this effort to entertain the public and satisfy the sponsor."[23]

Under questioning, Abrams conceded that he and his boss were more concerned by Jackson's complaint than Cohn's because of the publicity generated by Jackson, and he admitted that the close supervision of the shows by Revlon was unusual in the business, but he too defended the procedure, calling it "a good one. I think more sponsors and agencies should get into the act where their programs are concerned. Too many are prone to just leave the program alone and look at the ratings without trying to make their programs better."[24] Implicit here was a fear among sponsors and advertising people that the scandal had undermined the traditional arrangement by which they exercised autonomy over the television time they bought.

On the morning of Abrams's appearance, the newspapers reported that President Eisenhower, asked again by reporters about the quiz scandal, likened it to the fixing of the 1919 World Series:

> I think I share the American general reaction of almost bewilderment that people could conspire to confuse and deceive the American people. . . . Selfishness and greed occasionally get the ascendancy over those things that we like to think of as the ennobling virtues of man, his capacity for self-sacrifice, his readiness to help others. . . . Every economic unit should remember that self-discipline is the thing that will keep free government working on and on.[25]

Eisenhower promised that the Justice Department study of the quiz matter he had ordered would be completed by the end of the year. As for developments at the hearings, the newspapers reported that Congressmen Bennett and Derounian had repeated their demands that the attorney general examine the testimony for the possibility of perjury, and Harris promised the transcript would be sent to the Justice Department. On the New York Stock Exchange, the price of Revlon shares fell 5¼ points to $54.25. Several newspapers printed excerpts from the executive-session testimony released by the subcommittee. Captain Michael O'Rourke, whose participation in rigging was made public by the now-released testimony of Dowd and Felsher, insisted on his innocence and announced his resignation from the army in order to testify before Congress as a civilian; however, the subcommittee did not call him.

IN A LONG PUBLIC SESSION in the evening of November 4 the subcommittee turned to a matter which, had we known of it during the life of the Third September 1958 Grand Jury, might have given an entirely different turn to our investigation. Three witnesses—Kenneth Hoffer, a former "Question" contestant and employee of the Hess Brothers Department Store in Allentown, Pennsylvania; David Gottlieb, another Hess employee; and Max Hess, the department store owner—told the following tale.

In August 1955 Hoffer was a buyer of men's furnishings for the department store, nationally known because of its mail-order business. When Hess learned that Hoffer had applied to become a "$64,000 Question" contestant in the category of the Bible, he instructed his public relations chief, Max Levine, to coordinate an effort to back Hoffer's effort in order to publicize the store. Through the intermediary of Gertrude Bayne, a partner in a New York public relations firm that did work for Hess, an interview of Hoffer by Elroy Schwartz, a staff writer for the "Question," was set up at the Cowan offices. On this occasion, Hoffer drove from Allentown to New York in Hess's car, accompanied by Gottlieb, a Hess employee with show-business connections. At the meeting with Schwartz, Hoffer was not given any concrete indication that he would be made a contestant and neither was he examined on his knowledge of the Bible.

Unknown to Hoffer, Gottlieb had his orders plus $1,000 in his pocket provided by Hess. Gottlieb took Schwartz aside and offered him up to $2,000 to put Hoffer on the show. Schwartz, according to Gottlieb, indicated that the amount was not sufficient, since others besides him would have to be paid. Meanwhile, Hoffer met with Joseph Cates, the producer-director of the "Question," who told him the Bible category had been used too recently and suggested baseball as an alternative.

That evening back in Allentown, Gottlieb reported to Hess and Levine, and they put in a phone call to Schwartz. Accounts varied on who actually spoke to Schwartz, but an agreement was reached that in return for $10,000 in cash, Hoffer would become a contestant. The following day, Gottlieb returned to New York and, at lunch with Cates and Schwartz, they hammered out the details. Hoffer would be on the show at least once, in the category of baseball, and the Hess store would receive at least two plugs; the $10,000 would be paid in cash in two installments, the day of the broadcast and several days after. At the end of the week, Hoffer was notified that he would be on the next broadcast of the "Question," on August 9, 1955.

On that day, Gottlieb, carrying $5,000 in $50 and $100 bills given to him by Hess, met Schwartz at a restaurant and handed him an envelope containing the money, which Schwartz counted and put in his pocket. That night, after the opera expert Gino Prato disappointed America by declining a try at the $64,000 question, Hoffer was introduced on the air. In the interview segment, he mentioned twice that he worked for the Hess Department Store in Allentown, Pennsylvania, but he never made it to the isolation booth. He failed to answer correctly the third question, worth $256 ("Name the New York Yankees outfielder known as 'Old Reliable' "—Tommy Henrich) and was off the show.

But the plugs, carried to the huge audience that had tuned in to see Prato, were enough for Hess. Several days later on a New York street, Gottlieb handed Schwartz an envelope containing a second $5,000 in cash. Hess, the last of the three to testify, was a colorful, sometimes recalcitrant witness, but he freely admitted the transaction, insisting however he did not know the money was going to Schwartz by name. Hess revealed that such payments were a normal promotion practice, and he retained public relations specialists, like Bayne, known as "schlockmeisters" (Yiddish for "junk masters"), to place plugs on numerous television shows sponsored by other advertisers. The unusual thing about this transaction, according to Hess, was the importance of the "Question," the size of the payment, and the fact it was in cash and paid directly to personnel on the show.

He went on to say that he retained six to eight public relations firms to promote his name around the country, paid for their services by check, and reported the payments as legitimate business expenses for tax purposes. He named several television shows on which he had appeared as a guest himself as a result of payments, and cited "goodwill" payments of $1,000 each to several newspaper columnists to visit the store and possibly mention it in their columns.

Following Hess, Max Levine, Hess's public relations manager, corroborated his boss's account and handed over to the subcommittee a list covering five years of check payments, of roughly $500 for each plug, to five New York schlockmeisters for plugs on television shows on some fifty different occasions. The programs were mostly daytime quiz and game shows but included the "Today" and the "Tonight" variety shows on NBC as well as the highly regarded "Person to Person" on CBS. This program had come in for trouble after the first round of hearings and Stanton's decision to ban all "deceits," which included the showing in advance of questions to guests interviewed by Edward R. Murrow.

After Levine testified, Schwartz and Cates were summoned; both requested and were granted executive sessions. Schwartz confirmed receiving $10,000 in cash in two installments from Gottlieb, which he shared with Cates, and admitted to speaking with Hess on the phone on two occasions. In his version of events, however, Schwartz did not solicit the bribe; Gottlieb told him that Hess was accustomed to paying handsomely for plugs and had once, according to Gottlieb, offered the Duke and Duchess of Windsor $25,000 to have dinner with him. When Schwartz said no, Gottlieb, then Hess himself, simply upped the offer and insisted Schwartz have lunch with Gottlieb who handed him the first installment of cash.

The way Schwartz and Cates told it, it was not clear who at EPI decided to make Hoffer a contestant. Schwartz claimed he was instructed by Elaine Silverstein, Cowan's secretary, to "interview" Hoffer—not screen him—as if the decision to put him on the show had already been made; in fact, Hoffer seemed quite suitable, providing a contrast in personality and subject matter to Prato. Schwartz and Cates gave the impression they just happened to be in the right place when the money was handed out and were able, in the words of Cates, "to split the loot." Cates called the selection of Hoffer an unfortunate "accident" resulting from the fact that Bayne was a friend of Silverstein. The possibility that the incident could have reflected badly on Cowan was the reason Schwartz and Cates requested the executive session.[26]

After hearing Schwartz and Cates, the subcommittee reconvened in public in the late afternoon of November 5, to begin the last leg of the hearings with the testimony of Robert Kintner, the president of NBC, to be followed by Stanton of CBS. The newspapers were already full of reports relating to the Hess matter. In New York, Hogan told reporters we had known nothing of it but it did "smack a little of commercial bribery." If that were the case, the dates of Hoffer's appearance on the "Question," in the summer of 1955, probably made the payment by Hess unprosecutable under the statute of limitations, which ran for two years in cases of commercial bribery.

As for the scandal in general, Hogan went overboard by saying "of the 150 persons who went before the grand jury, perhaps 50 told the truth." A reporter asked in relation to the possibility of perjury prosecutions if there were two standards—one for ordinary people and another for celebrities.

Hogan snapped back angrily, "That's ridiculous. The law is clear," though, he acknowledged, perjury was difficult to prove. "Certainly and definitely" he would be consulting a new grand jury on whether to prosecute perjury, adding that it was Freedman's corrected grand jury testimony that persuaded Van Doren to tell the truth, not the viewer's letter cited by Van Doren in his Washington statement. The office was receiving a huge volume of mail urging Hogan to prosecute Van Doren. Only one in ten said Van Doren "has suffered enough." For his part, Hogan was amazed that a great percentage of the letter writers were "vindictive and almost sadistic."[27]

ROBERT KINTNER had the bluff manner of the newspaperman he had been early in his career. He had been president of NBC, reporting to the chairman, Robert Sarnoff, since July 1, 1958. In his opening statement, Kintner asserted that NBC had been deceived as much as the public "by a small group of people in the production field and the contestant field" but would not "abdicate a program responsibility in the quiz, audience-participation, panel-show field." It had set up a "standards and practices" investigatory unit, it favored making the rigging of quiz shows a crime, and it would offer its facilities to the subcommittee to present to the public its conclusions regarding the investigation and the television industry.[28]

Kintner brought up to date the account provided in the first round of hearings by Thomas Ervin, detailing NBC's moves in the last days of Van Doren's association with the company and the results of its decision to clean up its quizzes. Since May 1959 contestants had been required to sign forms stating they would not take assistance and would report all offers of help. In the time since the New York grand jury had completed its work, a "professionally equipped" standards and practices group of former FBI agents had interrogated some eighty former contestants in all parts of the country. As a result, two instances of wrongdoing had been turned up: a kickback scheme between audience members and two "warm-up men" and evidence of use of "controlled" questions, meaning easy questions for contestants the producers wished to retain, hard ones for those they wanted to be rid of. This information, Kintner said, had just been turned over to the Manhattan district attorney. In addition, NBC had revised its contracts with all packagers to require warranties as to the "honest conduct" of the programs provided, and the network had secured affidavits from every NBC executive, regardless of assignment, and all staff members connected with quiz or audience-participation

game shows, attesting to the honesty of their programs. These efforts, according to Kintner, would obviate the need for an industry "czar," which would
be no more workable for an industry as large and complex as broadcasting
than for the newspaper or magazine industries.

At the same time, Kintner asserted, it would not be in the public interest
for the networks to be required to directly produce all programs, but neither
should they be barred from owning and producing their own programs. In
sum, the content of broadcasting was the broadcaster's responsibility; government regulatory action would "inject the government into the program process itself," which would not only be counter to the "whole concept" of
broadcasting in this country but also be ineffective as regards quiz shows,
since it could not prevent a producer from conspiring with a contestant. On
the other hand, legislation "aimed directly at the wrongdoer" would be appropriate. In this connection, Kintner presented a draft federal statute making
it a crime to

> knowingly [participate] in any scheme or artifice to control the
> outcome of a contest portrayed on such program so that the pub-
> lic listening to or viewing such program is deceived into believing
> that the outcome of such contest is determined on the basis of the
> knowledge and skill of the participants in such contest in answer-
> ing questions put to them when in fact the outcome of such con-
> test has been predetermined by such scheme or artifice.[29]

But the subcommittee was more interested in Van Doren. One after another, the members asked almost identical questions about Van Doren's
October 7 telegram, apparently eager to prove that NBC higher-ups had
approved the contents, which Kintner denied vehemently. Before finishing
with him, the congressmen made light of his invitation for them to present
their findings to the public on NBC, saying they were afraid of what their
ratings would be and that they might be told what to say in advance.

On Friday, November 6, the morning newspapers focused on the fresh
allegations against a current quiz show, which the *New York Times* identified
as "Treasure Hunt," adding that the show's producer had announced the dismissal of the two "warm-up men" mentioned by Kintner. The *Times* also
reported a rally at Columbia University the night before, called to protest the
forced resignation of Van Doren, which was interrupted by booing from students opposed to his reinstatement.

At 10 A.M., the subcommittee convened to hear the last witness in the hearings. Refined and punctilious, notorious for his attention to detail, Frank Stanton had earned a Ph.D. in psychology prior to starting with CBS in 1935, doing research on audience reactions to programming. Though William Paley, the chairman, continued to rule CBS with an iron hand, Stanton had the role of representing the company before committees of Congress, industry and public policy associations, and at important awards dinners, fostering and maintaining the prestigious image of CBS as the leader of the broadcasting business and pillar of the public interest.

Stanton began with an apology that Cowan, still in the hospital, could not appear. Later under questioning, he defended Cowan, whom he had known since World War II, as "an idea man, a creator . . . not the man who has gone into the control room or into the studio and done the detail work. . . . I have no reason to question Mr. Cowan's integrity as far as *The $64,000 Question* show is concerned when he was in charge of it."[30] For his own part, Stanton claimed no knowledge of irregularities in CBS quizzes until August 8, 1958, and the "Dotto" matter. Acknowledging the network's responsibility for its programming, even if produced by outsiders, Stanton cited his decision to cancel all big-money quizzes as a step toward making CBS "the masters of our own house . . . to be more certain in the future that it is we and we alone who decide not only what is to appear on CBS Television Network, but how it is to appear." The next step would be, he promised, to issue rules "to assure that programs will be exactly what they appear to be."[31]

Stanton said the network was exploring the use of a new code of standards that would "eliminate legitimate complaints" regarding commercials; after all, he asserted, "in the long run it is as much to the advantage of the advertiser as to the broadcaster that there be public confidence in the medium of television and public support for its practices." Voicing support for a law "making it a crime to use deceitful practices in any game or contest or in any advertising medium," Stanton concluded his statement with confidence that the subcommittee "would not recommend legislation which would invade the areas of programming or result in censorship."[32]

Questioned about the *Time* and *Look* magazine pieces raising doubts about the quiz shows as early as 1957, Stanton observed that the motivations of the magazines had to be taken into consideration, in view of the fact they were "fighting for advertising dollars and information the same as we are. . . . This isn't to excuse us for not knowing more, but I say we weren't triggered and perhaps shouldn't have been" by the articles. He added that the magazine companies were competitors who also owned TV stations, which continued to carry the quizzes without complaint. CBS, he insisted, had taken "affirmative action" against the quizzes without waiting for "someone in Washington" to say something.[33]

By contrast to their previous treatment of the commission chairmen, the congressmen all but fawned on Stanton, taking turns congratulating him on the "forthrightness" of his position on television deceit, by implication—in a couple of cases openly—critical of his NBC counterpart for evading responsibility for the independently packaged quizzes presented on NBC. Stanton masterfully split hairs in responding to the question of whether there could be legitimate "controls on a so-called contest of skill and knowledge":

> I think the word "control" is a dirty word when read against one situation and . . . a good or clean word when read against another. . . . If you say that you are selecting someone because he has knowledge in a narrow field, and then you are going to ask him a series of questions, that is perfectly legitimate, because you are showing him off as an expert in Italian opera, in baseball, whatever it might be. But if you so control him, or if you select him so that you know beforehand that he can answer the precise question, or if you, through control, virtually give him the question, that is obviously the dirty application of the word "control". . . . Control isn't bad, but control with abuse is bad.[34]

Finally, Stanton resisted the notion of regulating networks by licensing them, saying that CBS was already regulated to the extent that it owned its flagship broadcasting stations, which in effect submitted it to licensing. Thus it was as a broadcaster in its own right, not as a network providing programming to independently owned affiliates, that CBS was "responsible" for the content of its programs. The questioning ended with effusive thanks from Harris for Stanton's willingness to assist the subcommittee. I gave silent thanks that my brief career as a Washington consultant had come to an end, but I had no way of imagining how much more the quiz affair had in store for me.

PART FIVE

A Change of Circumstances

CHAPTER SIXTEEN

Mass Perjury

(NOVEMBER 1959—MAY 1960)

For the public at large, the quiz scandal ended with the confession of Charles Van Doren, but for former contestants, the broadcasting and advertising industries, as well as the district attorney's office, the confession was an explosion with continuing fallout. In the following weeks, recriminations swirled at the highest levels of business and government, as regulatory commissioners, congressmen, network presidents, broadcasting and advertising association chiefs vied in issuing warnings of the dire consequences for American broadcasting if the industry did not clean house. These were accompanied by laments on the state of the American soul and loss of innocence, from religious leaders, editorial writers, columnists, and pundits.[1]

Richard Goodwin wrote an article for *Life* magazine pointing out that, though they were called "big money shows," the quizzes were in fact "one of the cheapest forms of advertising available on television." According to Goodwin, the attitude of many in the television business that "the airwaves belong to them" had to be "stamped out." The airwaves were "public property granted by the people to private enterprise. The powerful medium of television comes into our homes and helps shape the values of our children, the desires of our people. With this great responsibility, television's morality must be beyond reproach."[2] Goodwin became hoist by his own petard when a *Washington Post* editorial criticized him for exploiting his position to write the article and thereby profit from public service. Even though Goodwin had cleared the project with his superiors, the incident was embarrassing for Harris, who later announced a tightening of rules regarding the outside activities of his staff. But the astute Goodwin had already lined up a new job. Resigning from the subcommittee, he joined the campaign staff of Senator John F. Kennedy, an unannounced candidate for president.

BACK in the office after the hearings, I worked with Hogan and three recently hired assistant D.A.s—William Reilly, Allan Schwartz, and Marshall Witten—to map our future course in unresolved matters connected with the quiz affair. These included the possibility that crime of commercial bribery had been committed when Max Hess paid $10,000 to place Kenneth Hoffer on "The $64,000 Question." Under New York law, the promise or gift of a payment or gratuity to an employee without the consent of his or her employer, with the intent of influencing the employee's action in regard to the employer's business, was a misdemeanor, and either or both the giver and receiver could be prosecuted for it. The fact that Hess's money had been handed over in New York put the matter in our jurisdiction.

Even though New York law placed a limitation of two years on prosecution of commercial bribery, a wrinkle in the law might have permitted action even though the Hess payoff had taken place four and a half years before. The unrolling of the limitation period was *suspended* when a violator left the jurisdiction in order to avoid prosecution. Schwartz and Cates had been New York residents, but Hess and his employees resided in Pennsylvania; given that fact, the statute of limitations could have applied only to the time the Pennsylvanians spent in New York and, conceivably, that might not have exceeded two years. I assigned Reilly and Allan Schwartz to research the law in this connection and dig into the business of "schlockmeistering," to determine if the selling of plugs on television shows was going on without the knowledge of the shows' nominal sponsors, an indication of the possibility of fraud.

ANOTHER DEVELOPMENT was the gift horse from NBC's new in-house investigative unit, revealed in Washington by Robert Kintner. The evidence, concerning kickbacks on the show "Treasure Hunt," had been turned over in the form of a complaint to our Fraud Bureau. Jan Murray, the show's emcee, producer, and copackager, had become suspicious of two part-time staff members, Arthur Roberts and Barney Martin, the latter a former New York City policeman. These two were employed by several different game and variety programs not only to warm up studio audiences before broadcasts, but also to help select prospective contestants from among audience members. Murray alerted the NBC investigation unit, which found that Martin and Roberts had taken kickbacks from people they selected. Upon the unit's recommendation, Martin and Roberts were fired. On November 11, I met with

Murray, then had my associates begin calling in former "Treasure Hunt" contestants to determine the extent of the kickbacks.

ON NOVEMBER 19, Mitchell Schweitzer handed down his final word on the quiz grand jury's presentment, denying our application that the presentment be accepted. In an extremely cogent fourteen-page opinion, Schweitzer narrowed the central issue to whether a grand jury could report on the "activities and conduct of private persons engaged in private enterprise" and found that the applicable precedents and statutes required holding that the grand jury was not so empowered nor could the court properly accept the report.[3]

Whatever may have been the powers of the grand jury at common law, Schweitzer stated, in New York the powers of grand juries derived solely from the state constitution and Code of Criminal Procedure, despite the "prior indulgence" of courts in accepting reports from grand juries on matters outside their statutory warrant. Describing this "indulgence," Schweitzer quoted a 1955 article by Richard Kuh, a Manhattan assistant district attorney and Hogan's administrative assistant:

The continued appearance of these reports might be attributable to the common belief among lay jurors, uninstructed by the law, that they are a power unto themselves and can peer into any matter that their civic consciences indicate need investigation.

Possibly, reports continue because of a disregard of legal precedents by prosecutors who guide the grand jury and by judges who accept these reports and permit them to become matters of court record. Or conceivably, the knowledge of the rarity of motions to expunge may serve as an informal license to juries, prosecutors, and courts bursting with information that they believe will contribute to community enlightenment.[4]

Furthermore, Schweitzer wrote, the mere absence of names in the quiz presentment could not "validate an otherwise unauthorized" report. The people involved in television were few enough in number to be easily identified; at the same time, without naming names, the report could tar individuals in the business who had never engaged in deceptive practices. The possibility of this kind of damage was a factor in Schweitzer's sweeping aside the contention of the Grand Jury Association, made in its amicus brief, that the court was bound to accept filing of the report and only then could act on motions to expunge that aggrieved parties might make. "Patently," wrote the judge, "such procedure would permit the evil sought to be avoided to penetrate and destroy. Any relief granted thereafter would be illusory at best and the affected person would be left with the consolation of a pyrrhic victory. Such procedure would be a meaningless circuity."[5]

Use of the testimony that formed the basis for the report, however, was another matter. The law permitted making available the grand jury minutes to public agencies with a "legitimate interest," including committees of the U.S. Congress. Even if the tenacity of the grand jury and the district attorney developed a "morally fraudulent picture," the function of making it public, commendable as that might be, short of uncovering proof of violation of "any state penal violations," did not belong to the grand jury. Rather, that function:

> properly devolves upon the duly elected representatives of the American people or upon such Committees as they may legally designate. A federal Congressional Committee, conducting hearings designed to review the impact of existing federal laws and the performance of regulatory agencies, has powers that a County Grand Jury, probing for criminal conduct that may afford a basis for indictment, lacks.[6]

It was a bravura performance, an excellent piece of law-making, beautifully written and reasoned and impeccably documented. Schweitzer had every reason to be proud and called a press conference to present it to the world, where he revealed he had studied some 150 court decisions and taken his own opinion through sixteen drafts. He suggested that the state legislature clarify the law on grand jury reports vis-à-vis public officials. As for grand juries he himself would impanel in the future, he would make sure they knew the limits of their power to report.

Later in the day, Louis Hacker told reporters that Schweitzer had "struck a serious blow at the effectiveness of the grand jury" and added his hope that the Grand Jury Association would immediately seek a writ of mandamus in a higher court to order Schweitzer to accept and release the presentment.[7] The decision was unpopular with the press as well, which, in angry editorials, deplored the implications for the public's right to know. I had two problems with the opinion. The first was on the level of substance. Holding as he did that grand juries had no right to air matters of public concern with an end to pointing up the need for legislative action to provide a remedy, the judge had thrust aside three hundred years of history and hundreds of presentments handed up by grand juries since colonial times; what he called "usurpation" was a common-law right in existence long before the New York State constitution and statutes he cited were ever dreamed of. My other problem was in the realm of style. In my opinion, Schweitzer lacked the temperament and inclination to produce a piece of writing of such clarity and depth. I simply could not believe he had written the opinion. This raised the old question—what really had motivated him to quash the presentment in the first place—and a new one: who had written the masterful opinion above his signature?

BUT THE FATE of the presentment was a minor consideration for me. Hogan's impulsive comments concerning the extent of the perjury and his call for witnesses to correct their grand jury testimony produced a torrent of calls from former Barry and Enright contestants, or more precisely their lawyers. Hogan's statements had the effect of confusing and of even misleading contestants and lawyers, including at least two former assistant D.A.s, into believing that by setting the record straight somehow, the perjury could be expunged. But, with the original jury out of existence, the law permitted no such thing. Now that so many people wanted to tell us the truth, quietly dropping any prosecution of Van Doren and Bloomgarden, who had been the first to come in, was ruled out.

Complicating the situation was the two-witness rule. The eager confession of a perjurer by itself was not enough to make a case, no more than a confession of homicide would be without a dead body and evidence of foul play. Thus as far as "Tic Tac Dough" and "Twenty-One" contestants were concerned, Felsher and Freedman would have to testify anew if we were to proceed against the perjurers. Felsher remained within reach, but Freedman had returned to Mexico and, according to Hyman Zoloto, Enright's lawyer, Freedman had no intention of returning voluntarily at our bidding, for, in his view, he had more than lived up to his side of the bargain. If, without Freedman's further cooperation, we could not proceed against Van Doren or any other "Twenty-One" perjurer, we could not proceed against the small fry who had lied in connection with "Tic Tac Dough," even with the testimony of Felsher to make the cases. It would be perceived as a miscarriage of justice to prosecute "Tic Tac Dough" perjurers only, when it was a "Twenty-One" contestant, Van Doren, who had admitted publicly to lying to the grand jury.

Freedman's attitude was made clear as early as November 9, when the *New York Times* reported a statement he made in Mexico City defending the rigged quiz shows as "a breath of fresh air" in television programming "saturated with murder and violence." Lest he be faulted for recommending deceit as a substitute for violence, he attacked the characterization that the shows were deceptive. "The entertainment field, from time immemorial," he said,

> has been based on showmanship, spectacle, and illusion. The only function of entertainment is to entertain. Everyone knows that the magician doesn't saw the lady in half, that movies supposedly filmed in Egypt are actually shot in Hollywood studios. . . . Our only error was that we were too successful. The stakes were too high and quiz winners fused themselves into the home life and the hopes and aspirations of the viewers. . . . It is about time the television industry stopped apologizing for its existence and began to fight back. It should insist that sponsored programs be recognized and judged as entertainment and entertainment only.

It seemed unlikely that Enright, acutely aware of the "house-cleaning" binge underway in the industry, had put Freedman up to this. Freedman had become a loose cannon, giving vent to his frustration and anger at exile.

By the end of December 1959, we had talked to some two dozen former contestants who now admitted to lying to the Third September 1958 Grand Jury. The great majority of these had been named by Freedman and Felsher under oath. Others, whom we had not put before the grand jury, came forward to say they had lied in office interviews. These accounts began to clear up a big mystery of the quiz affair—how was it that so many respectable, otherwise law-abiding citizens had lied under oath en masse—but opened a new can of worms, the possibility of extensive subornation of perjury by lawyers, inducing grand jury witnesses to lie under oath.

The statement of Timothy Horan was a good illustration. Horan, an old friend of Felsher, had been assisted by the producer on daytime "Tic Tac Dough" and later became a nighttime champion. Now, thirteen months after his grand jury appearance, Horan not only admitted receiving questions and answers as a contestant, he also told us of a flurry of contacts between himself, Felsher, and the lawyer, Sol Gelb, before and after his grand jury testimony, which followed by two days Felsher's first grand jury appearance in October 1958. At these meetings, according to Horan, Gelb advised him that Felsher would be in trouble—having just testified under oath that he had not given assistance to anyone—if Horan did not corroborate this position. Gelb in effect solicited Horan's assurance he would not contradict Felsher, which

Horan gave. Later on, after testifying, Horan reassured Gelb he had no intention of changing his story.

Similar accounts were now given to us by nine other former "Tic Tac
Dough" contestants. All admitted to meeting, at Felsher's behest, with Gelb
for a pep talk on at least one occasion before their testimony. Gelb did not
ask them whether they had received assistance nor did he tell them directly
they should lie to us or the grand jury. Instead he warned them we would
employ pressure tactics, even yell and pound on the table, but the contestants
should not be intimidated and stick to their stories.

Gelb told one contestant the investigation was a witch-hunt—that even if
the contestant had been given assistance, no law was broken. To others he
explained the law of perjury by saying that even if a contestant stuck by a
story that he had received no answers and Felsher himself contradicted that,
the situation would still be a standoff, because it was a matter of one person's
word against another's. On one or two occasions, Gelb interpreted the two-
witness rule as meaning that the contestant was in no danger at all, thus it
would cost the contestant nothing to protect Felsher. All this indicated that
Gelb's conduct, if it did not cross the line into subornation of perjury, which
would have been almost impossible to prove, was unethical according to the
Canons of Ethics for lawyers—since he was giving legal advice to persons
whose own interests might be in conflict with that of his client, Felsher.

I was anxious to go over the whole story with Felsher again, since in his
previous recantation he had neglected to inform us of his lawyer's active role.
Moreover, he had neglected to name one of the contestants who had just told
us the truth, and we wanted to know why. But, aggrieved for having lost his
job, attributable to his recantation's falling into the hands of the Harris subcommittee, and feeling betrayed, Felsher wanted nothing more to do with us.
He retained a new attorney, Maurice Nessen, an aggressive young lawyer who
was a partner of Van Doren's lawyer, Rubino. Nessen informed me that
Felsher would answer additional questions only under the compulsion of a
subpoena.

We decided not to take that step until we completed the picture with
evidence from former "Twenty-One" contestants now coming in with new
statements of their own. The most unexpected of these was a pre-Stempel
contestant, the detective magazine editor, James Bowser. Now Bowser spilled
the beans, not only admitting being fed everything by Enright personally, but
also revealing the nature of his contacts with Enright during the investigation.
The day before his scheduled visit to the office in September 1958, Bowser

claimed, Enright advised him he needed no lawyer and urged him simply to tell us he received no help on the show. After the interview, he briefed Enright, then wrote to Enright saying he would sue for damages if it were shown that the contestant who defeated him on "Twenty-One" received assistance. The idea of the letter resulted from the prompting of friends and was intended to deflect suspicions by them and his employer that he himself had been fixed. On the same day, he mailed a postcard to Enright, which contained the following: "Dan—Disregards, MYERS." "Myers," Bowser revealed, was a code name he and Enright had arranged for communicating with each other. He further claimed that, upon receiving the letter and postcard, Enright called to acknowledge that he understood their meaning.

Bowser's story not only bolstered our knowledge of the extent to which Enright had orchestrated the mass perjury committed by contestants; it also impeached Enright's Washington testimony that Freedman and Felsher were the instigators, because Bowser had had no link at all with Freedman or Felsher. Pressed on exactly what had prompted him to lie, Bowser claimed to be motivated by "self-pride," not wanting to appear to have committed a crime, and the desire to help Enright who was in trouble.

Now I believed, with additional help from Felsher and Freedman, we could make a case for a conspiracy against Enright, Gelb, and Myron Greene to suborn perjury by various contestants. Freedman had more explaining to do as well: we had new statements from two former "Tic Tac Dough" contestants handled by him when he was that program's producer; he had named only one of them in his recantation of May 1959. The other, Terry Curtis, had won $2,800 on daytime "Tic Tac Dough," then later won $78,000 on the short-lived "High Low," which Freedman had also produced and Bloomgarden indicated was rigged. She had denied receiving assistance on either show to the Third September 1958 Grand Jury; now she was telling us that Freedman had assisted her on both.

While Zoloto continued to pour cold water on any notion of prevailing upon Freedman to return, the lawyer regaled me with gossip and advice on how to make life easier for everyone and tried pumping me for what we were learning from the former contestants. I conceded that some people had come in, and ultimately their cases would be submitted to a grand jury, which made Freedman's further cooperation essential. Zoloto then suggested if we would formally drop the outstanding perjury indictment against Freedman, all our problems would be solved; I countered that this was ruled out by the change of circumstances caused by the Van Doren explosion—hardly my fault. In fact, the indictment was the only leverage I had with Freedman. Since it was doubtful that Freedman was paying Zoloto, it was clear that Enright was still pulling the strings in the hope that any cases we had against the contestants would be dropped if he, Freedman, and Felsher could just sit it out.

ON DECEMBER 9, 1959, William Reilly and Allan Schwartz submitted a report of findings from their investigation of schlockmeistering. In the Hess affair, Max Hess himself, Elroy Schwartz, and Joseph Cates were the only possible targets. The fact that the testimony of the last two in executive session by the Harris subcommittee was not released indicated they might have incriminated themselves. Though willing to discuss other aspects of his experience with the $64,000 shows, Cates declined the opportunity to discuss the Hess affair when we interviewed him not long after my return from Washington. Now residing in California, Elroy Schwartz was out of reach.

Under a strict reading of section 439 of the Penal Law, commercial bribery could have been prosecuted if Louis Cowan would testify that he had never authorized any of his employees to accept payment in return for the kind of arrangements made on behalf of Hess. But we could not determine whether Schwartz had left New York before the statutory limitation of two years had run on the infraction, and the task of proving that Hess had been outside of New York long enough for the limitation not to have run out would be daunting. Richard Denzer advised me that a court probably would rule that the statute of limitations had run out in this situation.

Using the information provided to the Harris subcommittee concerning payments by Hess in the years 1954–1959, Reilly and Allan Schwartz had sought to determine if Hess had broken the law in his other dealings. Many of these transactions had been handled by a public relations agent named Paul Mosher. Since Mosher played no part at all in procuring the plug on "The $64,000 Question," he cooperated fully with us. His records revealed the scope and complexity of the schlockmeistering network of PR men and their clients, radio and TV producers, performers, writers, and so-called prize men, or agents who provided producers with merchandise and services to be given away in lieu of cash on quiz and game shows in return for discount prizes and/or plugs on the air for the manufacturers and/or retailers (like Hess).

A key skill of the schlockmeister was to develop and put into action ideas of how to subtly mention the names of clients on shows. Mosher wrote one-liners and jokes using the Hess name, then offered these to performers, writers, producers, or other publicity men connected with shows. The fees paid by Hess were in the range of $600 for each plug—half going to the contacts setting up the plug, half to Mosher. All of these transactions were paid for by check and carried on Mosher's books. Since 1958 Mosher had obtained some dozen plugs for Hess on a number of programs. During the 1958–59 winter season, when we were investigating "Name That Tune" for quiz rigging, Hess bought seven plugs on the show through Mosher, who used contacts with emcee George DeWitt or one of the program's writers. Each of the plugs was a mention of the fact that a "Name That Tune" board game was selling very well in Hess's store.

Hess was only one of Mosher's clients; the others included an airline, a perfume manufacturer, and a hotel, in addition to show-business celebrities. The nature of the plugs varied—some giveaway game shows were open to donated merchandise plus fees in return for plugs; with these fees, the producers would buy other merchandise to give away on their shows. In this connection, Mosher worked with a range of quiz producers, including Barry and Enright when they still operated their shows for NBC. Mosher secured plugs for Trans World Airlines on "Tic Tac Dough" on several occasions in 1959. These took the form of announcements at the end of broadcasts that the transportation of contestants was "arranged by TWA." Airline plugs in game and variety shows were a widespread practice, and NBC continued to utilize them on "Tic Tac Dough" after the ouster of Barry and Enright. In the purification campaign that followed the Washington quiz hearings, CBS decided to abolish them; ABC and NBC were still in the process of "studying" the problem.

By March 1960, after taking statements from numerous people involved in schlockmeistering, we decided that even though a pattern of abuse existed, the possibility of proving commercial bribery was slim. Much of the plugging going on was at the producers' behest, a trade-off for giveaway merchandise or transportation "arrangements," and these transactions were carried out openly and recorded in the books of the participants. The fact that scripts were read in advance and closely supervised by the representatives of networks and primary sponsors indicated that these parties tolerated "plugola" in the form of gifts of liquor and small amounts of cash off the books to writers and performers.

Our investigation of schlockmeistering coincided with a change in climate underway since the quiz hearings, especially since a reawakened Federal Trade Commission was looking into plugola as a form of hidden advertising. The networks created their own departments for the procuring of merchandise for giveaway programs, previously the province of the program produc-ers as an "above the line" cost. By March 1960, Mosher was nervously asking for reassurances that we would not impart to NBC what he had told us. The network had created a new position: manager of program merchandising. The job was to find merchandise to give away on the network's quizzes and game shows. There would no longer be fees involved; NBC would either buy the merchandise or get it free in return for plugs. None other than Paul Mo-sher had been hired by NBC for the new position of manager of program merchandising.

ON MAY 20, 1960, I boarded a plane for Mexico City. Since our effort through Zoloto to bring Freedman back to New York was going nowhere, Hogan agreed that a surprise visit by me might serve to shake him up. I spent the next week in daily sessions with Freedman, often with his wife, Esther, pres-ent. I explained that we had planned to drop his perjury indictment after the 1958 grand jury's term, but the suppression of the presentment, the ensuing involvement of Congress, and the explosion caused by Van Doren's confes-sion had forced us to investigate the matter of the perjured contestants. Since they had the right to appear before another grand jury to explain their con-duct and plead for forgiveness, their cases could not be resolved without his cooperation, and if he wanted the indictment dropped, then he had to return to New York to testify again.

Freedman replied that his life was a disaster. Blacklisted in U.S. show busi-ness, he had moved to Mexico because his wife had connections there from student days and spoke Spanish fluently. He had rented out the house he owned in New Rochelle and was borrowing money from Enright to make ends meet. After almost a year in Mexico, he was not making a living and owed Enright some $18,000. He had written a nightclub show, now in re-hearsal in Mexico City, but foresaw no real financial rewards from it. He claimed he had been misled into lying the first time before the grand jury; when he told us the truth and then went to Washington to tell the truth again, he was smeared by Van Doren's accusation that he had solicited a kickback of $5,000. Thus he could not face the ordeal of testifying again.

My rejoinder, that his reappearance before the grand jury and recantation were not legally a defense for perjury, touched a nerve. Bitterly criticizing the legal advice he had received, Freedman began to amplify. When Stempel's initial allegations were published, Freedman now said, he was shocked and frightened by their vehemence against Van Doren and shared his concerns with Enright, who sent him to confer with Arthur Franklin's lawyer, Edwin Slote. When Freedman told Slote the truth about Van Doren and subsequent "Twenty-One" contestants, the lawyer promised to help, but Freedman never heard from him again. Meanwhile, Van Doren called Freedman and asked for a lunch meeting. According to Freedman, Van Doren said if the truth got out, it would not only ruin his career but the shock could kill his father. Freedman reassured Van Doren he would tell nobody. This lunch, which occurred before the grand jury was impaneled, Freedman claimed, was the only occasion on which he saw Van Doren in person after the scandal broke.

At this point, Freedman said, he had already been in touch with Snodgrass, whom he believed to be the weakest link, since Snodgrass believed that he had been swindled out of $40,000, which he could have walked away with if Enright had followed the suggestion of Bloomgarden's accountant and divided the prize money in the wake of the "sacral-coccyx" flap. When Freedman asked Snodgrass to keep his mouth shut, Snodgrass, according to Freedman, simply laughed and told him in crude terms what he could do with the show and the other contestants. A few days later, when Snodgrass telephoned Freedman to suggest a meeting at his lawyer's office, Enright referred Freedman to his new lawyer, Greene.

Freedman admitted to Greene that he had rigged the Snodgrass-Bloomgarden match, and Greene recommended that he stay away from Snodgrass and his lawyer. After Freedman agreed to talk to us in the office the first time, he again conferred with Greene, admitting just about everything to the lawyer. Greene represented himself as a good friend of Schweitzer and wise in the ways of the district attorney's office; even if we yelled at him, Freedman was advised by Greene, it was only a technique designed to frighten witnesses; he would not be under oath or any compulsion to tell us the truth.

According to Freedman, Greene asked him if any third person was ever present when he provided questions and answers to contestants or rehearsed them for their appearances. Freedman assured the lawyer there was never anyone else present, and only Enright had known what was going on. When Freedman explained to the lawyer that if he conceded to us that he had rigged Snogdrass, he would also have to tell about Bloomgarden and Van Doren, Greene replied, "If that's your position, that's your position" and repeated there was nothing to worry about from us in the office and he, Greene, would be present throughout the interview.

But, at the interview, Freedman chose to advance his version of events, even after Greene, at my suggestion, decided to leave because of the possible conflict of interest, in that Greene also represented Enright. Still, Freedman reported back to Greene, who again advised him he had nothing to worry about, then referred him to Edward Levine, a former assistant district attorney in Brooklyn. According to Freedman, Levine was thorough and meticulous but unforceful and lackadaisical in his advice, and he failed to adequately prepare Freedman for his first grand jury appearance. Freedman told Levine the facts, adding that he had committed himself to the contestants and would not let them down. When Freedman told Levine there had been no third person present when he assisted contestants, the lawyer said that fact would make it difficult to prove rigging. Levine said nothing to Freedman about perjury.

When it came time to appear before the grand jury, Freedman expected a rehearsal, with Levine playing the part of the prosecutor, as depicted in the movies. Instead, at a meeting with Levine, Greene, and Enright, the lawyers advised that Freedman's options were to go in and tell the truth or refuse to testify and be cited for contempt. Freedman told them that if he did either, it would leak out and the publicity would be horrendous, so he had no choice but to go in and *not* tell the truth. The lawyers did not try to dissuade him. After his testimony, when he returned to Greene's office to report, the lawyers were concerned not that he had lied but that he had been asked a general question about rigging rather than specific questions about individual contestants. Freedman sensed that Levine was beginning to regret being involved.

Naturally I was intrigued by these disclosures, but I disabused Freedman of the notion they would serve to make me yield about his returning to New York. The prospect of the publicity that might ensue horrified him, so he tried overwhelming me with revelations. Saying he had not been entirely truthful in his recantation, he admitted having given assistance to Nearing, as we had suspected. He protected her because she, as a lawyer, could be disbarred if her perjury was discovered. He had also shielded a high-school teacher with a large family, as well as several others outside the jurisdiction—a policeman, a research chemist working on a government grant, and a minister—all of whom, he feared, could lose standing in their communities, even their livelihoods, as a result of his testimony.

Now seriously doubting I could convince Freedman to return, I wondered whether he could be forced out of Mexico. I sought advice from the legal staff at the U.S. Embassy about the possibility of having him extradited. The embassy suggested I go to the chief of police to determine whether the Freedmans were legal residents of Mexico City. Using a letter of introduction from a New York police inspector, I secured by telephone an appointment with the assistant chief of police. Arriving at police headquarters the next day, I was intercepted by John Foley, a U.S. FBI agent attached to the embassy. In a high-handed manner, Foley asked for my identification and reasons for being in Mexico. He then beckoned me to a balcony overlooking the street, where our conversation could not be overheard, and said I was wasting my time going through official channels. If I wanted Freedman, the best thing to do was bribe the Mexican police, who would then harass him and drive him out. When I told Foley that the Hogan office did not operate in that fashion, the FBI man shrugged, wished me well, and disappeared. My meeting with the police chief's amiable assistant was indeed a waste of time; he would relay my request to his boss when the latter returned from a hunting trip, but I heard nothing more.

I continued to see Freedman every day and several times socialized with him and his family. At our last meeting before my departure, I said I did not want to rush him into a decision—adding that the district attorney's office would pay his expenses for the trip to New York—but hoped he would let me know within a reasonable time.

CHAPTER SEVENTEEN

Second Grand Jury

(JUNE–NOVEMBER 1960)

Back in New York, I found the lawyers involved in the quiz affair in a state of near panic. Freedman had phoned Enright daily during my stay in Mexico, and the word had spread that we were investigating the lawyers, notably Greene and Gelb. Retained from the outset because of their touted contacts in the office, Greene and Gelb now brought every possible influence to bear. Gelb complained to David Worgan, Hogan's chief assistant, that I had not consulted with him before going to see Freedman and declared that it was unthinkable that he, a predecessor of Worgan, could suborn perjury. Called in for my side of the story, I told Worgan that Gelb was no longer Freedman's lawyer, and was whining precisely because his conduct with Felsher and the "Tic Tac Dough" contestants had been questionable. Whether such conduct amounted to subornation remained to be seen.

A few days later, Sal Camp, who had represented various "Dotto" figures during the investigation, dropped by to report a recent conversation with Gelb. When Camp expressed relief that his clients had cooperated with us from the start and so were soon done with the affair, Gelb replied that he would rather deal with a lawyer than a representative of the Better Business Bureau. This was a snide reference to my role in recent prosecutions resulting from our investigation of the advertising of Regimen, a phony diet pill, whose manufacturer Gelb represented at one stage. In Gelb's view, instead of according him the respect he deserved as my former superior and a Dewey-era racket buster, I was harassing his clients. After all, relayed Camp, Felsher and the others were only trying to save a commercial enterprise— they hadn't killed anyone.

Greene had no prior association with me, despite what he might have bragged to Enright at the start; the lawyer and I had not dealt directly since the time, early in the investigation, I ordered him out of my office for stalling over Barry and Enright's records. But he had many contacts. One of these was Al Felix, a politico close to the Manhattan Democratic party boss, Carmine DeSapio. Felix informed me that Sidney Baron, a public relations operator also close to DeSapio, wanted to smooth things out between Greene and me. Then I received a call from Joseph Ruggiero, chairman of the New York County Republican Law Committee, of which I was a member. Ruggiero said Bernard Newman, the New York County Republican leader, wanted to talk to me. Newman, who had steered Enright to Greene back at the very beginning, had never before given me the time of day. I concluded that Greene was covering the political spectrum to focus heavy guns on me.

Playing all the angles was Zoloto, who now represented Freedman in addition to being one of a gaggle of lawyers continuing to represent Enright. Having never dealt with the contestants during the investigation, he had nothing to fear from me. At our first meeting after my return from Mexico, Zoloto jovially paraded his knowledge of everything, including Gelb's visit to Worgan. If I wanted Freedman back in New York, Zoloto said, he would make it happen, and he did so, by degrees. The first step was to reassure Eli Katz, a Queens lawyer who was Freedman's brother-in-law, that if Freedman cooperated, we would drop the indictment. Several days after I explained the technicalities to Katz, Zoloto reported that the lawyers around Enright were now split: he and Katz were in favor of Freedman's returning and Greene and Gelb were opposed. Zoloto continued to regale me with confidences about the backbiting in the Enright camp, warnings about Greene, and admonitions to resist pressures being put on me at Greene's behest.

ON JUNE 3, 1960, Vivienne Nearing appeared with her attorney, Murray Gurfein, another former colleague of mine, to make a full confession that she had committed perjury. Gurfein, the model of the quick, hard-working, incorruptible assistant D.A., was brilliant, but a man of action, not one to ponder his moves. Now he was having his client stick her head into the lion's mouth by telling us the whole truth. As Nearing now told it, she was prevailed upon to play a couple of fixed tie games with Van Doren in order to create excitement on "Twenty-One"; when she was told she would replace him, she was promised she would be on her own, but this never materialized. Though she wanted out, at Freedman's insistence she continued until Bloomgarden was found to replace her. Just before her final appearance, Freedman said she would lose by a full 21 points to make Bloomgarden more interesting, but would receive $10,000 even though the loss would cut her posted winnings total back to $5,500. With the breaking of the scandal, Freedman was in constant touch with her. After his first grand jury testimony, he told her that he specifically testified he had not given her or anyone else assistance, and when her time came, she should testify to the "truth" that she had not received assistance. Now she was prepared to tell the real truth to a new grand jury.

Still another lawyer made an entrance. Irving Mendelson had been an assistant D.A. back in the 1930s, before the Dewey era, and was famous for his scrupulous attention to all clients, big and small. Earlier in the quiz affair, he had briefly represented two "Tic Tac Dough" contestants who admitted before the first grand jury to fixing by Felsher. Now he was representing Glorianne Rader, Freedman's former assistant, and Robert Noah, Enright's right-hand man. Before interviewing them, I talked to Arthur Franklin, Enright's former public relations man, and added Edwin Slote to the list of lawyers whose activities warranted scrutiny. Franklin's grievance that Slote, who had represented him for years before joining the Enright team, became willing to throw him to the wolves made him willing to testify that Slote urged him to lie to the old grand jury.

When Mendelson brought in Noah, the former producer admitted that he, Freedman, and Enright had thoroughly rigged "Twenty-One" and he was aware of what was happening on "Tic Tac Dough," but he was hazy about his dealings with Slote, Gelb, and Greene. He could recall only one meeting with Greene, early in the investigation, when the lawyer merely advised him not to be afraid of me. I suspected Noah was taking orders not to reveal anything about the lawyers or the possibility of suborning witnesses and began to worry that if Freedman returned to testify, he would play the same game and backpedal from what he had said in Mexico. I advised Mendelson that I would not give his client immunity if Noah would provide nothing in return; secretly I was alarmed by the possibility that Mendelson had been roped in to the cabal.

But Rader changed my mind when Mendelson brought her in at the end of June. She admitted that, as Freedman's assistant, she knew he was helping contestants and that most of the matches on "Twenty-One" were rigged; moreover, she personally assisted two "Tic Tac Dough" contestants: John Stewart, the elderly, former *New York Times* reporter in need of medical care, who had died in the meantime; and a sixteen-year-old boy who had testified before the old grand jury that he received no assistance. According to Rader, early in the scandal Enright called a meeting of the staff to denounce Stempel and introduced Slote as someone they could freely talk to. When Rader told Slote in general terms what she knew, he said he would "get back to her" but did not. Meanwhile, she continued, Enright instructed her to alter the screening-test scores of several contestants whose records had been requested by us; since some of the actual scores were lower than appropriate for "Twenty-One" contestants, that might have raised questions. (This also helped explain Greene's stalling in turning over the records.)

Before being questioned by us the first time, she told Greene everything, including her concern that we would detect the difference in inks on the contestant records. Greene laughed off her concerns, saying the investigation had been launched because Hogan was running for the Senate and everything would blow over after the election. He also told Rader he had talked to one of the contestants she had assisted, who intended to deny assistance, so there was no reason for her to upset the applecart. Since Enright, Freedman, and Noah were the only ones who knew of assistance and no third person was present when it was actually given, it could never be proved, Greene said, so she had nothing to fear. Before her first testimony, she was rehearsed by Noah and met again with Greene, who gave her the impression that she would hurt Freedman if she didn't hew to the line. After her first day before the jurors, when she reported back, Greene was alarmed that she had testified about Freedman's easy access to the questions before their use on the air. Greene instructed her to put across to the jurors the fact that others besides Freedman had access; following orders, she asked and received permission from the grand jury to clarify her previous testimony on that point.

I was grateful to Mendelson, because Rader's revelations could help make a case against Greene, similar to that against Gelb, for subornation of perjury at worst and a breach of ethics at the least. When Zoloto announced that Freedman was returning to New York on July 4, I was elated; if Freedman elaborated upon what he had told me in Mexico, then I could clinch the case against Greene, who, I was beginning to realize, had played the key role, as Enright's chief counsel, in encouraging Felsher's and Freedman's perjury and their mobilizing of the contestants in the effort.

Zoloto at this point informed me that Greene had devised the formula Felsher used to buck up contestants being called to testify, that is, "I told the truth to the grand jury that I did not give you questions and answers, and you should tell the truth that you did not receive questions and answers." If so,

Greene might have crossed the line into suborning false testimony. Zoloto also played to my suspicions regarding Schweitzer's authorship of his legal opinion in the presentment matter. According to Zoloto, his partner, Arthur Karger, and Schweitzer were close. From the beginning, writing the presentment opinion was rough going, and Schweitzer soon asked for Karger's help, which Karger initially refused, since his firm was involved in the case. One Saturday morning, Schweitzer telephoned Karger in great agitation to say the opinion was finished but needed going over by an expert. Meeting Schweitzer later in the morning with Zoloto present, Karger glanced at the draft, said it needed polishing and proceeded to do it. As he worked, Schweitzer became impatient, looking at his watch and telling Zoloto he would be late for an appointment. Schweitzer could no longer stand it, announced he had an important "conference," and departed, leaving the phone number of a hotel. After Karger spent hours working on the opinion, he and Zoloto delivered it to Schweitzer in the lobby of the hotel.

Finally, I discovered what appeared to be a crucial remaining stake in the whole affair for Enright. Among the assets Barry and Enright had not sold to NBC in 1957 was WGMA, a radio station in Hollywood, Florida. The station's broadcasting license had come up for renewal by the FCC, and the quiz scandal could make approval of the renewal application a bumpy road. Zoloto said Enright was now willing to tell me everything so long as he did not have to testify, because the testimony could be used against him in the license-renewal deliberations. I refused the offer.

On July 1, 1960, a grand jury directed the filing of informations against Bernard Martin and Arthur Roberts, charging the former "Treasure Hunt" staff members with the misdemeanors of requesting and accepting gifts and gratuities, as agent and employee of another, and conspiracy. Martin and Roberts were accused of soliciting cash kickbacks from ten contestants, who appeared on the show between October 1958 and October 1959. The amounts ranged from $200 to $1,400 and totaled $6,420. We had questioned half of the 250 contestants who had appeared on the show since its premiere in the fall of 1957, and found that some 30 percent of these had been selected as contestants with the participation of Martin and Roberts. The scheme depended on the fact that winners could take cash in lieu of merchandise prizes. Roberts and Martin made agreements with prospective contestants, many of them friends and acquaintances, assuring them of winning on the show in return for sharing the cash value of the prizes with them 50–50 after deducting 25 percent for income taxes. The informations covered only incidents on which the statute of limitations had not expired. Roberts and Martin were arrested and arraigned on July 8, and were released on their own recognizance pending a trial on the charges.

WITH FREEDMAN on his way back to New York, Hogan approved the impaneling of a new grand jury to hear the perjury cases and other matters related to the original investigation. On July 4 Zoloto and I met Freedman at the airport and brought him in to lodgings at a hotel. The next day, the Fourth Grand Jury of the July 1960 term was sworn in by Judge Charles Marks to consider charges of perjury, subornation of perjury, obstruction of justice, and conspiracy in connection with the 1958 quiz investigation. Coincidentally, on the same day, the Appellate Division of the New York Supreme Court denied the mandamus application by the Grand Jury Association against Schweitzer, ruling that there was no statutory mandate requiring Schweitzer to make public the presentment. Moreover, the higher court decided, the Association failed to establish the power under common law of grand juries to make such reports or that "if indeed there were such powers, they carry with them a corresponding obligation on the part of the court to accept and file such reports."[1] If indeed there was a dead duck, it was the Third September 1958 Grand Jury's presentment.

The new grand jury began work immediately, hearing readings by the original grand jury reporters of their minutes of 1958 and 1959 testimony by twenty former "Twenty-One" and "Tic Tac Dough" contestants who had agreed to waive immunity in order to testify anew. For nearly two weeks, Freedman, under a grant of immunity, testified almost daily. The cases were presented individually, and he was required to repeat in each instance the basic facts of the quizzes and his involvement. He was forthcoming except when it came to the role of Enright's lawyers. At one point he balked at answering questions about who had advised him he could cover up the fact regarding Nearing and others when he recanted in May 1959, and we had to threaten him with a contempt action to make him yield. This, plus Zoloto's constant disparaging of Freedman to me in private, made me wonder if Enright's latest strategy was to have Freedman purposely discredit himself and weaken our cases. Making matters worse was a second session in my office with Rader, who backed away from her previous assertions regarding Greene. Now she calmly claimed she had not told Greene of her assistance to "Tic Tac Dough" contestants until just before the Washington hearings. I exploded in anger, and Rader left the office in tears.

The pressure put on me by intermediaries on behalf of Greene intensified. Bernard Newman was concerned about rumors his name was being "bandied about" before the new grand jury, and he wanted to meet with me somewhere outside the office. I told his emissary, Joseph Ruggiero, that I could not say what did or did not happen before the grand jury, but Newman's name was not being bandied about by us. The same day, the ubiquitous Al Felix came by to say that Greene did not know that the Enright quizzes were rigged until after Freedman testified the first time.

A few days later I gave in to Felix's pestering and had lunch with him and Sidney Baron, to see how far Enright and Greene were willing to go. After assurances that he was not meeting with me regarding any matter pending in the office and that he had the highest respect for Hogan, Baron got down to business. He had decided that the television industry "needed" quiz programs that could be operated honestly, and, given my role in the investigation, I would make the ideal quiz show "czar." He would approach the networks and sell them the idea. Not that his motives were unselfish—he would earn $100,000 handling the public relations for the project.

Baron then said that he hoped nothing would happen to his friend, Greene. Schweitzer was also a good friend, and Baron hoped that the judge's action in the presentment matter had not caused bitterness on my part. Baron asked me not to mention this discussion to Hogan, because he didn't want "Frank" angry at him for trying to lure me away. Baron sweetened the deal by advising me to resign from the County Law Committee and change my voter registration to independent. This was because, he hinted with a twinkle in his eye, there were great plans afoot for Hogan, but not even he would be able to appoint a Republican to a judgeship.

The next time I talked to Zoloto, he called Baron's offer simply a ploy for Greene's consumption. Baron and Felix intended to extract a large fee from Greene for their efforts. Baron's organization, Zoloto added, owed its effectiveness in fixing things to the fact that DeSapio was a silent partner, but since Baron was cheating DeSapio in the enterprise, a big blowup was expected. A day or so later, I called Baron and declined his offer of the "czar" position, saying I had had enough of quiz shows. As if on cue, Felix came in, all smiles and full of anxiety, wanting to make sure that I reported our luncheon meeting to Hogan in the proper light, that is, the meeting had nothing to do with Greene. When I did make my report to Hogan, his biggest chuckle was over

Baron's "big plans" for him—to have him run for mayor of New York. It would be nothing more or less than another kiss of death from DeSapio.

DURING the last two weeks of July, following Freedman's testimony, the grand jurors heard former "Twenty-One" contestants who had formally requested permission to appear on their own behalf. After confirming they had waived immunity to appear, Paul Bain, Ruth Miller, David Mayer, and Richard Klein, in addition to Von Nardroff, Bloomgarden, and Van Doren, were informed they were defendants and were being given the opportunity to make statements in connection with the charges being presented against them. The first four, relatively unknown to the public, told the jurors that their perjury had stemmed from fear that tattling on Freedman would ruin him, and now they beat their breasts at the mistakes they had made. All had good backgrounds, were highly educated and model citizens in all aspects of their lives, and the jurors were inclined to pity them.

This was especially the case with Ruth Miller, who had left "Twenty-One" with $2,500 after a series of ties with Van Doren. According to her testimony, she needed the money to tide her over during convalescence from major surgery. The day after her testimony, the foreman, Harold Dunbar, received phone calls from three jurors expressing their concern for Miller. But the stern Dunbar wrapped himself in the dignity of the institution of the grand jury and insisted that perjury was a crime that must be punished. I advised Dunbar and the jurors that a compromise was possible; when the time came, they could vote to charge Miller and others with misdemeanors instead of felonies.

Von Nardroff, Bloomgarden, and Van Doren, whose arrivals and departures from the Criminal Courts Building were covered by reporters and photographers, did not provoke as much sympathy. Before the jurors, Von Nardroff tried to appear repentant but took a swipe at Freedman. When she had amassed $35,000 in winnings, she testified, Freedman told her she would probably be the first woman to reach $100,000—and, if so, he wanted $2,500, to which she agreed; several weeks after she was off the program she gave him the money in small bills, which she had begun to accumulate, long before receiving the check for her winnings, by putting aside change from grocery purchases. This was not so much of a bombshell as it appeared. Even if she had told us this before the statute of limitations had expired on the crime of commercial bribery she was alleging, additional corroboration would have been required to make a charge stick. When we called Freedman back before the jury, he vehemently denied her accusation. One or the other was lying, but there was no way of telling which one.

Bloomgarden was totally forthcoming and recounted his story as he had told it to me before the Washington hearings. At the end of his testimony, Bloomgarden said there was no defense for what he had done, yet he hoped the jurors would not cut him down, because he had much to offer society through his work in the public health field. If he were to be indicted and involved in public legal proceedings, for all intents and purposes, he would be through in terms of leading a useful life. "I might as well go out and get a job as a truck driver," he concluded.

The day before Van Doren testified I was visited by Rubino, seeking to know in advance what I intended to ask his client, an unusual tactic for a former assistant D.A. I outlined the general procedure and areas I would pursue; included, I pointed out, would be exactly what had motivated Van Doren finally to tell the truth. "Not relevant!" Rubino interjected, then asked why I had not called Van Doren back in right after Freedman purged himself. I pointed out that the law in New York was clear: a recantation had to be carried out promptly and when no reasonable likelihood existed that the witness had learned his perjury might become known to the authorities. For that matter, I realized, Rubino could have brought Van Doren in himself, if what Zoloto told me was true—that Greene informed Rubino of Freedman's return to the grand jury as soon as it took place. By the time Harris and Goodwin got in the act and the situation began to deteriorate, the old grand jury was out of existence and it was too late for recanting. Now that the office was probing the doings of the lawyers in the affair, Rubino was possibly concerned at the prospect that I would pursue Van Doren about his own lawyer's role, for the fact remained that Van Doren had committed perjury on Rubino's watch.

Appearing before the new grand jury on July 28, Van Doren took an hour to retell his familiar story. A few things still eluded resolution, even at this late date. The story of the $5,000 "loan" solicited by Freedman seemed to change with each telling, as did the account of meetings with Enright and Freedman after the scandal erupted. In Washington, Van Doren had given the impression that the initiative for covering up came from Freedman; now Van Doren corroborated the later assertion by Freedman that Van Doren had started it, fearing exposure would ruin him and hurt his family. Van Doren also now revealed that when Enright visited him before his first questioning by me, it had been to tip him off that we had subpoenaed the records; therefore Van Doren should own up to the advance given him at Christmastime 1956.

Van Doren revealed another topic of that meeting with Enright with which I was unfamiliar. Enright wanted to determine whether Van Doren harbored any resentment against him because of an employment contract he had signed with Barry and Enright the week before his last appearance on "Twenty-One." Under the terms of this contract, Van Doren would have been an "adviser" to the partnership shows for a salary of $125 a week. When shortly afterward, NBC offered him a deal at $50,000 a year, Van Doren prevailed upon Enright to cancel the employment contract in return for helping him with another quiz program. That turned out to be the short-lived "High Low," which two other targets of the new grand jury probe, Bloomgarden and Terry Curtis, had admitted was fixed. Van Doren's contribution to "High Low" was to arrange the services of his brother John Van Doren, also a college professor, as a panelist on the quiz, where John demonstrated a fund of information just as phenomenal as Charles's had appeared. Charles had breathed nothing of this to the Harris subcommittee, to avoid tarnishing the image he had put forward of wanting to put the quiz shows behind him as soon as he was off "Twenty-One" and to avoid dragging his brother into the mess.

As for exactly when he told Rubino the whole truth, Van Doren was vague; he did not recall telling Rubino about Freedman's offer of assistance and request for $5,000 until September 1959, several weeks before the Washington hearings. These were the tidbits he later trotted out, in the evening after Stempel's Washington testimony, in his first attempt to appease NBC. Nevertheless, Van Doren now conceded, Rubino was "an intelligent man" and could have guessed the truth long before.

AT THE END of July, I obtained from Judge Marks an extension of the Fourth July 1960 Grand Jury's life for three months and began preparations for a presentation against the "Tic Tac Dough" perjurers. These would include testimony by Felsher in repeated appearances as well as the testimony under waiver of immunity by twelve former contestants, ten of whom had been assisted by Felsher and two by Freedman. With long breaks in August for vacations, the "Tic Tac Dough" presentation dragged into September. On

September 20 Nearing, the last of the "Twenty-One" targets, returned from Europe to throw herself on the mercy of the grand jury by repeating what she had told me in the office at the beginning of the summer. With that, we had no further need of Freedman, who was free to return to Mexico. He was understandably bitter when I informed him that we still could not drop the indictment against him. In the event that any of the cases against "Twenty-One" contestants came to trial, we would require his presence again to testify in open court.

On October 3 the grand jury heard the last testimony in the twentieth and final case against the contestants. Patricia Nance, who had engaged in a series of ties against Michael O'Rourke on nighttime "Tic Tac Dough" before losing for a consolation prize of $4,200, threw everything she had at the jurors—motherhood, her reputation in the community, that she had studied very hard and could have answered the questions on her own, the fact that both her husband and father had been grand jurors—in an attempt to evoke pity. For Nance and each of the nineteen other defendants, Robert Donnelly, Marshall Witten, and I went through the same procedures I followed nearly two years before in regard to Freedman. We advised the jurors they could return an indictment for a felony or felonies, and/or order the filing of informations for misdemeanor charges, or vote to dismiss the charges. Second-degree perjury, the misdemeanor, we explained, was false testimony regarding immaterial matters.

We went over the requirements of the two-witness rule, which in these cases were satisfied by the testimony of Freedman or Felsher and each of the defendants themselves. It was pointed out that the defendants were exercising their right to appear before the grand jury, but in order to do so, had been required to waive immunity. If the jurors believed the testimony of Freedman or Felsher, then admissions made by the defendants constituted the corroboration to justify an indictment or information. In addition, second-degree perjury could be found if the jurors determined that the defendants made statements before them that simply contradicted statements they had made before the old grand jury. On the other hand, the jurors were obliged to consider whatever explanations the defendants now made before reaching decisions in their cases.

The appearances by the defendants made for a dramatically different situation than prevailed in our presentation against Freedman. The Fourth of July 1960 grand jurors, having seen and heard the defendants in person, were reluctant to find even misdemeanors in a number of cases. During the appearance of one defendant, a juror was on the verge of tears, and in the deliberation that followed, the foreman told me later, the juror called for reconsidering the already-decided cases of several defendants. Dunbar again argued the sanctity of the oath, the dignity of the grand jury, and the issue of law and order versus anarchy, and a majority of jurors sided with the foreman. Nevertheless, though the jurors considered both degrees of perjury against all the defendants, in every case they voted misdemeanor charges only.

On October 7, when the paperwork was completed, misdemeanor charges were filed against the former "Twenty-One" contestants Paul Bain, Henry Bloomgarden, Richard Klein, David Mayer, Ruth Miller, Vivienne Nearing, Charles Van Doren, and Elfrida Von Nardroff, and "Tic Tac Dough" contestants Terry Curtis, Henrietta Dudley, Charles Gilliam, Morton Harelik, Timothy Horan, Ruth Klein, Patricia Nance, Joseph Rosner, Patricia Sullivan, Michael Truppin, and Neil Wolfe. The twelfth "Tic Tac Dough" contestant charged was under age at the time of his perjury, making him a youthful offender, and proceedings against him were sealed.

Over the next few weeks the defendants turned themselves in. Two immediately entered not guilty pleas and were paroled on their own recognizance; the others were also released on parole but were granted delays in filing pleas. Aside from Van Doren, Von Nardroff, and Bloomgarden, the names of the defendants meant little to the public, which must have wondered how it was that these small fry were being prosecuted while the big shots, who had benefited most from quiz rigging—producers, advertising men, and sponsors—were getting off scot-free. This sentiment was a big factor in the grand jury's decision to treat the defendants as lightly as possible.

In fact, we were still after bigger game: the lawyers, whose role in orchestrating perjury had emerged clearly in the new testimony. As October drew to a close, we obtained a second extension, and the panel continued hearing evidence until December. Coming after the informations, the extension fueled new speculation. When the *New York Times* and *New York Post* reported that the lawyers in the quiz affair were being investigated, the reaction was immediate. Nessen called me to demand who was responsible for the articles, saying that these were blackening the reputation of his partner, Rubino. Rubino himself complained to me that reporters were asking him if he was being investigated, and demanded to know what the office was going to do about the leaks.

Joseph Ruggiero put in another appearance to say Bernard Newman wanted to see me. According to Ruggiero, Newman was deeply concerned by the investigation, even though he had done nothing beyond referring Enright to Greene back at the beginning; if Greene had violated the law or engaged in improper conduct for a lawyer, that was his problem. I showed no reaction to this transparent, obviously rehearsed dialogue. I told Ruggiero there was no need for messengers; Newman knew where to reach me.

Lawyers for the new defendants came in to complain as well. One was Frank Brenner, my former colleague who had brought in Mayer for a talk soon after the office confessions of Van Doren and Bloomgarden in October 1959 and now realized he had put his client's head in a noose. He fired at me with both barrels, not blaming himself or me, but what he regarded as Hogan's deceitfulness. He had misread Hogan, believing his call to the contestants meant they would be forgiven if they came in and owned up. I sat back and listened to Brenner with mixed feelings, understanding how he could have been misled.

On October 26 I told Hogan that the grand jury believed the extent of perjury was too great not to have been suborned. Though by no means "runaway," the jurors would not be satisfied simply to fold their tents. They were determined to probe more deeply and possibly proceed against Greene, Gelb, and Slote. To this end, I told Hogan, we might consider offering immunity to Enright himself, who had paid something in the area of $200,000 to various lawyers and no longer had any real reason to protect them.

My theory here was that even though Enright's rigging of television programs was not illegal, he had very good reasons at the beginning to conceal it and accordingly had paid his lawyers to assist in a cover-up. As far as the evidence showed, Enright had not personally advised anyone to lie under oath. Rather it was the lawyers, realizing that Enright was a gold mine, who provided the blueprints for the perjury and obstruction that dogged our investigation from the start. If Enright could be motivated to testify to the whole truth, then Barry and Noah, to say nothing of Felsher and Rader, would open up and provide enough evidence to support charges against Greene, Gelb, Slote, and possibly other lawyers. Even if the evidence was not enough to bring criminal charges, at the least it could enable the grand jury to recommend turning over its minutes to the Bar Association for possible action.

I should not have been surprised by Hogan's reaction. At the very beginning, when Hilgemeier blew the whistle on "Dotto," the Chief had been supportive, and when "Twenty-One" came under fire he backed our effort. But Stempel's charges against Columbia University's Van Doren made Hogan skeptical. Without consulting me, he publicly expressed doubts that any crimes had been committed even if the quiz shows were fixed. It was only after the Reverend Jackson's allegations that Hogan ordered a grand jury investigation, and that was to get reporters off his back. Craig's confession, while it exhilarated me, had disturbed Hogan, and Freedman's subsequent perjury and recantation jolted him.

When the time came for me to confirm his original assessment—that no real crimes had been committed by sponsors, networks, and advertising agencies—Hogan was relieved. During the writing of the 1958 grand jury's presentment, which he had never been enthusiastic about, Hogan quietly kept abreast of its contents, reading drafts and registering his approval of the process by which the shrillness of Hacker's attacks on the networks was toned down. He had called Hacker, a prominent figure at Columbia University, a friend, but I sensed Hogan did not have complete confidence in anyone in the very sensitive matter of the presentment. At the same time, he expected little to come of a congressional investigation and tacitly backed Schweitzer's decision to hand over the grand jury minutes to the Harris subcommittee. Still wanting to believe Van Doren's denial of involvement in the rigging, even in the face of Freedman's recanted testimony, Hogan expected the Harris investigation simply to warm over some of the grand jury's findings in a disorganized manner and show that we had been on the ball.

So it was that now, amiably and without fuss, the Chief demolished my proposal, reminding me that more than anyone else Enright had been responsible for quiz rigging; to grant the main perpetrator immunity to take the investigation in a new direction would be a public relations fiasco. What trial jury, Hogan asked me, would accept the testimony of Enright, the architect of the deceit, and contestants who had committed perjury in the grand jury against lawyers of the caliber of Gelb and Greene? At any rate, the evidence suggested we had a better case against Gelb than Greene or Slote; Hogan said he was not interested in hurting Gelb and was sure I felt the same way. Gelb could be aggressive and arrogant, but here he had simply made a mistake, and we didn't want to crucify him for that. "Let it go, Joe," Hogan said, "you have enough to do."

Two days later, Zoloto dropped in to say he had heard that Hogan had told Schweitzer about our meeting, specifically that I had pushed for an investigation of the lawyers. I brushed Zoloto off but was disturbed by this leak. I had never told Hogan directly what I suspected about Schweitzer, since I had little but hearsay, mostly via Zoloto, to back it up. I had hoped Hogan would draw the conclusion from what I did say, but now I could see he was

not so inclined. I finally realized that I was a mere soldier and had my orders—to bring the quiz investigation to a close.

THERE WAS one windmill I wanted to try a last pass at, and that was the case of
Joyce Brothers. The Hess department store affair and the private confession
to me by Richard McCutcheon had reinforced my suspicion that, despite the
grand jury and Washington testimonies of Koplin, Carlin, and Bernstein,
Brothers had not told everything she knew to the grand jury. If she did crack
and the second phase of the investigation were not limited simply to the
Barry and Enright quizzes, I believed we could justify the effort expended in
what otherwise appeared to be a wasteful anticlimax after the Washington
circus. Brothers, unlike "Twenty-One" and "Tic Tac Dough" contestants, had
made no move in the direction of coming in to set the record straight.

Even before the Fourth July Grand Jury was impaneled, I arranged separate interviews with two producers closely involved with Brothers as a contestant—Koplin and Joseph Cates. Koplin repeated his story that he
unknowingly used Nat Fleischer as a consultant in the writing of boxing questions while Fleischer (who continued to remain out of our reach as an official
of the Olympic Games in Rome) was advising Brothers. Otherwise Koplin
denied giving Brothers any form of assistance. When I pointed out he had
said the same thing about McCutcheon, Koplin said nothing.

Cates was equally adamant, recalling that at the beginning of Brothers's
appearances on the "Question," the Revsons expressed such distaste that he
and Koplin tried devising questions to knock her out, without success. Cates,
having jumped the $64,000 ship long before the scandal, had directed a
movie and was finding work in television. Unbending a bit, he told me of his
great admiration and loyalty to Cowan. According to Cates, Cowan built in
controls for his shows starting with "Quiz Kids"; but even before Cowan's
era, the writing of questions on the highly regarded "Information Please" had
played to the strengths of the panelists. Cowan was an "idea man" who had
nothing to do with the day-to-day operations, even before he left his production company for CBS, and was never at any meeting where controls were
discussed. On the other hand, Cates confided, he was not terribly impressed
by Cowan's failure to testify in Washington. When he learned that Cowan
could not appear before the subcommittee because he had a bad leg, his own
reaction was that Cowan did not have lockjaw.

I also interviewed Edward Eagan, the former Olympic champion, who had accompanied Brothers into the isolation booth when she answered the final question for $64,000. Eagan talked freely of his relationship with Brothers, who had asked him to be her on-camera "expert" when Fleischer declined the honor, but he knew nothing of Fleischer's role in her boxing education. In the isolation booth, Eagan claimed she did not know the answers to three out of the four items in the multipart question, which he supplied, as permitted of course under the rules.

After I interviewed Shirley Bernstein, who now admitted she had used playback in warming up Brothers for several appearances on the "Challenge," it was time for a showdown. Brothers agreed to an interview on the condition that she not be seen coming into the office, so we set an appointment for Election Day, November 8, 1960, when the Criminal Courts Building was all but shut down. She arrived without a lawyer, and I introduced her to Donnelly and Witten. I said we had evidence that she had not told the whole truth before the old grand jury on January 7, 1959. Specifically, she had been pretested prior to several quiz appearances, asked a series of thirty to forty warm-up questions, imbedded in which was material to be used on the air.

When I maintained in face of her denials that we had evidence of her being given help, she became upset. She had dreaded each appearance, she now said; she hated the studying and the tension. Her only happy moments during the entire ordeal were after each broadcast, when she could sit down and eat a good meal. But the tension would soon return and build up to a near paralysis of fear by the time of her next appearance. Asked what compelled her to continue, she answered that at the time her husband was earning $50 a month as a hospital intern; between that and her college teaching, they managed to eke out $4,000 a year. Their financial dependence on her parents had become degrading, but then she gave me no clear answer as to why she had gone on to become a "Challenge" contestant after winning $64,000 on the "Question."

Only after she read the Washington testimony of Carlin and Koplin did she realize that the shows had been controlled by the producers and sponsors. She had no idea what might have been done with other contestants, but it was hard work and perseverance that enabled her to answer the questions correctly. Now, she said, it was as if she had won the Congressional Medal of Honor and people were spitting on her. She had been cross-examined and tried by the executives of NBC, who had cleared her and allowed her to keep working on her weekly psychological advice program.

What then, I asked, could have motivated Bernstein to tell us about pretesting her? Perhaps Bernstein had done so with other contestants, Brothers replied, and unwittingly included her in the category. As Jay Goldberg had done two years before, Witten asked her questions she had answered correctly on the quizzes; again she could not answer and explained the technique of dumping from her mind information no longer needed. Bringing the interview to a close, I went through the motions of telling Brothers to reconsider what she had told us or we might have to charge her with perjury. She replied she had nothing to reconsider inasmuch as she was telling us the truth. I suggested she discuss the matter with a lawyer, but in fact she had done very well on her own.

IT REMAINED to bring the crusading grand jurors down gently, even as we pursued a careful examination of Felsher and Rader under oath in November. Rader more or less implicated Greene by recounting her close consultations with the lawyer at the time of her appearances before the old grand jury; Felsher performed the same function vis-à-vis Gelb but with less effect, inasmuch as Felsher waffled on how much he and Gelb had told each other in regard to the contestants he was rallying. He simply assumed that Gelb deduced that he had rigged the contestants he was sending over for pep talks. It was all very interesting for the jurors, but we could take it no further without testimony from other parties.

At the end of November the time came for a valedictory. We had been unable to produce the missing link required to establish a case against the lawyers. The missing link was Enright. Even if we were to grant him immunity and compel his testimony, his credibility would be zero in a courtroom and we could not count on his telling the whole truth in an area of inquiry not pursued in his testimony before the Harris subcommittee. This being the case, we could not ask the jurors to vote on additional charges. Puzzled and deeply disturbed by the irony that only contestants who had finally told the truth would be prosecuted, the jurors asked me many questions. I answered as best I could. They were then discharged with the thanks of the court.

CHAPTER EIGHTEEN

The Public Interest, Convenience, and Necessity

(NOVEMBER 1960–JULY 1966)

The penalty for second degree perjury was up to one year in prison and/or a fine of up to $500, but since the former quiz contestants were charged with first offenses and had confessed their crimes under oath with varying degrees of remorse, the likelihood of punishment was remote. Nevertheless, convictions would mean blots on their records and new barrages of publicity. For private and professional reasons, and because they felt betrayed in the expectation that the charges would be dropped along the way, all were determined to fight. The sparring began on November 7, 1960, the first court date after the arraignments in October. In the Court of Special Sessions, where misdemeanor cases were tried before one or three judges, not a jury, three defendants requested and were granted delays before entering pleas. The others had pleaded not guilty at their arraignments.

On November 14 Nearing, Von Nardroff, and others filed motions to dismiss the informations on a number of technical grounds. This halted our preparations for trial and we filed briefs in opposition to the defendants' motions. On December 2 Van Doren and six others who had not joined in the previous motions entered not-guilty pleas. Rubino told reporters that even though Van Doren had admitted committing perjury before the Harris subcommittee, his client could not plead guilty while the legality of the charges was in question. All the cases were adjourned until January 1961, pending a decision on the November 14 motions.

At the crux of these was the idea that the defendants could not be charged for falsely testifying about receiving assistance on a quiz show, because the 1958 grand jury had no business questioning them about something that was not a crime. That being the case, the defendants argued, the grand jury had not been legally empowered to administer the oath to them; this meant that an essential element of perjury was missing and required dismissal of the charges.

BY THIS TIME, though it had no bearing on the merits of the defendants' motions, giving or receiving assistance on quiz shows had become a federal crime, pursuant to a bill passed by Congress on August 30, 1960, and signed into law by Eisenhower two weeks later.[1] The tortured history of the legislation began at the end of 1959 when Robert Kintner, the president of NBC, himself proposed wording for such a law, at a time when the Harris subcommittee hearings had raised expectations of wide-ranging reforms to tighten government regulation of broadcasting and advertising. As the subcommittee prepared for a probe into "payola," the widespread music-recording industry practice of bribes to disc jockeys and other broadcasting personnel, Attorney General William Rogers submitted his "Report to the President on Deceptive Practices in Broadcasting Media," which was made public on December 30, 1959.

The bulk of the report was devoted to the role of the Federal Communications Commission and Federal Trade Commission in the quiz affair. A review of Supreme Court rulings, Rogers contended, showed that the commissions could exercise considerable power in relation to advertising and programming practices "in the context of licensing, rule-making or investigative proceedings . . . without running afoul" of constitutional safeguards of freedom of speech.[2] The FCC had the power, for example, to require honesty in presentation; it could ban deceptive contests as well as payola and plugola, compel broadcasting personnel to submit financial statements regarding outside earnings for promoting the sale of products, exercise greater scrutiny of broadcasters' practices before granting license renewals, and use cease and desist orders to assure compliance. In addition, the Commission could emphasize the responsibility of individual licensees in using material supplied by networks; likewise, networks that owned individual stations could be required to secure warranties from packagers and other outside sources of programming that the material supplied was what it purported to be. For its part, the FTC, Rogers found, could proceed against broadcasters as well as advertisers in cases of false or deceptive advertising; it could study the extent to which deception was used to stimulate sales, and formulate and urge adoption of a broadcasting advertising code.

Rogers recommended the passage of two new laws—one making payola and related practices, such as plugola, federal crimes, the other giving the FCC the power to punish with less drastic measures than the outright cancelation of licenses. With the power to temporarily suspend or to grant licenses on a provisional basis, the Commission would have more flexibility, and therefore more credibility in exacting compliance. He also recommended studying the extension of the FCC's injunction authority to all false advertising and placing in the FCC direct authority over networks. Eisenhower made no comment on the report, and nothing more at all was heard concerning Justice Department action about the possibility of perjury in the contradictory Washington testimony of such figures as Abrams and the Revsons.

Now under the gun, the FCC held nineteen days of its own hearings on broadcasting and commercial practices, in December 1959 and January 1960, with testimony from more than ninety witnesses. In the first round, various critics of broadcasting—representatives of associations of parents, educators, clerics, and consumer advocates—deplored the conditions that spawned the quiz scandal and recommended various schemes for raising and enforcing standards, including licensing of the networks. Other suggestions centered on taxing a percentage of broadcasters' profits as fees for the use of the airwaves, the proceeds to be spent on beefing up the FCC's monitoring and enforcement capability and financing a publicly owned network for the broadcasting of high-quality programming unbeholdened to commercial advertisers.[3]

But the preponderance of testimony shifted to industry advocates. On December 17 Elmo Roper presented the results of a public opinion poll concerning the quiz scandal, commissioned by the Television Information Office, a public relations bureau created earlier in the year by the National Association of Broadcasters. According to Roper, an extraordinarily high 89 percent of the two thousand people polled had heard of the scandal, but, asked to rate various propositions as to its cause, the public accepted the notion of bad apples in the barrel. Only 4 percent agreed with the proposition the quiz scandal showed "just how bad television is," while 65 percent agreed that even if quiz rigging was "very wrong . . . you can't condemn all television because of it." Summing up his findings, Roper declared that the public was "properly critical of abuses but they have not lost confidence in the medium as a whole."[4] Thus the blitz by the broadcasting industry to show that it was "assuming responsibility" and "housecleaning" was working; the ground-work was laid for a protracted effort to block any attempts to submit the business to stiffer regulation.

In January 1960 FCC chairman John Doerfer, addressing an industry asso-ciation, warned that the networks had to meet criticism by setting aside prime time on a rotating basis among them for "public service" programming. This idea was offered by the chairman as a way for broadcasters to deflect pres-sures growing on Congress to "do something" about television. The network chiefs agreed in principle to a modified version of "the Doerfer plan," pledg-ing to increase the amount of "cultural" programming on each network and its affiliates by an hour a week. Though the networks' offer amounted to little more than juggling previously announced documentary programming, Doer-fer hailed it as "a good start."[5]

After warnings by industry representatives that if advertisers were not al-lowed to have a say in programming, they would reduce "their commitment" to television with dire results, the FCC heard the three network chiefs, who rejected any regulation of programming, insisting that they could not be le-gally censored. But, deploying slogans like "progress through evolution," they offered to consider adherence to a broadcasting code formulated by themselves and to accept FCC requirements that license renewal applicants describe the means by which they determined the needs of their communi-ties and how these were being served. Conceding for the record that the FCC needed to provide something for the public interest, the chiefs insisted that for the Commission to regulate programming would be "to turn our backs on democracy," in the words of Frank Stanton, and to "cripple or retard" television's growth and "its ability to experiment, to be daring, to be vigorous and to enter into new fields," in the words of ABC president Leonard Goldenson.[6]

In early February, just after it began public hearings on disc jockey payola, the Harris subcommittee issued its own "Interim Report" on the quiz inves-tigation. The report denounced

> how far certain advertisers, producers and others will go to wring the last possible dollar out of the privilege of using the air-waves. . . . The sordid story demonstrates the futility of the theory underlying the present statute that the use of the airwaves in the public interest can be assured by holding only station licensees responsible for everything they broadcast. . . . Many licensees have virtually surrendered control of programming during the best

broadcasting time to the networks, who in turn have often abdicated control to advertisers."

The report's recommendations included making plugola and the broadcasting of programs with the intent of deceiving viewers illegal. The FCC would be given the power to license networks, to suspend licenses, tighten controls over the selling of licenses, and require public hearings in localities where licenses were up for renewal. In addition, the FTC would be given the power to regulate all advertising; broadcasting stations, networks, and advertising agencies, as well as manufacturers and sponsors, would be subject to criminal penalties for deceptive and misrepresentative advertising.

DURING the period of maximum zeal, two prominent scapegoats were found. On December 8, 1959, CBS forced the resignation of Louis Cowan. Cowan made public a letter to Stanton accusing the network chief of undermining him by leaks to the press of his impending resignation for reasons of health, even as he expressed confidence that Cowan had nothing to do with quiz rigging. The scapegoating of Cowan diverted attention from the fact that there was no other bloodletting among CBS executives.

Several months later, the second scapegoat was found, in the person of Doerfer. On March 4, 1960, two days before the Harris subcommittee opened a second round of public hearings into payola, newspapers reported rumors that Doerfer had been the guest on the yacht of George Storer, a Florida broadcaster. Interrogated by the Harris subcommittee about this, Doerfer admitted to having accepted Storer's hospitality, contradicting denials he had made when the rumors were first reported. When it was clear that Doerfer and the FCC would become issues in the fall election, Eisenhower forced his resignation, on March 10. His replacement was Frederick W. Ford, a former associate of Rogers in the Justice Department. Ford had publicly dissented from Doerfer's conservative position on the FCC powers and seemed to favor a more active role by the Commission.

During the spring, while payola made headlines, little attention was paid when Harris introduced legislation that backpedaled from the findings of his subcommittee's "Interim Report." His proposals would make the broadcasting of fixed quizzes a crime, tighten licensing requirements for broadcasters, and compel the licensing of networks, but he dropped the "Interim Report" 's recommendations for widening the powers of the FTC. The Harris bill and initiatives by the supposedly revitalized FCC and FTC represented the high point of official concern and attempts to bring government power to bear on the problems of abuse of the airwaves. From this point on, the networks and the big broadcasters, represented by lobbying groups, worked behind the scenes to water down the Harris bills.

When a revised bill was reported to the House by the full House Interstate and Foreign Commerce Committee on June 10, 1960, industry lobbying showed its effect. Although the provisions to make quiz rigging and payola illegal remained, the FCC would now be *permitted*, not *required*, to hold public hearings concerning license applications, and the provision to license networks was dropped. On June 28 this weakened legislation passed the House by a lopsided vote of 208–15, then moved to the Senate, allowing the lobbyists to whittle it down further. At the end of August a version passed the Senate without provisions for temporary suspension of licenses or heavy fines for violators of FCC regulations. The Senate version was hailed by Senator John Pastore as "a strong bill but not a punitive bill and not intended to harass or embarrass the broadcasting industry."[8] Whereas the House version had contained provisions for fines on broadcasters of $1,000 a day for up to three years, the Senate version restricted any fines to a total of $10,000, and these could be levied only when the FCC could prove "willful and repeated" violations by broadcasters after a notification in writing as soon as a violation was detected.

Eager to put the matter to rest before the elections, Harris endorsed the Senate version, which passed the House on August 30 and was signed into law by Eisenhower on September 13. Quiz rigging was henceforth a federal crime, but then the networks themselves had offered language for such a law as far back as the quiz hearings. The main legislative recommendations by Rogers and Harris's own report—to license networks and give the FCC new teeth to regulate broadcasting with the power to levy fines and temporarily suspend licenses—had fallen by the wayside. It was a quiet but important victory for the broadcasters and networks.

HALF A YEAR LATER, on April 7, 1961, Judge Gerald Culkin, of New York County's Court of General Sessions, ruled on the motions of Nearing and others for dismissal of the informations against them. Rejecting the argument that the

Third September 1958 Grand Jury was merely investigating the content of television programs, Culkin held that the grand jury was constituted for a legal purpose, which meant that the oaths sworn by the defendants were legally administered; the Penal Law prohibiting false testimony as to nonmaterial matters was a "valid exercise of the police power" of the state "in preserving the integrity of the oath."[9] The defendants could not have it both ways. Since there was no evidence before the old grand jury that the defendants had committed crimes, they were therefore not "targets" of prosecution whose privilege against self-incrimination had been violated; yet the grand jury had been entitled to examine them in order to determine the actions of other individuals who might have qualified as targets.

But Culkin also faulted us for not sufficiently apprising the defendants of their rights in connection with immunity and of the consequences of committing perjury. "Although everyone is presumed to know the law," he wrote, "we know that with the many complexities and ramifications of the law, the presumption is unwarranted. Therefore simple justice would require giving of this counsel to the witnesses prior to their testifying and in the presence of the grand jury."[10] Despite this slap on the wrist, the way was cleared for trials, which were scheduled to begin in the Court of Special Sessions on May 8, 1961.

One by one the defendants came to the end of their legal tethers. The first, Nearing, pleaded guilty on May 8 and received a suspended sentence. Thirteen more motions to dismiss the informations were filed on behalf of the remaining defendants, each requiring a rebuttal by us, each occasioning a delay of the final reckoning. In addition to fine points and variations on the theme of Nearing's previous motions regarding the legality of the original grand jury investigation and questions of self-incrimination and immunity, there were demands to examine grand jury minutes and a frivolous attempt to invalidate the charges on the basis of the contention that since I lived in Queens I was not legally an assistant district attorney of Manhattan.

Between June and the end of December 1961, Dudley, Horan, Miller, Rosner, and Truppin pleaded guilty and received suspended sentences. As 1962 opened, the cases of thirteen of the original twenty remained to be tried. Finally, on January 17, Van Doren, Von Nardroff, Bloomgarden, and the others pleaded guilty. Judge Breslin, a former chief assistant district attorney in the Bronx who on the bench dealt mostly with street crime, was mellow when he asked for my recommendation in sentencing. I told the judge I had lived with the cases for a long time and was in a position to say how contrite the defendants were. No one involved could see any point in punishing them more than they had already been. Breslin suspended the sentences without imposing probation.

SIX MONTHS LATER, in July 1962, I was again embroiled in the affair, this time at the behest of the FCC in connection with the license-renewal application of Barry and Enright for their radio station WGMA in Hollywood, Florida, a small town on the Atlantic coast between Miami and Fort Lauderdale. The ownership of WGMA was registered to Melody Music, Inc., a Barry and Enright company that held the copyrights of background and incidental music used on television shows.

Several weeks after the quiz hearings, the FCC had informed Melody Music that testimony before the Harris subcommittee had raised questions concerning the character qualifications of Enright and whether he was entitled to own and operate a radio station. The matter lay dormant until a year later, when Melody Music applied for a renewal of the station's license for a term of three years, to run until February 1, 1964. On April 12, 1961, the FCC declared it could not make the requisite finding that approving the application would "serve the public interest, convenience, and necessity," without airing in public before a hearing examiner the issue of whether Barry and Enright were qualified in terms of "character" to have a broadcasting license.

After a series of petitions submitted by Melody Music for reconsideration, clarification, and extensions plus a number of conferences, a preliminary hearing took place on March 12, 1962. The Commission's Broadcast Bureau on one side and lawyers for Melody Music on the other hashed out proposed stipulations and future procedures for a round of evidentiary hearings in the summer. At this point, I was visited in New York by two Broadcast Bureau lawyers, Lewis Cohen and William Kehoe, Jr., seeking material not aired by the Harris subcommittee. I agreed to testify about various aspects of our investigation. In the week before the evidentiary hearings opened, Zoloto appeared in my office, still representing Enright, although a Washington firm was representing Melody Music before the FCC. According to Zoloto, the FCC lawyers were "wild kids" determined to prove that Enright had committed a crime by personally sending Felsher out to instruct former contestants to lie before the 1958 grand jury.

On July 16, 1962, I went to Washington at the request of the Broadcast Bureau. When I entered the hearing room, Barry was testifying before the examiner, Elizabeth C. Smith. It was the first time Barry had been questioned under oath about the quiz affair, and now he admitted he had known in a general way that contestants were given assistance. Trying not to appear evasive, Barry claimed to have known nothing about Enright's handling of Stempel but admitted the falsity of both the statement he made on the air during the September 8, 1958, broadcast of "Twenty-One" denying the Stempel allegations and the affidavit he had signed for NBC to the same effect. He now conceded that the broadcast statement represented a gross error of judgment.

On July 17, 1962, Enright began three days of testimony. Adding little to his Washington account, he contended that he talked to only two contestants after the scandal broke, Van Doren and Richard Jackman, and at no time suggested to Van Doren what he ought to say to the investigators or the grand jury. At the last moment, both sides agreed to stipulate to, or accept, Van Doren's testimony before the Harris subcommittee and more recent statements he had made to the Broadcast Bureau lawyers. Thus it was entered into evidence that, in September 1958, Van Doren read in the newspapers that the financial records of Barry and Enright were being examined by the D.A. Fearing damage because he had been given an advance against his winnings, Van Doren went to Enright, who told him that it was not very important. Enright now added that Van Doren also wanted reassurance that the contract he signed with Barry and Enright before he signed with NBC would not become known. Portions of Jackman's Washington testimony were stipulated to as well.

At times Enright appeared humble and apologetic; at other times, he was bold enough to say that everyone was rigging programs, hinting that the networks were aware of and tolerated the practice. In my opinion, the FCC questioners were not seasoned enough to face this venerable showman. Moreover, Zoloto was on the scene, digging deep into his bag of tricks. He told me that during a recess he buttonholed Cohen and asked him if he liked government service, wondering how with a family to support Cohen could afford to work for the government; then he mentioned he was thinking of expanding his office in New York and looking for some young lawyers to join him.

The Melody Music lawyers soon sensed that the Broadcast Bureau had a trump card. On the morning of Enright's third day of testimony, his Washington lawyer, Benito Gaguine, asked that Enright be permitted to correct previous testimony as to the number of contestants he had talked to following the breaking of the scandal. Adopting the procedure used with the Harris subcommittee, Enright insisted on not naming contestants not previously linked in public with the scandal, and now admitted to meeting with "Mr. X," a third contestant. Mr. X had called in September or October 1958, Enright testified, to say he had been summoned by the district attorney. Since Mr. X was confused and apprehensive about the possibility of losing his job, Enright suggested he consult an attorney. To the best of Enright's recollection, he did not talk again to Mr. X between the latter's visit to the D.A. and his appearance before the grand jury.

Enright went on to deny discussing with Freedman and Felsher "stiffening up" the contestants by advising them to go to the D.A. and grand jury and "tell the truth that they had not received questions and answers in advance." Rather, Enright claimed, he urged Freedman to recant his false testimony by pointing out that if he were tried for perjury, the names of the contestants he helped would be publicly divulged, whereas a recantation would keep their identities secret. Freedman, who had moved back to the United States, was not subpoenaed by the FCC, and his testimony was stipulated to on the basis of what he told the Harris subcommittee. During the recess after Enright's testimony, Zoloto confided to me that he had battled with Barry and Enright over whether they should reveal that NBC in fact had known the quizzes were rigged, but to Zoloto's disgust, it was Barry who had finally vetoed the idea.

The Broadcast Bureau played its trump card by calling Mr. X, who turned out to be James Bowser, the detective magazine editor who had lied to the first grand jury, then came in after the Washington hearings to spill the beans. He was the key to the Broadcast Bureau's case, because Enright's contacts with him could be construed as an attempt to suborn perjury. Bowser was on the stand for three days, during which some not very telling inconsistencies between his and Enright's versions of their contacts were developed. Enright's lawyers countered by depicting Bowser as a devious operator, if not an outright extortionist, and a patsy of the D.A. in a vendetta against Enright, scoring points by noting that despite Bowser's sworn statement admitting perjury, he had not been prosecuted subsequently along with other contestants.

Bowser was followed to the stand by Bloomgarden on July 24. Bloomgarden's October 5, 1959, statement to me was introduced as a key piece of evidence, because of Bloomgarden's description of contacts with Enright in a belated attempt by the latter to derail the Harris hearings or, failing that, to have Bloomgarden make himself scarce. But Enright's side had anticipated this testimony, and Enright had already denied Bloomgarden's allegations of an offer of money for people in Washington and any discussion at all about the possibility of Bloomgarden's leaving the country. Enright conceded that a meeting did take place toward the end of September 1959, but claimed its purpose was to inform Bloomgarden that Freedman had implicated him. According to Enright, Bloomgarden on his own proposed visiting someone he knew in Washington who could "shed light" on the upcoming hearings; Enright simply said Bloomgarden should "go down and visit the man" if he wanted to.

The Melody Music lawyers put Zoloto on the stand to corroborate Enright in these assertions. As I listened to Zoloto deny any discussion about interfering with the hearings, about senators or Senate committees, about Bloomgarden's leaving the country, or about money, I recalled his boasting back in the summer of 1960 about his own contacts with various politicians "close to" Harris at the time. None of this came out now, of course, since I could not share such hearsay with the Broadcast Bureau.

Thomas Gilchrist, the alumnus of the D.A.'s office whom Enright had retained early in the investigation, took the stand after Zoloto. Saying he initially believed what he was told about the honesty of "Twenty-One," Gilchrist testified that he used a list provided by Enright to secure affidavits from a score of New York area contestants, all of whom denied receiving assistance. But Enright had earlier testified that he did not know what Gilchrist was doing aside from interviewing contestants. Gilchrist himself now admitted that the affidavits were his own idea, simply lawyer strategy. After all, he said, he was being paid and had to do something.

Felsher took the stand on July 31. As the examination proceeded, the strain showed on Felsher, who said at one point, "I am so confused that I will not testify to anything with any degree of accuracy or any authority at all."[11] He was excused to find new counsel, and the hearings were recessed until September. Melody Music then moved, in Supreme Court, New York County (the successor to the Court of General Sessions under a reorganization of the state's judiciary earlier in the year), to examine the minutes of Felsher's testimony before both the Third September 1958 and Fourth July 1960 grand juries. We moved to dismiss the motion on the grounds that Melody Music, as a litigant in a civil administrative proceeding with only a private pecuniary interest at stake, lacked the standing to lift grand jury secrecy. Melody Music's motion was denied by the court without comment.

In September a more composed Felsher attempted to corroborate Enright's FCC testimony that he had not suggested to Felsher to advise contestants about what he planned to tell the first grand jury. As to the extent Enright encouraged or discouraged him in his attempts to induce the contestants to lie, Felsher waffled, as he had before the grand jury in 1960. When asked if he actually told Enright of his intention to get the contestants to lie, he answered that he might have, but he could not remember whether Enright had told him *not* to suborn the contestants.

Finally, it was my turn on the stand, and I testified in detail about the roadblocks put in the way of the 1958 investigation. Though I was questioned closely about Bowser by both sides, I was not given the opportunity to refute the innuendo about Bowser's not being prosecuted for perjury. The hearings ended without my being able to explain to the examiner the nature of the two-witness requirement for proving perjury; Enright himself and he alone had handled Bowser as a contestant, but since he was one of the targets of the investigation, he had never testified before the grand jury, which ruled out proceeding against Bowser for perjury.

IN OCTOBER 1962, we entered a motion in Supreme Court, New York County, recommending dismissal of the outstanding perjury indictment against Freedman. Though, we noted, Freedman's reappearance before the 1958 grand jury did not constitute recantation as a defense to perjury, his ultimate cooperation with the grand jury did significantly help the jury in its work, and we cited his later cooperation with the Harris subcommittee and the work of the 1960 grand jury. The motion was granted by the court and the indictment against Freedman was dismissed. This was the end of my official involvement in the quiz show affair.

On April 26, 1963, Smith handed down her decision on the WGMA license renewal, subject to review by the commissioners themselves. In the conclusion of her thoughtful report, which ran to sixty-five printed pages,[12] she noted that no matter how "repugnant to good conscience and moral sensibilities" quiz rigging was, it did not violate federal, state, or local laws when it took place. Furthermore, in Smith's opinion, the evidence did not support the conclusion that either Barry or Enright was responsible for the perjury committed by others. Only one perjurer, Bowser, had alleged being advised or requested by Enright to testify falsely, and Smith gave Enright the benefit of the doubt raised by Bowser's contradictory account of the chronology of their meetings. The fact that the 1960 grand jury returned no indictment against Bowser had, for Smith, diminished the weight of his evidence.

As for the core issue, Smith wrote, the fact that both Barry and Enright made false statements about quiz operations did "reflect adversely upon their character qualifications," but this was mitigated by the fact that the use of controls was general and "symptomatic of the moral climate" in the television industry:

> The attitude of those in the industry who were not directly in-
> volved appears to have been either that of extreme naivete or of
> not wanting to know . . . so long as the ratings were good and the
> public was kept in the dark. . . . Simple justice requires that Barry
> and Enright's conduct be considered in the light of the then-exist-
> ing circumstances. Certainly the networks which broadcast these
> then highly rated programs had both network and licensee re-
> sponsibility, since the programs were broadcast over their own
> stations as well as those of their affiliates.[13]

Equally important for Smith was the fact "that none of these actions [by Barry and Enright], then or now, in any way carried over into the operation of station WGMA," which she praised for its improvement since its purchase by Barry and Enright in terms of the criterion of "performance versus prom-ise." She then cited legal precedents, notably the recent matter of the renewal of the licenses of Westinghouse Broadcasting. The Commission had found that the "outstanding broadcast record" of Westinghouse "constituted suffi-cient countervailing circumstances to warrant renewal" even when the offi-cers and directors of the parent corporation were indicted and convicted for the crimes of fixing prices and rigging bids in the sale of electronic equip-ment.[14] On these bases, then, Smith ordered that Melody Music's license re-newal for WGMA be granted.

The Broadcast Bureau appealed the case to the full Commission, and more petitions, oppositions, and denials followed from both sides, leading to oral arguments before the commissioners sitting en banc on January 9, 1964. Ar-guing for the Broadcast Bureau, Kehoe stressed Enright's attempts to mislead the district attorney, NBC, and the public before the demise of "Twenty-One," as well as Barry's on-air denial of fixing. Ridiculing Smith's crediting of En-right over Bowser, Kehoe called Enright "a liar à la carte. Anyway you want it, he has served it upon this record, fried, fricasseed. . . . He lies to his lawyers who are representing him before the grand jury. He lies to the public. He calls a press conference and lies. He uses a statement that he deliberately knows is false, and files a libel suit on the basis of that statement. And he is to be believed over Bowser? It is unthinkable."[15] Asked what this had to do with WGMA, Kehoe argued that the rejection of a license renewal was not a penalty but denial of a privilege that Enright, for reasons of character, did not deserve.

Appearing for Melody Music was Marcus Cohn, accompanied by Zoloto's partner, Arthur Karger. Cohn kept up the attack on Bowser, stressing Enright's candor about his misdeeds, which were not committed as a licensee. Cohn contended that Enright could not have deceived NBC, which knew or should have known that quiz rigging was common. Asked how people who committed fraud could be deserving of a broadcast license, Cohn answered that FCC denials of licenses had always involved at least one of three elements: the station's performance and programming had not been adequate, the principals had lied to or deceived the Commission, or they had violated the law. None of these conditions applied here. Moreover, WGMA had not carried the fixed quizzes, while newspaper and magazine publishers who had exposed or questioned the quizzes before the scandal did continue to carry them on the television stations they owned. Finally, Cohn noted, the FCC had neither revoked nor denied the renewal of any licenses to stations whose personnel had been involved in payola and whose owners had admitted being aware of the practice.

On April 15, 1964, the Commission reversed Smith. Melody Music's application for renewal of the license was denied, and it was given until July 20, 1964, to operate WGMA and wind up its affairs. The commissioners found that even if Enright never attempted to procure false testimony or induce anyone to lie to the grand jury, Barry and Enright had attempted to "discourage and to frustrate" the investigation and "remained silent while they knew that former contestants and their employees, in testifying before the grand jury, were falsely denying that questions and answers had been supplied to contestants on their quiz programs."[16] In the opinion of the Commission, it was the applicant's conduct in the *broadcast field* that distinguished this from the Westinghouse case. Westinghouse's rigging the prices of electronic products, though serious, even criminal, was not in the broadcast field, and the company's excellent broadcasting record since 1920 "demonstrated an outstanding contribution to the public interest." In the case of Barry and Enright, the Commission was "concerned with the activities of the corporate principals in the broadcast field, and a broadcast record of relatively short duration."[17]

Dissenting, Commissioner Robert Lee was scornful of the majority's interpretation of the Westinghouse decision, especially what he called the inference that "if misconduct takes place in a non-broadcast field, the blood is not so corrupted that a person's qualifications to engage in broadcasting are really impaired."[18] He cited a decision in which the FCC denied a broadcaster a license application in one locality for a number of misdeeds, but granted the same broadcaster a renewal for a station he owned in a different location. Therefore, Barry and Enright's misdeeds in New York should not have made them unfit to operate a radio station in Florida.

In the period that the FCC was considering the WGMA matter, NBC was seeking renewals of its own radio and television stations in Philadelphia. One of these was challenged by the Philco Broadcasting Co. in a bid to wrest the Philadelphia television channel away from NBC. Among other issues raised by Philco was NBC's role in televising rigged quiz shows, notably those packaged, then sold to NBC, by Barry and Enright. On November 20, 1963, a hearing examiner granted NBC's application on the grounds that even if NBC was negligent in not discovering quiz rigging before the scandal and it looked the other way as long as the public continued to watch the shows, this was not "guilty knowledge" of the rigging; offsetting NBC's negligence were the facts that it took steps to ascertain the facts once the scandal began, it cooperated with the district attorney, it assumed direct production control of the Barry and Enright programs, it eliminated all dishonest practices, and it undertook to prevent dishonesty in the future. Moreover, the examiner held, NBC's faults in connection with quiz rigging were counterweighed by its long and meritorious past conduct in the broadcasting field.[19]

Philco took exception, and the case was pending when the full Commission ruled in the WGMA matter in April 1964. Melody Music immediately filed for the Commission to vacate its order pending a decision in the NBC case, which request the Commission denied on July 24. Yet only days later it granted NBC's license renewal request without any mention of the network's role vis-à-vis quiz rigging. Melody Music promptly appealed to the U.S. Circuit Court of Appeals for the District of Columbia Circuit in Washington. On April 8, 1965, the Circuit Court remanded the case for further proceedings, ordering the Commission to reconsider Melody Music's case. Writing for the three-judge court, Chief Judge David Bazelon faulted the Commission for its "refusal at least to explain its different treatment" of Melody Music and NBC: "Both were connected with the deceptive practices and their renewal applications were considered by the Commission at virtually the same time. Yet one was held disqualified and the other was not. . . . We think the differences are not so 'obvious' as to remove the need for explanation."[20]

After new briefs and arguments, the Commission, on March 6, 1966, reversed its 1964 decision and granted the renewal of the license of WGMA for one year, with the condition that the licensee divest itself of all broadcast interests by assigning the license to a qualified applicant within sixty days. Thus the Commission, in a tortuous opinion with dissent by two commissioners, conceded the Appeal Court's point that denying the Melody Music license was "to set a higher standard for small than for large corporations, and to permit large corporations greater latitude than is permitted small corporations."[21]

The Commission still found that the misconduct of Barry and Enright created "doubts as to their possible future course in the operation of a broadcasting station" and decided that the public interest would be served if WGMA was sold along with its license: this course would "take full account of any doubts that may exist as to future conduct that arises out of the past conduct of Enright and Barry. On the other hand, wholly to forfeit the license of WGMA would be . . . to penalize Enright and Barry without serving any statutory purpose the Commission is authorized to serve."[22]

In his dissent, Chairman William E. Henry excoriated the pusillanimity of the majority's finding, which he called an attempt to "avoid an unpleasant decision in this case by giving Barry and Enright a chance to go away." In Henry's view, since Barry and Enright were unqualified to run a radio station, they had forfeited their license in effect and should not profit from its sale; the failure of NBC to be vigilant could not be equated with the "personal, direct responsibility" of Barry and Enright for the quiz rigging and the subsequent attempts to cover it up; though NBC's faults were outweighed by its record as a broadcaster, "no such mitigation" existed in regard to Barry and Enright and WGMA.[23]

On July 27, 1966, the FCC announced that it had granted the assignment of the license of station WGMA by Melody Music to a new owner. The sum paid to Barry and Enright for WGMA was not made public.

Conclusion
Legacy of a Fraud

"It is something past. It is part of a business experience."
—Charles Revson, Subcommittee Hearings

Barry and Enright and the perjury defendants were not the only private parties to engage in legal struggles as a result of the quiz affair. From the outset of the scandal, a number of former contestants filed suit against producers, networks, sponsors, and advertising agencies claiming damages in connection with having been on rigged programs. One cannot make an educated guess as to how many of these suits were actually initiated before being settled or dropped; only a handful have left a trace on legal records, as a result of motions being argued and ruled upon by higher courts. The decisions made by judges in these cases indicate that none ever reached trial. There is no record whatsoever of any cash payments that might have been made, since, as permitted by law, these could be hidden as a condition of settlement.

The most publicized law suit in connection with the quiz programs was initiated in New York federal court a year and a half *before* the scandal, by the former "Big Surprise" contestant Dale Logue, against EPI, in December 1956, claiming damages for being ousted by being given on the air a question she was unable to answer in a warm-up. The Logue suit, reported in *Variety* on January 16, 1957, figured in the speculative articles about the quizzes that appeared in *Time* and *Look* later that year. On June 1, 1959, a stipulation was filed in the court that the Logue case was settled and discontinued, effectively sealing from public scrutiny the nature of any settlement reached.[1] Between October 1958 and September 1961 a number of former "Tic Tac Dough" and "Twenty-One" contestants brought suits for damages in varying amounts against Barry and Enright, NBC, sponsors, and other contestants on various grounds: defamation, damage to credit rating and reputation and consequent financial losses, and breach of contract. In addition, Doll Goostree, one of several former $64,000 program contestants to sue CBS and

EPI, alleged that as a result of losing on "The $64,000 Challenge," she not only lost the $4,000 which Charles Jackson won in the rigged match, she was deprived of the opportunity to go on to win the top prize.

All the suits that reached higher courts as a result of various motions by one or the other side were dismissed piecemeal in subsequent stages. The findings of the higher courts clustered around several areas. In the area of contracts, even if a cause of action could lie to recover damages incurred by reason of a fraudulent inducement to enter a contract, that is, to agree to be a contestant on a quiz program that was fixed, the plaintiff, in order to recover, had to "state clearly a cause for the recovery of damage . . . stating factual allegations from which a conclusion of damage may be inferred."[2] That is to say, plaintiffs had to show specific financial losses that occurred as a result of their being on the programs, which the courts found they had not done.

Likewise, the courts found there was nothing inherently defamatory about a quiz show, even a rigged one, and the defamation alleged by the plaintiffs was disclosed only by reason of the later exposure of the rigging and there was no effort alleged that the defendants intended to hurt the plaintiffs by involving them in rigging; thus, since the plaintiffs were not defamed in a prima facie sense, they had to allege special damages. Moreover, the courts did not accept the claim by Goostree and others that they were entitled to recover amounts they might have won if the quizzes were not rigged against them. The final decision in these cases was by the New York Court of Appeals, in May 1967, in the suit of a university professor against NBC, Barry and Enright, Pharmaceuticals, and Elfrida Von Nardroff. The plaintiff demanded special damages of $7,500 for being turned down for a Guggenheim Fellowship, which he claimed he was denied because of his involvement with "Twenty-One." In his opinion, Chief Justice Stanley Fuld found that the plaintiff's "speculations" concerning the reasons for his failure to obtain the fellowship were "simply not adequate" to allege special damages. Furthermore, the court ruled, even if the professor had a cause of action, his complaint, filed in September 1961, three and a half years after he was a contestant, had to be dismissed because the statute of limitations of one year to claims of libel or slander applied.[3]

THE FAILURE of these suits underscored the unique feature of the quiz affair as an example of fraud. Despite the national scale of the fraud and the amount of money it generated, there were, strictly speaking in a legal sense, no victims. Those who were "deceived" by the packagers into sponsoring and broadcasting the fixed quizzes suffered increased sales and profits; even the patsy contestants, who played in good faith against rigged contestants, were rewarded, at the very least, as noted by Edward Jurist of "Dotto," with the excitement of being on television. Instances of bribes or kickbacks were limited to the activities of the two low-level employees of "Treasure Hunt" and the payment by Max Hess to place his employee as a contestant on "The $64,000 Question"; as far as we could determine, there was no instance whatsoever that anyone who became involved with the quiz programs lost money out of pocket as a result. Significantly, the whistle-blowers in the affair—Hilgemeier, Stempel, Jackson, and Snodgrass—had not been swindled, but for one reason or another came to believe that they hadn't gotten *enough*.

In a larger sense, not lost on the Manhattan grand jury, the victims were the television audience, which was suckered into accepting the appearances of Van Doren, Von Nardroff, McCutcheon, and O'Rourke (to name the very popular contestants who were consciously in on the rigging) as genuine. These attractive and respectable folks lent their personal luster to the products advertised, prompting viewers to buy them; if that had not been the case, the shows would not have survived as long as they did.

The quiz show scheme, if such it was, was brilliant because it turned on the mysterious tendency of consumers to buy a product because it is advertised on a program they like, even though what they like about the show has nothing to do with what the product may or may not do for them. The public may have been disappointed, upset, even angry about the quiz scandal, but as far as I knew, no one ever filed a complaint or tried to recover the money spent for the products of rigged quiz sponsors. But in fact, scores of millions of dollars flowed in dribs and drabs from a national public upwards of fifty million people as a result of their watching the shows, thereby enriching manufacturers, broadcasters, advertising agencies, as well as program packagers and a score or more of contestants. Not only was it a gigantic fraud but it was legal; what made it unique was the possibility that it had the most victims ever, yet not one of them was consciously aware this was the case.

BECAUSE of the stakes Enright had in preserving the appearance of integrity of his shows, and the lengths to which he was willing to go to counter the published allegations of Stempel, the district attorney's office was drawn precipitously into a full-fledged grand jury presentation before we could determine whether any crimes had been committed; by the time we realized that the operation per se of rigged quizzes broke no laws, we were confronted by mass perjury, engineered with the compliance, if not the connivance, of influence-peddling lawyers. The ultimate result, the conviction of twenty former contestants, the majority of them only small winners, was interpreted as a miscarriage of justice by some, including members of the grand jury issuing the charges.

In part, this was the result of what might have been my mistake in judgment in not siding with Louis Hacker and other members of the 1958 grand jury who wanted to summon figures like Louis Cowan, William Paley, Robert Kintner, and Robert Sarnoff instead of settling for versions of events put forward by network spokesmen like Thomas Fisher and Thomas Ervin. At that point I had no knowledge of the fixing of McCutcheon or of the Hess bribe, both of which took place at the time Cowan was still very close to the operation of "The $64,000 Question"; on the other hand, the versions of Koplin and Carlin, exonerating Cowan from specific knowledge of rigging, might well have been sustained. But the opportunity to examine Cowan under oath as to steps he personally took in regard to his own creations when he was first notified of the "Dotto" problem, for example, might have provided truly explosive material for the presentment. As it turned out, although the grand jury gained a detailed knowledge of the operation of the quizzes, the nature of decision-making at the highest corporate levels that led to the proliferation of fixed quizzes on the air was never brought out. A bigger picture would have included scrutiny as well of the claims made in the commercials for Geritol and other products advertised on the quizzes.

The mystery of the extent of the knowledge of CBS higher-ups as to the true nature of the Cowan creations has remained tantalizing, especially in light of a claim made by Fred W. Friendly in his memoir of his career at CBS in association with Edward R. Murrow. In 1958, before the scandal, Friendly asserted, he was tipped off by William Golden, CBS's director of advertising, that there was evidence the big-money quiz shows were rigged and Friendly and Murrow would do well to make a special documentary "exposing the whole nasty mess." When Friendly expressed interest, Golden volunteered to "use his good offices" to secure time on the network for such a presentation. Friendly heard nothing more from Golden until one day after the first round of the Washington quiz hearings, when Golden confided that CBS's lawyers had vetoed the idea. "They said it would have been in bad taste," Golden told Friendly, then asked rhetorically, "What the hell do lawyers have to do with deciding what's good taste on the air and what isn't?"[4] That night, Golden, at the age of forty-eight, died of a heart attack, and with him a possible lead to what and when the CBS higher-ups knew about rigging.

ANOTHER unsolved mystery for me was the real nature of Mitchell Schweitzer's role in the presentment matter. It must have been gratifying for Schweitzer to see his eloquent November 19, 1959, decision upholding his own sealing of the presentment footnoted in a landmark decision by the Court of Appeals of New York in February 1961, which struck down the grand jury's presentment power altogether. Ruling for the first time since 1905 on the legality of grand jury reports, a majority of the state's highest court reasoned that if the grand jury had the power and duty to report on any matter it considered, it had the power and duty to report on all matters it considered, a consequence that hardly could have been intended by the original legislators in granting the grand jury its powers.

Chief Justice Fuld, writing for the majority, pointed out that the concept of willful and corrupt official misconduct which state law empowered the grand jury to consider was "self-contradictory and meaningless" if it did not amount to a crime, but the grand jury was empowered to deal with crime through the indictment power. Thus, Fuld concluded, if a grand jury could not find sufficient evidence for an indictment, it had no choice but to "dismiss the charge or remain silent."[5] In vigorous dissents, two justices cited the long history of grand jury reports as well as New York legislative history mandating that any misconduct of public officials that did not amount to a crime was still a proper area of grand jury inquiry; they called the notion of investigating without the power to report "nonsensical." "The public, too, has rights," wrote Justice Froessel, and it was up to the public through the legislature, not the courts, to strike down a practice that "has continued for so many years."[6]

In 1964, in a reversal, the state legislature enacted a law restoring to grand juries the power to issue reports concerning "misconduct, nonfeasance or neglect in public office by a public servant" or to propose "recommendations for legislative, executive or administrative action in the public interest based upon stated findings."[7] Under the new law, reports could not be critical of named or identifiable private persons, while named public officials were given the opportunity to respond to charges before a report was filed and made public. Since that time, grand juries in New York have issued reports on a variety of matters, not limited to the conduct of public officials, including one in December 1986 recommending legislation and action to tighten the supervision of hospital emergency-room procedures and operations. Though the report named no person or hospital, that information was well known or easily deducible, since the grand jury investigation, which produced no indictments, resulted from pressure on the district attorney by a prominent journalist after the emergency-room death of his daughter.[8]

ON JANUARY 21, 1971, Judge Fuld convened a Court on the Judiciary, an ad hoc procedure provided for by the state constitution to deal with misconduct by judges, to consider charges adduced in hearings before the New York Joint Legislative Committee on Crime against Mitchell Schweitzer. On September 23, 1971, Lawrence E. Walsh, counsel to the Court of the Judiciary, after an extensive investigation, brought charges of misconduct against Schweitzer, that is, for conspiracy to obstruct justice by using his office to secure lenient treatment for imprisoned organized crime figures, engaging in private business activities inconsistent with his judicial duties, including moneylending, and failure to be candid about his activities before various official bodies. The court suspended Schweitzer from office.

When hearings on the charges were set for January 24, 1972, Schweitzer's lawyer, Myron Greene, filed for a discontinuance of the proceedings on the grounds they were moot, for Schweitzer had submitted his resignation from the bench. When Greene relayed the commitment by Schweitzer never again to seek or accept public office nor to seek back pay from the date of his suspension, the Court on the Judiciary closed the proceeding.[9] Schweitzer's convivial, free-wheeling style, though it helped make him one of the most productive judges in New York in terms of cases disposed of, had caught up with him and he was driven from the bench. The charges did not touch on his conduct concerning the quiz grand jury. But the presence of Schweitzer's old friend Greene as his advocate confirmed for me what my own experience with Greene at several stages during the quiz investigation, my previous knowledge of Schweitzer's activities, and the loud hints of Hyman Zoloto all had led me to believe—in the quiz matter, Schweitzer danced to Enright's tune.

THE BIG-MONEY quiz programs were quickly forgotten by the public as new fads, filmed westerns and detective shows, took over prime-time television. The quiz scandal coincided with a profound and permanent shift in the financial relations of the main players in the television business, as the networks junked the traditional arrangements with advertising agencies for the sponsorship of broadcast time and took total control of the content of the programs they broadcast. Now the networks were commissioning programming directly or produced it themselves, then sold commercial time during the broadcast to advertisers in what was known as the "magazine-ad" approach. At the same time, a varying-rate system for charging advertisers was introduced, by which advertisers paid for airtime on the basis of the size of the audience their commercials reached; this compensated for the old practice by which the commercial sponsors tinkered with the content of the programs they controlled in order to raise ratings and eliminate all conceivable references to their competitors.[10]

It is ironic that the quiz shows, touted in their time as "educational" and an alternative to "violence," fell victim to scandal and left the field for the return of schlock on an unprecedented scale, as NBC and CBS were taken over by programmers shaped in the more overtly commercial mold of ABC, which, again ironically, had eschewed the big-money quizzes during their heyday and thus came under no scrutiny in the quiz hearings. Another trend given a fillip by the quiz scandal would ultimately strip away the need for the networks to even pretend to be providing the public with anything but commercial entertainment—the rise of educational or "public" (as opposed to private profit-making) television. In the wake of the quiz hearings, influential columnists like Walter Lippmann called for the creation of a British Broadcasting Corporation–type setup to provide high-quality programming not dependent on advertising by being publicly funded, if not actually directed by the government.

The election of John Kennedy as president in 1960 brought a new chairman to the FCC in 1961, Newton Minow, who became nationally known overnight for a speech in which he called commercial television "a vast wasteland. . . . a procession of game shows, violence, audience participation shows, formula comedies about totally unbelievable families, blood and thunder, mayhem, violence, sadism, murder, western badmen, western good men, private eyes, more violence, and cartoons. And endlessly, commercials—many screaming, cajoling, and offending. And most of all, boredom."[11] Minow also used his good offices to arrange the sale and license transfer of New York's Channel 13 to a noncommercial broadcasting group in the New York metropolitan area and later prevailed upon Congress to pass legislation requiring television-set manufacturers to equip all sets to receive UHF stations from January 1963 on, moves that were crucial to the growth and spread of noncommercial television, even after the accession to the presidency of Lyndon Johnson, the owner himself of a television station in Texas and a close friend of Frank Stanton of CBS.[12]

Despite new laws and a reorganization of the television business, the nature of the content of commercial broadcasting changed little; indeed, it was not long before quiz shows, better known as game shows, began to make a comeback, with smaller prizes, easier questions, replacing solemnity and long-term suspense with an emphasis on chance and fun. Though CBS canceled all its quizzes, along with canned laughter, in the period of purification following on the Washington hearings—including "Name That Tune"—it retained several prime-time celebrity guessing game shows like "What's My Line." NBC kept two of its Barry and Enright creations in the daytime schedule, "Concentration" and "Dough Re Mi," after canceling the tainted "Tic Tac Dough" at the time of Felsher's Washington testimony. "Dough Re Mi" survived till early 1961, and "Concentration" endured until 1973.

At CBS, Stanton's purification campaign did not last. Canned laughter and applause quickly returned, such deceptions labeled with phrases like "portions of this program were prerecorded." In the summer of 1960 the network introduced an experimental daytime game show called "Video Village," where contestants moved about the studio, "Monopoly"-style, winning merchandise prizes. In early 1961 two new efforts included "Double Exposure," a "Dotto"-like quiz in which a pair of contestants competed by guessing the identity of a famous face in a jigsaw puzzle.

Though the three networks continued to play game shows on the daytime schedule, trying out new ones with regularity, the efforts in prime time were sporadic. The important new market for quiz and game shows—no longer broadcast live but videotaped—was syndication, previously the domain of reruns of old network shows, that is, the leasing of programs by production companies or others directly to individual television stations, whether network affiliates or independents, for local broadcasting. Thus by the mid-1960s the daytime network game show lineups included several enduring successes like "Jeopardy!" and "The Dating Game," but also functioned to showcase efforts that might survive only a season or two before going to new lives in syndication. In 1971 the importance of syndication increased when the FCC issued a new regulation limiting network prime-time broadcasting to three hours each weekday night, in effect removing the 7–8 P.M. time slot from the network lineup. The idea behind the regulation was to make network affiliates more responsive to local community needs—and the full beneficiary of advertising revenue for the slot. But instead of going to the expense of producing their own programming, local stations tended to turn to syndicators for material recorded on videotape and relayed by satellite technology.

The result was a Renaissance of the quiz show by the mid-1970s. In the fall of 1975, there were more than thirty quiz and game shows on the air, half of them in network daytime schedules (none in prime time), the remainder distributed through syndication. So strong was the demand for game show ideas that the producers began recycling prescandal "classics" in new formats. Among them was "The New Name That Tune" introduced on NBC in 1973, where it lasted two years before going into syndication. Another was "The New Treasure Hunt" introduced directly into syndication in 1974. Also in syndication was "Classic Concentration," a refurbished version of the old Barry and Enright creation, canceled by its previous owner, NBC, in 1973. In that year, the veteran panel show packager, Goodson and Todman, bought the rights and reintroduced "Concentration" into syndication in 1974, hosted by Jack Narz and produced by Howard Felsher, now a member of the staff of Goodson and Todman.

Among the shows canceled in the banner year 1975 was "The Joker Is Wild," introduced on daytime CBS in 1972, produced and emceed by Jack Barry. The show had represented a comeback for Barry who, after a checkered career in the wake of the scandal, had been a consultant to other producers, emceed game shows in Canada, run an FM radio station in California, and hosted a short-lived panel quiz called "Generation Gap" (reminiscent of his and Enright's early 1950s venture, "The Wisdom of the Ages"), on ABC in 1969. In 1976 Barry was able to revive "The Joker Is Wild" for syndication, calling in Enright to help with the effort. Thus the partnership was reborn, now based in Los Angeles. In the summer of 1978, the new Barry and Enright bought back the rights from NBC and launched "New Tic Tac Dough" on CBS for a season before taking it into syndication. In its first year, a navy lieutenant named Thom McKee appeared on forty-seven broadcasts in a row and won $312,750, a new quiz record.[13]

Meanwhile, in March 1975 Viacom Enterprises, an entertainment syndicator with important interests in the burgeoning field of cable television, announced it had acquired the rights to "The $64,000 Question" and had formed a syndicate of CBS affiliates to broadcast the show anew in the 7:30 P.M. time slot, starting in 1976, complete with an isolation booth and expert contestants. A month later, the CBS-owned stations in the deal bowed out because of a CBS policy limiting to $25,000 the cash winnings on game shows broadcast by the network, but these were replaced by independent stations. With Steve Carlin credited as an executive producer, the show debuted on September 18, 1976, on Saturday nights on approximately one-hundred stations, its name changed to "The $128,000 Question." According to Henry Gillespie, president of Viacom, the program had safeguards that would make it impossible for any contestant to receive answers in advance, and he explained the doubling of the top prize: "Times have changed, and we wish to change with them. We feel $128,000 is a proper reward for extraordinary knowledge."[14] Two months after the debut of the new show, the man who started it all, Louis Cowan, at the age of sixty-seven, died in a fire in his penthouse apartment in Manhattan. After his departure from CBS, Cowan had become director of the Brandeis University Communications Research Center, then joined Columbia University as a professor in the School of Journalism, where he was a founder of the *Columbia Journalism Review*. Though "The $128,000 Question" lasted until 1978 in syndication, it generated none of the excitement of Cowan's masterpiece.

Though truly big prize money has never really come back, quiz shows remain a fixture of television, providing popular entertainment and large profits at a minimum production cost, which is why so many have been tried out over the years. At this writing, two shows that became popular in the 1980s continued their dominance in the so-called evening prime-time access slots, "Jeopardy!" and "Wheel of Fortune," while in the mornings and afternoons in network lineups and in syndication to independent stations and cable operators, some twenty games and quizzes jostled, including "Name That Tune," "Classic Concentration," and "Tic Tac Dough." In the fall of 1990, "Quiz Kids Challenge" was introduced on CBS, broadcast on weekday mornings and in the prime-time access slot on Saturday evenings. In this quiz, a panel of high-school students, changed every week, competed with a panel of grown-ups changed daily. The new show was produced by Geoffrey Cowan, son of the creator of the original "Quiz Kids."

One of the most important differences between contemporary game shows and the scandal quizzes is that the latter were live broadcasts and the former are videotaped and edited to create flow and eliminate "fluffs." The questions used are not esoteric and do not require vast funds of expert knowledge; the home viewers have the thrill of being able to answer a large proportion themselves, though usually not as quickly as the contestants. Magazine articles and other publicity promoting the shows, in addition to describing in detail the manner in which prospective contestants are recruited and auditioned, often en masse, emphasize the elaborate precautions taken to keep the questions secret and insulate potential contestants from the shows' production personnel. (After all, ever since 1960, it has been a federal crime to fix a television quiz show.) Perhaps the most important difference is that the *contestants* no longer fuel the shows' success; unlike Charles Van Doren three decades ago, today's contestants are a blur.

But some things have not changed. In recent years accounts written by former champions of the biggest current quizzes have abounded, appearing even in the pages of newspapers like the *New York Times* and the *Wall Street Journal*,[15] reminiscent of the explanations provided to me by former "Twenty-One" and "Tic Tac Dough" contestants who answered questions in a number of knowledge categories. Like their predecessors of thirty years ago, today's champions say they have studied the *program*, to figure out and master the recurring categories. My guess is that the current crop are too young to remember the 1950s scandal directly and are unaware that they have written inadvertent spoofs of the kind of how-I-studied piece penned by Von Nardroff and published after her departure from "Twenty-One" on the eve of the scandal.

To be sure, the prize money hasn't kept up with inflation, Thom McKee's 1978 record and "The $128,000 Question" notwithstanding. Winners no longer make the cover of *Time* magazine. The emphasis nowadays is on speed in answering the questions; in the old days, the contestants were ordered to hesitate, agonize, sweat it out for dramatic effect before giving the correct answers. Nevertheless, it is reassuring to know that the television business still puts a high premium on knowledge for its own sake; the word is getting out that anyone can win who hangs in there and works very hard. The American dream is alive and well.

On the other hand, it can be argued that, after children's programming, quiz shows are the most manipulative of viewers, providing vicarious participation in something that appears spontaneous, democratic, and harmless, but appeals directly and solely to the dream fantasy of sudden riches. If a "Quiz Kids"-like show, for example, were to give young panelists open-ended stints, this would be an ominous sign of the revival of the use of the personalities of contestants to drive the shows and raise the question whether "controls" were being employed to keep the most attractive contestants on the air.

The popularity of a new TV fad—home-made videotapes sent in by viewers competing for prize money—raised the possibility that the supply of genuinely clever and fresh material from viewers could dry up and producers might begin covertly to provide professional help—even scripts—to willing participants. Short of that, producers have issued public warnings to prospective participants to avoid endangering themselves by coming up with difficult stunts for the purpose of taping.

Even barring the return of quiz and game show rigging, the situation already has been made ominous by the growth of state-run gambling in the form of lotteries, horse-race betting and, most recently, football betting schemes, as well as legalized casino and riverboat gambling. All of these enterprises use television advertising to stimulate participation by the public, yet the FTC does not apply laws against unfair methods of competition or deceptive commercial practices to state-run monopolies.[16] The combination of get-rich-quick quiz shows and deceptive advertising that promotes gambling, in an age when money-making has been glorified as never before and government regulation of business has been all but dismantled, may well add up to an atmosphere in which corruption flourishes. If so, once again, the losers will be the public, which can still be gulled by the rationalization that it is not "paying" for what is on television. As in the 1950s, the truly big winners will not be contestants, but the packager-producers, now known as syndicators, the broadcasters and programmers, the advertisers and their agents, and, last but not least, if the going gets rough, the lawyers.

NOTES

A note on sources: Quotations not cited—mostly dialogue in interviews conducted by Joseph Stone during the course of his investigation of the television quiz programs— are reconstructions by Stone based on his recollections and those of his colleagues in the Manhattan district attorney's office.

CHAPTER 1, Connecting the Dots

1. *Investigation of Television Quiz Shows*, Hearings before a Subcommittee of the Committee on Interstate and Foreign Commerce, House of Representatives, 86th Cong., 1st sess., Washington, D.C.: U.S. Government Printing Office, 1960 (hereafter cited as *Hearings*), p. 288.
2. Ibid., p. 296.
3. *New York Journal-American,* August 27, 1958.
4. Ibid.

CHAPTER 2, "I'm Perfectly Willing to Need Help"

1. See *Hearings,* p. 24.
2. *New York Times,* August 29, 1958.
3. Ibid.
4. *New York Mirror,* August 30, 1958.
5. See *New York Times,* September 1, 1958.
6. *New York Daily News,* September 3, 1958.

CHAPTER 3, Straws in the Wind

1. *New York Herald-Tribune,* and *New York Journal-American,* September 7, 1958.
2. *Hearings,* p. 191.
3. *New York Times,* September 13, 1958.

CHAPTER 4, The People against John Doe

1. *New York Journal-American,* September 13, 1958.
2. *Hearings,* p. 476.
3. Ibid., p. 1117.
4. Ibid., p. 1118.
5. Ibid., p. 400.
6. Ibid., p. 465.

CHAPTER 5, The People against Richard Roe

1. *Hearings,* p. 75.
2. Ibid., p. 83.
3. Ibid., p. 84.

CHAPTER 6, The Two-Witness Rule

1. New York Penal Law, sec. 1620 (1958).
2. *United States v. Palese,* 133 F. 2d 600 (3rd Cir. 1943).
3. *New York Times,* October 4, 1958.
4. Ibid., October 11, 1958.

CHAPTER 7, The People against Albert Freedman

1. *New York Herald-Tribune,* October 17, 1958.
2. *New York Times,* November 8, 1958.
3. Ibid.
4. Ibid.

CHAPTER 8, The $64,000 Empire

1. "Are Quiz Shows Fixed? Let's Just Say Controlled," *New York World Telegram & Sun,* April 19, 1957.
2. *New York Times,* November 5, 1958.

CHAPTER 9, Shaking the Tree

1. Elfrida Von Nardroff, as told to Leslie Lieber, "My Quarter-Million Dollar Secret," *This Week,* July 20, 1958.

CHAPTER 10, The People against Peter Poe

1. *Hearings,* p. 439.
2. See Ralph Lee Smith, *The Health Hucksters* (New York: Thomas Y. Crowell Company, 1960), p. 17.
3. See *Hearings,* p. 167.

CHAPTER 11, Recantations

1. *People of the State of New York v. Isaac Ezaugi,* 2 N.Y. 2d 439 (1957); emphasis added.
2. See *Matter of Osborne,* 68 Misc. 597 (1910).
3. *New York Herald-Tribune,* June 11, 1959.
4. Ibid.
5. Ibid.
6. *New York Post,* June 11, 1959.
7. Ibid.

CHAPTER 12, Congress in the Act

1. *New York World Telegram & Sun,* June 12, 1959.
2. "In the Matter of the Report of the Third September 1958 Grand Jury Relating to the Investigation of Television Quiz Programs," Memorandum of Law submitted July 13, 1959, by Frank S. Hogan, District Attorney, County of New York, Court of General Sessions, County of New York. See *Hearings,* p. 608.
3. *In re Monmouth County Grand Jury,* 24 N.J. 318, 131 Atl. 2d 751. (1957).
4. *Application of United Electrical, Radio and Machine Workers of America,* 111 Fed. Supp. 858 (S.D.N.Y.1953).
5. *Hearings,* p. 611.
6. *New York Times,* July 31, 1959.
7. *New York Daily News,* July 31, 1959.
8. For an account of Schwartz's brief but spectacular tenure with the subcommittee, see his memoir, *The Professor and the Commissions* (New York: Alfred Knopf, 1959).
9. *Before We Sleep* (New York: G. P. Putnam, 1958).

CHAPTER 13, Washington Circus

1. *Hearings,* p. 59.
2. Ibid., p. 245.
3. Ibid., p. 249.
4. Ibid., p. 252.
5. Ibid., pp. 283–284.

6. See ibid., p. 303.
7. Ibid., p. 324.
8. Ibid., p. 326.
9. Ibid., p. 332.
10. Ibid., p. 342.
11. Ibid., p. 404.
12. Ibid., p. 443.
13. Ibid., p. 446.
14. Ibid., p. 452.
15. Ibid., p. 456.
16. Ibid., p. 458.
17. Ibid., p. 487.
18. Ibid., p. 515.
19. Ibid., pp. 522–523.
20. Ibid., p. 547.
21. Ibid., p. 548.
22. Ibid., p. 265.
23. Ibid., p. 554.
24. Ibid., p. 592.
25. *New York Mirror,* October 12, 1959.
26. *Hearings,* pp. 578, 579.
27. Ibid., p. 619.

CHAPTER 14, Intermission

1. Richard Goodwin, *Remembering America: A Voice from the Sixties* (Boston: Little, Brown and Company, 1988), p. 55.
2. *New York Herald-Tribune*, October 14, 1959.
3. *New York Mirror*, October 14, 1959.
4. *New York Post*, October 15, 1959.
5. Ibid.
6. *New York Times*, October 15, 1959.
7. Ibid., October 16, 1959.
8. Ibid., October 17, 1959.
9. *New York Herald-Tribune*, October 18, 1959.
10. *New York Times*, October 26, 1959.

CHAPTER 15, Second Round

1. *Hearings*, p. 624.
2. Ibid., p. 625.
3. Ibid., p. 627.
4. Ibid., pp. 627–628.
5. Ibid., pp. 629, 630.
6. Ibid., p. 632.
7. Ibid., p. 636.
8. Ibid., pp. 645, 646.

9. Ibid., p. 656.

10. *New York Times*, November 3, 1959.

11. *Hearings*, pp. 701, 702.

12. See Patty Duke Astin, with Kenneth Turan, *Call Me Anna* (New York: Bantam Books, 1987), pp. 51–56.

13. *Hearings*, p. 923.

14. Ibid., p. 925.

15. Ibid., p. 794.

16. *New York Times*, November 4, 1959.

17. Ibid., November 5, 1959.

18. *Hearings*, p. 836.

19. Ibid., p. 838.

20. Ibid., p. 847.

21. Ibid., p. 891.

22. Ibid., p. 981.

23. Ibid., p. 985.

24. Ibid., p. 996.

25. *New York Times*, November 5, 1959.

26. U.S. House of Representatives, Report of Proceedings, Hearing held before the Special Subcommittee on Legislative Oversight, Committee on Interstate and Foreign Commerce: "Television Quiz Show Programs," November 5, 1959, Executive Session Testimony of Elroy Schwartz, Testimony of Joseph Cates, Further Testimony of Elroy Schwartz, Washington, U.S. Archives, Legislative Division. These transcripts were released to Joseph Stone by vote of the U.S. House of Representatives, Subcommittee on Oversight and Investigations of the Committee on Energy and Commerce, May 1, 1990.

27. *New York Herald-Tribune*, November 6, 1959.

28. *Hearings*, p. 1026.

29. Ibid., p. 1039.

30. Ibid., p. 1100.

31. Ibid., p. 1090.

32. Ibid., p. 1091.

33. Ibid., p. 1096.

34. Ibid., p. 1115.

CHAPTER 16, Mass Perjury

1. See Kent Anderson, "Are We a Nation of Liars and Cheats?" in *Television Fraud: The History and Implications of the Quiz Show Scandals* (Westport, Conn.: Greenwood Press, 1978), pp. 147–167.

2. Richard Goodwin, "Committee Investigator Reveals How Fixers Seduced Innocents," *Life*, November 16, 1959.

3. *Matter of Application of the Third September, 1958 Grand Jury to Submit and File Its Report Concerning Its Investigation of Certain Television Quiz Programs*, 19 Misc. 2d 682, 193 N.Y.S. 2d 553 (General Sessions, N.Y. Co., 1959).

4. Ibid. 565–566. See also Richard Kuh, "The Grand Jury 'Presentment': Foul Ball or Fair Play?" *Columbia Law Review*, December, 1955, pp. 1103, 1104–1105.

5. *Matter of Application*, p. 567.

6. Ibid., pp. 569, 570.

6. Ibid., 569, 570.
7. *New York Herald-Tribune*, November 20, 1959.

CHAPTER 17, Second Grand Jury

1. *Grand Jury Association of New York County, Inc., v. Schweitzer*, 11 A.D. 2d 761, 202 N.Y.S. 2d 376 (1960).

CHAPTER 18, The Public Interest, Convenience, and Necessity

1. 47 U.S. Code, annotated, sec. 509 (1960).

2. See *New York Times*, January 1, 1960.

3. See Meyer Weinberg, *TV in America: The Morality of Hard Cash* (New York: Ballantine Books, 1962), pp. 113–118.

4. Elmo Roper, "The Public's Reaction to Television Following the Quiz Investigations," statement before FCC, December 17, 1959. See Elmo Roper, "Rigged Quizzes: The Public View," *Saturday Review*, February 13, 1960.

5. See Weinberg, *TV in America*, pp. 147–150.

6. See ibid., pp. 119–122.

7. *New York Times*, February 6, 1960.

8. See Weinberg, *TV in America*, p. 167.

9. *People v. Michael Truppin*, 213 N.Y.S. 2d 469, 471 (General Sessions, N.Y. Co., 1961).

10. Ibid., p. 473.

11. 36 F.C.C. 710 (1963), p. 749.

12. See ibid., pp. 710–775.

13. Ibid., p. 769.

14. *Re: Renewal of Westinghouse Broadcasting's Station Licenses*, F.C.C. 62-243, 22 Pike & Fisher, R.R. 1023 (1962).

15. Official Report of Oral Arguments before the F.C.C. on January 9, 1964, for Renewal of License for Broadcast Station WGMA, Hollywood, Florida, p. 2683.

16. 36 F.C.C. 701 (1964), p. 705.

17. Ibid., p. 707.

18. Ibid., pp. 708, 709.

19. See *National Broadcasting Company*, 37 F.C.C. 427 (1964).

20. *Melody Music, Inc. v. F.C.C.*, 345 F. 2d 730 (1965), pp. 732–733.

21. 2 F.C.C. 2d 958 (1966), p. 962.

22. Ibid.

23. Ibid., pp. 965, 968, 969.

CONCLUSION, Legacy of a Fraud

1. See Weinberg, *TV in America*, pp. 1–2.

2. *Davidson v. National Broadcasting Company, Inc., et al.*, 26 Misc. 2d 936, 204 N.Y.S. 2d 532, p. 536 (Sup. Ct, N.Y. Co., 1960).

3. *Morrison v. National Broadcasting Company, Inc., et al.*, 19 N.Y. 2d 453, p. 458, 280 N.Y.S. 2d 641 (1967).

4. Fred W. Friendly, *Due to Circumstances Beyond Our Control . . .* (New York: Vintage Books, 1968), pp. 96–97.

5. *Wood v. Hughes*, 9 N.Y. 2d 144, 212 N.Y.S. 2d 33, pp. 38, 39 (1961).

6. Ibid., p. 51.

7. New York State Criminal Procedure Law, sec. 190.85, subdiv. 1.

8. Report of the Fourth Grand Jury for the April/May Term of 1986 Concerning the Care and Treatment of a Patient and the Supervision of Interns and Junior Residents at a Hospital in New York County, New York Supreme Court, New York County, December 31, 1986; see also "The Legacy of Libby Zion" (editorial), *New York Times*, June 8, 1987.

9. See "In the Matter of the Proceedings Pursuant to Section 22 of Article VI of the Constitution of the State of New York in Relation to Mitchell D. Schweitzer," 29 N.Y. 2d (insert a-ss). (1971).

10. See Anderson, *Television Fraud*, pp. 166–167; Erik Barnouw, *The Image Empire: A History of Broadcasting in the United States, vol. 3—from 1953* (New York: Oxford University Press, 1970), p. 150; William Boddy, *Fifties Television: The Industry and Its Critics* (Urbana and Chicago: University of Illinois Press, 1990).

11. *New York Times*, May 10, 1961.

12. See Barnouw, *The Image Empire*, pp. 199–201, 237–238.

13. See Jefferson Graham, *Come on Down!!!: The TV Game Show Book* (New York: Abbeville Press, 1988), pp. 42, 100.

14. *New York Times*, August 19, 1976.

15. See Mark M. Lowenthal, "It's Time to Play Final 'Jeopardy!' " *New York Times*, January 22, 1989; Eugene Finerman, "My Hour of Fame on 'Super Jeopardy!' " *Wall Street Journal*, September 6, 1990.

16. See Jonathan Karl, "Lotto Baloney: The Great State Lottery Swindle," *The New Republic*, March 4, 1991, pp. 13–15.

BIBLIOGRAPHY

Abrams, George A. *How I Made a Million Dollars with Ideas*. Chicago: Playboy Press, 1972.

Anderson, Kent A. *Television Fraud: The History and Implications of the Quiz Show Scandals*. Westport, Conn.: Greenwood Press, 1978.

Astin, Patty Duke, and Kenneth Turan. *Call Me Anna: The Autobiography of Patty Duke*. New York: Bantam Books, 1988.

Barnouw, Erik. *The Image Empire: A History of Broadcasting in the United States, vol. 3—from 1953*. New York: Oxford University Press, 1970.

Boddy, William. *Fifties Television: The Industry and Its Critics*. Urbana and Chicago: University of Illinois Press, 1990.

———. "The Seven Dwarfs and the Money Grubbers: The Public Relations Crisis of US Television in the Late 1950s." In Patricia Mellencamp, ed., *Logics of Television: Essays in Cultural Criticism*. Bloomington: Indiana University Press, 1990.

Castleman, Harry, and Walter J. Podrazik. *The TV Schedule Book: Four Decades of Network Programming from Sign-On to Sign-off*. New York: McGraw-Hill Book Company, 1984.

———. *Watching TV: Four Decades of American Television*. New York: McGraw-Hill Book Company, 1982.

Cowan, Paul. *An Orphan in History: Retrieving a Jewish Legacy*. New York: Doubleday, 1982.

Cunningham, Barry, and Mike Pearl. *Mr. District Attorney*. New York: Mason/Charter, 1977.

DeLong, Thomas A. *Quiz Craze: America's Infatuation with the Radio and Television Game Show*. Westport, Conn.: Praeger Publishers, 1991.

Dunning, John. *Tune in Yesterday: The Ultimate Encyclopedia of Old-time Radio, 1925–1976*. Englewood Cliffs, N.J.: Prentice-Hall, 1976.

Fabe, Maxene. *TV Game Shows*. New York: Doubleday, 1979.

Feldman, Ruth Dinkin. *Whatever Happened to the Quiz Kids: Perils and Profits of Growing Up Gifted*. Chicago: Chicago Review Press, 1982.

Friendly, Fred W. *Due to Circumstances Beyond Our Control . . . .* New York: Vintage Books, 1968.

Goodwin, Richard N. *Remembering America: A Voice from the Sixties*. Boston: Little, Brown and Company, 1988.

Graham, Jefferson. *Come on Down!!!: The TV Game Show Book*. New York: Abbeville Press, 1988.

Halberstam, David. *The Powers That Be*. New York: Alfred A. Knopf, Inc., 1979.

Independent Regulatory Commissions. Report of the Special Subcommittee on Legislative Oversight of the Committee on Interstate and Foreign Commerce, House of Representatives, 86th Cong., 2d sess. Washington, D.C.: U.S. Government Printing Office, 1961.

Investigation of Television Quiz Shows, Hearings before a Subcommittee of the Committee on Interstate and Foreign Commerce, House of Representatives, 86th Cong., 1st sess. Washington, D.C.: U.S. Government Printing Office, 1960.

Payola and Other Deceptive Practices in the Broadcasting Field. Hearings before a Subcommittee of the Committee on Interstate and Foreign Commerce, House of Representatives, 86th Cong., 2d sess., parts 1 and 2. Washington, D.C.: U.S. Government Printing Office, 1960.

Regulation of Broadcasting: Half a Century of Government Regulation of Broadcasting and the Need for Further Legislative Action. Study for the Committee on Interstate and Foreign Commerce Committee, House of Representatives, 85th Cong., 2d sess. Washington, D.C.: U.S. Government Printing Office, [n.d.].

Schwartz, Bernard. *The Professor and the Commissions*. New York: Alfred A. Knopf, Inc., 1959.

Schwartz, David; Steve Ryan; and Fred Wostbrock. *The Encyclopedia of TV Game Shows*. New York: New York Zoetrope, 1987.

Seitel, Irving. *A Pictorial History of Radio*. New York: Grosset & Dunlap, 1960.

Smith, Ralph Lee. *The Health Hucksters*. New York: Thomas Y. Crowell Company, 1960.

Sperber, Ann M. *Murrow: His Life and Times*. New York: Freundlich Books, 1986.

Steinberg, Cobbett. *TV Facts*. New York: Facts on File, Inc., 1980.

Terrace, Vincent. *Encyclopedia of TV Series, Plots, and Specials, 1937–1973*. New York: New York Zoetrope, 1986.

Tobias, Andrew. *Fire and Ice: The Story of Charles Revson—The Man Who Built the Revlon Empire*. New York: William Morrow and Company, 1976.

Weinberg, Meyer. *TV in America: The Morality of Hard Cash*. New York: Ballantine Books, 1962.

INDEX